Hotels & Guest Houses

Where to Stay Guide 2006

visitscotland.com
0845 22 55 121

Scotland is split into eight tourist areas. You will find accommodation listed alphabetically by location within each of these areas. There is an index at the back of this book of all associated accommodation operators in VisitScotland's Quality Assurance Schemes which may also help you.

Introduction

Welcome to Scotland ii
Using this book iii-v
Disclaimer v
Signs you need to know vi-xiii
Travellers' Tips xiv-xvi
Prize Draw xvii-xviii
Maps xix-xxiv

Accommodation

A South of Scotland 2
Ayrshire and Arran, Dumfries and Galloway, Scottish Borders
B Edinburgh and Lothians 21
C Greater Glasgow and Clyde Valley 52
D West Highlands & Islands Loch Lomond, Stirling and Trossachs 66
E Perthshire, Angus and Dundee and the Kingdom of Fife 90
F Aberdeen and Grampian Highlands – Scotland's Castle and Whisky Country 120
G The Highlands and Skye 138
H Outer Islands: 182
Outer Hebrides, Orkney, Shetland

Appendix

Visitors with disabilities 191
Index by location 267

More Accommodation

Directory of all VisitScotland Quality Assured Serviced Establishments 210

Welcome to Scotland

Hotels & Guest Houses

From world famous hotels to friendly guest houses, you'll find a variety of Scotland reflected in the wide choice available in this guide.

Hundreds of hotels in all kinds of locations, are listed each with their own special character and atmosphere.

There are city hotels, located within walking distance of all the main attractions, which also offer the high-tech and sophisticated facilities for the business traveller, as well as some of the best conference and function facilities in Europe. Outwith the city, there is an exciting range of country retreats, where you can relax in luxurious and peaceful surroundings, which are ideal for a spot of golf, fishing or stress-relieving spa treatments.

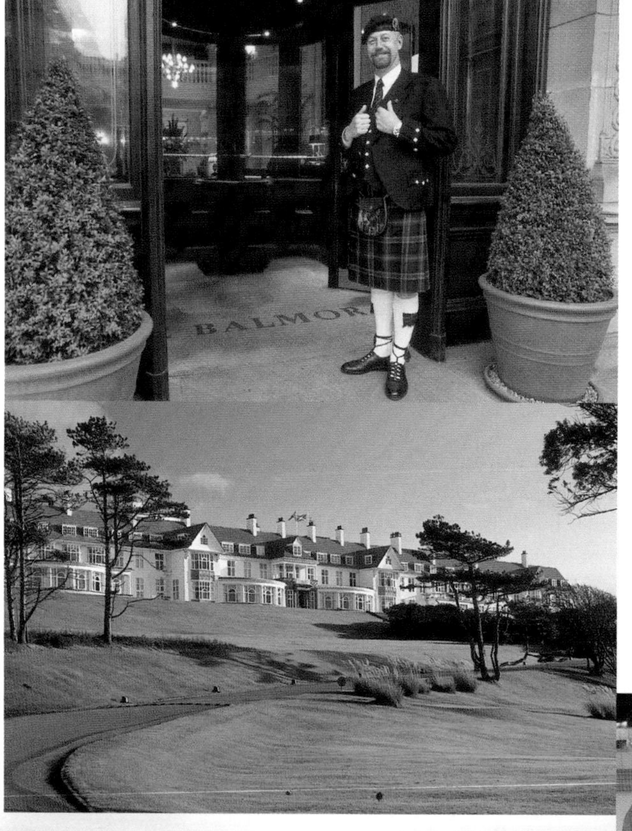

Scotland also provides numerous friendly and welcoming family hotels, with sports, activities and entertainment for all ages, and excellent value for weekend breaks. Many of these large hotels have modern leisure complexes, for a work-out, swim or sun-tan, whatever the weather.

Staying in one of Scotland's hotels or guest houses give you the ideal opportunity to tempt your taste buds with the distinctive quality of Scottish produce. In addition, these guest houses are friendly and economical, and almost all are family-run to provide great value and comfort in a homely atmosphere.

From the furthest-flung islands to the busy hub of Scotland's capital, there is something to suit everyone's taste – so go out and experience the very best of Scotland's traditional welcome and hospitality!

Using This Book

Hotels & Guest Houses

Where to Stay...?

Over 1500 answers to the age-old question!

Revised annually, this is the most comprehensive guide to serviced accommodation in Scotland.

Every property in the guide has been graded by VisitScotland Quality Advisors.
See page vi for details.

How to find accommodation

This book has been split into eight areas of Scotland:

A	South of Scotland *Ayrshire and Arran, Dumfries and Galloway, Scottish Borders*	2
B	Edinburgh and Lothians	21
C	Greater Glasgow and Clyde Valley	52
D	West Highlands & Islands Loch Lomond, Stirling and Trossachs	66
E	Perthshire, Angus and Dundee and the Kingdom of Fife	90
F	Aberdeen and Grampian Highlands – Scotland's Castle and Whisky Country	120
G	The Highlands and Skye	138
H	Outer Islands: *Outer Hebrides, Orkney and Shetland*	182

The map on page xix shows these areas. Within each area section you will find accommodation listed alphabetically by location.

Alternatively there is an index at the back of this book listing alphabetically the accommodation locations in Scotland.

More Accommodation

There is also a complete directory of all VisitScotland Quality Assured Serviced Establishments on page 210.

Using This Book

Hotels & Guest Houses

Learn to use the symbols in each entry – they will contain a mine of information! There is a key to symbols on the back flap.

Naturally, it is always advisable to confirm with the establishment that a particular facility is still available.

Prices in this guide are quoted per person and represent the minimum and maximum charges expected to apply to most rooms in the establishment. They include VAT at the appropriate rate and service charges where applicable.

The prices of accommodation, services and facilities are supplied to us by the accommodation operators and were, to the best of our knowledge, correct at the time of going to press. However, prices can change at any time during the lifetime of the publication, and you should check again when you book.

Bookings can be made direct to the establishment, through local Tourist Information Centres, through a travel agent or through **Scotland's National Booking and Information Centre –** Tel: 0845 22 55 121. or, from outside the UK: +44 (0)1506 832121

A £3 booking fee applies to telephone bookings through the National Booking Centre.

The prices stated are inclusive of a 10% agency commission where applicable.

Remember, when you accept accommodation by telephone or in writing, you are entering a legally binding contract which must be fulfilled on both sides. Should you fail to take up accommodation, you may not only forfeit any deposit already paid, but may also have to compensate the establishment if the accommodation cannot be re-let.

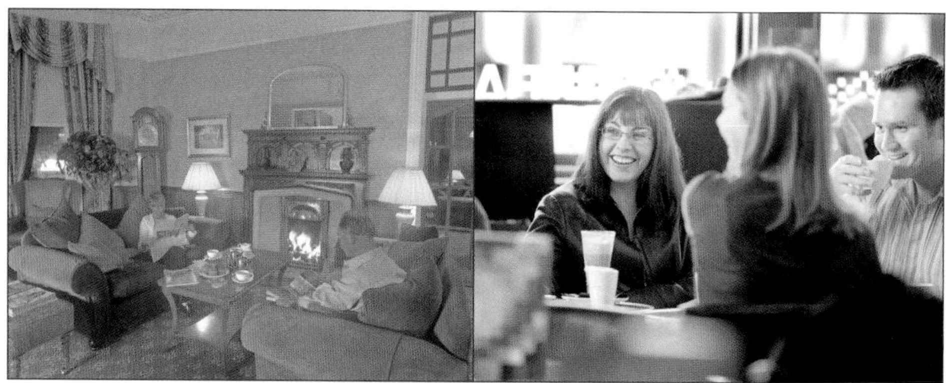

Using This Book

Hotels & Guest Houses

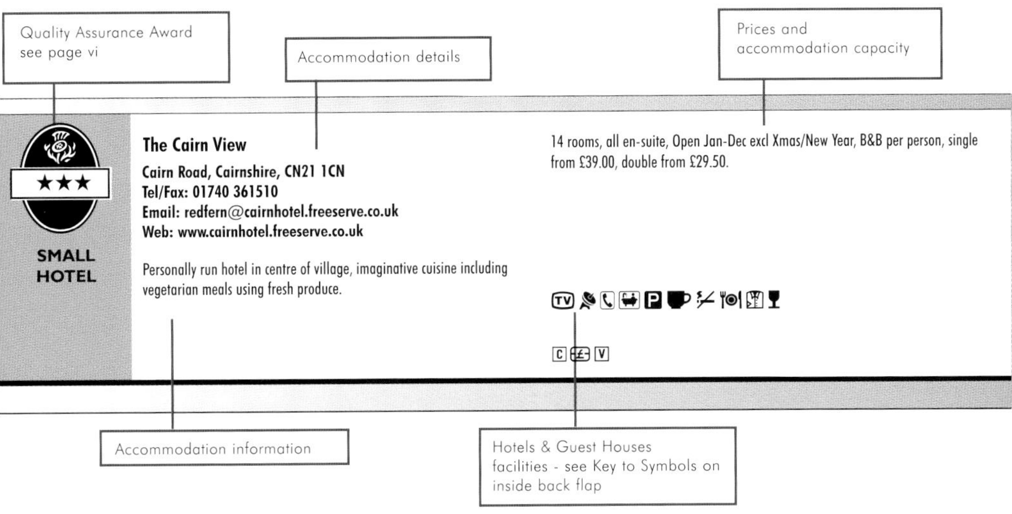

Disclaimer

VisitScotland has published this guide in good faith to reflect information submitted to it by the proprietors of the premises listed who have paid for their entries to be included. Although VisitScotland has taken reasonable steps to confirm the information contained in the guide at the time of going to press, it cannot guarantee that the information published is and remains accurate.

Accordingly, VisitScotland recommends that all information is checked with the proprietor of the premises prior to booking to ensure that the accommodation, its price and all other aspects of the premises are satisfactory.

VisitScotland accepts no responsibility for any error or misrepresentation contained in the guide and excludes all liability for loss or damage caused by any reliance placed on the information contained in the guide. VisitScotland also cannot accept any liability for loss caused by the bankruptcy, or liquidation, or insolvency, or cessation of trade of any company, firm or individual contained in this guide.

Signs You Need To Know

Quality Grading

Follow the stars and you won't be disappointed when you get to the inn.

The VisitScotland Star System is a world-first. Quality is what determines our star awards, not a checklist of facilities. We've made your priorities our priorities.

Quality makes or breaks a visit. This is why the most important aspects of your stay; the warmth of welcome, efficiency and friendliness of service, the quality of the food and the cleanliness and condition of the furnishings, fittings and decor earn VisitScotland Stars, not the size of the accommodation or the range of available facilities.

This easy to understand system tells you at a glance the quality standard of all types and sizes of accommodation from the smallest B&B and self-catering cottage to the largest countryside and city centre hotels.

Quality Assurance awards correct at end September 2005

Look out for this distinctive sign of Quality Assured Accommodation.

VisitScotland star grading schemes take the guesswork out of arranging a holiday in Scotland. Branded under the Scottish Tourist Board label, the schemes are impartial, reliable and easy to understand.

Signs You Need To Know

Quality Grading

The standards you can expect:

★★★★★ Exceptional
★★★★ Excellent
★★★ Very good
★★ Good
★ Fair and Acceptable

A trained VisitScotland Quality Advisor grades each property every year to give you the reassurance that you can choose accommodation of the quality standard you want.

To help you further in your choice the VisitScotland System also tells you the type of accommodation and the range of facilities and services available.

Please turn over for details.

For further information call into any Tourist Information Centre, or contact VisitScotland.

More details available from:

Quality and Standards Department
VisitScotland
Thistle House
Beechwood Park North
INVERNESS
IV2 3ED

Tel: 01463 723040
Fax: 01463 717244
Email: qa@visitscotland.com

If you have a complaint about your accommodation, make it known to the management as soon as possible so that they can take action to investigate and resolve the problem. You should not feel reluctant to complain if you are dissatisfied with some aspect of your accommodation. Indeed, it is always the best policy to draw attention to the problem on the spot. Proprietors and their staff want you to return and for you to recommend what they provide to your friends. If you let them know what displeases you at the time they have an opportunity to put matters right. However, if you do have a problem with one of our Quality Assured properties which has not been resolved by the proprietor, please contact us at the above address.

Signs You Need To Know

Quality Grading

Accommodation Types:

Self Catering
A house, cottage, apartment, chalet or similar accommodation which is let normally on a weekly basis to individuals where facilities are provided to cater for yourselves.

Serviced Apartments
Serviced apartments are essentially self catering apartments where services such as a cleaning service is available and meals and drinks may be available. Meals and drinks would normally be provided to each apartment or in a restaurant and/or bar which is on site.

Guest House
A guest house is usually a commercial business and will normally have a minimum of 4 letting bedrooms, of which some will have ensuite or private facilities. Breakfast will be available and evening meals may be provided.

B&B
Accommodation offering bed and breakfast, usually in a private house. B&B's will normally accommodate no more than 6 guests, and may or may not serve an evening meal.

Hotel
A hotel will normally have a minimum of 20 letting bedrooms, of which the majority will have ensuite or private bathroom facilities. A hotel will normally have a drinks licence (may be a restricted licence) and will serve breakfast, dinner and normally lunch.

Small Hotel
A small hotel will normally have a maximum of 20 letting bedrooms and a minimum of 6. The majority of the bedrooms will have ensuite or private facilities. A small hotel will be licenced (may be a restricted licence) and will serve breakfast, dinner and normally lunch. It will normally be run by owner(s) and reflect their style and personal input.

International Resort Hotel
A hotel achieving a 5 Star quality award which owns and offers a range of leisure and sporting facilities including an 18 hole golf course, swimming and leisure centre and country pursuits.

Lodge
Primarily purpose-built overnight accommodation, often situated close to a major road or in a city centre. Reception hours may be restricted and payment may be required on check in. There may be associated restaurant facilities.

Inn
Bed and breakfast accommodation provided within a traditional inn or pub environment. A restaurant and bar will be open to non-residents and will provide restaurant or bar food at lunchtime and in the evening.

Restaurant with Rooms
In a restaurant with rooms, the restaurant is the most significant part of the business. It is usually open to non-residents. Accommodation is available, and breakfast is usually provided.

Campus Accommodation
Campus accommodation is provided by colleges and universities for their students and is made available - with meals - for individuals, families or groups at certain times of the year. These typically include the main Summer holiday period as well as Easter and Christmas.

Signs You Need To Know

Quality Grading

Serviced Accommodation: Facility and Service Symbols

- TV in bedrooms
- Satellite/cable TV
- Tea/coffee making facilities in bedrooms
- Telephone in bedrooms
- Hairdryer in bedrooms
- Evening meal available
- Room service
- Restaurant
- Leisure facilities
- Indoor swimming pool
- Laundry service
- Porterage
- Lounge
- TV Lounge
- Full alcohol drinks licence
- Restricted alcohol drinks licence
- Non-smoking establishment
- Smoking restricted
- Payphone provided
- Washbasin in bedrooms
- Ensuite bath and/or shower for all bedrooms
- Ensuite bath and/or shower for some bedrooms
- Private bath and/or shower for all bedrooms
- Private bath and/or shower for some bedrooms
- Private parking
- Limited parking
- No TV

Signs You Need To Know

For a Quality Destination

You not only want to be sure of the standard of accommodation you choose to stay in, whichever type it may be, you want to be sure you make the most of your time.

VisitScotland not only grades every type of accommodation every year, but also a wide range of visitor attractions every second year to grade the standard of customer care provided for visitors.

The grading scheme for visitor attractions provides you with the assurance that an attraction has been assessed for the condition and standard of the facilities and services provided – the warmth of welcome, efficiency of service, level of cleanliness, standard of visitor interpretation and of the toilets, restaurant and shop, if provided.

A large world famous castle, or small local museum can attain high grades if their services for the visitor are of a high standard.

The Standards You Can Expect:

★★★★★	Exceptional
★★★★	Excellent
★★★	Very good
★★	Good
★	Fair and Acceptable

In addition to the star grades, every attraction is categorised under one of the following types to help give the visitor an indication of the type of experience on offer:

Visitor Attraction
Castle
Historic Attraction
Museum
Tour
Garden
Activity Centre
Tourist Shop
Leisure Centre
Arts Venue
Historic House
Garden Centre

Look for the VisitScotland/Scottish Tourist Board sign of quality:

Signs You Need To Know

Mobility Needs

Visitors with particular mobility needs must be able to be secure in the knowledge that suitable accommodation is available to match these requirements. Advance knowledge of accessible entrances, bedrooms and facilities is important to enable visitors to enjoy their stay.

Along with the quality awards which apply to all the establishments in this, and every VisitScotland guide, we operate a national accessibility scheme. By inspecting establishments to set criteria, we can identify and promote places that meet the requirements of visitors with mobility needs.

The three categories of accessibility – drawn up in close consultation with specialist organisations are:

Unassisted wheelchair access for residents

Assisted wheelchair access for residents

Access for residents with mobility difficulties

Look out for these symbols in establishments, in advertising and brochures. They assure you that entrances, ramps, passageways, doors, restaurant facilities, bathrooms and toilets, as well as kitchens in self catering properties, have been inspected with reference to the needs of wheelchair users, and those with mobility difficulties. Write or telephone for details of the standards in each category – address on page vii.

For more information about travel, specialist organisations who can provide information and a list of all the Scottish accommodation which has had the access inspection, get in touch with our **National Information and Booking Line on:** **0845 22 55 121** or e-mail: **info@visitscotland.com** (or ask at a Tourist Information Centre) for the VisitScotland booklet "Accessible Scotland".

A £3 booking fee applies to telephone bookings of accommodation.

Tourism for All
The Hawkins Suite
Enham Place
Enham Alamein
Andover
Hampshire SP11 6JS

Tel: **0845 124 9971**
Fax: **0845 124 9972**
Minicom: **0845 124 9976**
Email: **info@holidaycare.org**
Web: **www.tourismforall.org.uk**

In addition, a referral service to put enquirers in touch with local disability advice centres is:

Update
27 Beaverhall Road
Edinburgh
EH7 4JE

Tel: **0131 558 5200**
Fax: **0131 558 5201**
Minicom: **0131 558 5202**
Email: **info@update.org.uk**
Web: **www.update.org.uk**

Signs You Need To Know

Quality Grading

Over 1200 quality assured accommodation providers are offering an extra warm welcome for visitors who are cycling or walking for all, or part, of their holiday in Scotland.

As well as having had the quality of the welcome, service, food and comfort assessed by VisitScotland, they will be able to offer the following:-

★ hot drink on arrival
★ packed lunch/flask filling option
★ late evening meal option
★ early breakfast option
★ drying facilities for wet clothes
★ local walking and/or cycling information
★ daily weather forecast
★ local public transport information
★ secure, lockable, covered area for bike storage
★ details of local cycle specialists

Walkers Welcome Scheme

Cyclists Welcome Scheme

Look out for the logos in this guide and other accommodation listings.

Green Tourism

In response to the increasing need for businesses throughout the world to operate in an environmentally friendly way, VisitScotland has developed the Green Tourism Business Scheme.

Where tourism businesses are taking steps to reduce waste and pollution, to recycle and to be efficient with resources they are credited in this Scheme with a "Green Award". In our assessment of the degree of environmental good practice the business is demonstrating they are awarded one of the following;

Bronze award BRONZE

for achieving a good level

Silver award SILVER

for achieving a very good level

Gold award GOLD

for achieving an excellent level

Signs You Need To Know

Eat Scotland

Eating out in Scotland... the choice is yours... but where?

Perhaps you feel like dining in a beautiful restaurant, with first-class ingredients carefully prepared by talented chefs. Or you might be looking for something quicker, simpler. You might be on holiday, or maybe you live in Scotland and you like to eat out now and then. Where do you turn for advice?

VisitScotland has come up with the answer. To help you choose, there is now a consistent, reliable, authoritative and, most important of all, comprehensive guide to quality eating in Scotland.

EatScotland is the new food quality assurance scheme for Scotland and of course only places offering good quality food can participate in the scheme. Hundreds of restaurants, tea rooms, coffee shops, pubs, self-service restaurants and takeaways across the length and breadth of Scotland have already been assessed, ensuring these businesses meet EatScotland's rigorous standards, not only in terms of good quality food, but also ambience, cleanliness and service.

The new website, www.eatscotland.com, will be your definitive guide to great places to eat and drink in Scotland. This site will provide you with everything you need to know to get the best out of Scotland's larder.

Haggis and whisky might hold the position of "most recognised" traditional Scottish fare, and maybe porridge. Why not add to the list Cullen Skink, Arbroath smokies, clapshot, cranachan, clootie dumpling and howtowdie wi' droppit eggs... discover the tastes that match such romantic and ancient names.

Even if you don't go for traditional fare, you'll find eating out in Scotland an experience in itself.

Scotland's quality produce is a source of inspiration for many enterprising chefs with our world famous beef, venison, grouse, seafood, cakes, fruit and vegetables and the number of world-class restaurants has increased dramatically over the last few years.

Restaurant design has moved with the times and there are some stunning new eating places around the country, from glass walled restaurants on the banks of a river to rooftop eyries with stunning views. You can have afternoon tea in an ancient castle steeped in dramatic legend, or sip your café latte in the cool sophistication of the 21st century.

The choice is yours, and EatScotland is there to help, no matter whether you are looking for a first-class gourmet dinner, a humble fish supper or a nice, refreshing cup of tea.

So look out for the EatScotland logo of food and drink outlets throughout the country and log onto the website at www.eatscotland.com

Traveller's Tips

Scotland is a small country and travel is easy. There are direct air links with UK cities, Europe and North America. There is also an internal air network bringing the islands of the North and West within easy reach.

Scotland's rail network not only includes excellent cross-border services but also a good internal network. All major towns are linked by rail and there are also links to the western seaboard at Mallaig (for ferry connections from Skye and the Outer Hebrides) and to Aberdeen, Thurso and Wick for ferries to Orkney and Shetland.

All the usual discount cards are valid but there are also FirstScotRail Rovers (multi journey tickets allowing you to save on rail fares) and the Freedom of Scotland Travelpass, a combined rail and ferry pass allowing unlimited travel on Caledonian MacBrayne ferry services to the islands and all of the rail network. In addition Travelpass also offers discounts on bus services.

Cross-border rail services are available from all major centres, for example: Birmingham, Carlisle, Crewe, Manchester, Newcastle, Penzance, Peterborough, Preston, Plymouth, York and many others.

There are frequent rail departures from Kings Cross and Euston stations to Edinburgh and Glasgow. The journey time from Kings Cross to Edinburgh is around 4.5 hours and from Euston to Glasgow around 5 hours.

Coach connections include express services to Scotland from all over the UK; local bus companies in Scotland offer explorer tickets and discount cards. Postbuses (normally minibuses) take passengers on over 130 rural routes throughout Scotland.

Ferries to and around the islands are regular and reliable, most ferries carry vehicles, although some travelling to smaller islands convey only passengers.

Contact **Scotland's National Booking and Information Line – Tel: 0845 22 55 121,** or any Tourist Information Centre, for details of travel and transport.

Traveller's Tips

Getting Around

Many visitors choose to see Scotland by road – distances are short and driving on the quiet roads of the Highlands is a new and different experience. In remoter areas, some roads are still single track, and passing places must be used. When vehicles approach from different directions, the car nearest to a passing place must stop in or opposite it. Please do not use passing places to park in!

Speed limits on Scottish roads:
Dual carriageways 70mph/112kph;
single carriageways 60mph/96kph;
built-up areas 30mph/48kph.

The driver and front-seat passenger in a car must wear seatbelts; rear seatbelts, if fitted, must be used. Small children and babies must at all times be restrained in a child seat or carrier.

Traveller's Tips

Getting Around

Opening Times

Public holidays: Christmas and New Year's Day are holidays in Scotland, taken by almost everyone. Scottish banks, and many offices close. Scottish towns also take Spring and Autumn holidays which may vary from place to place, but are usually on a Monday.

Banking hours: In general, banks open Monday to Friday, 0930 to 1700, with some closing later on a Thursday. Banks in cities, particularly in or near the main shopping centres, may be open at weekends. Cash machines in hundreds of branches allow you to withdraw cash outside banking hours, using the appropriate cards.

Pubs and restaurants: Pubs and restaurants are allowed to serve alcoholic drinks between 1100 hours and 2300 hours Monday through to Saturday; Sundays 1230 hours until 1430 hours then again from 1830 hours until 2300 hours.

Residents in hotels may have drinks served at any time, subject to the proprietors discretion.

Extended licensing hours are subject to local council applications.

Telephone codes

If you are calling from abroad, first dial your own country's international access code (usually 00, but do please check). Next, dial the UK code, 44, then the area code except for the first 0, then the remainder of the number as normal.

Bring your pet

The Pet Travel Scheme (PETS) means you are able to bring your dog or cat into the United Kingdom from certain countries and territories without it first having to go into Quarantine, provided the rules of the scheme are met. PETS only operates on certain air, rail and sea routes and your own government should be able to provide you with details. Alternatively you may wish to obtain detailed information from:

Department of Environment
Food and Rural Affairs
1a Page Street
London
SW1P 4PQ

Tel: **0870 241 1710**
Fax: **0207 904 6834**
E-mail:
pets.helpline@defra.gsi.gov.uk
Web:
www.defra.gov.uk/animalh/quarantine

Scotland on the net

Visit our web site at:
visitscotland.com

"VisitScotland is committed to ensuring that our natural environment, upon which our tourism is so dependent, is safeguarded for future generations to enjoy."

Prize Draw

The perfect companion to your holiday.

February Draw
Entries must be received before 1st February 2006

May Draw
Entries must be received before 1st May 2006

September Draw
Entries must be received before 1st September 2006

Fill in the form overleaf to have the opportunity of winning this great prize.

Prize Draw

Send Entries to VisitScotland, Where To Stay Prize Draw, Ocean Point One, 94 Ocean Drive, Edinburgh EH6 6JH

Title: Mr, Mrs, Miss, Ms

Name:

Address:

Postcode:

Home telephone number:

E-mail address

Date of Birth dd/mm/yy

Data Protection:

We'd like to keep you informed of special offers from VisitScotland/visitscotland.com
Would you like to receive these?

Yes, by post ☐ Yes, by e-mail ☐ Both No ☐

In future VisitScotland may wish to contact you for research purposes. Is this okay?

Yes ☐ No ☐

From time to time we permit other tourism organisations to write to you about their products or services. Would you like to receive these?

Yes, by post ☐ Yes, by e-mail ☐ Both No ☐

Are you interested in any of the following activities?

Adventure Sports	☐	Festive Breaks	☐	Island Hopping	☐	Trekking & Riding	☐
Archeology	☐	Field Sports	☐	Mountain Biking	☐	Visiting Gardens	☐
City Breaks	☐	Fishing	☐	Off-road Driving	☐	Walking	☐
Romantic Breaks	☐	Cruising	☐	Food & Drink	☐	Sailing	☐
Watersports	☐	Culture	☐	Geneology	☐	Shopping	☐
Wildlife Watching	☐	Cycling	☐	Golf	☐	Snowsports	☐
Winter Breaks	☐	Events	☐	Hiking	☐	Spring Breaks	☐
Family Attractions	☐	Historic Sites	☐	Touring	☐		

Other (please state)

Prize draw rules:

1. Closing date for entry into the free prize draws are as follows: February Prize Draw entries must be received by the 1st February 2006; May Prize Draw entries must be received by the 1st May 2006; September Prize Draw entries must be received by the 1st September 2006.
2. Only one entry per household.
3. Employees of VisitScotland, visitscotland.com, their agencies and immediate families are not eligible to enter.
4. The winners will be notified by post as follows: February Draw winner by 15th February 2006; May Draw winner by 15th May 2006; and September Draw winner by 15th September 2006.
5. The winners' names will be available after the dates above (15th February, 15th May and 15th September 2006) by applying in writing enclosing a stamped, self-addressed envelope and writing to:
   VisitScotland Where To Stay Prize Draw, Ocean Point One, 94 Ocean Drive, Edinburgh EH6 6JH within 6 weeks of the closing date.
6. Prizes are non-transferable and no cash alternative will be offered.
7. All entrants must be UK residents and aged 18 or over.
8. The prize is a beautiful hamper full of wonderful delights to make your holiday or party that little bit special.
9. The promoter of this prize draw is VisitScotland.The promoter's decision is final and no correspondence will be entered into.
10. In the event of unforseen circumstances the Promoter reserves the right to offer an alternative prize of equal or greater value. Entry implies acceptance of rules.
11. Entries must not be sent through agents or third parties. Any such entries will be invalid.

Maps

Scotland's Tourist Areas

Accommodation

A	South of Scotland *Ayrshire and Arran, Dumfries and Galloway, Scottish Borders*	2
B	Edinburgh and Lothians	21
C	Greater Glasgow and Clyde Valley	52
D	West Highlands & Islands Loch Lomond, Stirling and Trossachs	66
E	Perthshire, Angus and Dundee and the Kingdom of Fife	90
F	Aberdeen and Grampian Highlands – Scotland's Castle and Whisky Country	120
G	The Highlands and Skye	138
H	Outer Islands: *Outer Hebrides, Orkney, Shetland*	182

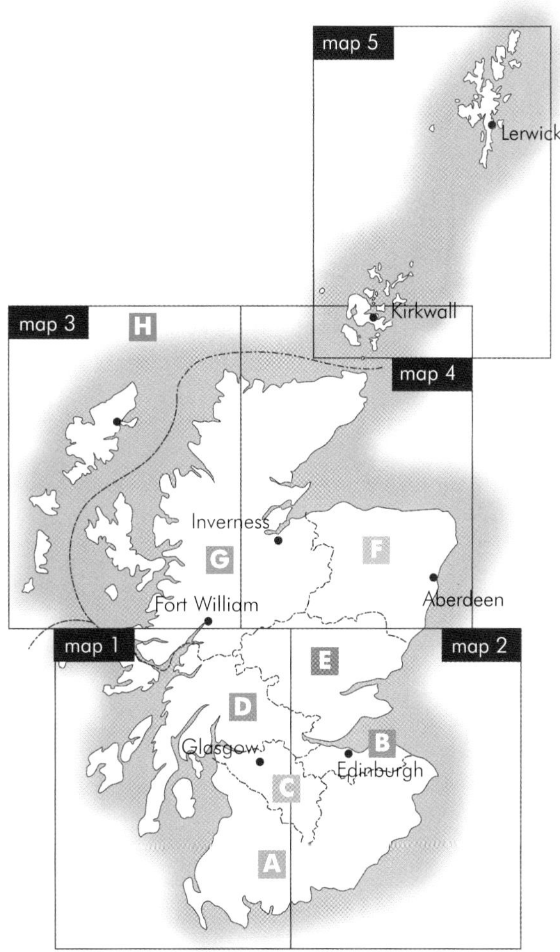

Map 1

A
B
C
D
E
F
G
H
1
2
3
4
5
6
7
8
9
10
11
12
Kilchoan
Strontian
Glencoe
Loch Leven
Ballachulish
Arinagour
COLL
Isle of Coll
Tobermory
Dervaig
Calgary
G
Lochaline
Scarinish
TIREE
Isle of Tiree
Fishnish
Lismore
Craignure
Barcaldine
Ardchattan
Connel
Oban
Killin
Loch Tay
MULL
Isle of Iona
Bunessan
Pennyghael
Dalmally
Kilchrenan
Crianlarich
Lochearnhead
Balquhidder
Strathyre
Ardlui
Cairndow
Inversnaid
D
Kilmelford
Inveraray
Arrochar
Tarbet
Port of Menteith
Ardfern
Loch Awe
Strachur
COLONSAY
JURA
Scalasaig
Isle of Colonsay
Luss
Loch Lomond
Drymen
Aberfoyle
Lochgilphead
Ardrishaig
Fintry
Helensburgh
Balloch
Alexandria
Isle of Jura
Dunoon
Gourock
Cardross
Port Askaig
Feolin
Rhubodach
Tighnabruaich
Colintraive
Inverkip
Wemyss Bay
Glasgow Airport
Paisley
GLASGOW
ISLAY
Ballygrant
Tarbert
Portavadie
Rothesay
Kennacraig
BUTE
(winter only)
Largs
Howwood
Cumbrae
CUMBRAE
Port Charlotte
Bowmore
Claonaig
Kilchattan Bay
Millport
Uplawmoor
Lochranza
Seamill
Isle of Gigha
Ardminish
Ardrossan
Kilwinning
Kilmarnock
Port Ellen
Tayinloan
Irvine
ARRAN
Carradale
Brodick
Firth of Clyde
Troon
Prestwick
ATLANTIC OCEAN
Blackwaterfoot
Whiting Bay
Kildonan
Ayr
Cumnock
Campbeltown
Dalrymple
Turnberry
Girvan
Car ferries and terminals:
Brodick
Ardrossan
Scale 1:1 300 000
0
10
20 miles
© Collins Bartholomew Ltd 2005
Cairnryan
Newton Stewart
Stranraer
Portpatrick
Creetown
Wigtown
Gatehouse of Fleet
Luce Bay
Larne
These maps show locations of establishments appearing in the Main Advertising Section of this guide. For route planning and touring please use a current road atlas.
Isle of Whithorn
BELFAST
To Douglas, Isle of Man
To Liverpool
MAP 1
MAP 2

Map 2

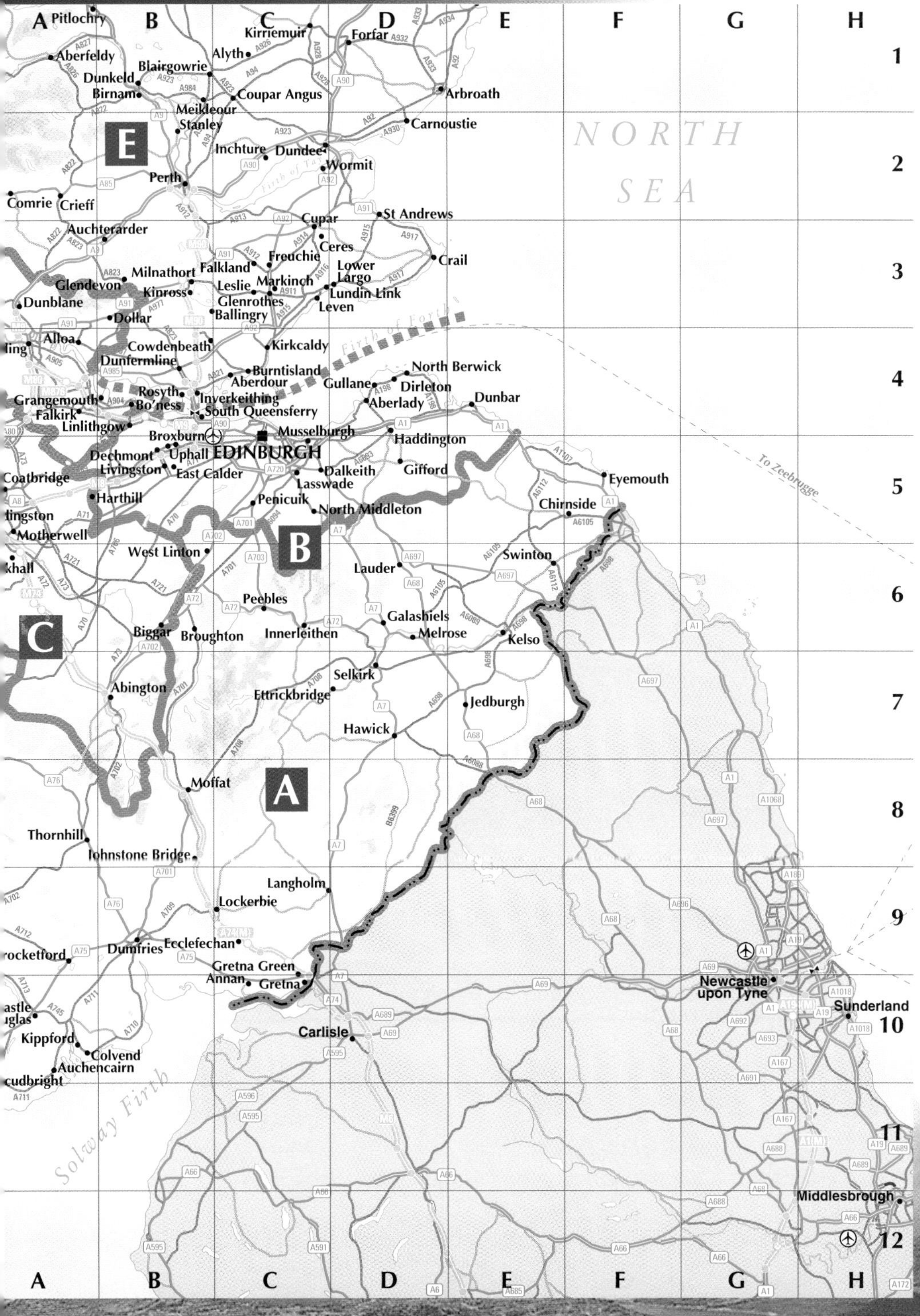

A B C D E F G H

1 2 3 4 5 6 7 8 9 10 11 12

Pitlochry
Aberfeldy
Kirriemuir
Forfar
Alyth
Blairgowrie
Dunkeld
Birnam
Coupar Angus
Arbroath
Meikleour
Stanley
Carnoustie
E
NORTH SEA
Inchture
Dundee
Wormit
Firth of Tay
Perth
Comrie
Crieff
St Andrews
Cupar
Auchterarder
Ceres
Freuchie
Crail
Milnathort
Falkland
Lower Largo
Glendevon
Kinross
Leslie
Markinch
Lundin Link
Dunblane
Glenrothes
Leven
Dollar
Ballingry
Firth of Forth
Alloa
Kirkcaldy
Cowdenbeath
Dunfermline
Burntisland
North Berwick
Aberdour
Gullane
Dirleton
Rosyth
Grangemouth
Bo'ness
Inverkeithing
Aberlady
Dunbar
Falkirk
South Queensferry
Linlithgow
Musselburgh
Haddington
Broxburn
Dechmont
Uphall
EDINBURGH
To Zeebrugge
Livingston
East Calder
Dalkeith
Gifford
Coatbridge
Lasswade
Eyemouth
Harthill
Penicuik
Chirnside
North Middleton
Motherwell
B
West Linton
Swinton
Lauder
Peebles
Galashiels
Biggar
Broughton
Innerleithen
Melrose
Kelso
C
Selkirk
Abington
Ettrickbridge
Jedburgh
Hawick
Moffat
A
Thornhill
Johnstone Bridge
Langholm
Lockerbie
Ecclefechan
Dumfries
Gretna Green
Annan
Gretna
Newcastle upon Tyne
Kippford
Colvend
Auchencairn
Carlisle
Sunderland
Solway Firth
Middlesbrough

Map 3

These maps show locations of establishments appearing in the Main Advertising Section of this guide. For route planning and touring please use a current road atlas.

A B C D E F G H

1 2 3 4 5 6 7 8 9 10 11 12

MAP 3 MAP 4

OUTER HEBRIDES

LEWIS

Stornoway
Callanish
Achmore

H

Ardhasaig
Tarbert
Kyles
HARRIS
Leverburgh
Otternish
Lochmaddy
Locheport
Carinish
NORTH UIST
BENBECULA
Liniclate
Creagorry
Lochcarnan
SOUTH UIST
Lochboisdale (Lochbaghasdail)
Daliburgh (Dalabrog)
Eriskay
BARRA
Tangasdale
Northbay
Castlebay
CANNA
RUM
EIGG
MUCK
ARDNAMURCHAN

The Minch

Duntulm
Staffin
Uig
Waternish
Dunvegan
Skeabost
Portree
RAASAY
Isle of Raasay
Raasay
Portnalong
Sconser
SKYE
Broadford
Breakish
Kyle of Lochalsh
Kyleakin
Kylerhea
Glenelg
Armadale
Ardvasar
Sleat
Mallaig
Morar
Arisaig
Loch Morar
Acharacle

Kinlochbervie
Rhicon
Scourie
Kylesku
Lochinver
ASSYNT
Achiltibuie
Ullapool
Aultbea
Dundonnell
Poolewe
Gairloch
Kinlochew
Achnasheen

G

Shieldaig
Torridon
Applecross
Kishorn
Lochcarron
Cannic
Ardelve
Dornie
Glenshiel
Invergarry
Loch Lochy
Spean Bridge
Glenfinnan
Roy Bridg
Fort William
Ardgour
Kinlochleven
Onich

Map 4

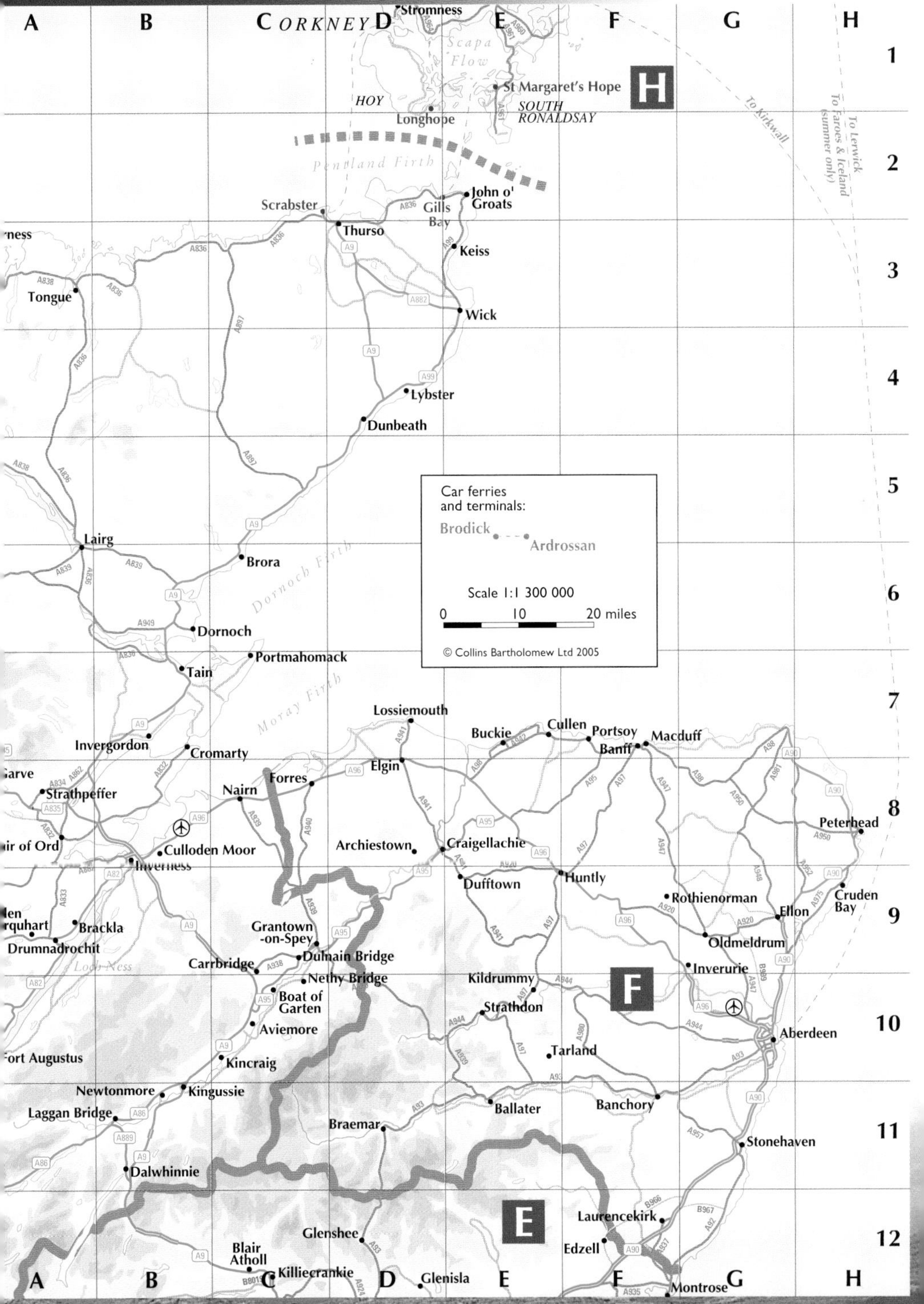

A B C D E F G H

1 2 3 4 5 6 7 8 9 10 11 12

ORKNEY
Stromness
Scapa Flow
HOY
Longhope
St Margaret's Hope
SOUTH RONALDSAY
H
To Kirkwall
To Faroes & Iceland (summer only)
To Lerwick
Pentland Firth
Scrabster
Thurso
Gills Bay
John o' Groats
Keiss
Tongue
Wick
Lybster
Dunbeath
Lairg
Brora
Dornoch Firth
Dornoch
Portmahomack
Tain
Moray Firth
Invergordon
Cromarty
Strathpeffer
Nairn
Forres
Culloden Moor
Inverness
Lossiemouth
Elgin
Buckie
Cullen
Portsoy
Banff
Macduff
Peterhead
Cruden Bay
Archiestown
Craigellachie
Dufftown
Huntly
Rothienorman
Ellon
Oldmeldrum
Inverurie
Brackla
Drumnadrochit
Loch Ness
Fort Augustus
Grantown-on-Spey
Dulnain Bridge
Carrbridge
Nethy Bridge
Boat of Garten
Aviemore
Kincraig
Kingussie
Newtonmore
Laggan Bridge
Dalwhinnie
Kildrummy
Strathdon
F
Aberdeen
Tarland
Ballater
Banchory
Braemar
Stonehaven
E
Laurencekirk
Glenshee
Edzell
Blair Atholl
Killiecrankie
Glenisla
Montrose

Car ferries and terminals:
Brodick - - - Ardrossan

Scale 1:1 300 000
0 10 20 miles

Map 5

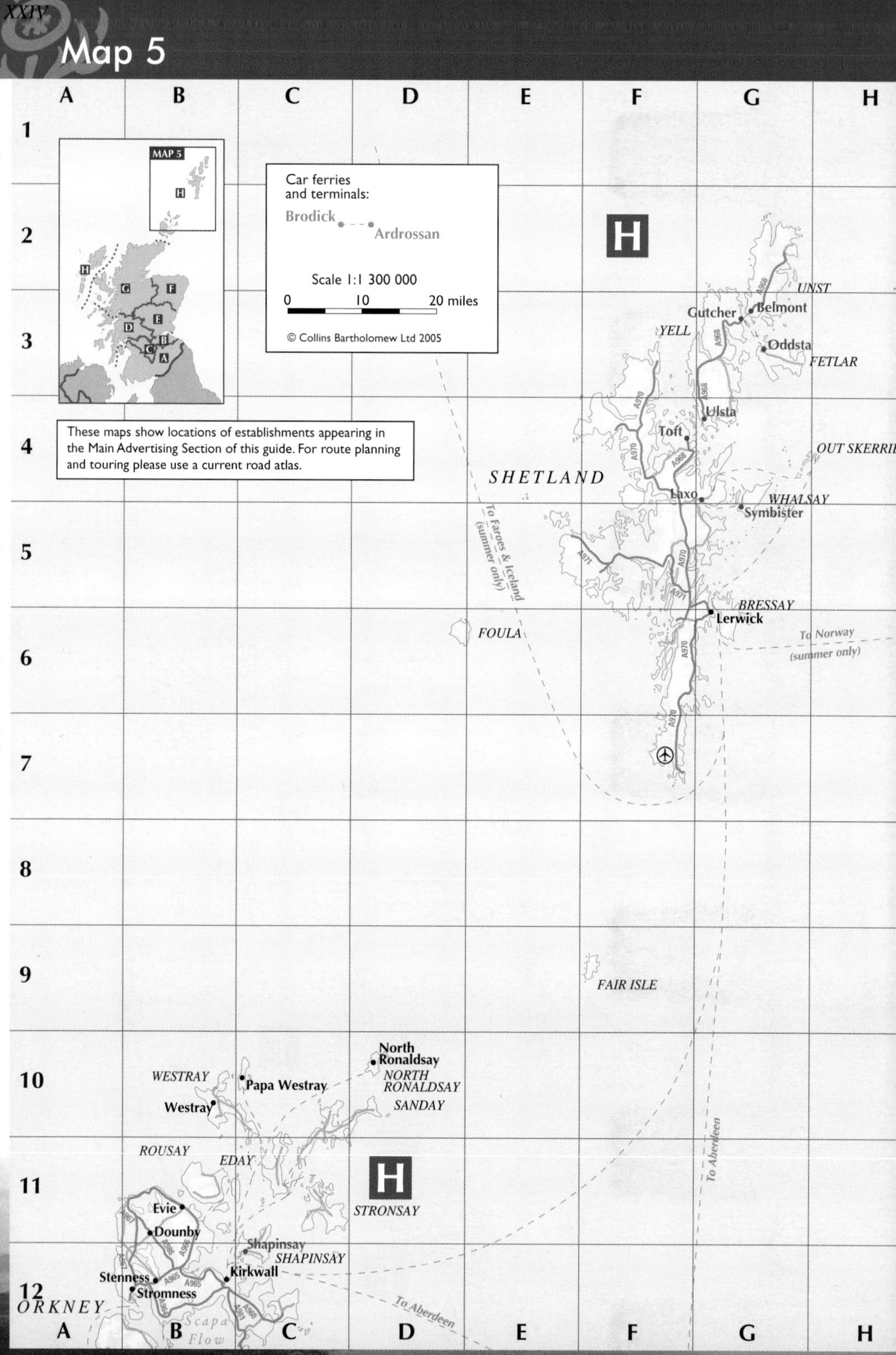

A B C D E F G H
1 2 3 4 5 6 7 8 9 10 11 12
MAP 5
Car ferries and terminals:
Brodick
Ardrossan
Scale 1:1 300 000
0 10 20 miles
© Collins Bartholomew Ltd 2005
These maps show locations of establishments appearing in the Main Advertising Section of this guide. For route planning and touring please use a current road atlas.
H
UNST
Gutcher
Belmont
YELL
Oddsta
FETLAR
Ulsta
Toft
OUT SKERRIE
SHETLAND
Laxo
WHALSAY
Symbister
To Faroes & Iceland (summer only)
BRESSAY
Lerwick
FOULA
To Norway (summer only)
A968
A970
A971
FAIR ISLE
North Ronaldsay
NORTH RONALDSAY
WESTRAY
Papa Westray
Westray
SANDAY
ROUSAY
EDAY
To Aberdeen
STRONSAY
Evie
Dounby
Shapinsay
SHAPINSAY
Kirkwall
Stenness
Stromness
ORKNEY
Scapa Flow
A965
A960
A961
A967
A986

Hotels & Guest Houses

Where to Stay Guide 2006

visitscotland.com
0845 22 55 121

Welcome to Scotland

South of Scotland: Ayrshire and Arran, Dumfries and Galloway, Scottish Borders

Scotland starts here in the south: rolling hills, legends of Scottish independence, and golf courses by the name of Troon, Turnberry and Prestwick. But it gets better…

Turnberry Championship Golf Course

You're spoilt for choice in these regions. Sports, castle spotting, sandy beaches, quaint villages, gardens, poets, fishing – the list goes on. The Borders, essentially Scotland's Deep South, is a place where Scottish armies 'negotiated' independence with England. Robert the Bruce and William Wallace won battles here, and Smailholm tower, near Kelso, is an example of the square towers that defended the Borders in the 16th century.

Beautiful scars remain in the Abbey ruins of Dryburgh, Jedburgh, Kelso and especially Melrose, where Robert the Bruce's heart is allegedly buried. Finding fish in the nearby Tweed River is easier. Try your hand at fly-fishing and hook yourself Scotland's finest salmon or trout. For insight into different worlds, visit The Edwardian mansion of Manderston and Georgian house of Mellerstain. Or walk in the Eildon Hills starting at Melrose and see romantic Scotland through the eyes of famous poet, Sir Walter Scott. More exciting, Glentress mountain biking in Peebles was recently voted the UK's best mountain biking route, providing tracks from mild to manic. To the east lie rich farmlands, ending abruptly in the cliffs of St Abbs, a must for birdwatchers.

Villages are dotted along the Solway Firth, but for gravitas, Caerlaverock Castle owns the coast. Look overhead and trace the flight of oyster-catchers to the nearby Wildfowl and Wetlands trust centre. Dumfries is a bustling market town with the warmth of red-sandstone houses. The 20 bookshops of Wigtown, plus an annual literary festival in September, make this Scotland's National Book Town.

South of Scotland:

South of Scotland: Ayrshire and Arran, Dumfries and Galloway, Scottish Borders

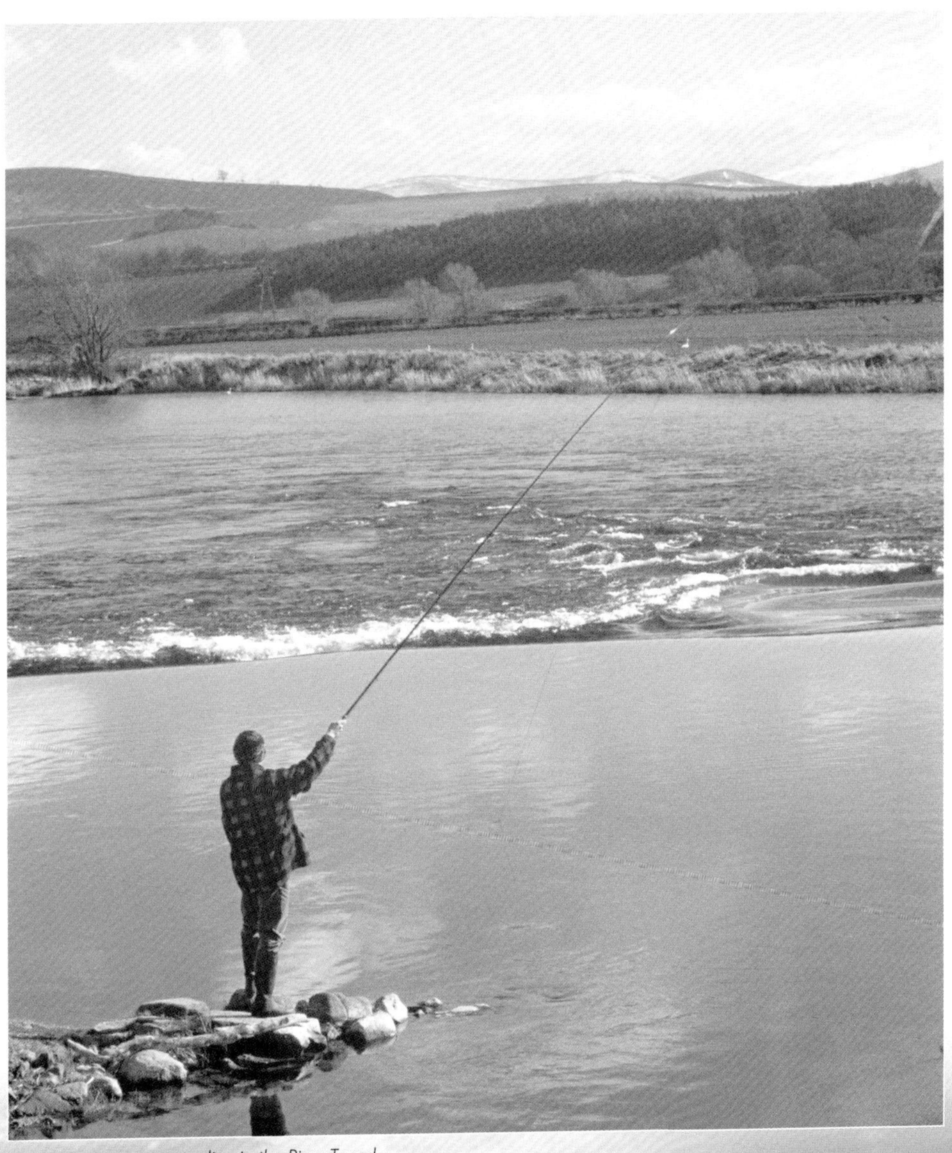

Any moment now... cast a line in the River Tweed

South of Scotland:

South of Scotland: Ayrshire and Arran, Dumfries and Galloway, Scottish Borders

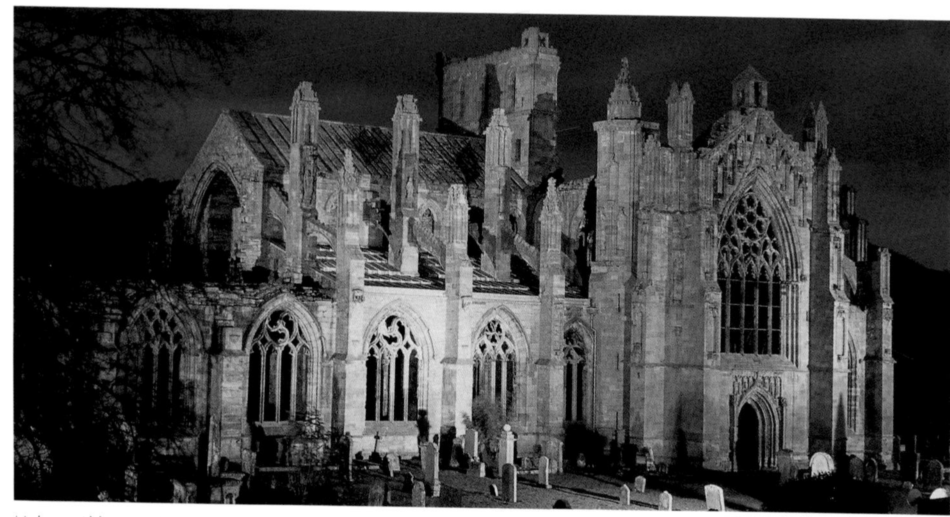

Melrose Abbey. A plaque marks the spot where Robert The Bruce's heart is allegedly buried.

Ayrshire rings with the name of Robert Burns, Scotland's star poet who, among other things, gave the English-speaking world that well known tune, *Auld Lang Syne*. There are related sites throughout the region, but Alloway is home to the Burns National heritage Park and a cracking folklore festival in May. It's easy to see other reasons for visiting, sandy beaches have made Ayr the leading family seaside resort on the Firth of Clyde. Largs has similar appeal, plus a chance to rub shoulders with Vikings at the Vikingar! Centre.

Culzean castle is arguably the finest castle in these parts. Lashings of tapestries, paintings and French windows are in a castellated mansion overlooking the Isle of Arran. Don't stop there – an hour's sail will take you to a place of quiet beaches, mountains, and drams at the Isle of Arran Distillery. Not to mention the seven golf courses.

As you can guess, the golf is bliss, not just at Championship greats but with scores of smaller clubs too. There's also 400 miles of the National Cycle network.

And you can always go for walk along the 212 mile coast-to-coast Southern Upland Way.

Events

South of Scotland: Ayrshire and Arran, Dumfries and Galloway, Scottish Borders

8 APRIL
MELROSE SEVENS
Traditional rugby competition with teams of seven players.
Tel: 01896 822993
www.melrose7s.com

21-22 APRIL
SCOTTISH GRAND NATIONAL, Ayr
The highlight of the Scottish horseracing year.
Tel: 01292 264179
www.ayr-racecourse.co.uk

12-14 MAY
NEWTON STEWART WALKING FESTIVAL, Ayrshire
Tel: 01671 403676
www.newtonstewartwalkfest.co.uk

20-29 MAY
BURNS AN' A' THAT, Ayrshire
A celebration of life and contemporary Scottish culture.
Tel: 01292 678100
www.burnsfestival.com

26 MAY-4 JUNE
DUMFRIES AND GALLOWAY ARTS FESTIVAL
Multi arts festival featuring music, dance, theatre and literature.
Tel: 01387 260447
www.dgartsfestival.org.uk

16 JUNE
SELKIRK COMMON RIDING
The battle of Flodden in commemorated with the casting of colours in the market place and the traditional riding of the marches.
Tel: 01750 21954

21-22 JULY
WICKERMAN FESTIVAL, Nr Kirkcudbright
Scotland's alternative music, dance and arts festival.
Tel: 01738 449430
www.thewickermanfestival.co.uk

5 AUGUST
BRODICK HIGHLAND GAMES, Isle of Arran
Traditional Highland games with pipe bands, athletic events and highland dancing.
Tel: 01770 302290

18 AUGUST-29 OCTOBER
GAELFORCE 2006
Arts festival celebrating Celtic culture.
Tel: 01387 262084
www.gaelforcefestival.co.uk

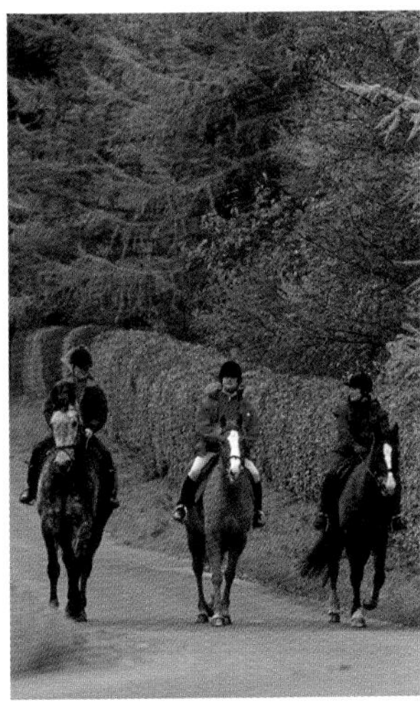

Cars and horses share the backroads of Peebles.

22 SEPTEMBER-1 OCTOBER
WIGTOWN BOOKTOWN FESTIVAL
A celebration of books and literature in Scotland's national book town.
Tel: 01988 402036
www.wigtown-booktown.co.uk

** denotes provisional date, event details are subject to change please check before travelling*

South of Scotland: Ayrshire and Arran, Dumfries and Galloway, Scottish Borders

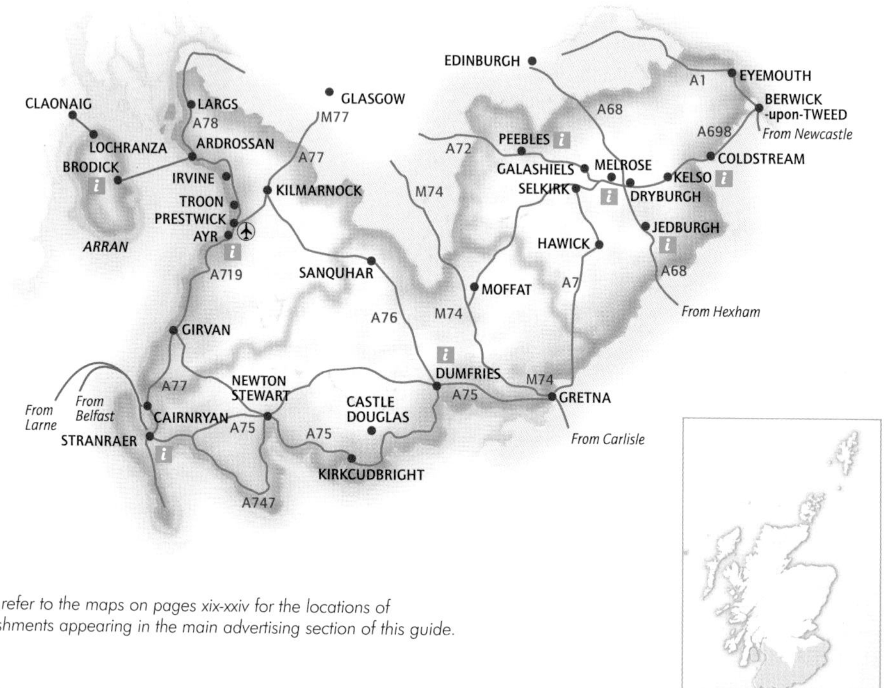

Please refer to the maps on pages xix-xxiv for the locations of establishments appearing in the main advertising section of this guide.

Finding out more...

For practical advice, ideas and information about exploring Scotland and to book your accommodation:

Tel: 0845 22 55 121*
or if calling from outside the UK: +44 (0) 1506 832121

Email: info@visitscotland.com
Web: www.visitscotland.com

* A £3 booking fee applies to telephone bookings of accommodation.

Tourist Information Centres

South of Scotland: Ayrshire and Arran, Dumfries and Galloway, Scottish Borders

Ayrshire and Arran

Ayr
22 Sandgate
Tel: (0845) 22 55 121
Jan – Dec

Brodick
The Pier, Isle of Arran
Tel: (0845) 22 55 121
Jan – Dec

Largs
The Railway Station
Main St
Tel: (0845) 22 55 121
Apr – Oct

Dumfries and Galloway

Castle Douglas
Markethill Car Park
Tel: (01556) 502611
Easter – Oct

Dumfries
64 Whitesands
Tel: (01387) 253862
Jan – Dec

Gatehouse of Fleet
Car Park
Tel: (01557) 814212
Easter – Oct

Gretna Green
Gretna Gateway
Tel: (01461) 337834
Easter – Oct

Kirkcudbright
Harbour Square
Tel: (01557) 330494
Easter – Oct (restricted winter opening)

Moffat
Unit 1, Ladyknowe
Tel: (01683) 220620
Easter – Oct

Newton Stewart
Dashwood Square
Tel: (01671) 402431
Easter – Oct

Stranraer
28 Harbour Street
Tel: (01776) 702595
Jan – Dec

Scottish Borders

Eyemouth
Auld Kirk, Manse Road
Tel: (0870) 6080404
Easter – Oct

Hawick
Drumlanrig's Tower
Tel: (0870) 608 0404
Apr – Oct

Jedburgh
Murray's Green
Tel: (0870) 608 0404
Jan – Dec

Kelso
Town House, The Square
Tel: (0870) 608 0404
Jan – Dec

Melrose
Abbey House, Abbey Street
Tel: (0870) 608 0404
Jan – Dec

Peebles
High Street
Tel: (0870) 608 0404
Jan – Dec

Selkirk
Halliwell's House
Tel: (0870) 608 0404
Apr – Oct

Brodick, Isle of Arran

Map Ref: 1F7

GUEST HOUSE

Dunvegan House
Shore Road, Brodick, Isle of Arran, KA27 8AJ
Tel/Fax:01770 302811

Superb sea and mountain views, conveniently situated for ferry terminal. Licensed. Dinner using fresh local produce when available. Private parking. Ground floor bedrooms available.

11 rooms, some en-suite, Open Jan-Dec, B&B per person, single from £35.00, double from £30.00, BB & Eve.Meal from £48.00.

GUEST HOUSE

Glencloy Farm Guest House
Glen Cloy Road, Brodick, Isle of Arran, KA27 8DA
Tel:01770 302351
Email:glencloyfarm@aol.com
Web:www.SmoothHound.co.uk/hotels/glencloy

A Farmhouse full of character set in a peaceful glen with views of hills and sea. A good base for exploring all that Arran has to offer. You will receive a very warm family welcome from Neil, Caroline and their chicks, a real home from home. Our 5 rooms are comfortable and individual with TV/Video and access to a video library. Breakfast is served in our cosy drawing room with some of the freshest eggs you will have eaten.

5 rooms, some en-suite, Open Jan-Dec, B&B pppn, single £27.00-35.00, double £25.00-40.00.

SMALL HOTEL

Ormidale Hotel
Brodick, Isle of Arran, KA27 8BY
Tel:01770 302293 Fax:01770 302098
Email:reception@ormidale-hotel.co.uk
Web:www.ormidale-hotel.co.uk

Family run Victorian Hotel built in the 1800s, set in mature woodland by the golf course. Home cooked meals for the family served in the conservatory. CAMRA approved. Good pub atmosphere.

7 rooms, all en-suite, Open Apr-Sep, B&B per person, single from £34.00, double from £34.00.

Kildonan, Isle of Arran

Map Ref: 1F7

INN

Breadalbane Hotel
Kildonan, Isle of Arran, KA27 8SE
Tel:01770 820284
Email:yvonne@breadalbanehotel.co.uk
Web:www.breadalbanehotel.co.uk

Situated on the Shore Road in the quiet village of Kildonan. The Breadalbane Hotel enjoys superb views to the islands of Pladda and the famous Ailsa Craig. A warm and friendly atmosphere in this personally run establishment offering freshly prepared food.

5 rooms, all en-suite, Open Jan-Dec, B&B per person, single from £25.00, double from £25.00.

Lochranza, Isle of Arran

Map Ref: 1E6

GUEST HOUSE

Apple Lodge
Lochranza, Isle of Arran, KA27 8HJ
Tel/Fax:01770 830229

A charming intimate country house set amidst spectacular scenery where deer and eagles are often sighted. Taste of Scotland.

4 rooms, Open Jan-Dec, B&B per person single from £48.00, double from £35.00.

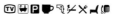

Important: Prices stated are estimates and may be subject to amendments

Whiting Bay, Isle of Arran

Map Ref: 1F7

GUEST HOUSE

View Bank House

Golf Course Road, Whiting Bay, Isle of Arran, KA27 8QT
Tel/Fax:01770 700326
Email:viewbank@btopenworld.com
Web:www.viewbank-arran.co.uk

Family run Guest House, the ideal haven for a relaxing holiday or a short break where you can unwind with superb elevated views and a short walk to the shore and nearest golf course. Six delightful bedrooms, Singles, Double, Family, some with sea views, most are ensuite. Warm friendly welcome and memorable breakfasts assured.

6 rooms, Open Jan-Dec, B&B per person, single from £22.00, double from £25.00.

Auchencairn, by Castle Douglas, Kirkcudbrightshire

Map Ref: 2A10

INN

The Old Smugglers Inn

Main Street, Auchencairn, Dumfries & Galloway, DG7 1QU
Tel:01556 640331
Email:jacvin@btopenworld.com
Web:www.oldsmugglersinn.freeserve.co.uk

Cosy Inn dating from 17th Century located in picturesque village on Solway Coast. Secluded Beer Garden with children's play area and burn running through it. Extensive menu with daily specials using fresh local produce.

3 rooms, all en-suite, Open Jan-Dec, B&B per person, single from £27.50, double from £25.00.

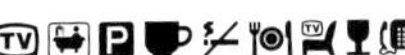

Ayr

Map Ref: 1G7

GUEST HOUSE

Belmont Guest House

15 Park Circus, Ayr, KA7 2DJ
Tel:01292 265588 Fax:01292 290303
Email:belmontguesthouse@btinternet.com
Web:www.belmontguesthouse.co.uk

Victorian townhouse in a quiet tree lined conservation area, within easy walking distance of town centre. Ground-floor bedrooms, all with ensuite facilities. Guest lounge with extensive book collection. On street and private car parking. Credit/Debit cards are accepted.

5 rooms, all en-suite, Open Jan-Dec excl Xmas/New Year, B&B per person, single from £28.00, double /twin from £26.00, family from £26.00.

HOTEL

Horizon Hotel

Esplanade, Ayr, KA7 1DT
Tel:01292 264384 Fax:01292 264011
Email:reception@horizonhotel.com
Web:www.horizonhotel.com

Family run hotel on seafront, views to the Isle of Arran. Refurbished Conservatory Restaurant serves meals all day. Ground floor bedroom with en suite disabled facilities. Lift to all floors. Golf breaks a speciality. Special winter offers such as 3 nights for the price of 2.

25 rooms, all en-suite, Open Jan-Dec, B&B per person, single from £45.00, double from £35.00, BB & Eve.Meal from £49.50.

GUEST HOUSE

The Richmond

38 Park Circus, Ayr, KA7 2DL
Tel:01292 265153 Fax:01292 288816
Email:Richmond38@btinternet.com
Web:www.richmond-guest-house.co.uk

Traditional stone built town house with many period features. Easy walking distance to sea front and town centre with all its amenities including a variety of eating establishments. Credit Cards accepted.

6 rooms, 5 en-suite, 1 priv.facilities, Open Jan-Dec, B&B per person, single from £30.00, double from £25.00.

VAT is shown at 17.5%: changes in this rate may affect prices.

Key to symbols is on back flap.

Ayr

Map Ref: 1G7

SMALL HOTEL

St Andrews Hotel

7 Prestwick Road, Ayr, KA8 8LD
Tel:01292 263211 Fax:01292 290738
Email:st_andrews_ayr@yahoo.com

St Andrews is a family run hotel. The hotel has a lounge bar, public bar, games room and a newly fitted dining room. The hotel is close to Ayr town centre, railway station and Prestwick Airport. Private parking. Golf packages available, member of South Ayrshire Golf.

7 rooms, some en-suite, Open Jan-Dec, B&B per person, single from £30.00, double from £25.00, family from £30.00, BB & Eve.Meal from £35.00.

SMALL HOTEL

Savoy Park Hotel

16 Racecourse Road, Ayr, KA7 2UT
Tel:01292 266112 Fax:01292 611488
Email:mail@savoypark.com
Web:www.savoypark.com

A contemporary, classic Scottish home, recently refurbished to today's quality standards. Ideally located in Ayr's premier residential area. Relax in homely surroundings and experience friendly service. Comfortable, inviting and excellent value.

15 rooms, all en-suite, Open Jan-Dec, B&B per room, single from £75.00, double from £105.00.

Castle Douglas, Kirkcudbrightshire

Map Ref: 2A10

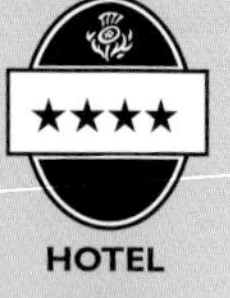

HOTEL

Balcary Bay Hotel

Shore Road, Auchencairn, by Castle Douglas
Kirkcudbrightshire, DG7 1QZ
Tel:01556 640217 Fax:01556 640272
Email:reservations@balcary-bay-hotel.co.uk
Web:www.balcary-bay-hotel.co.uk

A lovely country house hotel, with past smuggling associations dating back to 1625. Stands in over 3 acres of garden in a secluded and enchanting situation on the shores of the bay. Cuisine based on local delicacies: Galloway beef, lamb, lobster and of course, Balcary Bay salmon.

20 rooms, all en-suite, Open Feb-Dec, B&B per person, single from £63.00, double from £56.00, BB & Eve.Meal from £85.00.

Important: Prices stated are estimates and may be subject to amendments

Castle Douglas, Kirkcudbrightshire

Map Ref: 2A10

SMALL HOTEL

The Imperial Hotel

35 King Street, Castle Douglas, DG7 1AA
Tel:01556 502086 Fax:01556 503009
Email:david@thegolfhotel.co.uk
Web:www.thegolfhotel.co.uk

Privately owned hotel in market town, close to local leisure facilities. Ideal base for touring Galloway. Individual and group golfing holidays arranged. Private secure parking.

12 rooms, all en-suite, Open Jan-Dec excl Xmas/New Year, B&B per person, single £42.00-54.00, double £33.00-35.00.

Colvend, Kirkcudbrightshire

Map Ref: 2A10

SMALL HOTEL

Clonyard House Hotel

Colvend, Dalbeattie, Kircudbrightshire, DG5 4QW
Tel:01556 630372 Fax:01556 630422
Email:info.clonyard@virgin.net
Web:www.clonyardhotel.co.uk

Situated in 7 acres of mature gardens and woodlands, in a secluded position on the Solway Coast between Rockcliffe and Kippford. Choice of modern or traditional rooms, many on the ground floor, with their own private patio.

14 rooms, all en-suite, Open Jan-Dec, B&B per person, single from £40.00, double from £34.00, BB & Eve.Meal from £46.00.

Creetown, Wigtownshire

Map Ref: 1H10

SMALL HOTEL

Ellangowan Hotel

St John Street, Creetown, Dumfries & Galloway, DG8 7JF
Tel:01671 820201 Fax:01671 820226
Email:enquiries@ellangowan.co.uk
Web:www.ellangowan.co.uk

Impressive granite built hotel on the edge of the village Square. Personally run, with emphasis on cuisine using fresh local produce. Adjacent public parking area. Ideally situated for golf, walking, cycling and birdwatching breaks. Special rates for group bookings. Storage and drying facilities.

8 rooms, Open Jan-Dec, B&B per person, single from £36.00, double from £28.00, BB & Eve.Meal from £36.00.

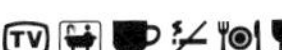

Crocketford, Dumfries

Map Ref: 2A9

SMALL HOTEL

Galloway Arms Hotel

Crocketford, nr Dumfries, Dumfries & Galloway, DG2 8RA
Tel.01556 690248 Fax:01556 690266
Email:info@gallowayarmshotel.co.uk
Web:www.gallowayarmshotel.co.uk

Historic Coaching Inn being upgraded and ideally situated on A75 only 9 miles from Dumfries and Castle Douglas on A75. A perfect location for touring 'The Land O'Burns' and the beautiful Solway coastline through which runs the Burns Heritage Trail. Popular base for golfing parties with many courses within a short driving distance. Popular locally for good hearty fayre.

10 rooms, some en-suite, Open all year, single room £37.50, double/twin £60.00 per room, family £75.00 per room.

Dalrymple, Ayrshire

Map Ref: 1G7

INN

The Kirkton Inn

1 Main Street, Dalrymple, Ayrshire, KA6 6DF
Tel:01292 560241 Fax:01292 560835
Email:kirkton@cqm.co.uk
Web:www.kirktoninn.co.uk

We organise the PERFECT BREAK for golf, fishing, touring, walking and any other outdoor pursuit. Outstanding Scottish and International food is served in our restaurant and a true Scottish evening may be enjoyed in our Malt Room and bars. Trained and qualified staff ensure the best of Scottish hospitality at all times. Living up to our motto 'There are no strangers here only friends who have never met!' we are sure to exceed your expectations.

11 rooms, all en-suite, Open Jan-Dec, Room only with breakfast: single £45.00, twin £80.00, triple £90.00, family £100.00, Eve.Meal from £16.95.

VAT is shown at 17.5%: changes in this rate may affect prices.

Key to symbols is on back flap.

Dumfries

Map Ref: 2B9

HOTEL

Cairndale Hotel & Leisure Club

English Street, Dumfries, DG1 2DF
Tel:01387 254111 Fax:01387 250555
Email:info@cairndalehotel.co.uk
Web:www.cairndalehotel.co.uk

Family run hotel in town centre. Executive rooms with jacuzzis. Extensive leisure facilities. Range of dining options.

91 rooms, all en suite.

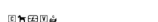

SMALL HOTEL

Moreig Hotel

67 Annan Road, Dumfries, DG1 3EG
Tel:01387 255524 Fax:01387 267105
Email:enquiries@moreighotel.co.uk
Web:www.moreighotel.co.uk

Originally built as a private residence, this family-run hotel is close to the town centre and has been sympathetically modernised for the comfort of both the Business and Leisure Traveller. Non-residents very welcome. Often used as a base by golf parties.

10 rooms, all en-suite, Open Jan-Dec, B&B per person, single from £45.00, double from £32.50, BB & Eve.Meal from £55.00.

Ettrickbridge, by Selkirk, Selkirkshire

Map Ref: 2D7

SMALL HOTEL

Ettrickshaws Country House Hotel

Ettrick Bridge, by Selkirk, TD7 5HW
Tel:01750 52229 Fax:01750 52377
Email:jenny@ettrickshaws.co.uk
Web:www.ettrickshaws.co.uk

Victorian Country house in 12 acre woodland setting. Elegant, spacious accommodation and home cooked food. Salmon fishing - guest concessions. Walking and cycling available within grounds and surrounding areas, where local wildlife and wild birds are seen in abundance.

5 rooms, all en-suite, Open Jan-Dec, B&B per person, single from £50.00, double from £47.00, BB & Eve.Meal from £67.50.

Galashiels, Selkirkshire

Map Ref: 2D6

SMALL HOTEL

Kingsknowes Hotel

Selkirk Road, Galashiels, Selkirkshire, TD1 3HY
Tel:01896 758375 Fax:001896 750377
Email:enquiries@kingsknowes.co.uk
Web:www.kingsknowes.co.uk

Family owned and run hotel, built in 1869 overlooking the River Tweed and Eildon Hills. 'A' listed former mansion house with original conservatory and set in its own well tended gardens. Ample parking. Sporting activities can be arranged nearby, golf, fishing, riding, walking, shooting, etc.

12 rooms, all en-suite, Open Jan-Dec excl Xmas/New Year, B&B per person, single from £59.00, double from £44.00.

Gatehouse of Fleet, Kirkcudbrightshire

Map Ref: 1H10

GUEST HOUSE

Bobbin Guest House

36 High Street, Gatehouse-of-Fleet
Kirkcudbrightshire, DG7 2HP
Tel/Fax:01557 814229
Web:www.visitscotland.com

Family run guest house in centre of village with ample parking. Ideally situated for touring Dumfries and Galloway. Home cooking with local produce. All en-suite facilities.

5 rooms, all en-suite, Open Jan-Dec, B&B per person, double £25.00-28.00.

Important: Prices stated are estimates and may be subject to amendments

Gatehouse of Fleet, Kirkcudbrightshire — Map Ref: 1H10

★★★

SMALL HOTEL

Murray Arms Hotel

High Street, Gatehouse of Fleet, Castle Douglas, DG7 2HY
Tel:01557 814207
Email:murrayarmshotel@ukonline.co.uk
Web:www.murrayarms.com

Built c1760, an attractive old Posting Inn where Robert Burns is known to have written 'Scots Wha Hae'. Discounted golf, fishing and tennis for residents. Warm friendly service. Ample parking available at hotel frontage.

12 rooms, all en-suite, Open Jan-Dec, B&B per person, single from £55.00, double from £47.50, BB & Eve.Meal from £70.00.

Girvan, Ayrshire — Map Ref: 1F8

★★

HOTEL

Westcliffe Hotel

15-17 Louisa Drive, Girvan, KA26 9AH
Tel/Fax:01465 712128

A family hotel, run by the Jardine family for 35 years, on the seafront overlooking the promenade, putting green and boating lake. Views across the Firth of Clyde to Ailsa Craig, Isle of Arran, Kintyre and Irish coast. Ground floor accommodation. Relax after a days sightseeing, golfing, fishing, walking, in the whirlpool spa, steam room, toning table or exercise gym. Limited secure private parking, unrestricted street parking.

24 rooms, all en-suite, Open Jan-Dec, B&B per person, single from £28.00, double from £28.00, BB & Eve.Meal from £36.00.

Gretna Green, Dumfriesshire — Map Ref: 2C10

★★★

SMALL HOTEL

Hunters Lodge Hotel

Annan Road, Gretna, Dumfriesshire, DG16 5DL
Tel:01461 338214
Email:Reception@HuntersLodgeHotel.co.uk
Web:www.HuntersLodgeHotel.co.uk

Closest hotel to the famous Gretna Registration Office. Cross the border into Scotland. Hunters Lodge Hotel is close to major routes. The chef proprietor creates freshly prepared dishes in attractive dining room with its tartan carpet giving a real flavour of Scotland. Staff are warm and welcoming as are the many different malt whiskies in the well stocked bar. Rooms are ensuite and well appointed. Full disabled facilities available.

11 rooms, all en-suite, Open Jan-Dec excl Xmas, B&B per person, single from £50.00, double from £35.00.

★★★

LODGE

The Mill

Grahamshill, Kirkpatrick Fleming, Lockerbie, DG11 3BQ
Tel:01461 800344 Fax:01461 800255
Email:info@themill.co.uk
Web:www.themill.co.uk

Converted farm steading and mill with stone built chalet style, en-suite accommodation. Just off the M74 near Gretna Green. Fully licensed bar/restaurant and function room. Purpose built, churchlike Forge building for marriage ceremonies in attractive grounds.

32 rooms, all en-suite, Open Jan-Dec, B&B per person, single from £55.00, double from £40.00.

by Hawick, Roxburghshire — Map Ref: 2D7

★★★★

SMALL HOTEL

Glenteviot Park Hotel

Hassendeanburn, by Hawick, Roxburghshire, TD9 8RU
Tel:01450 870660 Fax:01450 870154
Email:enquiries@glenteviotpark.com
Web:www.glenteviotpark.com

Traditional country house hotel located in a rural estate between Hawick and Jedburgh with stunning views across the River Teviot. Luxurious accommodation, excellent cuisine and genuine hospitality are just some of the reasons why discerning guests return time and time again. Available to adult residents only, tranquillity and a sense of calm relaxation is ensured. Golf, walking, horse riding, fishing, cycling and other pursuits.

5 rooms, all en-suite, Open Jan-Dec, B&B per person, single £75.00, double from £48.00, BB & Eve.Meal from £76.00.

nr Irvine, Ayrshire

Map Ref: 1G6

HOTEL

Montgreenan Mansion House Hotel

Montgreenan Estate, Kilwinning, Ayrshire, KA13 7QZ
Tel:01294 850005 Fax:01294 850397
Email:info@montgreenanhotel.com
Web:www.montgreenanhotel.com

A listed country mansion in 50 acres of garden. Near championship golf courses - Royal Troon, Old Prestwick and Turnberry. Hotel has 3 hole practice golf course, tennis courts, billiard room, bar & restaurant. Ideal base for touring Burns Country, Arran and the Isles.

21 rooms, all en-suite, Open Jan-Dec, B&B per person, single from £65.00, double from £40.00, BB & Eve.Meal from £65.00.

Isle of Whithorn, Wigtownshire

Map Ref: 1H11

INN

Steam Packet Inn

Harbour Row, Isle of Whithorn, Wigtownshire, DG8 8LL
Tel:01988 500334 Fax:01988 500627
Email:steampacketinn@btconnect.com
Web:www.steampacketinn.com

Personally run, on harbour front. Sea fishing. Access to walks, birdwatching and archaeological sites. Children and dogs welcome. Excellent value food with the emphasis on fresh local seafood, meat and game. Separate children's menu. Extensive wine list and range of malt whiskies. Real ales. Traditional Sunday lunches and buffet. Lunches served 12-2pm. Bar meals and restaurant. Conservatory and beer garden. No smoking areas. Open fires.

7 rooms, all en-suite, Open Jan-Dec excl Xmas, B&B per person, single from £30.00, double from £30.00. Evening meals 6.30-9pm.

Jedburgh, Roxburghshire

Map Ref: 2E7

SMALL HOTEL

Jedforest Hotel

Camptown, Jedburgh, Roxburghshire, TD8 6PJ
Tel:01835 840222 Fax:01835 840226
Email:info@jedforesthotel.com
Web:www.jedforesthotel.com

First hotel in Scotland on A68 route. High quality accommodation. All rooms en-suite. Taste of Scotland restaurant. Country setting, in 35 acres of grounds with 1 mile of trout fishing on the Jed Water. Scottish hospitality with a Continental flavour. 2 Red rosettes for cuisine.

12 rooms, all en-suite, Open Jan-Dec, B&B per person, single from £60.00. Dinner B&B from £70.00 per person.

Kelso, Roxburghshire

Map Ref: 2E6

GUEST HOUSE

Bellevue House

Bowmont Street, Kelso, TD5 7DZ
Tel:01573 224588
Email:bellevuekelso@aol.com
Web:www.bellevuehouse.co.uk

House of character in residential part of the historic town of Kelso. Minutes to the Tweed, town square and Floors Castle. Convenient for a good selection of restaurants, close to race course, ideally situated for local golf course and fishing. Private parking. Non smoking. All rooms ensuite.

6 rooms, all en-suite, Open Jan-Dec excl Xmas/New Year, B&B per person, single from £35.00, double from £29.00.

HOTEL

Cross Keys Hotel

36-37 The Square, Kelso, TD5 7HL
Tel:01573 223303 Fax:01573 225792
Email:cross-keys-hotel@easynet.co.uk
Web:www.cross-keys-hotel.co.uk

One of Scotland's oldest coaching Inns, recently re-furbished to a high standard. Enjoying prominent position overlooking the cobbled Flemish style square. A la carte restaurant and Bistro specialising in both local and Continental cuisine. 1999 winner of Best Eating Place in the Borders.

25 rooms, all en-suite, Open Jan-Dec excl Xmas, B&B per person, single from £42.90, double from £31.00 (subject to season).

Important: Prices stated are estimates and may be subject to amendments

Largs, Ayrshire

Map Ref: 1F5

GUEST HOUSE

Lea-Mar Guest House

20 Douglas Street, Largs, Ayrshire, KA30 8PS
Tel/Fax:01475 672447
Email:leamar.guesthouse@fsbdial.co.uk

4 rooms, all en-suite, Open Mar-Jan excl Xmas/New Year and Feb, B&B per person, from £28.00 double/twin room.

Detached bungalow in quiet area, yet close to town. 100 yards from the promenade and beach. Ideal base for touring. Private parking. All rooms ensuite.

HOTEL

Willowbank Hotel

96 Greenock Road, Largs, North Ayrshire, KA30 8PG
Tel:01475 672311 Fax:01475 689027
Email:iaincsmith@btconnect.com

30 rooms, all en-suite, Open Jan-Dec, B&B per person, single from £60.00, double from £45.00, BB & Eve.Meal from £56.00.

Modern hotel offering bedrooms on ground floor and 1st floor only, in tree-lined location on edge of town. Mid week and weekend entertainment. Bar meals, high teas and dinner available daily.

Lockerbie, Dumfriesshire

Map Ref: 2C9

SMALL HOTEL

Kings Arms Hotel

29 High Street, Lockerbie, Dumfriesshire, DG11 2JL
Tel/Fax:01576 202410
Email:reception@kingsarmshotel.co.uk
Web:www.kingsarmshotel.co.uk

13 rooms, all en-suite, Open Jan-Dec, B&B per person, single from £40.00, double from £35.00, BB & Eve.Meal from £47.50.

This family-run hotel is centrally situated within the town just off the M74 Motorway. The bedrooms and en-suites are currently being upgraded and the hotel is popular locally for food and drink. The function rooms can accommodate weddings and dances.

SMALL HOTEL

Ravenshill House Hotel

12 Dumfries Road, Lockerbie, Dumfriesshire, DG11 2EF
Tel/Fax:01576 202882
Email:reservations@RavenshillHotelLockerbie.co.uk
Web:www.RavenshillHotelLockerbie.co.uk

8 rooms, most en-suite, Open Jan-Dec, B&B per person, single from £40.00, double from £30.00, BB & Eve.Meal from £40.00.

A family run hotel set in 2.5 acres of garden in a quiet residential area, yet convenient for town centre and M6/M74. With a chef proprietor the hotel enjoys a reputation for good food, comfortable accommodation and friendly service. Weekend, short and golfing breaks.

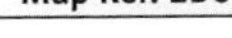

Melrose, Roxburghshire

Map Ref: 2D6

SMALL HOTEL

Burts Hotel

Market Square, Melrose, Roxburghshire, TD6 9PL
Tel:01896 822285 Fax:01896 822870
Email:enquiries@burtshotel.co.uk
Web:www.burtshotel.co.uk

20 rooms, all en-suite, Open Jan-Dec, B&B per person, single from £55.00, double from £50.00, BB & Eve.Meal from £60.00-90.00.

Family owned and run town house hotel - great bistro food and fine dining. 2 AA Rosette restaurant. AA Pub of the Year for Scotland 2005.

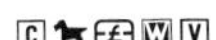

VAT is shown at 17.5%: changes in this rate may affect prices.

Key to symbols is on back flap.

Melrose, Roxburghshire

Map Ref: 2D6

SMALL HOTEL

The Townhouse Hotel

Market Square, Melrose, Roxburghshire, TD6 9PQ
Tel:01896 822645 Fax:01896 823474
Email:enquiries@thetownhousemelrose.co.uk
Web:www.thetownhousemelrose.co.uk

Situated in the heart of historic Borders town, this delightful family run hotel offers excellent food and wines and best local produce. Eleven well appointed bedrooms. Ideally located for fishers, walkers and cyclists (facilities available). Direct access to St Cuthberts and Southern Upland Ways.

11 rooms, all en-suite, Open Jan-Dec, B&B per person, single from £54.00, double from £45.00, BB & Eve.Meal from £60.00.

HOTEL

Waverley Castle Hotel

Skirmish Hill, Waverley Road, Melrose, TD6 9AA
Tel:01942 824824
Email:reservations@WAshearings.com
Web:www.shearingsholidays.com

Entertainment every night.

81 rooms, all en-suite, Open Feb-Dec, B&B per person, double from £35.00.

by Melrose, Roxburghshire

Map Ref: 2D6

B&B

Whitehouse

St Boswells, Roxburghshire, TD6 OED
Tel:01573 460343
Email:tyrer.whitehouse@lineone.net
Web:www.aboutscotland.com/south/whitehouse.html

Large country house decorated to a high standard, luxurious bedrooms and spacious bathrooms. Full of character, relaxed atmosphere, log fires. Delicious dinners using much of our own or local produce. Kelso, Melrose and Scott's View are all within 10 minutes drive.

3 rooms, all en-suite, Open Jan-Dec, B&B per person, double from £42.00, BB & Eve.Meal from £64.00.

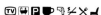

Moffat, Dumfriesshire

Map Ref: 2B8

SMALL HOTEL

Annandale Arms Hotel

High Street, Moffat, Dumfriesshire, DG10 9HF
Tel:01683 220013 Fax:01683 221395
Email:vs@annandalearmshotel.co.uk
Web:www.annandalearmshotel.co.uk

Imposing Georgian hotel (1760) set on the tree lined High Street of Moffat. Renowned for good food, hospitality and relaxed atmosphere. Bar and restaurant. Lounge. Private car park. Pets welcome, no extra charge.

11 rooms, all en-suite, Open Jan-Dec excl Christmas & Boxing Day, B&B per person, single from £50.00, double from £40.00.

Important: Prices stated are estimates and may be subject to amendments

Moffat, Dumfriesshire

Map Ref: 2B8

GUEST HOUSE

Barnhill Springs Country Guest House

Moffat, Dumfries & Galloway, DG10 9QS
Tel:01683 220580

Barnhill Springs is an early Victorian country house standing in its own grounds overlooking upper Annandale. It is a quiet family run guest house situated ½ a mile from the A74/M at the Moffat junction no.15. Barnhill Springs is ideally situated as a centre for touring Southern Scotland, for walking and cycling on the Southern Upland Way or for a relaxing overnight stop for holiday makers heading North or South. AA 3 Diamonds.

5 rooms, Open Jan-Dec, B&B per person, single from £25.00, double from £25.00, BB & Eve.Meal from £41.00.

GUEST HOUSE

Buchan Guest House

Beechgrove, Moffat, Dumfriesshire, DG10 9RS
Tel:01683 220378
Email:mailto:buchanguesthouse@moffatbroadband.net
Web:www.buchanguesthouse.co.uk

Victorian house in quiet residential area, close to centre of Moffat. Ideal base for touring.

8 rooms, most en-suite, Open Jan-Dec excl Xmas, B&B per person, single from £30.00, double from £25.00.

SMALL HOTEL

The Famous Star Hotel

44 High Street, Moffat, DG10 9EF
Tel:01683 220156 Fax:01683 221524
Email:tim@famousstarhotel.com
Web:www.famousstarhotel.com

A warm welcome is assured at this family run hotel in the centre of the popular Border town of Moffat. As the narrowest hotel in the United Kingdom, mentioned in the Guiness Book of Records. Popular with golfers and locally for food, drink and Real Ales.

8 rooms, Open Jan-Dec, B&B tariff, single en-suite £50.00, twin/double en-suite £60.00, family room from £70.00.

GUEST HOUSE

Hartfell House

Hartfell Crescent, Moffat, Dumfriesshire, DG10 9AL
Tel:01683 220153
Email:enquiries@hartfellhouse.co.uk
Web:www.hartfellhouse.co.uk

An elegant Victorian family run guest house with spacious, comfortable rooms in a quiet location only four minutes walk from High Street.

7 rooms, all en-suite, Open Mar-Dec excl Xmas, B&B per person, single from £30.00, double from £27.50.

SMALL HOTEL

Moffat House Hotel

High Street, Moffat, DG10 9HL
Tel:01683 220039 Fax:01683 221288
Email:moffat@talk21.com
Web:www.moffathouse.co.uk

18c Adam mansion with magnificent staircase, set in own grounds with country views to rear, yet in the centre of the award winning 'Scotland in Bloom' village of Moffat. All rooms en suite, ground floor rooms available including a self contained cottage. Lounge food plus fine dining in Hopetoun Restaurant.

20 ensuite rooms, Open Jan-Dec, B&B per person, single £65.00-70.00, double £49.00-58.00.

VAT is shown at 17.5%: changes in this rate may affect prices.

Key to symbols is on back flap.

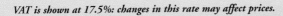

Moffat, Dumfriesshire

Map Ref: 2B8

SMALL HOTEL ★★★★

Well View Hotel

Ballplay Road, Moffat, Dumfriesshire, DG10 9JU
Tel:01683 220184
Email:info@wellview.co.uk
Web:www.wellview.co.uk

Mid-Victorian house converted to comfortable, family run hotel. Overlooking town and surrounding hills, with its own large garden. Innovative and original use of fresh local ingredients, in our attractive award winning restaurant.

3 rooms, all en-suite, Open Jan-Dec, B&B per person, single from £70.00, double from £55.00, BB & Eve.Meal from £85.00.

Newton Stewart, Wigtownshire

Map Ref: 1G10

SMALL HOTEL ★★★

Creebridge House Hotel

Newton Stewart, Wigtownshire, DG8 6NP
Tel:01671 402121 Fax:01671 403258
Email:info@creebridge.co.uk
Web:www.creebridge.co.uk

Traditional, Scottish country house hotel, offering modern comforts, situated in 3 acres of gardens, yet close to town centre. Relax in the elegant lounges with log fires in winter. We provide innovative meals in either the Brasserie or the Restaurant using fresh, local produce when available. Ideal base for golfers and walkers with Galloway Forest nearby. CAMRA Good Beer Guide. Taste of Scotland.

18 rooms, all en-suite, Open Jan-Dec, B&B per person, single from £50.00, double from £50.00, BB & Eve.Meal from £70.00.

GUEST HOUSE ★★★

Flowerbank Guest House

Millcroft Road, Minnigaff, Newton Stewart, DG8 6PJ
Tel:01671 402629
Web:www.flowerbankgh.com

Detatched 18th Century stone house set in one acre of wooded garden on the banks of the River Cree. Situated in a quiet and pretty village yet within easy walking distance of the bustling market town of Newton Stewart. Totally non-smoking.

5 rooms, most en-suite, Open Mar-Nov, B&B per person, double from £24.00, BB & Eve.Meal from £35.00.

Peebles

Map Ref: 2C6

INN ★★

Cross Keys Hotel

24 Northgate, Peebles, EH45 8RS
Tel:01721 724222 Fax:01721 724333
Email:crosskeyspeebles@aol.com

17th Century coaching inn in town centre. Brasserie serving bar suppers, a' la carte,and lunches. Bar and beer garden serving real ales.

5 rooms, all en-suite, Open Jan-Dec excl Xmas/New Year, B&B per person, single from £32.00, double from £29.00, family from £65.00.

HOTEL ★★★

Park Hotel

Innerleithen Road, Peebles, EH45 8BA
Tel:01721 720451 Fax:01721 723510
Email:reserve@parkpeebles.co.uk
Web:www.parkpeebles.co.uk

Quiet and comfortable, with extensive gardens and fine hill views. Ideal touring centre, and only 22 miles (35kms) from Edinburgh.

24 rooms, all en-suite, Open Jan-Dec, B&B per person, single from £59.50, double from £53.50.

Important: Prices stated are estimates and may be subject to amendments

by Peebles

Map Ref: 2C6

HOTEL

Cardrona Hotel Golf & Country Club

Cardrona, Peebles, EH45 6LZ
Tel:01896 833600
Email:cardrona@macdonald-hotels.co.uk
Web:www.cardrona-hotel.co.uk

The Cardrona Hotel, Golf & Country Club is set within the rolling hills of the Scottish Borders, yet is only 20 miles from Edinburgh. This 99 bedroom hotel features an 18 hole par 72 golf course designed by former Ryder Cup player Dave Thomas. In addition, the Cardrona Hotel offers guests state-of-the-art spa and leisure facilities.

99 rooms, all en-suite, Open Jan-Dec, B&B per person, single from £85.00, double from £60.00, BB & Eve.Meal from £80.00 pp.

Prestwick, Ayrshire

Map Ref: 1G7

HOTEL

Parkstone Hotel

Central Esplanade, Prestwick, Ayrshire, KA9 1QN
Tel:01292 477286 Fax:01292 477671
Email:info@parkstonehotel.co.uk
Web:www.parkstonehotel.co.uk

On the seafront overlooking a sandy beach on the Firth of Clyde. Close to many good golf courses and local amenities, and the town centre. Ideally situated for railway station and Prestwick airport.

30 rooms, all en-suite, Open Jan-Dec, B&B per person, single from £49.00, double from £41.00.

St Boswells, Roxburghshire

Map Ref: 2D7

HOTEL

Dryburgh Abbey Hotel

St Boswells, Melrose, Scottish Borders, TD6 0RQ
Tel:01835 822261 Fax:01835 823945
Email:enquiries@dryburgh.co.uk
Web:www.dryburgh.co.uk

Country house hotel on banks of River Tweed overlooked by 12c Dryburgh Abbey. Ideal base for fishing, shooting or exploring this historic area. Indoor pool, putting green and mountain bikes, trout rights on the Tweed.

38 rooms, all en-suite, Open Jan-Dec, B&B per person, single from £55.00, BB & Eve.Meal from £69.00 Single.

nr Stranraer, Wigtownshire

Map Ref: 1F10

SMALL HOTEL

Corsewall Lighthouse Hotel

Kirkcolm, Stranraer, DG9 0QG
Tel:01776 853220 Fax:01776 854231
Email:info@lighthousehotel.co.uk
Web:www.lighthousehotel.co.uk

Corsewall Lighthouse Hotel offers the charm and romance of an 1815 functional lighthouse with its cosy bedrooms each individually furnished. Spectacular sea views. The award-winning restaurant caters for a wide range of tastes including local beef, lamb, seafood and vegetarian dishes. Additionally there are 3 self-contained suites in the grounds. AA 3 Star and One Rosette.

9 rooms, some en-suite, Open Jan-Dec, B&B per person, single from £90.00, double from £50.00, BB & Eve.Meal from £65.00.

Swinton, Berwickshire

Map Ref: 2E6

RESTAURANT WITH ROOMS

The Wheatsheaf

Swinton, Berwickshire, TD11 3JJ
Tel:01890 860257 Fax:01890 860688
Email:reception@wheatsheaf-swinton.co.uk
Web:www.wheatsheaf-swinton.co.uk

Award winning restaurant with rooms, personally run by owners . Emphasis on hospitality and customer care and high class cuisine using local produce creatively. Convenient location for touring the Borders. All rooms en-suite. Open 7 days for lunch and dinner. 'Highly Commended' - Scottish Gastro Pub Chef of the Year - 2005.

7 rooms, all en-suite, Open Jan-Dec, B&B per person, single from £62.00, double from £47.50.

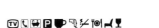

VAT is shown at 17.5%: changes in this rate may affect prices.

Key to symbols is on back flap.

Troon, Ayrshire

Map Ref: 1G7

HOTEL

South Beach Hotel

South Beach, Troon, Ayrshire, KA10 6EG
Tel:01292 312033 Fax:01292 318438
Email:info@southbeach.co.uk
Web:www.southbeach.co.uk

Privately owned hotel facing the sea on main road and about 0.5 miles (1km) from town centre. Convenient for Troon championship golf course.

34 rooms, all en-suite, Open Jan-Dec, B&B per person, single from £35.00, double from £30.00.

Turnberry, Ayrshire

Map Ref: 1G8

INTERNATIONAL RESORT HOTEL

The Westin Turnberry Resort

Turnberry, Ayrshire, KA26 9LT
Tel:01655 331000 Fax:01655 331706
Email:turnberry@westin.com
Web:www.westin.com/turnberry

Located just 50 minutes from Glasgow, this world famous resort offers Open Championship golf, award winning spa facilities and exhilarating outdoor pursuits.

219 rooms, all en-suite, Open Jan-Dec excl Xmas, B&B per room, single from £135.00, double from £159.00.

Welcome to Scotland

Edinburgh and Lothians

Why do visitors travel thousands of miles to walk The Royal Mile? If one street has this effect on people, imagine what the whole city can do…

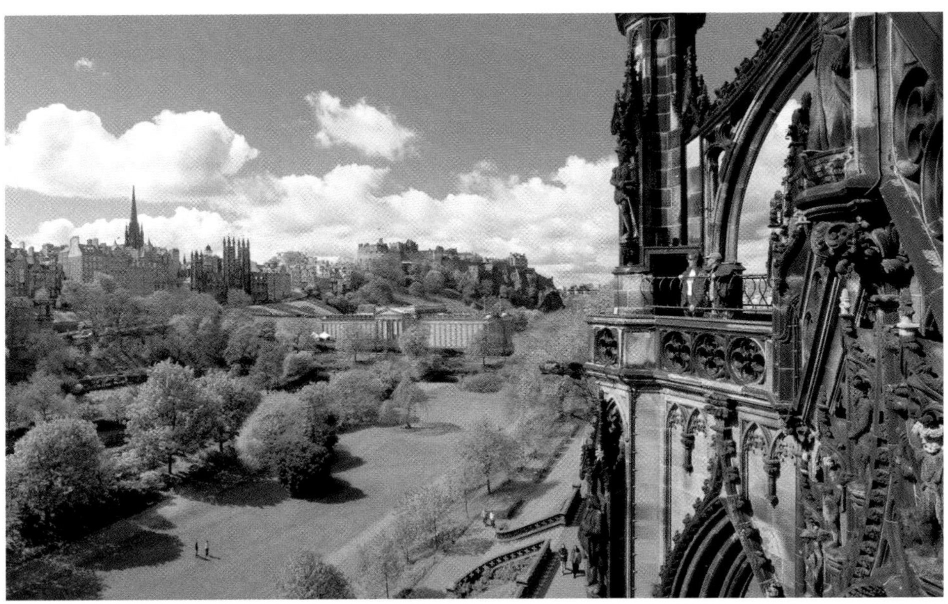

Climb the Scott Monument to see Edinburgh from a bird's view.

Everybody knows the name. Edinburgh is larger than life, offering more than you can fit into one holiday. It's also a city that continues to influence the world, which is remarkable when you consider it has a population of just half a million.

This is a city for time travel – just take The Royal Mile. At the southern end is the pomp and splendour of Holyrood House, official residence for the Royal Family in Scotland. A short walk will take you to the new Scottish Parliament, a bold architectural nod to the future of government. Then step back five billion years to see how the planet was created at Dynamic Earth, an interactive science museum. At the top of the hill is a castle - the castle. Once a royal palace and then a military fortress, Edinburgh Castle is still imposing, but not discouraging to a million visitors every year.

Head down the cobbled streets behind the castle, or try a walking tour of the old cemetery if you dare. Are you prepared for the MacKenzie Poltergeist? You're less likely to bump into witches and grave robbers today, just friendly locals who inhabit the bars and clubs nestled by The Old Town. And there's no shortage of them. Edinburgh has 700 bars in total. Many are located in the New Town, an elegant legacy of the

Street performers during Edinburgh's Fringe Festival in August.

Edinburgh and Lothians

The Union Canal, Ratho.

1800s when the city achieved new wealth and status, and Scots colonised distant lands. Princes Street combines Georgian facades with high fashion, much to the delight of shoppers. But for the priceless, you have to visit the museums and galleries. A weighty collection of Scottish and European masters is on display at The National Gallery of Scotland. Thousands of everyday objects, costumes and machines relive the country's evolution at the Museum of Scotland, adjoining the Royal Museum.

Above all, Edinburgh has a knack for turning traditions on their head. That's why you'll find comedians like, 'The Giant Pineapple Boys' hamming it up at the Fringe Festival.

A different reality lies a few miles away. From the summit of Arthur's Seat, Edinburgh's ex-volcano, you can see the hills and coastline of the Lothians. Nature reserves, sandy beaches and seaside resorts beckon.

Don't miss seeing the finest medieval stone carving in Scotland at Rosslyn Chapel, also rumoured to be the last resting place for the Holy Grail. If castle visiting is on the agenda visit the wildly romantic Dirleton Castle in East Lothian, and the dramatic ruins of Tantallon Castle with its views to Bass Rock. A bracing walk along the beaches in East Lothian is another treat, just 30 minutes from the city. Climbers will have a field day at Ratho Adventure Centre, which is simply the world's largest indoor climbing area with 2.4 square kilometres of artificial terrain.

Events

Edinburgh and Lothians

1 JANUARY
LOONY DOOK
On the first day of every year a brave few leap into the freezing cold water of the Firth of Forth at South Queensferry.
www.hogmanay.net

30 APRIL
BELTANE FIRE FESTIVAL
A celebration of summer's arrival.
Tel: 0131 228 5353
www.beltane.org

2-4 JUNE
GARDENING SCOTLAND
The biggest gardening and outdoor living show in Scotland.
Tel: 0131 333 0969
www.gardeningscotland.com

22-25 JUNE
ROYAL HIGHLAND SHOW
The highlight of the Scottish country calendar.
Tel: 0131 335 6200
www.rhass.org.uk

4-26 AUGUST
EDINBURGH MILITARY TATTOO
The capital's annual military extravaganza featuring a unique blend of music, dance, drama and pageantry set against the dramatic backdrop of Edinburgh Castle.
Tel: 08707 555 1188
www.edintattoo.co.uk

6-28 AUGUST
EDINBURGH FESTIVAL FRINGE
The largest arts festival in the world showcasing comedy, theatre and music.
Tel: 0131 226 0026
www.edfringe.com

12-28 AUGUST
EDINBURGH INTERNATIONAL BOOK FESTIVAL
This prestigious literary festival includes readings, author interviews and discussions.
Tel: 0131 228 5444
www.edbookfest.co.uk

13 AUGUST-2 SEPTEMBER
EDINBURGH INTERNATIONAL FESTIVAL
One of the world's most prestigious arts festivals offering the very best in international opera, theatre, music and dance.
Tel: 0131 473 2001
www.eif.co.uk

23-25 SEPTMEBER
BELHAVEN BEST TRADITIONAL MUSIC FESTIVAL, Dunbar
Popular music festival with concerts, sessions and dancing.
Tel: 01368 863301
dtmf.dunbar.org.uk

24 NOVEMBER-24 DECEMBER
EDINBURGH'S CHRISTMAS
Edinburgh's Christmas opens with the annual Christmas lights switch-on and includes many festive events including the Edinburgh Wheel, ice skating and the Christmas market.
Tel: 0131 529 4310
www.edinburghschristmas.co.uk

** denotes provisional date, event details are subject to change please check before travelling.*

Edinburgh and Lothians

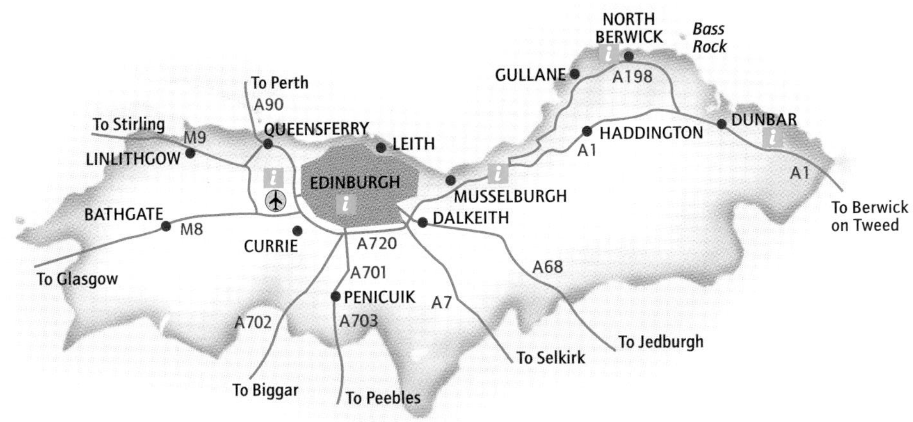

Please refer to the maps on pages xix-xxiv for the locations of establishments appearing in the main advertising section of this guide.

Finding out more...

For practical advice, ideas and information about exploring Scotland and to book your accommodation:

Tel: 0845 22 55 121*
or if calling from outside the UK: +44 (0) 1506 832121

Email: info@visitscotland.com
Web: www.visitscotland.com

* A £3 booking fee applies to telephone bookings of accommodation.

Tourist Information Centres

Edinburgh and Lothians

Edinburgh and Lothians

Dunbar
143A High Street
Tel: (0845) 22 55 121
Apr – Oct

Edinburgh
Edinburgh & Scotland
Information Centre
3 Princes Street
Tel: (0845) 22 55 121
Jan – Dec

Edinburgh Airport
Main Concourse
Tel: (0845) 22 55 121
Jan – Dec

Linlithgow
Burgh Halls
The Cross
Tel: (0845) 22 55 121
April – Oct

Newtongrange
Scottish Mining Museum
Tel: (0845) 22 55 121
Easter – Oct

North Berwick
Quality Street
Tel: (0845) 22 55 121
Jan – Dec

Old Craighall
Old Craighall Service Area (A1)
Tel: (0845) 22 55 121
Apr – Oct

Broxburn, West Lothian

Map Ref: 2B5

GUEST HOUSE

Bankhead Farm

Dechmont, Broxburn, West Lothian, EH52 6NB
Tel:01506 811209 Fax:01506 811815
Email:bankheadbb@aol.com
Web:www.bankheadfarm.com

Perfectly placed for Edinburgh and airport. Stay in a traditional farmhouse with modern en-suite bedrooms. Panoramic views of Scottish countryside.

7 rooms, all en-suite, Open Jan-Dec excl Xmas, B&B per person, single from £40.00, double from £35.00.

Dalkeith, Midlothian

Map Ref: 2C5

GUEST HOUSE

The Guesthouse@Eskbank

Rathan, 45 Eskbank Road, Eskbank, Dalkeith, EH22 3BH
Tel/Fax:0131 663 3291
Email:guesthouse@eskbank.scot.cc
Web:www.eskbank.guest.scot.cc

Award winning B&B with tranquil childsecure walled garden, croquet lawn and private parking. Set in the leafy Eskbank conservation area. Excellent park & ride base for Edinburgh. Low fat 'Highland' breakfasts and vegetarian option.

6 rooms, all en-suite, Open Feb-Dec excl Xmas, B&B per person, single from £35.00, double from £35.00.

Dunbar, East Lothian

Map Ref: 2E4

SMALL HOTEL

The Barns Ness Hotel

Station Road, Dunbar, East Lothian, EH42 1JY
Tel:01368 863231 Fax:01368 865200
Email:info@barnsnesshotel.com
Web:www.barnsnesshotel.com

Comfortable family run hotel offering superb Scottish hospitality. 16 en-suite bedrooms some with sea views. Excellent food in fine restaurant and bar. Easy travelling to Edinburgh on upgraded A1 road or 20 mins by train - station 2 mins walk. Golfers welcome. Private parking.

16 rooms, all en-suite, Open Jan-Dec, B&B per person, single from £55.00, double from £37.50, family from £85.00.

GUEST HOUSE

Springfield Guest House

Belhaven Road, Dunbar, East Lothian, EH42 1NH
Tel:01368 862502
Email:smeed@tesco.net

An elegant 19c villa with attractive garden. Family run with home-cooking. Ground floor room with private bathrooms available. Ideal base for golfing and touring East Lothian, Edinburgh and the Borders.

5 rooms, Open Jan-Nov excl Xmas/New Year, B&B per person, single from £25.00, double from £22.00.

East Calder, West Lothian

Map Ref: 2B5

GUEST HOUSE

Ashcroft Farmhouse

East Calder, Nr Edinburgh, EH53 0ET
Tel:01506 881810 Fax:01506 884327
Email:scottashcroft7@aol.com
Web:www.ashcroftfarmhouse.com

A warm Scottish welcome awaits you. Runner-up AA Landlady of the Year Awards 2005. Award winning landscaped gardens. Superior Guest House accommodation. Bus/train Edinburgh city centre 10 miles; airport 5 miles; M8/M9/A720 5 miles. Superb choice of breakfasts.
AA & RAC ◆◆◆◆◆

6 rooms, all en-suite, Open Jan-Dec, B&B per person, single from £45.00, double from £32.00.

VAT is shown at 17.5%: changes in this rate may affect prices.

Key to symbols is on back flap.

Edinburgh

Map Ref: 2C5

Abcorn Guest House

4 Mayfield Gardens, Edinburgh, EH9 2BU
Tel:0131 667 6548 Fax:0131 667 9969
Email:sales@abcorn.co.uk
Web:www.abcorn.co.uk

Personally managed by the owners Jimmy and Marjorie Kellacher, this detached guest house is centrally located, on a frequent bus route to the city centre. Ample private parking. Ground floor accommodation available.

7 rooms, all en-suite, Open Jan-Dec excl Xmas, B&B per person, single £28.00-42.00, double £28.00-42.00.

Adria Hotel

11-12 Royal Terrace, Edinburgh, EH7 5AB
Tel:0131 556 7875 Fax:0131 558 7782
Email:manager@adriahotel.co.uk
Web:www.adriahotel.co.uk

Friendly family run private hotel in quiet Georgian terrace. Spacious bedrooms. A pleasant short walk to Princes Street, Waverley Train Station and bus terminal. Totally non-smoking.

23 rooms, some en-suite, Open Feb-Nov, B&B per person, single from £30.00, double from £25.00.

Aeon-Kirklands Guest House

128 Old Dalkeith Road, Edinburgh, EH16 4SD
Tel:0131 664 2755 Fax:0131 621 0866
Email:dot@baigan.freeserve.co.uk
Web:www.aeon-kirklands.co.uk

Ideal base for sightseeing many of this city's historic attractions. Some ground floor en suite annexe accommodation. On main bus route to city centre. Close to Craigmillar Castle. Within walking distance of Royal Edinburgh Infirmary.

9 rooms, all ensuite, Open Jan-Dec, B&B per person, single from £35.00, double from £22.50. Family room available.

Afton Guest House

1 Hartington Gardens, Edinburgh, EH10 4LD
Tel/Fax:0131 229 1019
Email:info@aftonguesthouse.co.uk
Web:www.aftonguesthouse.co.uk

Newly refurbished end terraced Victorian house in residential area but near main bus route to city centre. Variety of restaurants nearby. Ensuite and private facilities throughout.

7 rooms, some en-suite, Open Jan-Dec, B&B per person, single from £25.00, double from £25.00.

A Haven Townhouse

180 Ferry Road, Edinburgh, EH6 4NS
Tel:0131 554 6559 Fax:0131 554 5252
Email:reservations@a-haven.co.uk
Web:www.a-haven.co.uk

Privately owned Townhouse Hotel. Near city centre and on main bus route. Scottish welcome and hospitality including a hearty Highland breakfast. Variety of restaurants nearby or dinner by prior arrangement. 2 new high quality bedrooms in garden annexe.

14 rooms, all en-suite, Open Jan-Dec excl Xmas, B&B per person, single from £30.00, double from £30.00.

Important: Prices stated are estimates and may be subject to amendments

Edinburgh **Map Ref: 2C5**

Ailsa Craig Hotel

24 Royal Terrace, Edinburgh EH7 5AH
Tel: 0131-556 1022/6055 Fax: 0131-556 6055
e.mail: ailsacraighotel@ednet.co.uk Web: www.townhousehotels.co.uk

Elegant Georgian town house hotel. Ideal city centre location within walking distance to Waverley Station, Princes Street, Edinburgh Castle and Playhouse Theatre. Combining traditional features with modern facilities, the hotel offers superb views, private gardens and friendly atmosphere providing the perfect blend of history and hospitality. Free wi-fi internet access.

SMALL HOTEL

Ailsa Craig Hotel

24 Royal Terrace, Edinburgh, EH7 5AH
Tel:0131 556 6055/1022 Fax:0131 556 6055
Email:ailsacraighotel@ednet.co.uk
Web:www.townhousehotels.co.uk

Elegant Georgian town house in city centre with tastefully decorated bedrooms, situated in quiet residential area overlooking landscaped public gardens. Front facing top floor bedrooms have views across Edinburgh to the Firth of Forth and the Fife Coast.

18 rooms, some en-suite, Open Jan-Dec, B&B per person, single from £35.00, double from £25.00.

C £ W V

GUEST HOUSE

Alexander Guest House

35 Mayfield Gardens, Edinburgh, EH9 2BX
Tel:0131 258 4028 Fax:0131 258 1247
Email:info@thealexanderguesthouse.co.uk
Web:www.thealexanderguesthouse.co.uk

Elegantly furnished four star Victorian villa situated one mile from Edinburgh's famous Royal Mile, Castle and Holyrood. Close to the University and Royal Infirmary.

6 rooms, some en-suite, Open Jan-Dec, B&B per person, single from £25.00, double from £25.00.

GUEST HOUSE

Allison House

17 Mayfield Gardens, Edinburgh, EH9 2AX
Tel:0131 667 8049 Fax:0131 667 5001
Email:info@allisonhousehotel.com
Web:www.allisonhousehotel.com

On main route into the city, convenient for all attractions, private parking and regular bus service. All rooms double glazed. One room has private bathroom.

11 rooms, 10 en-suite, Open Jan-Dec, B&B per person, single from £40.00, double/twin from £30.00.

C £ V

GUEST HOUSE

Alloway Guest House

96 Pilrig Street, Edinburgh, EH6 5AY
Tel:0131 554 1786 Fax:0131 554 2060
Email:alloway@eh65ay.fsnet.co.uk

Family run Victorian guest house, within easy reach of the city centre. Unrestricted street parking. Short stroll to Leith Walk with its many restaurants, theatres etc. Frequent bus service to city centre.

6 rooms, some en-suite, 1 room with priv.facilities (twin). Open Jan-Dec, B&B per person, single from £25.00, double/twin from £28.00.

£

Edinburgh Map Ref: 2C5

Apex Hotels, Edinburgh

31-35 Grassmarket, Edinburgh EH1 2HS
Telephone: 0845 3650000 or 0044 131 666 5124, Quote VS.
Fax: 0131 666 5128
e.mail: reservations@apexhotels.co.uk
Web: www.apexhotels.co.uk

Apex International Hotel lies below the Castle in Edinburgh's historic Old Town. Contemporary design with stunning views. Heights restaurant has the best Castle and skyline views in town. Metro Brasserie, a three storey brasserie for relaxed dining. Apex City Hotel, a Deluxe Hotel, sitting alongside the Apex International in the historic Grassmarket. The chic bedrooms are creatively designed with wide screen TV's and CD/DVD players. Agua Restaurant offers uplifting cuisine. Apex European Hotel, contemporary in style, perfectly located at the West End of the city centre. Metro Brasserie offers classic and contemporary dishes in a relaxed environment.

HOTEL

Apex International Hotel
31/35 Grassmarket, Edinburgh, EH1 2HS
Tel:0845 365 0000 Fax:0131 666 5128
Email:reservations@apexhotels.co.uk
Web:www.apexhotels.co.uk

Modern hotel in city centre with views towards Edinburgh Castle. Roof top restaurant with spectacular views of the castle. Private car parking. Ideal location for visitors to city without a car.

171 rooms, all en-suite, Open Jan-Dec, B&B per person, single from £80.00, double from £40.00, BB & Eve.Meal from £57.00 pppn.

C £ V

Ardenlee Guest House

9 Eyre Place, Edinburgh EH3 5ES. Telephone: 0131 556 2838
e.mail: info@ardenlee.co.uk Web: www.ardenlee.co.uk

Beautiful Grade 'B' listed Victorian town house in the very centre of Edinburgh (off Dundas Street). Only half a mile from Princes Street and within easy walking distance of all main attractions, train and bus stations. Family run offering a warm welcome, spacious comfortable rooms and a fully cooked breakfast.

GUEST HOUSE

Ardenlee Guest House
9 Eyre Place, Edinburgh, EH3 5ES
Tel:0131 556 2838 Fax:0131 557 0937
Email:info@ardenlee.co.uk
Web:www.ardenlee.co.uk

Personally run terraced guest house, in New Town approximately 0.5 mile (1km) from Princes Street and city centre. Ideal touring base. Non-smoking house. Variety of shops and restaurants nearby. Most rooms en-suite.

9 rooms, some en-suite, Open Jan-Dec, B&B per person, single from £27.50, double from £27.50.

C £ V

Important: Prices stated are estimates and may be subject to amendments

Edinburgh

Map Ref: 2C5

GUEST HOUSE

Ardgarth Guest House

1 St Mary's Place, Portobello, Edinburgh, EH15 2QF
Tel:0131 669 3021 Fax:0131 468 1221
Email:stay@ardgarth.com
Web:www.ardgarth.com

Comfortable accommodation in friendly guest house. Close to sea. Special diets catered for, full ensuite disabled facilities, With roll-in showers. French spoken. On street parking available.

9 rooms, some en-suite, Open Jan-Dec excl Xmas, B&B per person, single from £17.00, double from £17.00.

GUEST HOUSE

Ardleigh Guest House

260 Ferry Road, Edinburgh, EH5 3AN
Tel:0131 552 1833 Fax:0131 552 4951
Email:info@ardleighhouse.com
Web:www.ardleighhouse.com

Panoramic views of the city and the castle, on the bus routes to the centre - 1.5 miles. Free parking.

7 rooms, 5 en-suite, Open Jan-Dec, B&B per person, single from £25.00, double from £20.00.

SMALL HOTEL

Ardmillan Hotel

9-10 Ardmillan Terrace, Edinburgh, EH11 2JW
Tel:0131 337 9588 Fax:0131 346 1895
Email:hotelardmillan@hotmail.com
Web:www.ardmillanhotel.com

Small family run hotel, with recently refurbished popular bar restaurant. Located on bus route to city centre and a short walk to Princes Street. Murrayfield Leisure and Tynecastle Stadium are close-by.

10 rooms, mostly en-suite, Open all year, B&B single from £39.00, double room from £59.00. Eve.meal 3 course from £10.00.

GUEST HOUSE

Ashgrove House

12 Osborne Terrace, Edinburgh, EH12 5HG
Tel:0131 337 5014 Fax:0131 313 5043
Email:info@theashgrovehouse.com
Web:www.theashgrovehouse.com

Family run guest house on main road leading into Edinburgh City, from the airport. Non smoking house, private parking, within easy walking distance to Princes Street and Murrayfield Stadium. Also close to Haymarket railway station.

7 rooms, some en-suite, Open Jan-Dec, B&B per person, single £35.00-60.00, double £33.00-50.00.

GUEST HOUSE

Ashlyn Guest House

42 Inverleith Row, Edinburgh, EH3 5PY
Tel/Fax:0131 552 2954
Email:reservations@ashlyn-edinburgh.com
Web:www.ashlyn-edinburgh.com

Semi-detached Georgian family home, only 5 minutes walk from the beautiful Botanical Gardens. This listed building retains many original features with ornate cornicing and period fire places. 20 minute walk to Princes Street and the Castle with frequent bus service on the door step. Unrestricted free street parking nearby.

7 rooms, most en-suite/private bathrooms. Open Jan-Dec excl Xmas, B&B single from £30.00, double from £60.00.

VAT is shown at 17.5%: changes in this rate may affect prices.

Key to symbols is on back flap.

Edinburgh

Map Ref: 2C5

★★★★★

HOTEL

The Balmoral

1 Princes Street, Edinburgh, EH2 2EQ
Tel:0870 460 7040 Fax:0131 557 8740
Email:reservations@thebalmoralhotel.com
Web:www.roccofortehotels.com

Edinburgh's landmark hotel at Edinburgh's most prestigious address.

188 rooms, all en-suite, Open Jan-Dec, Room rate: single from £270.00, classic double from £320.00.

★★

GUEST HOUSE

Barossa Guest House

21 Pilrig Street, Edinburgh, EH6 5AN
Tel:0131 554 3700

Family run Georgian house only a short walk from city centre on main bus routes. Ensuite rooms available. Unrestricted street parking.

6 rooms, some en-suite, Open Jan-Dec, B&B per person, double £27.00-45.00.

★★★

GUEST HOUSE

Ben Cruachan

17 McDonald Road, Edinburgh, EH7 4LX
Tel:0131 556 3709
Email:nan@bencruachan.com
Web:www.bencruachan.com

Centrally located, personally run, terraced house 0.5 mile (1 km) to Princes St. All ensuite bedrooms. Unrestricted street parking. Excellent selection of restaurants nearby, Playhouse Theatre, 0.25 mile.

3 rooms, all en-suite, Open Jan-Dec, B&B per person, double £26.00-40.00.

★★★★

GUEST HOUSE

Ben Doran

11 Mayfield Gardens, Edinburgh, EH9 2AX
Tel:0131 667 8488 Fax:0131 667 0076
Email:info@ben-doran.com
Web:www.ben-doran.com

Charming and historically listed Georgian townhouse, elegantly refurbished. Central, on bus routes, close to City Centre and Edinburgh attractions. Lovely city and hillside views from the windows. The Ben Doran is run with pride.

11 rooms, most en-suite, Open Jan-Dec, B&B per person, single from £35.00, double from £32.50.

Important: Prices stated are estimates and may be subject to amendments

Edinburgh **Map Ref: 2C5**

GUEST HOUSE

Beresford Hotel

32 Coates Gardens, Edinburgh, EH12 5LE
Tel:0131 337 0850
Email:bookings@beresford-edinburgh.com
Web:www.beresford-edinburgh.com

Family run establishment close to city centre and Haymarket station. Most rooms en-suite. Children very welcome.

12 rooms, 10 en-suite, Open Jan-Dec, B&B per person, single from £30.00, double from £22.50.

HOTEL

Best Western Bruntsfield Hotel

69 Bruntsfield Place, Edinburgh, EH10 4HH
Tel:0131 229 1393 Fax:0131 229 5634
Email:reservations@thebruntsfield.co.uk
Web:www.thebruntsfield.co.uk

Overlooking a park close to the city centre, the Best Western Bruntsfield Hotel is a well appointed townhouse hotel with friendly & professional service. The 71 comfortably furnished bedrooms offer all facilities & services required by both business & leisure travellers.The Cardoon Restaurant serves modern Scottish cuisine in an elegant but informal atmosphere. A relaxing lounge & stylish bar add to the distinctive character of The Bruntsfield.

71 rooms, all en-suite, Open Jan-Dec excl Xmas, B&B per person, single from £85.00, double from £75.00 per person per night.

HOTEL

Best Western Kings Manor Hotel

100 Milton Road East, Edinburgh, EH15 2NP
Tel:0131 468 8003 Fax:0131 669 6650
Email:reservations@kingsmanor.com
Web:www.kingsmanor.com

Family run hotel 4 miles (6kms) east of city centre, handy for beach and all major road routes. Extensive modern leisure facilities.

67 rooms, all en-suite, Open Jan-Dec, B&B per person, single from £60.00, double from £45.00, BB & Eve.Meal from £60.00.

GUEST HOUSE

The Beverley

40 Murrayfield Avenue, Edinburgh, EH12 6AY
Tel:0131 337 1128 Fax:0131 313 3275
Email:enquiries@thebeverley.com
Web:www.thebeverley.com

An elegant Victorian terraced house, situated in a quiet tree-lined avenue offering ample free parking. Only minutes from Edinburgh's historic city centre and within fifteen minutes of all main coach, rail and air terminals. Non-smoking throughout. TV/DVDs in all bedrooms. Wireless Broadband Network.

8 rooms, all en-suite, Open Jan-Dec, B&B per person, single £35.00-50.00, double £30.00-50.00.

GUEST HOUSE

Blossom House

8 Minto Street, Edinburgh, EH9 1RG
Tel:0131 667 5353 Fax:0131 667 2813
Email:blossom_house@hotmail.com
Web:www.blossomguesthouse.co.uk

Comfortable, family run guest house. City centre within walking distance. Excellent bus service. Private car park. Close to Commonwealth pool and Royal College of Surgeons.

7 rooms, some en-suite, Open Jan-Dec, B&B per person, single from £25.00, double from £20.00.

VAT is shown at 17.5%: changes in this rate may affect prices.

Key to symbols is on back flap.

Edinburgh

Map Ref: 2C5

GUEST HOUSE ★★★

Boisdale Hotel

9 Coates Gardens, Edinburgh, EH12 5LG
Tel:0131 337 1134 Fax:0131 313 0048

10 rooms, all en-suite, Open Jan-Dec, B&B per person, single £30.00-45.00, double £30.00-45.00.

Victorian terraced house, close to Haymarket station. All rooms have full private facilities.

HOTEL ★★★★

The Bonham

35 Drumsheugh Gardens, Edinburgh, EH3 7RN
Tel:0131 274 7400 Fax:0131 274 7405
Email:reserve@thebonham.com
Web:www.thebonham.com

48 rooms, all en suite, Open Jan-Dec, B&B per person double from £73.00, single from £108.00.

The Bonham is the coolest hotel in Edinburgh, where you'll enjoy an uplifting contemporary ambience within the classic atmosphere of a Victorian town house. During your stay, experience Edinburgh's most timeless contemporary restaurant - Restaurant at the Bonham. You'll be tempted by distinct European-inspired food and enticed by provocative wines.

AWAITING INSPECTION

Bonnington Guest House

202 Ferry Road, Edinburgh, EH6 4NW
Tel/Fax:0131 554 7610
Email:bonningtongh@btinternet.com
Web:www.bonnington-guest-house-edinburgh.co.uk

6 rooms, some en-suite, Open Jan-Dec, B&B per person, single from £35.00, double from £28.00.

GUEST HOUSE ★★★

Briggend Guest House

19 Old Dalkeith Road, Edinburgh, EH16 4TE
Tel:0131 258 0810 Fax:0131 620 2873
Email:reservations@briggend.com
Web:www.briggend.com

4 rooms, all ensuite, Open Jan-Dec, B&B per person, single from £35.00, double from £22.50. Family room available.

Recently extended traditional cottage, now providing 4 ensuite bedrooms, all on ground level, on south side of city with very easy access to main routes, the new Edinburgh Royal Infirmary, Universities and many of the city's attractions. Also on main bus route.

GUEST HOUSE ★★

Caravel Guest House

30 London Street, Edinburgh, EH3 6NA
Tel:0131 556 4444 Fax:0131 557 3615
Email:caravelguest@hotmail.com
Web:www.caravelhouse.co.uk

11 rooms, some en-suite, Open Jan-Dec, B&B per person, single from £30.00, double from £25.00.

A warm welcome at this guest house with spacious, en-suite bedrooms. This Georgian house is situated in the heart of Edinburgh's New Town only a short distance from Princes Street and close to Waverley Station and the bus station.

Edinburgh

Map Ref: 2C5

GUEST HOUSE

Carrington Guest House

38 Pilrig Street, Edinburgh, EH6 5AL
Tel:0131 554 4769

7 rooms, some en-suite, Open Feb-Nov, B&B per person, double £27.00-45.00.

Large family run guest house convenient for all city centre attractions. On street parking. Open for holiday guests and business people only.

HOTEL

Channings

12-16 South Learmonth Gardens, Edinburgh, EH4 1EZ
Tel:0131 274 7401 Fax:0131 274 7402
Email:reserve@channings.co.uk
Web:www.channings.co.uk

41 rooms, all en suite, Open Jan-Dec, B&B double from £65.50 pppn, single from £101.00.

Channings is the friendliest hotel in Edinburgh, where you'll enjoy country-style tranquillity in a city setting and be charmed by our people. During your stay, experience great food and flavoursome wine in a warm and welcoming ambience in Channings Restaurant.

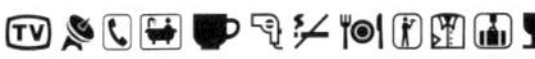

SMALL HOTEL

Clan Campbell Hotel

11 Brunswick Street, Edinburgh, EH7 5JB
Tel:0131 557 6910 Fax:0131 557 6929
Email:clan.campbell@virgin.net
Web:www.clancampbellhotel.co.uk

8 rooms, all en-suite, Open Mar-Nov, B&B per person, single from £25.00, double from £25.00.

Former Black Watch Club, now a small hotel set in central Georgian town house. On street parking with no charge. French and Spanish spoken. Dinner is not available but there are many restaurants within walking distance.

HOTEL

Clarendon Hotel

25-33 Shandwick Place, Edinburgh, EH2 4RG
Tel:0131 229 1467 Fax:0131 229 7549
Email:res@clarendonhoteledi.co.uk
Web:www.clarendonhoteledi.co.uk

66 rooms, all en-suite, Open all year, B&B per person, single from £30.00, double from £25.00.

Situated in the heart of the city, approximately 20 yards from Edinburgh's famous Princes Street. Ideally situated for the city's financial district, tourist attractions, theatres, restaurants and the International Conference Centre (EICC), all within minutes walking distance. If arriving at Edinburgh International Airport, the Airport bus drops off and picks up opposite the hotel. Located between Waverley and Haymarket Railway stations, both within easy walking distance.

Edinburgh **Map Ref: 2C5**

The Corstorphine House

188 St Johns Road, Edinburgh, EH12 8SG
Tel:0131 539 4237 Fax:0131 539 4945
Email:corsthouse@aol.com
Web:www.corstorphinehotels.co.uk

Pleasant Victorian house providing a warm welcome and excellent facilities. Close to city centre, Edinburgh airport, and all major attractions. On excellent frequent bus route. Off street parking. Extensive walled garden to rear for guests to use.

5 rooms, all en-suite, Open Jan-Dec, B&B per person, single £25.00-59.00, double £24.00-59.00 per person.

Corstorphine Lodge Hotel

186 St Johns Road, Edinburgh, EH12 8SG
Tel:0131 476 7116 Fax:0131 476 7117
Email:corstlodge@aol.com
Web:www.corstorphinehotels.co.uk

Spacious, family run Victorian house providing a warm welcome and very good facilities, Private parking and convenient for airport and city centre. Ensuite facilities available. Guests are welcome to enjoy the garden.

12 rooms, all en-suite, Open Jan-Dec, B&B per person, single £25.00-89.00 pppn, double from £24.00-69.00 pppn.

Crioch Guest House

23 East Hermitage Place, Leith Links, Edinburgh EH6 8AD
Tel/Fax:0131 554 5494
Email:welcome@crioch.com
Web:www.crioch.com

Set on a frequent bus route to the city centre, Crioch overlooks the leafy park of Leith Links. All rooms have ensuite shower or private bathroom, TV, radio alarm and welcome tray. You can choose from continental or full cooked breakfast. Free parking and the frequent bus service leaves you to enjoy Edinburgh's sights on foot, and a short stroll takes you to Leith's fine cafes, bars and restaurants.

6 rooms, some en-suite, Open Jan-Dec, B&B per person, single from £25.00, double from £22.50.

Cumberland Hotel

1-2 West Coates, Edinburgh, EH12 5JQ
Tel:0131 337 1198 Fax:0131 337 1022
Email:cumblhotel@aol.com
Web:www.corstorphinehotels.co.uk

Family run property in listed Victorian detached houses, A short walk from the West End of the city centre. 10 - 15 min drive to the airport and Ingliston Highland Showground. Murrayfield Stadium within walking distance. The Cumberland offers a choice of continental, traditional or vegetarian breakfasts. There are several restaurants providing a variety of cuisine within easy walking distance of the property.

17 rooms, all en-suite, Open Jan-Dec, B&B per person, single £39.00-99.00, double £25.00-69.00 pppn.

Dene Guest House

7 Eyre Place, off Dundas Street, Edinburgh EH3 5ES
Tel:0131 556 2700 Fax:0131 557 9876
Email:deneguesthouse@yahoo.co.uk
Web:www.deneguesthouse.com

Charming Georgian townhouse, situated in the famous 'New Town' of Edinburgh's city centre, providing you with the perfect location to experience the capital's culture, history, shops, restaurants and bars. Enjoy a comfortable stay in a relaxed and informal atmosphere from only £19.50-£40.00 pppn, including a hearty breakfast.

11 rooms, some en-suite, Open Jan-Dec, B&B per person, single from £19.50, double from £19.50.

Important: Prices stated are estimates and may be subject to amendments

Edinburgh **Map Ref: 2C5**

DUNSTANE HOUSE HOTEL

4 West Coates, Haymarket, Edinburgh EH12 5JQ
Tel: 0131 337 6169 Fax: 0131 337 6060
e.mail: reservations@dunstanehousehotel.co.uk
Web: www.dunstane-hotel-edinburgh.co.uk

Impressive Victorian mansion dating 1850's retaining spectacular original features. All rooms luxuriously refurbished. Four poster deluxe rooms available. Unique bar and restaurant themed on the Scottish islands. Excellent range of malt whiskies stocked. Located in the heart of the city, only minutes from Princes Street, the Castle, conference centre and Edinburgh Airport. Private car park.

SMALL HOTEL

Dunstane House Hotel
4 West Coates, Haymarket, Edinburgh, EH12 5JQ
Tel:0131 337 6169 Fax:0131 337 6060
Email:reservations@dunstanehousehotel.co.uk
Web:www.dunstane-hotel-edinburgh.co.uk

16 rooms, all en-suite, Open Jan-Dec, B&B per person, single from £59.00, double from £49.00, BB & Eve.Meal from £69.00.

Impressive Listed Victorian mansion retaining many original features enjoying imposing position within large grounds on the A8 airport road (major bus route). 10 mins walk from city centre. Close to Edinburgh Conference Centre, Murrayfield and Edinburgh Zoo. Private secluded car park. Unique lounge bar and restaurant themed on the Scottish Islands.

DUTHUS LODGE

5 West Coates, Edinburgh EH12 5JG
Tel: 0131 337 6876 Fax: 0131 313 2264
e.mail: duthus.lodge@ukgateway.net
Web: www.duthuslodge.com

Splendid detached family run Victorian establishment offering accommodation in tastefully decorated and comfortable surroundings. A perfect base to explore Edinburgh. All bedrooms are ensuite. Private parking, close to the city centre, conference centre and Murrayfield stadium.

GUEST HOUSE

Duthus Lodge
5 West Coates, Edinburgh, EH12 5JG
Tel:0131 337 6876 Fax:0131 313 2264
Email:duthus.lodge@ukgateway.net
Web:www.duthuslodge.com

8 rooms, all en-suite, Open Jan-Dec, B&B per person, single £35.00-55.00, double £25.00-50.00.

Magnificent detached sandstone building with attractive walled gardens. Ideal base for exploring Edinburgh. Close to the city centre, conference centre, zoo and Murrayfield stadium.

GUEST HOUSE

Edinburgh House
11 McDonald Road, Edinburgh, EH7 4LX
Tel/Fax:0131 556 3434
Web:www.edinburgh-house.co.uk

4 rooms, all en-suite, Open Jan-Dec, B&B per person, double £27.00-45.00.

Small personally run guest house in a traditional tenement building approx 0.5 ml from Princes Street. Good bus service to city centre with all its amenities. Variety of restaurants nearby. Non-smoking house.

Edinburgh

Map Ref: 2C5

HOTEL

Edinburgh Marriott Hotel

111 Glasgow Road, Edinburgh, EH12 8NF
Tel:0131 334 9191 Fax:0131 316 4507
Email:reservations.edinburgh@marriotthotels.co.uk
Web:www.marriotthotels.com/edieb

A recently refurbished modern hotel ideally situated to enjoy Edinburgh's attractions and surrounding areas. The hotel offers a fully equipped leisure club, health and beauty clinic, 2 Bars and Restaurants, Executive Lounge and extremely large bedrooms. The hotel's public areas are all on one level making us a good choice for special needs guests.

245 rooms, all en-suite, Open Jan-Dec, B&B per person, single from £96.00, double from £48.00, BB & Eve.Meal from £71.00.

HOTEL

The Edinburgh Residence

7 Rothesay Terrace, Edinburgh, EH3 7RY
Tel:0131 274 7403 Fax:0131 274 7405
Email:reserve@theedinburghresidence.com
Web:www.theedinburghresidence.com

The Edinburgh Residence is the most distinguished collection of luxury townhouse suites in Edinburgh, offering a refreshing alternative to a five star hotel where you will enjoy an experience to remember. Comprising three beautiful architectural Georgian townhouses and situated in Edinburgh's West End, close to both the city's financial district and main shopping area, The Edinburgh Residence enjoys a peaceful yet central location only 5 minutes walk from Edinburgh's main tourist attractions.

29 rooms, all en suite, Open Jan-Dec, B&B per person double from £85.00, single from £135.00.

GUEST HOUSE

Elder York Guest House

38 Elder Street, Edinburgh, EH1 3DX
Tel:0131 556 1926 Fax:0131 624 7140
Email:info@elderyork.co.uk
Web:www.elderyork.co.uk

Recently refurbished family run Guest House, centrally located, very close to large car park. Totally Non-smoking.

13 rooms, some en-suite, Open Jan-Dec, B&B per person, single £30.00-60.00, double £25.00-60.00.

GUEST HOUSE

Ellesmere Guest House

11 Glengyle Terrace, Edinburgh, EH3 9LN
Tel:0131 229 4823
Email:celia@edinburghbandb.co.uk
Web:www.edinburghbandb.co.uk

City centre Victorian terraced house in quiet location overlooking Bruntsfield Links. Kings Theatre, Conference Centre and all amenities within walking distance. All rooms en suite. Full Scottish Breakfast is served and a warm welcome is extended to all guests.

4 rooms, all en-suite, Open Jan-Dec, B&B per person, single from £35.00, double from £35.00.

Edinburgh **Map Ref: 2C5**

GUEST HOUSE ★

Falcon Crest Guest House
70 South Trinity Road, Edinburgh, EH5 3NX
Tel/Fax:0131 552 5294
Email:kathryn@falconcrest.co.uk
Web:www.falconcrest.co.uk

Victorian terraced family home in attractive residential area, near main bus route to city centre. Free on street parking.

6 rooms, some en-suite, (1 single, 2 twin, 2 double, 1 family), from £18.00 Single, double from £18.00.

TV P C V

SERVICED APARTMENTS ★★★★

Fountain Court Apartments
123 Grove Street, Edinburgh, EH3 8AA
Tel:0131 622 6677 Fax:0131 622 6679
Email:enq@fountaincourtapartments.com
Web:www.fountaincourtapartments.com

These city centre apartments offer a great "home away from home" and feature fully equipped kitchens with oven, hob, fridge/freezer, microwave, washer/tumble dryer. Cable TV, CD player, free internet access, linen, towels, cots, highchairs and daily maid service provided.

32 flats/apartments, 1 pub rm, 5 grd.flr beds, sleeps 1-5, total sleeping capacity 104, £595.00-1,295.00, Jan-Dec, bus nearby, rail nearby, airport 10 km.

TV

VAT is shown at 17.5%: changes in this rate may affect prices.

Key to symbols is on back flap.

Edinburgh | Map Ref: 2C5

Fountain Court EQ-2 Apartments

1 Lower Gilmore Bank, 'Edinburgh Quay', Edinburgh EH3 9QP
Tel: 0131 622 6677 Fax: 0131 622 6679
e.mail: enq@fountaincourtapartments.com
Web: www.eq-2.co.uk

EQ-2 is Edinburgh's most exciting city centre accommodation development in a beautifully regenerated canalside setting. Just a stone's throw away from the EICC and Princes Street, these stunning state of the art serviced apartments have all the style and comfort of a boutique hotel, with added space. Available from 1 night onwards.

SERVICED APARTMENTS

Fountain Court EQ-2 Apartments
1 Lower Gilmore Bank, 'Edinburgh Quay', Edinburgh, EH3 9QP
Tel:0131 622 6677 Fax:0131 622 6679
Email:enq@fountaincourtapartments.com
Web:www.eq-2.co.uk

Stunning state-of-the-art serviced apartments with Italian designer furniture throughout. Cable TV, CD player, wi-fi broadband access, room safe. Kitchens feature Smeg oven, hob, fridge/freezer, microwave, washer/tumble dryer. Fully tiled bathrooms with Grohe showers and luxury toiletries.

40 one, two and three bedroom luxury apartments minutes from the heart of the city. £135.00-400.00 per apartment per night. Open Jan-Dec.

Frederick House Hotel

42 Frederick St, Edinburgh, EH2 1EX
Tel: 0131 226 1999 Fax: 0131 624 7064
e.mail: frederickhouse@ednet.co.uk Web: www.townhousehotels.co.uk

Offering an atmosphere of comfort and tradition. Situated in the very heart of Edinburgh's city centre with Princes Street practically on our door step. All 45 rooms have en-suite, satellite TV, telephone/modem, refrigerators, tea/coffee, trouser press and hairdryers.
Free wi-fi internet access. We aim to make your stay as comfortable as possible.

LODGE

Frederick House Hotel
42 Frederick Street, Edinburgh, EH2 1EX
Tel:0131 226 1999 Fax:0131 624 7064
Email:frederickhouse@ednet.co.uk
Web:www.townhousehotels.co.uk

Situated in the heart of Edinburgh close to all city centre amenities and with a wide variety of restaurants and bars in the immediate vicinity. Georgian building with all rooms to a high standard with en-suite facilities, fridges and modem points. Princes Street just 150 yards away. Breakfast available across the road at the award winning Rick's Bar/Restaurant. Street parking.

45 rooms, all en-suite, Open Jan-Dec, B&B per person, single from £35.00, double from £25.00 per person subject to availability and season.

Important: Prices stated are estimates and may be subject to amendments

Edinburgh

Map Ref: 2C5

The George Hotel

19-21 George Street, Edinburgh EH2 2PB
Tel: +44 (0) 131 225 1251
Fax: +44 (0) 131 226 5644
e.mail: george.reservations@principal-hotels.com
Web: www.principal-hotels.com

This traditional Georgian property is located in the heart of Edinburgh. As one of the city's premier hotels, The George is ideally positioned close to many major attractions and quality shops. Only a short walk from Waverley Station and a 20 minute journey from Edinburgh Airport. The George Hotel provides the perfect setting for an opulent and affordable Scottish City break. B&B from £70 per person per night.

AWAITING INSPECTION

The George Hotel
19-21 George Street, Edinburgh, EH2 2PB
Tel:0131 225 1251 Fax:0131 226 5644
Email:george.reservations@principal-hotels.com
Web:www.principal-hotels.com

195 rooms, all en-suite, Open Jan-Dec, B&B per person, single from £70.00, double from £80.00, BB & Eve.Meal from £100.00.

C £ V

GUEST HOUSE

Gifford House
103 Dalkeith Road, Edinburgh, EH16 5AJ
Tel/Fax:0131 667 4688
Email:giffordhotel@btinternet.com
Web:www.giffordhousehotel.co.uk

A well appointed Victorian stone built house situated on one of the main routes into Edinburgh. Close to Holyrood Park and Arthur's Seat and only 300 metres from Royal Commonwealth Swimming Pool. Regular bus services to all city amenities. Well positioned for conference centre.

7 rooms, all en-suite, Open Jan-Dec excl Xmas, B&B per person, single £35.00-75.00, double from £30.00-55.00.

£ V

GUEST HOUSE

Gildun Guest House
9 Spence Street, Edinburgh, EH16 5AG
Tel:0131 667 1368 Fax:0131 668 4989
Email:gildun.edin@btinternet.com
Web:www.gildun.co.uk

A warm and friendly run guest house recently refurbished to an excellent standard situated in cul de sac with private parking. Close to Commonwealth Pool and bus route to city centre. Cameron Toll Shopping Centre nearby and situated near University Halls of Residence. A variety of eating establishments within walking distance.

8 rooms, some en-suite, Open Jan-Dec, B&B per person, single from £24.00, double from £24.00.

£ V

VAT is shown at 17.5%: changes in this rate may affect prices.

Key to symbols is on back flap.

Edinburgh **Map Ref: 2C5**

GUEST HOUSE

Glenora Hotel

14 Rosebery Crescent, Edinburgh, EH12 5JY
Tel:0131 337 1186 Fax:0131 337 1119
Email:reservations@glenorahotel.co.uk
Web:www.glenorahotel.co.uk

Victorian terraced town house a short walk to city centre and within easy reach of city's tourist attractions. Airport bus stops next to hotel.

11 rooms, single from £40.00, double from £35.00. Telephones and modem points in rooms. Buffet & full cooked breakfasts, all entirely organic.

GUEST HOUSE

Hanover House Hotel

26 Windsor Street, Edinburgh, EH7 5JR
Tel:0131 556 1325
Email:info@hanoverhousehotel.co.uk
Web:www.hanover-house-hotel.co.uk

A recently refurbished family run Guest House offering comfortable accommodation in quiet area, close to city centre. Ideal for Playhouse Theatre, Restaurants, Cinemas and shopping. On street parking available.

5 rooms, all en-suite, Open Jan-Dec excl Xmas, B&B per person, single £35.00-50.00, double £25.00-50.00.

HOTEL

Herald House Hotel

70 Grove Street, Edinburgh, EH3 8AP
Tel:0131 228 2323 Fax:0131 228 3101
Email:info@heraldhousehotel.co.uk
Web:www.heraldhousehotel.co.uk

A friendly hotel located in a quite area of the city yet only 15 minutes walk from the centre's main attractions (Princes Street and Edinburgh Castle). All 45 bedrooms have en-suite shower room and there is a breakfast room and brasserie/bar serving drinks and snacks including Internet access. Staff are very helpful and to start the day a full breakfast is served and included in the price.

45 rooms, all en-suite, Open Jan-Dec, B&B from £25.00 pppn sharing.

SMALL HOTEL

The Howard

34 Great King Street, Edinburgh, EH3 6QH
Tel:0131 274 7402 Fax:0131 274 7405
Email:reserve@thehoward.com
Web:www.thehoward.com

The Howard is the most discreet 5-star hotel in Edinburgh - attention to detail together with the personal touch will ensure you feel special. 'Dining at The Atholl' is an experience full of decadent pleasures. You'll enjoy dinner, which will be meticulously prepared by our dedicated team of chefs, in this warm and exclusive Georgian setting. Alternatively, you can be served dinner in the comfort of your room.

17 rooms, all en suite, B&B single from £108.00, double from £90.00 pppn.

Important: Prices stated are estimates and may be subject to amendments

Edinburgh

Map Ref: 2C5

GUEST HOUSE

Ivy Guest House

7 Mayfield Gardens, Edinburgh, EH9 2AX
Tel:0131 667 3411 Fax:0131 620 1422
Email:dolly@ivyguesthouse.com
Web:www.ivyguesthouse.com

Warm and friendly welcome assured at this established Victorian listed town house. With rear parking. Centrally situated on bus route to Edinburgh's many cultural attractions, parks and restaurants.

8 rooms, some en-suite, B&B per person, single from £30.00, double from £25.00.

HOTEL

Jurys Inn Edinburgh

43 Jeffrey Street, Edinburgh, Lothian, EH1 1DH
Tel:0131 200 3300 Fax:0131 200 0400
Email:brenda_kirkland@jurysdoyle.com
Web:www.bookajurysinn.com

Jury's Inn's superb city centre location (adjacent to Royal Mile, Princes Street and Waverley Station) is combined with incredible value for money. For a fixed rate your room can accommodate up to 3 adults or 2 adults and 2 children. All rooms are ensuite and have direct dial phone, satellite TV, hairdryer, modem and tea and coffee making facilities. Warm welcome and friendly prices in the Inn Pub and Arches restaurant.

186 rooms, all en-suite, Open Jan-Dec excl Xmas, B&B per person, single from £50.00, double from £35.00 per person.

GUEST HOUSE

Kariba Guest House

10 Granville Terrace, Edinburgh, EH10 4PQ
Tel:0131 229 3773 Fax:0131 229 4968
Email:karibaguesthouse@hotmail.com
Web:www.karibaguesthouse.co.uk

A Victorian house on major bus route to city centre about 10 minutes away. Restaurants, theatres and International Conference Centre all within easy reach. Private car parking.

9 rooms, some en-suite, Open Jan-Dec, B&B per person, single from £35.00, double £20.00-40.00.

GUEST HOUSE

Kenvie Guest House

16 Kilmaurs Road, Edinburgh, EH16 5DA
Tel:0131 668 1964 Fax:0131 668 1926
Email:dorothy@kenvie.co.uk
Web:www.kenvie.co.uk

A charming, comfortable, warm, friendly family run Victorian town house in a quiet residential street. Very close to bus routes and the city by-pass. We offer for your comfort, lots of caring touches including complimentary tea / coffee, colour TV, hairdryers and no-smoking rooms. En-suite available and vegetarians catered for. You are guaranteed a warm welcome from Richard and Dorothy.

5 rooms, some en-suite, Open Jan-Dec, B&B per person, single from £27.00, double from £25.00.

VAT is shown at 17.5%: changes in this rate may affect prices.

Key to symbols is on back flap.

Edinburgh

Map Ref: 2C5

SMALL HOTEL

Kildonan Lodge Hotel

27 Craigmillar Park, Edinburgh, EH16 5PE
Tel:0131 667 2793 Fax:0131 667 9777
Email:info@kildonanlodgehotel.co.uk
Web:www.kildonanlodgehotel.co.uk

Kildonan Lodge is an outstanding example of Victorian elegance, beautifully restored to capture the atmosphere of a by-gone era and situated close to the city centre. Individually designed bedrooms have spa baths and 4-poster beds in selected rooms. There is a private car park and the residents lounge contains an open fire where a dram can be savoured from the Honesty Bar.

12 rooms, all en-suite, Open Jan-Dec excl Xmas, B&B per person, single from £56.00, double from £42.00 pppn.

GUEST HOUSE

Kingsview Guest House

28 Gilmore Place, Edinburgh, EH3 9NQ
Tel/Fax:0131 229 8004
Email:kingsviewguesthouse@talk21.com
Web:www.kingsviewguesthouse.com

Family run, city centre guest house conveniently situated near the Kings Theatre. Close to all main bus routes.

9 rooms, all en-suite, Open Jan-Dec, B&B per person, double from £22.50.

SERVICED APARTMENTS

The Knight Residence

12 Lauriston Street Edinburgh, Lothian, EH3 9DJ
Tel:0131 622 8120 Fax:0131 622 7363
Email:info@theknightresidence.co.uk
Web:www.theknightresidence.co.uk

Tastefully furnished, quality serviced apartments available for one night or more, in the centre of Edinburgh. Private, secure parking for each apartment on site. Excellent location for castle, theatres and restaurants.

19 rooms, Open Jan-Dec, from £95.00 per apartment per night.

GUEST HOUSE

McDonald Guest House

5 McDonald Road, Edinburgh, EH7 4LX
Tel/Fax:0131 557 5935
Email:white@5mcdonaldroad.co.uk
Web:www.5mcdonaldroad.co.uk

Comfortable accommodation a short walk from Princes Street. Adjacent to main bus routes. Many good restaurants locally. Playhouse Theatre nearby. Free on street parking. French and German spoken.

4 rooms, some en-suite, Open Mar-Dec incl New/Year, B&B per person, single from £28.00, double from £25.00.

Edinburgh

Map Ref: 2C5

GUEST HOUSE

Mackenzie Guest House

2 East Hermitage Place, Edinburgh, EH6 8AA
Tel:0131 554 3763 Fax:0131 554 0853
Email:info@mackenzieguesthouse.co.uk
Web:www.mackenzieguesthouse.co.uk

A warm welcome awaits you at the Mackenzie Guest House, set in an excellent location overlooking Leith Links and only a 10-15 minute ride from the City Centre. Leith Waterfront with its Bars & Restaurants, Ocean Terminal & the Royal Yacht Britannia are all within walking distance.

5 rooms, some en-suite, Open Jan-Dec, B&B per person, single from £25.00-50.00, double/twin from £24.00-45.00.

HOTEL

Menzies Belford Hotel

69 Belford Road, Edinburgh, EH4 3DG
Tel:0131 332 2545 Fax:0131 332 3805
Email:belford@menzies-hotels.co.uk
Web:www.bookmenzies.com

On the banks of the Water of Leith in a quiet secluded area, yet close to the city centre, the hotel offers the best of both worlds. The Forth Road Bridge and both of Edinburgh's main railway stations are only a short drive away and many of the city's local attractions, including the Dean Gallery and Princes Street are just a short walk from the hotel. Extensive private parking, which is free for all residents.

146 rooms, all en-suite, Open Jan-Dec, B&B per person, single from £85.00, double from £55.00.

GUEST HOUSE

Menzies Guest House

33 Leamington Terrace, Edinburgh, EH10 4JS
Tel/Fax:0131 229 4629
Email:menzies33@blueyonder.co.uk
Web:www.menzies-guesthouse.co.uk

Situated in residential area near Bruntsfield Links and close to main bus route to city centre. Private parking. Princes Street and West End with theatres and restaurants approx. 0.75 mile.

7 rooms, some en-suite, Open Jan-Dec, B&B per person, single from £15.00, double from £15.00.

HOTEL

Norton House Hotel

Ingliston, Edinburgh, EH28 8LX
Tel:0131 333 1275 Fax:0131 333 5305
Email:nortonhouse@handpicked.co.uk
Web:www.handpicked.co.uk/nortonhouse

Ideally situated in wooded grounds, an elegant mansion house, 8 miles (13kms) west of the city centre, close to the airport. Choice of restaurants. Conference and banqueting facilities available.

47 rooms, all en-suite, Open Jan-Dec, B&B per person, single from £135.00, double from £80.00, BB & Eve.Meal from £82.50.

HOTEL

Parliament House Hotel

15 Calton Hill, Edinburgh, EH1 3BJ
Tel:0131 478 4000 Fax:0131 478 4001
Email:info@parliamenthouse-hotel.co.uk
Web:www.parliamenthouse-hotel.co.uk

Town house hotel in city centre location and situated on historic Calton Hill a few minutes walk from Princes Street and the Playhouse Theatre. 3 minutes walk from Waverley Train Station. Discount Parking at nearby Greenside Multi-storey. 'MP's' Bistro available for dinner and non-residents welcome.

53 rooms, all en-suite, B&B per person, single from £60.00, double from £35.00.

VAT is shown at 17.5%: changes in this rate may affect prices.

Key to symbols is on back flap.

Edinburgh Map Ref: 2C5

Piries Hotel

4/8 Coates Gardens, Edinburgh EH12 5LB

Tel: 0131 337 1108 Fax: 0131 346 0279

e.mail: manager@thepiries.com Web: www.pirieshotel.com

Privately owned Georgian style hotel comprising of 3 town houses. Located in the West End of the city centre. Few minutes walk to Princes Street and Conference Centre. Close proximity to main tourist attractions. All rooms ensuite with facilities. Licensed bar and restaurant. B&B from £25 to £45 per person per night. Group enquiries welcome.

★★★ HOTEL

Piries Hotel

4-8 Coates Gardens, Edinburgh, EH12 5LB
Tel:0131 337 1108 Fax:0131 346 0279
Email:manager@thepiries.com
Web:www.pirieshotel.com

Comfortably furnished privately owned, stone terraced building in West End of city. City centre location, within walking distance of Princes Street, and EICC. Selection of bar meals available. Supper is available by prior arrangement only and there are a number of restaurants within easy walking distance. On street parking is payable from 8.30am-6.30pm.

30 rooms, all en-suite, Open Jan-Dec, B&B per person, single from £35.00, double from £25.00.

★★★ GUEST HOUSE

Priestville Guest House

10 Priestfield Road, Edinburgh, EH16 5HJ
Tel/Fax:0131 667 2435
Email:priestville@hotmail.com
Web:www.priestville.com

Friendly Scottish Hospitality in Victorian Townhouse, quiet residential area. 20 minute walk to city centre. Excellent bus service. Full fry, Smoked Salmon or Haggis for breakfast. Close to Commonwealth Pool, Holyrood Park and Golf Course. Broadband and wireless Internet access and Parking Available.

6 rooms, some en-suite, Open Jan-Dec, B&B per person, single from £25.00, double from £20.00.

★★★★ HOTEL

Radisson SAS Hotel, Edinburgh

80 High Street, The Royal Mile, Edinburgh, EH1 1TH
Tel:0131 473 6590 Fax:0131 557 9789
Email:reservations.edinburgh@radissonsas.com
Web:www.radissonsas.com

This modern, city centre hotel offers first class facilities including 238 en-suite bedrooms, restaurant, lounge, bar, onsite parking for 135 cars, Leisure club with indoor pool, fitness room, saunas, solarium and treatment room.

238 air-conditioned rooms, all en-suite (fully refurbished May 2005), Open Jan-Dec excl Xmas/New Year, B&B per person, single from £120.00, double from £65.00.

★★ HOTEL

Ritz Hotel

14-18 Grosvenor Street, Edinburgh, EH12 5EG
Tel:0131 337 4315 Fax:0131 346 0597

On five floors, each room of individual character, some featuring four poster beds. Within easy walking distance of Haymarket railway station and West End of Princes Street. There is a wide range of restaurants available in the city centre.

36 rooms, all en-suite, Open Jan-Dec, B&B per person, single £50.00-61.00, double £35.00-50.00.

Important: Prices stated are estimates and may be subject to amendments

Edinburgh **Map Ref: 2C5**

★★★

SMALL HOTEL

Rosehall Hotel

101 Dalkeith Road, Newington, Edinburgh, EH16 5AJ
Tel/Fax:0131 667 9372
Email:info@rosehallhotel.co.uk
Web:www.rosehallhotel.co.uk

This small, recently refurbished hotel retains many fine period features restored to their original Victorian splendour. One room has a 4-Poster bed. Free on-street parking is available nearby. The hotel is located around 1.5 miles from Princes Street.

8 rooms, 7 en-suite, Open Jan-Dec, B&B per person, single £30.00-65.00, double £25.00-50.00.

TV C £ W V

★★

GUEST HOUSE

St Bernards Guest House

22 St Bernards Crescent, Edinburgh, EH4 1NS
Tel:0131 332 2339 Fax:0131 332 8842
Email:alex.stbernards@aol.com

Elegant terrace house in Georgian New Town area of the city. Convenient for Princes Street. Many excellent restaurants within walking distance. A warm and friendly welcome.

8 rooms, some en-suite, Open Jan-Dec, B&B per person, single from £30.00, double from £25.00.

TV £ V

★★★

GUEST HOUSE

The St Valery

36 Coates Gardens, Edinburgh, EH12 5LE
Tel:0131 337 1893 Fax:0131 346 8529
Email:info@stvalery.co.uk
Web:www.stvalery.com

Traditional guest house, centrally situated in West End of Edinburgh. 1 mile from Princes Street. 3 minutes walk from Haymarket Station. Evening meal on request. Internet facilities now available.

11 rooms, some en-suite, Open Jan-Dec, B&B per person, single from £25.00-48.00, double from £25.00-48.00.

C £ V

★

GUEST HOUSE

Sakura House

18 West Preston Street, Edinburgh, EH8 9PU
Tel/Fax:0131 668 1204

Victorian house in central location, close to castle and shopping centre. Numerous good restaurants and pubs in immediate vicinity. On main bus route. Video recorders in bedroom and a selection of videos for guests use. Single guests welcome.

6 rooms, some en-suite, Open Jan-Dec, B&B per person, single from £18.00, double from £18.00.

TV

VAT is shown at 17.5%: changes in this rate may affect prices.

Key to symbols is on back flap.

Edinburgh **Map Ref: 2C5**

GUEST HOUSE ★★★★

Sandaig Guest House

5 East Hermitage Place, Leith Links, Edinburgh EH6 8AA
Tel:0131 554 7357 Fax:0131 467 6389
Email:info@sandaigguesthouse.co.uk
Web:www.sandaigguesthouse.co.uk

Marina and Derek personally welcome you to their delightful Victorian terraced villa overlooking historic Leith Links. Unrestricted street parking. Variety of restaurants nearby or frequent bus service to Princes Street with all its amenities. Totally non-smoking house.

8 rooms, all en-suite, Open Jan-Dec, B&B per person, single from £35.00, double from £30.00.

C £ W V

B&B

Mr Semlali

56 East Claremont Street, Edinburgh, EH7 4JR
Tel: 0131 478 4463
Email:enquiriesandbookings@karenbridges.co.uk
Web:www.karenbridges.co.uk

Comfortable B&B, furnished to a high standard, within easy reach of city centre. 10 minutes walk to Princes Street and main attractions.

2 rooms, all en-suite. Open Jan-Dec. B&B per person per night: single £20.00-50.00, double £20.00-40.00, family £20.00-40.00.

C £ V

HOTEL

Sheraton Grand Hotel & Spa

1 Festival Square, Edinburgh, EH3 9SR
Tel:0131 229 9131 Fax:0131 221 9631
Email:grandedinburgh.sheraton@sheraton.com
Web:www.sheraton.com/grandedinburgh

This luxurious hotel is ideally situated in the heart of the city with magnificent views of Edinburgh Castle. Theatres, shops, restaurants and nightlife are within walking distance. Includes 4 outstanding restaurants and Europe's most advanced city spa. Unsurpassed Scottish hospitality ensures a truely memorable stay at Edinburgh's most welcoming hotel.

269 rooms, all en-suite, Open Jan-Dec, B&B per person, double from £90.00.

£ V

GUEST HOUSE

Sheridan Guest House

1 Bonnington Terrace, Edinburgh, EH6 4BP
Tel:0131 554 4107 Fax:0131 554 8494
Email:info@sheridanedinburgh.co.uk
Web:www.sheridanedinburgh.co.uk

Contemporary furnished, sensitively restored, elegant Georgian townhouse with 8 en-suite bedrooms. Good food, warm welcome. Unrestricted street parking. On excellent bus route. Strictly non-smoking.

8 rooms, Open Jan-Dec, B&B per person single from £35.00, double from £28.00, family from £27.50, room only single from £35.00. double from £56.00, family from £56.00.

C £ V

Important: Prices stated are estimates and may be subject to amendments

Edinburgh

Map Ref: 2C5

GUEST HOUSE

Smiths' Guest House

77 Mayfield Road, Edinburgh, EH9 3AA
Tel:0131 667 2524 Fax:0131 668 4455
Email:mail@smithsgh.com
Web:www.smithsgh.com

Victorian town house, recently refurbished. Near to city centre.

7 rooms, all en-suite, Open Jan-Dec, B&B per person, single from £18.00, double from £18.00.

GUEST HOUSE

Tania Guest House

19 Minto Street, Edinburgh, EH9 1RQ
Tel:0131 667 4144

Traditional Guest House, welcoming families, conveniently situated on main bus route from city centre. Limited private parking. Choice of restaurants available locally. Non-smoking house.

6 rooms, some en-suite, Open Jan-Dec excl Xmas, B&B per person, single from £20.00, double from £20.00.

GUEST HOUSE

Terrace Hotel

37 Royal Terrace, Edinburgh, EH7 5AH
Tel:0131 556 3423 Fax:0131 556 2520
Email:terracehotel@btinternet.com
Web:www.terracehotel.co.uk

Personally run guest house in impressive Georgian terrace close to city centre, shopping and all amenities. Excellent views.

14 rooms, some en-suite, Open Jan-Dec, B&B per person, single from £30.00, double from £25.00.

HOTEL

Thistle Edinburgh

107 Leith Street, Edinburgh, EH1 3SW
Tel:0870 3339153 Fax:0870 3339253
Email:edinburgh@thistle.co.uk
Web:www.thistle.com/edinburgh

Modern hotel in city centre location with friendly and efficient staff. Craigs restaurant, Boston Bean cocktail bar.

139 rooms, all en-suite, Open Jan-Dec, B&B per person, single from £65.00, double from £65.00, BB & Eve.Meal from £85.00.

INN

Toby Carvery & Innkeepers Lodge Edin/Wes

114-116 St Johns Road, Edinburgh, EH12 8AX
Tel:0131 334 8235 Fax:0131 316 5012
Web:www.innkeeperslodge.com

Completely re-furbished (2002), this former Coaching Inn is situated on the main route to/from Airport (3Miles) and to the city centre. On-site Toby Carvery and popular bar. Fixed price per room includes complimentary continental breakfast. The inn is a popular base for both business travellers and tourists alike.

28 rooms, all en-suite, Open Jan-Dec, £62.00 per room.

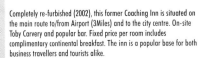

VAT is shown at 17.5%: changes in this rate may affect prices.

Key to symbols is on back flap.

Edinburgh

Map Ref: 2C5

GUEST HOUSE ★★★★

The Town House

65 Gilmore Place, Edinburgh, EH3 9NU
Tel:0131 229 1985
Email:Susan@thetownhouse.com
Web:www.thetownhouse.com

An elegant Victorian town house c1876, situated in the city centre. Easy walking distance of West End, Princes Street and Kings Theatre. A skilful mix of modern and period furnishings enhanced by stylish decor makes for a very warm and comfortable stay.

5 rooms, all en-suite, Open Jan-Dec, single & double rooms from £35.00-45.00 per person per night.

TV P V

GUEST HOUSE ★★★★

Turret Guest House

8 Kilmaurs Terrace, Edinburgh, EH16 5DR
Tel:0131 667 6704 Fax:0131 668 1368
Email:contact@turretguesthouse.co.uk
Web:www.turretguesthouse.co.uk

Listed Victorian house in quiet residential area, furnished to a high standard. Easy access to city centre. Commonwealth Pool and Queens Park nearby.

8 rooms, most en-suite, Open Jan-Dec excl Xmas, B&B per person, single from £28.00, double from £23.00.

TV C £ V

GUEST HOUSE ★★★

Western Manor House Hotel

92 Corstorphine Road, Murrayfield, Edinburgh,EH12 6JG
Tel:0131 538 7490
Email:info@westernmanorhousehotel.co.uk
Web:www.westernmanorhousehotel.co.uk

Well-appointed family run hotel where a warm, friendly Scottish welcome awaits you from Julie and Adam. Conveniently located only 2 miles from Edinburgh Castle and city centre, with a regular bus service (every 10mins) outside the gates. Ground floor disabled room available. Secure parking. Totally non-smoking house. Within easy walking distance of Murrayfield Stadium and Edinburgh Zoo. Coffee, snacks, bar lunches and evening meals served.

11 rooms (31 guests), some en-suite, Open Jan-Dec, B&B per person, single from £40.00, double from £30.00.

£ V

Gullane, East Lothian

Map Ref: 2D4

HOTEL ★★★

Greywalls

Muirfield, Gullane, East Lothian, EH31 2EG
Tel:01620 842144 Fax:01620 842241
Email:hotel@greywalls.co.uk
Web:www.greywalls.co.uk

Renowned family owned Lutyens house with friendly atmosphere, gardens by Gertrude Jekyll. Adjacent to Muirfield Golf Course. Views over Forth. Award winning cuisine also attracts a strong following locally.

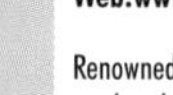

23 rooms, all en-suite, B&B per person, single from £140.00, double from £140.00.

TV P C £ V

Haddington, East Lothian

Map Ref: 2D4

SMALL HOTEL ★★★

Browns Hotel

1 West Road, Haddington, EH41 3RD
Tel/Fax:01620 822254
Email:info@browns-hotel.com
Web:www.browns-hotel.com

Regency town house, elegant furnishings and decor with contemporary Scottish paintings. Private parking within the grounds. Restaurant noted in many guides. Easy access to A1, approx. 20 golf courses of all standards close by. Many award winning beached and picturesque villages nearby.

5 rooms, all en-suite, Open Jan-Dec, B&B per person, single from £55.00, double from £45.00, BB & Eve.Meal from £75.00.

C £ V

Important: Prices stated are estimates and may be subject to amendments

Haddington, East Lothian

Map Ref: 2D4

Maitlandfield House Hotel

HOTEL

24 Sidegate, Haddington, East Lothian, EH41 4BZ
Tel:01620 826513 Fax:01620 826713
Email:info@maitlandfieldhouse.co.uk
Web:www.maitlandfieldhouse.co.uk

A country house hotel at the edge of town. Ideally located to visit Edinburgh and the Lothian's. A mecca for golf and walking. Splendid facilities for weddings and conferences.

25 rooms, all en-suite, Open Jan-Dec, B&B per person, single from £60.00, double from £55.00 pp, BB & Eve.Meal from £48.50.

North Berwick, East Lothian

Map Ref: 2D4

The Golf Hotel

SMALL HOTEL

34 Dirleton Avenue, North Berwick, East Lothian EH39 4BH
Tel:01620 892202 Fax:01620 892290
Email:emma@thegolfhotel.net
Web:www.thegolfhotel.net

Friendly family run hotel offering tailor-made golf packages incorporating all of East Lothian's 19 golf courses. East Lothian offers an abundance of historic castles and homes to visit and the exceptional visitor attractions of the Scottish Seabird Centre within walking distance.

12 rooms, some en-suite, Open Jan-Dec excl Xmas, B&B per person, single from £45.00, double from £40.00.

Nether Abbey Hotel

SMALL HOTEL

20 Dirleton Avenue, North Berwick, EH39 4BQ
Tel:01620 892802 Fax:01620 895298
Email:bookings@netherabbey.co.uk
Web:www.netherabbey.co.uk

Stone built hotel with character, situated in attractive grounds. 2 minutes walk to sandy beach and west links. 19 golf courses within 10 mile radius. 30 minute train service to Edinburgh.

13 rooms, all en-suite, Open Jan-Dec, B&B per person, single £35.00-65.00, double £30.00-45.00, BB & Eve.Meal from £50.00.

South Queensferry, West Lothian

Map Ref: 2B4

Priory Lodge

GUEST HOUSE

8 The Loan, South Queensferry, West Lothian EH30 9NS
Tel:0131 331 4345 Fax:0131 331 4345
Email:calmyn@aol.com
Web:www.queensferry.com

Traditional Scottish hospitality in this friendly family run guest house located in the picturesque village of South Queensferry. Edinburgh city centre 7 miles: Airport / Royal Highland Exhibition grounds 3 miles. Priory Lodge is within walking distance of the village shops, variety of eating establishments, Forth Bridges and Dalmeny train station. Internet access available. Non-smoking establishment.

5 rooms, all en-suite, Open Jan-Dec excl Xmas, B&B per person, single from £50.00, double from £30.00.

Uphall, West Lothian

Map Ref: 2B5

Houstoun House Hotel

HOTEL

Uphall, West Lothian, EH52 6JS
Tel:01506 853831 Fax:01506 854220
Email:events.houstoun@macdonald-hotels.co.uk
Web:www.houstounhouse.co.uk

Early 16th Century, this unique tower house offers 71 bedrooms with 21 in the original tower steading. Set in 20 acres of glorious gardens yet only 10 minutes from Edinburgh airport. New leisure club offers an extensive range of facilities together with informal steakhouse and floodlit tennis court. Log fires, 8 conference suites & award winning dining room. Beauty Spa now available.

71 rooms, all en-suite, Open Jan-Dec, B&B per person, single from £100.00, double from £60.00, BB & Eve.Meal from £80.00.

VAT is shown at 17.5%: changes in this rate may affect prices.

Key to symbols is on back flap.

Welcome to Scotland

Greater Glasgow and Clyde Valley

Ever since James Watts invented the steam engine, Glasgow has led a revolution. There was industry, then architecture, and now style. Join the cause…

Explore Glasgow by night – in your party shoes

Glasgow is a tour de force of character. The friendliness of locals is infectious, whether in a bar or simply asking for directions. They love their city, and they want you to love it too.

At first glance, Glasgow is an exciting fusion of style. From the rooftops you can see the Gothic, Art Nouveau, post-modern, and Victorian buildings vying for attention. When Britannia ruled the waves, this city exploded with new ideas, technology, and wealth. That attitude has shaped the streets, including George Square, home to the neoclassical façade and rich marble of Glasgow City Chambers.

Walk through Merchant City to see old Victorian warehouses restored as homes with edge. The West End is student bohemia set against terraces, sandstone mansions and galleries. Straddling the streets, Glasgow Cathedral is one of the few Gothic churches to have remained intact over the centuries. But for the definitive 'Glasgow Style', you have to visit the Glasgow School of Art, where Charles Rennie Mackintosh threw the book at art establishment. Critics said he led the 'Spook school', but Mackintosh blended Celtic with Japanese influences to create Art Nouveau and iconic high-backed chairs.

It's a style of passion, or obsession, which can be seen in more than 20 galleries. Essential places include the Burrell Collection, where a man's life is expressed through 8000 pieces of art from every corner of the world.

Princes Square Shopping Centre, Glasgow

Greater Glasgow and Clyde Valley

The Clyde weaves through the gentle farmlands of South Lanarkshire.

Or the sumptuous European masters of Kelvingrove Art Gallery and Museum.

Glasgow has elevated another pastime to the status of 'art'. Shopping. Experience the A-list of designer garb in malls resembling palaces or galleries. Princes Square is style central; Argyll Arcade is Paris indoors; St Enoch Complex is a glass juggernaut; and The Italian Centre of Merchant City boasts Ralph Lauren, Armani, Versace and Boss.

But the streets really sizzle with local charm and quirkiness. This is where you can find Doctor Who's TARDIS, a time machine in the shape of a Police Box, turned into a coffee stall. Follow the tongue-in-cheek from 'Where The Monkey Sleeps' café to 'King Tut's Wah Wah Hut' music club. King Tut's and Barrowland Ballroom are where you're also likely to see the next big thing – Radiohead and Oasis had early gigs there. Clubbers can get their fix of edgy sounds at The Arches and Sub Club.

Discerners of the classics can breathe easy. The city is home to Scottish Opera, Scottish Ballet and the Royal Scottish National Orchestra.

Leave the city behind for Renfrewshire's gentle hills, or the Inverclyde coastline. Take a trip aboard the Waverley, the world's last sea-going steamer. You can also visit New Lanark – an immaculately preserved mill town and a World Heritage Site in its own right.

Paisley, home of the Paisley Pattern, is just a short journey from the city and the whole story of the distinctive design is told in the town's Museum and Art Gallery. Paisley Abbey, dating back to 1163, with its inspiring stained glass and 10th Century cross, is also well worth a visit.

Events

Greater Glasgow and Clyde Valley

11-29 JANUARY
CELTIC CONNECTIONS
Celebration of Celtic music.
Tel: 0141 353 8000
www.celticconnections.com

16-26 FEBRUARY
GLASGOW WORLD FILM FESTIVAL
Showcase of movies from around the world.
Tel: 0141 332 6535
www.glasgowfilmfestival.org.uk

9-25 MARCH
GLASGOW COMEDY FESTIVAL
Festival featuring stand-up, cabaret and theatre.
Tel: 0141 552 2070
www.glasgowcomedyfestival.com

19 APRIL-1 MAY
GLASGOW INTERNATIONAL
Colourful festival of contemporary art.
www.glasgowinternational.org

3 JUNE
SHOTTS HIGHLAND GAMES
Traditional Highland games.
Tel: 01501 823560
www.shottshighlandgames.org.uk

8 JUNE
LANIMER CELEBRATIONS, Lanark
100 year old traditional procession through the town of Lanark culminating with the crowning of the Lanimer Queen.
Tel: 01555 663251
www.lanarklanimers.co.uk

9-26 JUNE
WEST END FESTIVAL
A varied festival of music, dance, theatre, comedy and much more.
Tel: 0141 341 0844
www.westendfestival.co.uk

23 JUNE-2 JULY
ROYAL BANK GLASGOW JAZZ FESTIVAL
Annual international jazz festival with a whole host of big name acts and local talent.
Tel: 0141 552 3552
www.jazzfest.co.uk

15-16 JULY
GLASGOW RIVER FESTIVAL
Rollicking family entertainment on the Clyde River and shore.
Tel: 0871 700 0685
www.glasgowriverfestival.co.uk

12 AUGUST
WORLD PIPE BAND CHAMPIONSHIP
Pipe bands from all over the world compete for the prestigious title.
Tel: 0141 221 5414
www.rspba.co.uk

7-13 AUGUST
PIPING LIVE!
A sizzling international piping event of the highest calibre.
Tel: 0141 353 0220
www.pipingfestival.co.uk

31 DECEMBER
GLASGOW'S HOGMANAY
Join the celebrations and take in the New Year with live music and entertainment.
Tel: 0141 204 4480
www.glasgowshogmanay.org.uk

** denotes provisional date, event details are subject to change please check before travelling*

Greater Glasgow and Clyde Valley

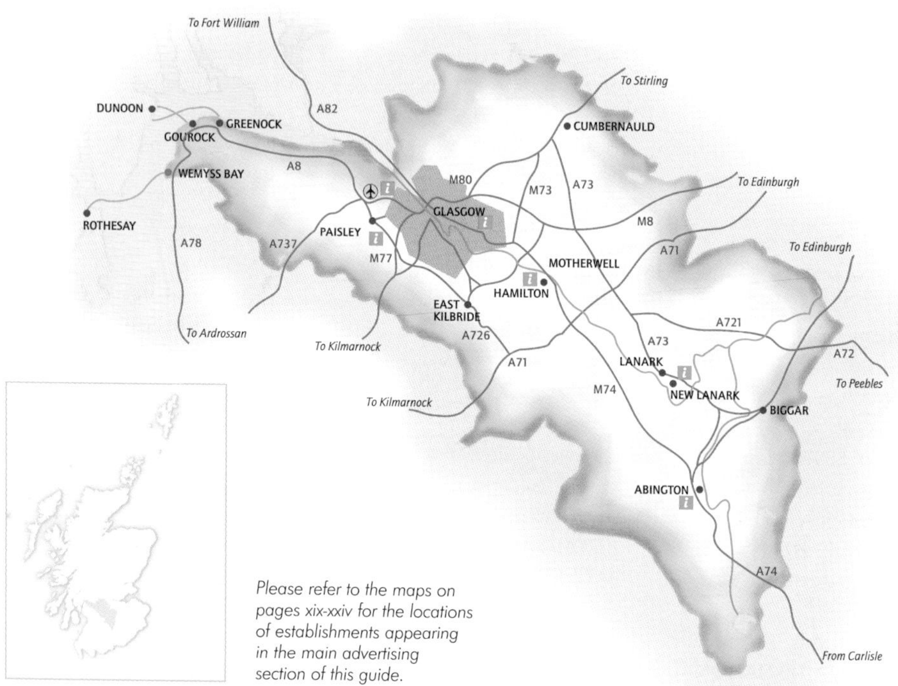

Please refer to the maps on pages xix-xxiv for the locations of establishments appearing in the main advertising section of this guide.

Finding out more...

For practical advice, ideas and information about exploring Scotland and to book your accommodation:

Tel: 0845 22 55 121*
or if calling from outside the UK: +44 (0) 1506 832121

Email: info@visitscotland.com
Web: www.visitscotland.com

* A £3 booking fee applies to telephone bookings of accommodation.

Tourist Information Centres

Greater Glasgow and Clyde Valley

Greater Glasgow and Clyde Valley

Abington
Welcome Break Service Area
Junction 13, M74
Tel: (01864) 502436
Jan-Dec

Biggar
155 High Street,
Tel: (01899) 221066
Easter-Sep

Glasgow
11 George Square
Tel: (0141) 204 4400
Jan-Dec

Glasgow Airport
Tourist Information Desk
Tel: (0141) 848 4440
Jan-Dec

Hamilton
Road Chef Services
M74 Northbound
Tel: (01698) 285590
Jan-Dec

Lanark
Horsemarket, Ladyacre Road
Tel: (01555) 661661
Jan-Dec

Paisley
9a Gilmour Street
Tel: (0141) 889 0711
Jan-Dec

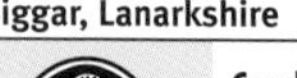

Biggar, Lanarkshire — Map Ref: 2B6

SMALL HOTEL ★★★

Cornhill House Hotel

Cornhill Road, Coulter, Biggar, Clyde Valley ML12 6QE
Tel:01899 220001 Fax:01899 220112
Email:enquiries@cornhillhousehotel.com
Web:www.cornhillhousehotel.com

A castellated Mansion House in the style of a Renaissance French Chateau. Sensitively restored to a Country House Hotel offering comfortable accommodation and excellent food.

7 rooms, all en-suite, Open Jan-Dec, B&B per person, single from £58.00, double from £40.00.

Glasgow — Map Ref: 1H5

SMALL HOTEL ★★★

Albion Hotel

405 North Woodside Road, Glasgow, G20 6NN
Tel:0141 339 8620 Fax:0141 334 8159
Email:albion@glasgowhotelsandapartments.co.uk
Web:www.glasgowhotelsandapartments.co.uk

Conveniently located in the heart of Glasgow's highly desirable West End, yet only 1 mile from the City Centre. Ideal for public transport, museums and art galleries. All rooms ensuite.

17 rooms, all en-suite, Open Jan-Dec, B&B per person, single from £48.00, double from £61.00.

GUEST HOUSE ★★

Alison Guest House

26 Circus Drive, Glasgow, G31 2JH
Tel/Fax:0141 556 1431
Email:circusdrive@aol.com

Victorian semi-villa in quiet residential area of East End yet only 15 minutes walk from city centre, 10 minutes walk from Cathedral, Royal Infirmary, Strathclyde University Campus. One ground floor room. Limited access to kitchen available for takeaway's for evening dining. Ideally situated for Celtic Park.

7 rooms, 3 ensuite, Open Jan-Dec, B&B per person, single from £22.00, double from £17.50. 3 Family en-suite rooms available.

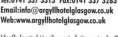

HOTEL ★★★

Argyll Hotel

973 Sauchiehall Street, Glasgow, G3 7TQ
Tel:0141 337 3313 Fax:0141 337 3283
Email:info@argyllhotelglasgow.co.uk
Web:www.argyllhotelglasgow.co.uk

Ideally located ½ mile west of city centre by Kelvingrove Park, the Argyll Hotel is within easy reach of the Scottish Exhibition and Conference Centre, Kelvingrove Art Galleries & Museum, The Glasgow Science Centre and Glasgow University. Excellent accommodation, warm Scottish hospitality, fine food and above all value for money.

38 rooms, all en-suite, Open Jan-Dec, B&B per person, single from £49.00-59.00, twin/double from £66.00-78.00 per room, Dinner available.

HOTEL ★★★★

Arthouse Hotel

129 Bath Street, Glasgow, G2 2SZ
Tel:0141 221 6789 Fax:0141 221 6777
Email:info@arthousehotel.com
Web:www.arthousehotel.com

Combining Henry E. Clifford's neo-classical architecture with Ronald MacColl's modern interior design to produce an ambience that is both vibrant and intriguing. This new addition to Glasgow's portfolio is ideally placed just off Sauchiehall Street in the heart of the city. Arthouse Bar and Grill and fine dining add to the experience.

63 rooms, all en-suite, Open Jan-Dec excl Xmas/New Year, B&B per person, double from £55.00.

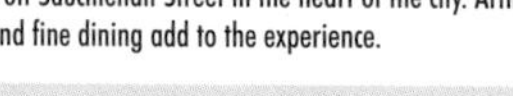

Important: Prices stated are estimates and may be subject to amendments

Glasgow | Map Ref: 1H5

GUEST HOUSE

Belgrave Guest House

2 Belgrave Terrace, Hillhead, Glasgow, G12 8JD
Tel:0141 337 1850 Fax:0141 337 1741
Email:belgraveglasgow@aol.com
Web:www.belgraveguesthouse.co.uk

Refurbished guest house, in the West End. Convenient for Botanic Gardens, other local attractions and amenities. 5 minute walk from two tube stations. Many restaurants, cafes and bus a few minutes walk away. Small private car-park to rear. Ensuite rooms available.

11 rooms, Open Jan-Dec, B&B per person, single from £25.00, double from £20.00.

HOTEL

Bewleys Hotel

110 Bath Street, Glasgow, G2 2EN
Tel:0845 234 5959/0141 353 0800
Fax:0141 353 0900
Email:gla@bewleyshotels.com Web:www.bewleyshotels.com

Contemporary, relaxed and informal that is the ethos of the Bewley's Hotel Glasgow. The rooms, which have been designed with both the tourist and business traveller in mind, are spacious and the top two floors have large windows with spectacular views over the City. Loop bar and restaurant provides a relaxed, informal dining experience. Food is served throughout the day.

103 rooms, all en-suite, Open Jan-Dec excl Xmas, from £69.00 Room Only.

HOTEL

Bothwell Bridge Hotel

89 Main Street, Bothwell, Glasgow, G71 8EU
Tel:01698 852246 Fax:01698 854686
Email:enquiries@bothwellbridge-hotel.com
Web:www.bothwellbridge-hotel.com

Family run hotel, 9 miles (14kms) from Glasgow city centre and convenient for motorway. Business meeting rooms. Ample parking. Wireless broadband available for conferences and guest rooms.

90 rooms, all en-suite, Open Jan-Dec, B&B per room, single from £60.00, double from £70.00.

HOTEL

Buchanan Hotel

185 Buchanan Street, Glasgow, G1 2JY
Tel:0141 332 7284 Fax:0141 333 0635
Email:salesbuchanan@strathmorehotels.com
Web:www.strathmorehotels.com

City centre hotel near to Queen Street Station and Buchanan Street Bus Station. Ideally situated for shopping, Royal Concert Hall and major theatres.

60 rooms, all en-suite, Open Jan-Dec, B&B per person, single from £35.00, double from £39.00, BB & Eve.Meal from £45.00.

Glasgow — **Map Ref: 1H5**

★★★
HOTEL

Campanile Hotel Glasgow

Tunnel Street, Glasgow, G3 8HL
Tel:0141 287 7700 Fax:0141 287 7701
Email:glasgow@campanile.com
Web:www.campanile.com

The Campanile is Glasgows newest waterside hotel and suitable for both corporate and leisure visitors. All rooms are ensuite with power shower and have working space with desk, modem, direct dial telephone and satellite TV. Our cafe' bistro restaurant offers a wide selection of finest seasonal products designed to bring you quality and freshness all year round.

106 rooms, all en-suite, Open Jan-Dec, B&B per person, double from £33.45.

The Georgian House

29 Buckingham Terrace, Great Western Road
Hillhead, Glasgow, G12 8ED
Tel:0141 339 0008
Email:thegeorgianhouse@yahoo.com
Web:www.georgianhousehotel.com

Restored Georgian townhouse, retaining many original features, set in the heart of the vibrant West End on the road to Loch Lomond. Close to Botanic Gardens, University of Glasgow, BBC, SECC and many other local attractions as well as a range of cafes and restaurants to suit all tastes. Comfortable rooms of varying sizes all with private or en suite facilities. Private parking.

15 rooms, some en-suite, Open Jan-Dec, B&B per person, single from £25.00, double from £25.00 per person.

The Heritage Hotel

4-5 Alfred Terrace, Glasgow, G12 8RF
Tel/Fax:0141 339 6955
Email:bookings@heritagehotel.fsbusiness.co.uk

Privately owned hotel, close to Botanic Garden, University, SECC and the major hospitals. Short walk to Underground.

27 rooms, all en-suite, Open Jan-Dec excl Xmas, B&B per person, single from £35.00, double from £27.50, family from £25.00.

Hilton Hotel Glasgow

1 William Street, Glasgow, G3 8HT
Tel:0141 204 5555 Fax:0141 204 5004
Email:sales.glasgow@hilton.com
Web:www.hilton.com

Built in 1992, this hotel is a stunning 20 storey landmark offering panoramic views across the city. There are 319 luxurious bedrooms which include 5 floors of non-smoking rooms. Enjoy fine dining in Camerons restaurant or dine in the more informal Minsky's New York Deli. Extensive conference business and leisure facilities.

319 rooms, all en-suite, Open Jan-Dec, B&B per person, single from £99.00, double from £109.00.

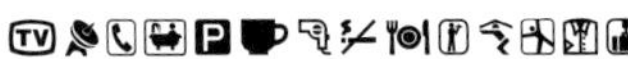

Holiday Inn Glasgow City Centre

Theatreland, 161 West Nile Street, Glasgow, G1 2RL
Tel:0141 352 8300 Fax:0141 352 8311
Email:reservations@higlasgow.com
Web:www.higlasgow.com

In the heart of the city, five minutes walk from theatres and transport. Award winning brasserie style restaurant. All 113 rooms refurbished in 2004 including Penthouse Suites and Junior Suites.

113 rooms, all en-suite, Open Jan-Dec, B&B per person, single from £75.00, double from £45.00, BB & Eve.Meal from £59.00.

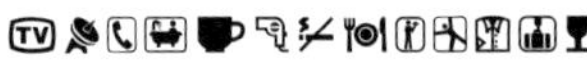

Important: Prices stated are estimates and may be subject to amendments

Glasgow | **Map Ref: 1H5**

HOTEL ★★★

Holiday Inn Glasgow City West

Bothwell Street, Glasgow, G2 7EN
Tel:0870 4009032 Fax:0141 221 8986
Email:sales.glasgowcity@6c.com
Web:www.holiday-inn.co.uk

City centre location with easy access from M8. Choice of dining in Carvery or 'Jules' themed restaurant and bar.

275 rooms, all en-suite, Open Jan-Dec, B&B per person, single from £58.00, double from £60.00, Eve.Meal from £12.95.

GUEST HOUSE

Kelvingrove Hotel

944 Sauchiehall Street, Glasgow, G3 7TH
Tel:0141 339 5011 Fax:0141 339 6566
Email:info@kelvingrovehotel.com
Web:www.kelvingrovehotel.com

A warm and welcoming family run hotel situated adjacent to Kelvingrove Park. Ideally situated close to main City attractions including the SECC, Science Centre, galleries and museums, famous parks and a variety of bars and restaurants. All 22 versatile and well-appointed rooms boast ensuite facilities, colour TVs, hospitality trays and a 24-hour reception service. Being on Sauchiehall Street, the hotel is conveniently located just 15 minutes walk from the City Centre and some of the best shopping in the UK.

22 rooms, all en-suite, Open Jan-Dec, B&B per person, single from £45.00, double from £30.00. Family rooms available.

HOTEL

Langs Hotel

2 Port Dundas Place, Glasgow, G2 3LD
Tel:0141 333 1500 Fax:0141 333 5700
Email:reservations@langshotels.co.uk
Web:www.langshotels.co.uk

A new and stylishly different experience in the centre of Glasgow. Ideally located for theatres and concert hall or for business and shopping. Hotel facilities include spa, gymnasium, 'Aurora' restaurant (2 AA Rosettes), and the unique Oshi........for a quite different and less formal meal.

100 rooms, all en suite, Open Jan-Dec, B&B per person single from £80.00, double/family from £45.00 per person.

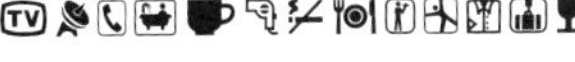

Glasgow

Map Ref: 1H5

LODGE

The Sandyford Hotel

904 Sauchiehall Street, Glasgow, G3 7TF
Tel:0141 334 0000 Fax:0141 337 1812

55 rooms, all en-suite, Open Jan-Dec excl Xmas, B&B per person, single from £32.00, double from £26.00.

Recently refurbished hotel, enjoying a convenient location in the West End, close to museums, Kelvingrove Park and SECC. On main bus route to city centre, and within walking distance of a host of Glasgow's major attractions.

GUEST HOUSE

Seton Guest House

6 Seton Terrace, Dennistoun, Glasgow, G31 2HY
Tel:0141 556 7654
Email:setonguesthouse@btconnect.com
Web:www.prestel.seton.co.uk

7 rooms, Open Jan-Dec, B&B per person, single from £22.00, shared from £18.00.

Stone built townhouse c.1850 in conservation area of East End. Close to city centre and all amenities. Public transport of rail & bus a 2 minute walk away.

HOTEL

Sherbrooke Castle Hotel

11 Sherbrooke Avenue, Glasgow, G41 4PG
Tel:0141 427 4227 Fax:0141 427 5685
Email:mail@sherbrooke.co.uk
Web:www.sherbrooke.co.uk

21 rooms, all en-suite, Open Jan-Dec, B&B per person, single from £68.00, double from £44.00.

The Sherbrooke Castle is situated in Glasgow's most prestigious of residential areas, Pollockshields. This magnificent baronial building crafted in rich red sandstone, combines traditional grace with modern efficiency. The fully air conditioned restaurant serves fresh local produce, prepared by award winning chefs, complimented with an interesting wine cellar. Some annexe accommodation.

CAMPUS ACCOMMODATION

University of Strathclyde

Residence and Catering Services,
50 Richmond Street, Glasgow, G1 1XP
Tel:0141 553 4148 Fax:0141 553 4149
Email:rescat@mis.strath.ac.uk
Web:www.rescat.strath.ac.uk

600 rooms, including 300 en-suite, Open Jun-Sep, B&B per person, single from £21.25, double from £22.00.

Modern, purpose-built halls of residence on city centre campus. Attractive bar/restaurant on site. Ideal centre for exploring the city.

Important: Prices stated are estimates and may be subject to amendments

Glasgow Airport, Renfrewshire Map Ref: 1H5

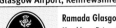

★★★ HOTEL

Ramada Glasgow Airport

Marchburn Drive, Glasgow Airport Business Park
Paisley, PA3 2SJ
Tel:0141 840 2200 Fax:0141 889 6830
Email:sales.glasgowairport@ramadajarvis.co.uk
Web:www.ramadaglasgowairport.co.uk

A chic, contemporary hotel opened in 2002. Free parking during your stay and just 500m from the airport. The hotel has Bagio's, an Italian style cafe bar serving pizzas from the wood burning oven.

108 rooms, all en-suite, Open Jan-Dec, B&B per person, double from £26.50.

by Glasgow Map Ref: 1H5

★★★ HOTEL

The Westerwood

St Andrews Drive, Cumbernauld, by Glasgow, G68 0EW
Tel:01236 457171 Fax:01236 738478
Email:westerwoodrooms@morton-hotels.com
Web:www.morton-hotels.com

Modern hotel, with leisure complex, and 18 hole championship golf course. The hotel provides a choice of eating and drinking options, including the Hotel Restaurant and The Clubhouse bar. Conference and function facilities are available.

100 rooms, all en-suite, Open Jan-Dec, B&B per person, single from £98.00, double from £60.00 per person, BB & Eve.Meal from £85.00 pp.

nr Glasgow Map Ref: 1H5

★★★ SMALL HOTEL

Uplawmoor Hotel

Neilston Road, Uplawmoor, Glasgow, G78 4AF
Tel:01505 850565 Fax:01505 850689
Email:info@uplawmoor.co.uk
Web:www.uplawmoor.co.uk

Quality eighteenth century Coaching Inn situated in quiet picturesque village just thirty minutes from Glasgow City Centre and airport, gateway to Burns Country.

14 rooms, all en-suite, Open Jan-Dec excl Xmas/New Year, B&B per person, single from £39.00, double from £29.50.

★★ RESTAURANT WITH ROOMS

Wallace Hotel

1 Yieldshields Road, Carluke, Lanarkshire, ML8 4QG
Tel:01555 773000
Email:info@wallacehotel.co.uk
Web:www.wallacehotel.com

A new purpose built and spacious family run restaurant with rooms. Easy access to major road network (M74, M8, A73) with Edinburgh, Glasgow, Stirling, Ayrshire and the Scottish Borders all within easy reach. 5 golf courses within 5 miles.

10 rooms, all en-suite, Open Jan-Dec, from £40.00 Room Only.

VAT is shown at 17.5%: changes in this rate may affect prices.

Key to symbols is on back flap.

Harthill, by Shotts, Lanarkshire

Map Ref: 2A5

GUEST HOUSE

Blairmains Guest House

Harthill, Shotts, Lanarkshire, ML7 5TJ
Tel:01501 751278 Fax:01501 753383
Email:Heather@blairmains.freeserve.co.uk
Web:www.blairmains.co.uk

Comfortable accommodation in separate unit adjacent to farmhouse. Conveniently situated directly beside M8 making it an ideal base for visiting Edinburgh, Glasgow and Stirling (all within 30 mins drive). Ensuite rooms available. Ample private parking. Well behaved pets welcome. Evening meals by prior arrangement.

5 rooms, some en-suite, Open Jan-Dec, B&B per person, single from £20.00, double from £18.00, BB & Eve.Meal from £25.50.

Inverkip, Renfrewshire

Map Ref: 1F5

SMALL HOTEL

Inverkip Hotel

Main Street, Inverkip, Renfrewshire, PA16 OAS
Tel:01475 521478 Fax:01475 522065
Email:enquiries@inverkip.co.uk
Web:www.inverkip.co.uk

Family run hotel, on main tourist route adjacent to Scotland's No 1 yachting marina. Reputation for good food. Sports can be arranged. Busy restaurant. Ideally positioned for the Clyde ferries to Dunoon and beyond or trips to Loch Lomond, Stirling and the Trossachs. 45 mins drive to Royal Troon.

5 rooms, all en-suite, Open Jan-Dec, B&B per person, single from £45.00, double from £34.00.

by Larkhall, Lanarkshire

Map Ref: 2A6

LODGE

Shawlands Hotel

Ayr Road, Canderside Toll, by Larkhall
Lanarkshire, ML9 2TZ
Tel/Fax:01698 791111

Privately owned and family run travel lodge with emphasis on quality food and drink at affordable prices. In central Scotland just off M74, 20 mins from Glasgow and 40 mins travel to Edinburgh. Refurbished function room with conservatory.

21 rooms, all en-suite, Open Jan-Dec, £50.00 per room per night.

Motherwell, Lanarkshire

Map Ref: 2A5

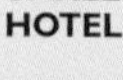

SMALL HOTEL

The Bentley Hotel

19 High Road, Motherwell, ML1 3HU
Tel:01698 265588 Fax:01698 253418
Email:thebentleyhotel@barbox.net
Web:www.thebentleyhotel.net

Privately owned, 19thC building centrally located, close to railway station and opposite the Motherwell Heritage Centre. Only 3 minutes drive from the M74, 15 miles south of Glasgow.

16 rooms, all en-suite, Open Jan-Dec excl Xmas/New Year, B&B per person, single from £45.00, double from £30.00.

HOTEL

Moorings Hotel

114 Hamilton Road, Motherwell, ML1 3DG
Tel:01698 258131
Email:enquiries@mooringsmotherwell.co.uk
Web:www.mooringsmotherwell.co.uk

The Moorings Hotel originates from a custom built 19th Century home of one of Scotlands foremost steel families (The Colvilles). Ideally situated a few minutes from the M74 and M8 motorways. Ample parking.

31 rooms, all en-suite, Open Jan-Dec, B&B per person, single from £52.00, twin/double from £35.00.

Important: Prices stated are estimates and may be subject to amendments

Motherwell, Lanarkshire

Map Ref: 2A5

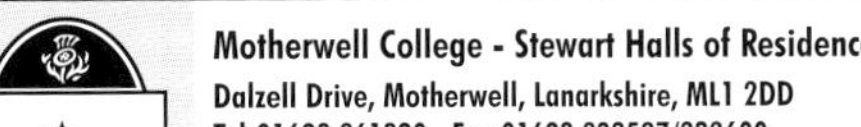

★ CAMPUS ACCOMMODATION

Motherwell College - Stewart Halls of Residence

Dalzell Drive, Motherwell, Lanarkshire, ML1 2DD
Tel:01698 261890 Fax:01698 232527/232600
Email:m.col@motherwell.co.uk
Web:www.motherwell.ac.uk

On college campus and all on one level. Close to Strathclyde Park and M8/M74 motorway link for Glasgow and Edinburgh.

52 rooms, Open Jan-Dec excl Xmas/New Year, B&B per person, single from £20.00.

Paisley, Renfrewshire

Map Ref: 1H5

★★ GUEST HOUSE

Dryesdale Guest House

37 Inchinnan Road, Paisley, Renfrewshire, PA3 2PR
Tel:0141 889 7178
Email:dd@paisley2001.freeserve.co.uk
Web:www.ga-taxis.co.uk/dryesdale.html

Personally run guest house 0.5 mile (1km) from Glasgow Airport and M8 access. Close to Paisley with its station for the 15 minute journey to Glasgow city centre. Ideal for touring Loch Lomond, Oban and Edinburgh. Some ground floor rooms.

7 rooms, Open Jan-Dec, B&B per person, single from £25.00, double from £22.50.

★★★ GUEST HOUSE

Makerston House & Spa

19 Park Road, Paisley, Renfrewshire PA2 6JP
Tel/Fax:0141 884 2520
Email:stay@makerston.co.uk
Web:www.makerston.co.uk

Mansion house, in a tranquil retreat set in one of Paisley's most private leafy enclaves. Recently and sympathetically refurbished under new ownership.

7 rooms, all en-suite, Open Jan-Dec excl Xmas/New Year, B&B per room, single from £35.00, double from £55.00. Evening meals available.

Uddingston, Lanarkshire

Map Ref: 2A5

★★★ SMALL HOTEL

Redstones Hotel

8-10 Glasgow Road, Uddingston, Glasgow, G71 7AS
Tel:01698 813744 Fax:01698 815319
Email:info@redstoneshotel.com
Web:www.redstoneshotel.com

Linked Victorian villas retaining original features and with modern facilities. Situated within easy access to M74, within 10mins of Glasgow.

12 rooms, all en-suite, Open Jan-Dec excl Xmas/New Year, B&B per person, single from £50.00, double from £60.00.

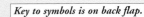

VAT is shown at 17.5%: changes in this rate may affect prices.

Key to symbols is on back flap.

Welcome to Scotland

West Highlands and Islands, Loch Lomond, Stirling and Trossachs

Between the Lowlands and the Highlands is an area of startling personality - or multiple personalities. Romantic, epic, and quirky, prepare to be charmed...

The Falkirk Wheel is unique for being the world's only rotating boat lift.

The endless list of things to do is a reflection of the landscape and people. Spanning the full width of the country, from Falkirk to the far-flung islands in the west, the area is a range of colourful personalities.

As a gateway to the mountainous north, Stirling is the cradle of independence and Scotland's newest city. The famous castle, once the hallowed throne of Scottish Kings, sits loftily above the Old Town. Visible from a nearby hill, the William Wallace monument pays homage to Scotland's first freedom-fighter. Or feel your skin crawl at Bannockburn, an outlying battleground where brutal fighting secured 300 years of freedom.

Behind the medieval stone is a kinetic city driven by students and young professionals. Why don't you join the throng at Cambio, Pivo or Best Bar None? And when the night closes in, go clubbing at The Beat, Fubar, or The Yard. Connoisseurs of fine dining will savour the flavours and impeccable service of Hermanns.

Continuing west from Stirling, hopeless romantics will be seduced by the sparkling beauty of Loch Lomond. Scotland's largest loch offers plenty of cruising options, and is part of a National Park extending into the Trossachs. The postcard towns of Callander and Aberfoyle provide easy access to an area rendered in hills, woods and wild glens. Ever had romantic thoughts about cattle rustlers? The heroic exploits of Rob Roy MacGregor, clan chief and wrongly accused outlaw, were immortalised by romantic poet, Sir Walter Scott. Delve into his legend at the Rob Roy Visitor Centre, Callander.

The 'bristly country' of Scott's poetry inspires walking, whether meandering through hills on a lazy

Loch Lomond

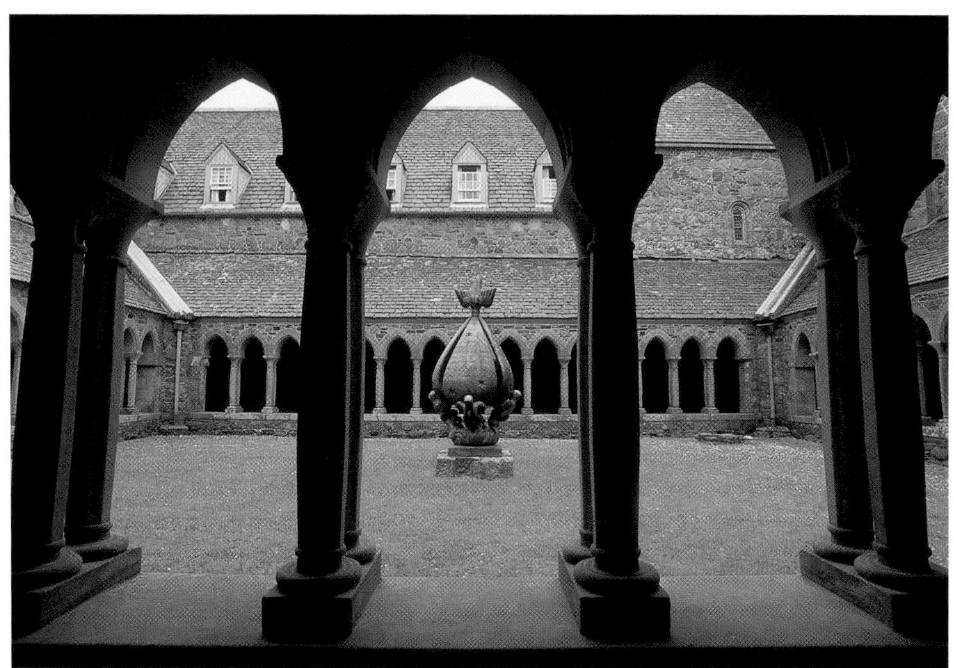

A tiny island with a big role. Iona introduced Scotland to Christianity.

picnic, or hiking the entire West Highland Way – that's a cool 95 miles. Spice up your holiday with some high-octane fun at Croft na Caber, at Kenmore on Loch Tay. Take your pick of jet skiing, canoeing, and quad biking.

Continue west and happen across a land of giants. Enclosed by dense, towering forests, the Cowal Peninsula has a primal majesty. Closer to monoliths than trees, the redwoods of Benmore Botanic Gardens elicit awe. Let your imagination go wild - in true pagan style - among the prehistoric stone circles at Kilmartin, near Lochgilphead. The Scots arrived here from Ireland in the 6th century, putting an end to iffy rituals and uniting scattered tribes into the first kingdom. Escape to sandy beaches and island fantasies farther down Kintyre peninsula. It's just a short ferry ride to one of the outlying islands: Gigha, Jura, Islay or Colonsay. Islay abounds in whisky, crafting a variety of distinct malts from its seven distilleries. Jura is defiantly minimal, opting for space to soothe the senses.

Heading further north, Mull attracts birdwatchers eager for a glimpse of the re-introduced white-tailed sea eagle. And children of all ages will recognise Tobermory's brightly-painted houses from the popular children's programme, 'Balamory'.

Neighbouring Iona is a tiny island with a far-reaching influence on Christianity. A burial place of Scottish Kings, Iona expresses the beauty of faith through Celtic crosses and sturdy chapels. And Oban is a popular coastal resort providing easy access to Mull and Iona.

Events

West Highlands and Islands, Loch Lomond, Stirling and Trossachs

15-22 APRIL
WALKISLAY, Islay and Jura
The routes allow you to visit local historical sites and appreciate the abundance of wildlife, you might even spot a golden eagle or the odd otter as well as the fantastic views across to Mull and Arran.
Tel: 01496 850382
www.walkislay.co.uk

27 APRIL-1 MAY
ISLE OF BUTE JAZZ FESTIVAL
The big names of jazz flock to this small island for a festival of dazzling music.
Tel: 01700 502151
www.butejazz.com

MAY-4 JUNE
ISLAY FESTIVAL OF MALT AND MUSIC
Whisky and song come together in this joyous collaboration.
www.feisile.org

27-28 MAY
LOCH FYNE FOOD FAIR
A feast of West-Coast seafood and quality local produce.
Tel: 01499 600264
www.loch-fyne.com

6-9 JULY
BARCLAYS SCOTTISH OPEN, Loch Lomond
Major PGA European Tour golf tournament.
Tel: 01436 655555
www.lochlomond.com

28-30 JULY
LOMOND FOLK FESTIVAL
A unique weekend of high quality traditional and folk music including concerts, ceilidh, workshops, open sessions, competitions, craft fair and street entertainment.
Tel: 01389 603278
www.lomondfolkfestival.com

29-30 JULY
WORLD CHAMPIONSHIP HIGHLAND GAMES, Callander
Traditional Highland games and Highland dancing competitions.
Tel: 01877 330919

23-24 AUGUST
ARGYLLSHIRE GATHERING, Oban
Traditional Highland games and Highland dancing.
Tel: 01631 562671
www.obangames.com

24-26 AUGUST
COWAL HIGHLAND GATHERING, Dunoon
One of the largest and most spectacular Highland games in the world featuring Highland dancing and pipe band championships.
Tel: 01369 703206
www.cowalgathering.com

13-15 OCTOBER
TUNNOCK'S TOUR OF MULL CAR RALLY
High-octane thrills on the Isle of Mull.
www.2300club.org

13-21 OCTOBER
THE ROYAL NATIONAL MOD IN DUNOON
The premier festival of Gaelic arts and culture.
Tel: 01463 709705
www.the-mod.co.uk

** denotes provisional date, event details are subject to change please check before travelling*

West Highlands and Islands, Loch Lomond, Stirling and Trossachs

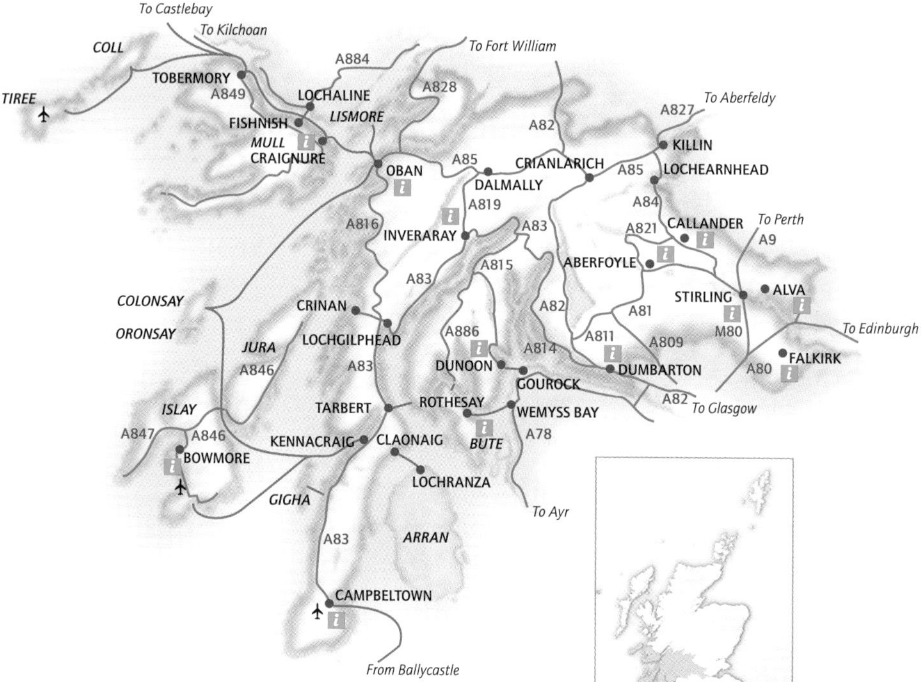

Please refer to the maps on pages xix-xxiv for the locations of establishments appearing in the main advertising section of this guide.

Finding out more...

For practical advice, ideas and information about exploring Scotland and to book your accommodation:

Tel: 0845 22 55 121*
or if calling from outside the UK: +44 (0) 1506 832121

Email: info@visitscotland.com
Web: www.visitscotland.com

* A £3 booking fee applies to telephone bookings of accommodation.

Tourist Information Centres

West Highlands and Islands, Loch Lomond, Stirling and Trossachs

Aberfoyle
Trossachs Discovery Centre
Main Street
Tel: (08707) 200604
Jan – Dec

Alva
Mill Trail Visitor Centre
Tel: (08707) 200605
Jan-Dec

Ardgartan
Arrochar
Tel: (08707) 200606
Apr-Oct

Balloch
The Old Station Building
Tel: (08707) 200607
Apr-Oct

Bo'ness
Seaview Car Park
Tel: (08707) 200608
May-Sep

Bowmore
Isle of Islay
Tel: (08707) 200617
Jan-Dec

Callander
Rob Roy and Trossachs
Visitor Centre, Ancaster Square
Tel: (08707) 200628
Mar-Dec
Jan and Feb weekends only

Campbeltown
Mackinnon House
The Pier, Argyll
Tel: (08707) 200609
Jan-Dec

Craignure
The Pier, Isle of Mull
Tel: (08707) 200610
Jan-Dec

Drymen
Drymen Library, The Square
Tel: (08707) 200611
May-Sep

Dumbarton
Milton, A82 Northbound
Tel: (08707) 200612
Jan-Dec

Dunblane
Stirling Road
Tel: (08707) 200613
May-Sep

Dunoon
7 Alexandra Parade, Argyll
Tel: (08707) 200629
Jan-Dec

Falkirk
2-4 Glebe Street
Tel: (08707) 200614
Jan-Dec

Helensburgh
The Clock Tower
Tel: (08707) 200615
Apr-Oct

Inveraray
Front Street, Argyll
Tel: (08707) 200616
Jan-Dec

Killin
Breadalbane Folklore Centre
Tel: (08707) 200627
Mar-Oct Feb weekends only

Lochgilphead
Lochnell Street, Argyll
Tel: (08707) 200618
Apr-Oct

Loch Lomond
Loch Lomond Gateway Centre
Loch Lomond Shores, Balloch
Tel: (08707) 200631
Jan – Dec

Oban
Argyll Square, Argyll
Tel: (08707) 200630
Jan-Dec

Rothesay
Discovery Centre, Winter
Gardens, Isle of Bute
Tel: (08707) 200619
Jan-Dec

Stirling
41 Dumbarton Road
Tel: (08707) 200620
Jan-Dec

Stirling
Royal Burgh of Stirling
Visitor Centre
Castle Esplanade
Tel: (08707) 200622
Jan-Dec

Stirling
Pirnhall Motorway Service Area
Junction 9, M9
Tel: (08707) 200621
Apr-Oct

Tarbert, Loch Fyne
Harbour Street
Argyll
Tel: (08707) 200624
Apr-Oct

Tarbet-Loch Lomond
Main Street
Tel: (08707) 200623
Apr-Oct

Tobermory
The Pier, Isle of Mull
Tel: (08707) 200625
Apr-Oct

Tyndrum
Main Street
Tel: (08707) 200626
Apr-Oct

Aberfoyle, Stirlingshire

Map Ref: 1H3

GUEST HOUSE

Creag-Ard House

Aberfoyle, Stirling, FK8 3TQ
Tel/Fax:01877 382297
Email:cara@creag-ardhouse.co.uk
Web:www.creag-ardhouse.co.uk

Welcoming Guest House with superb views over Loch Ard 3kms from the centre of Aberfoyle Village in the heart of Trossachs. A haven of peace and tranquility. Delicious breakfast with homebaking.

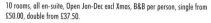

6 rooms, all en-suite, Open Mar-Oct, B&B per person, single from £45.00, double from £32.00.

Ardlui, Argyll

Map Ref: 1G3

SMALL HOTEL

Ardlui Hotel

Ardlui, Loch Lomond, Argyll, G83 7EB
Tel:01301 704269/243 Fax:01301 704268
Email:info@ardlui.co.uk
Web:www.ardlui.co.uk

Former shooting lodge on A82 and on the banks of Loch Lomond with private gardens to shore. Caravan site adjacent. Moorings available. 1 hour from Glasgow or Oban & 1½ hours from Fort William via Glencoe.

10 rooms, all en-suite, Open Jan-Dec excl Xmas, B&B per person, single from £50.00, double from £37.50.

Ardrishaig, by Lochgilphead, Argyll

Map Ref: 1E4

SMALL HOTEL

Allt-Na-Craig House

Tarbert Road, Ardrishaig, Argyll, PA30 8EP
Tel:01546 603245
Email:information@allt-na-craig.co.uk
Web:www.allt-na-craig.co.uk

A Victorian Mansion set in picturesque grounds, with magnificent views across Loch Fyne. Entrance to Crinan Canal nearby. Home cooking. Hill-walking, bird-watching, fishing, golf, riding, diving, wind-surfing and many other outdoor activities are available in the area.

5 rooms, all en-suite, Open Jan-Dec excl Xmas/New Year, B&B per person, single from £35.00, double from £35.00.

Balloch, Dunbartonshire

Map Ref: 1G4

GUEST HOUSE

Anchorage Guest House

31 Balloch Road, Balloch, Loch Lomond, G83 8SS
Tel:01389 753336
Email:anchorage_gh@hotmail.com

Extended cottage in centre of village, near river. Railway station and all other amenities nearby. Ideal touring base. All rooms ground floor.

5 rooms, all en-suite, Open Jan-Dec, B&B per person, single from £25.00, double from £25.00.

Bo'ness, West Lothian

Map Ref: 2B4

GUEST HOUSE

Carriden House

Carriden Brae, Bo'ness, West Lothian, EH51 9SN
Tel:01506 829811 Fax:01506 826888
Email:carriden_house@compuserve.com

16th century turreted mansion house set in 25 acres of mature parkland - an ideal quiet and peaceful setting. Only 15 mins drive to Edinburgh airport and easy access to all major routes in central Scotland.

5 rooms, all en-suite, Open Jan-Dec, B&B per person, single from £40.00, double from £35.00.

Important: Prices stated are estimates and may be subject to amendments

Rothesay, Isle of Bute

Map Ref: 1F5

HOTEL

The Ardyne Hotel

38 Mountstuart Road, Rothesay, Isle of Bute, PA20 9EB
Tel:01700 502052 Fax:01700 505129
Email:ardyne.hotel@virgin.net
Web:www.rothesay-scotland.com

Elegant, licensed Victorian hotel, with spectacular seafront views. All bedrooms en-suite. Reputation for comfortable accommodation and excellent restaurant.

20 rooms, all en-suite, Open Jan-Dec, B&B per person, single from £32.50, double from £29.50, BB & Eve.Meal from £47.00.

HOTEL

Glenburn Hotel

Mount Stuart Road, Rothesay, Isle of Bute, PA20 9JB
Tel:01942 824824
Email:reservations@WAshearings.com
Web:www.shearingsholidays.com

Fine Victorian building in an outstanding position above its own terraced gardens overlooking the sea. Entertainment every night.

127 rooms, all en-suite, Open Feb-Dec, B&B per person, double from £25.00.

SMALL HOTEL

The Regent Hotel

23 Battery Place, Rothesay, Isle of Bute, PA20 9DU
Tel:01700 502006
Email:info@theregent.co.uk
Web:www.theregent.co.uk

A warm welcome awaits you at this small hotel situated a short walk from the town centre. Comfortable rooms are complemented by an a' la carte restaurant, with a choice of Scottish Fayre and Mediterranean-style cuisine. Enjoy a drink on the sea-facing deck or in Dizzy's Bar which has twice-weekly cabaret entertainment.

8 rooms, some en-suite, Open Jan-Dec, B&B per person, single from £25.00, double from £27.50, BB & Eve.Meal from £45.00.

Cairndow, Argyll

Map Ref: 1F3

INN

Cairndow Stagecoach Inn

Cairndow, Argyll, PA26 8BN
Tel:01499 600286 Fax:01499 600220
Email:cairndowinn@aol.com

Old Coaching Inn on Loch Fyne. Ideal centre for touring Western Highlands. 9 bedrooms with loch view - all en-suite - all fully appointed. 2 rooms with 2 person spa baths. Stables restaurant and lounge meals all day. Half-price golf at Inveraray. Beer garden. Sauna, solarium and multi-gym.

13 rooms, all en-suite, Open Jan-Dec, B&B per person, single from £30.00, double from £35.00, BB & Eve.Meal from £48.00.

VAT is shown at 17.5%: changes in this rate may affect prices.

Key to symbols is on back flap.

Callander, Perthshire

Map Ref: 1H3

GUEST HOUSE

Annfield Guest House

North Church Street, Callander, Perthshire, FK17 8EG
Tel:01877 330204 Fax:01877 330674
Email:janet-greenfield@amserve.com

Centrally situated in a quiet area of the town in close proximity to shops and restaurants. Stepping stone to the Highlands. Ideal for an overnight stop.

7 rooms, some en-suite, Open Jan-Dec, B&B per person, single from £25.00, double from £24.00.

SMALL HOTEL

Coppice Hotel

Leny Road, Callander, Perthshire, FK17 8AL
Tel:01877 330188

Personally run hotel with emphasis on cuisine using fresh local produce when available. Ideal base for touring the Trossachs or day trips to Stirling with its Castle and the Wallace Monument.

5 rooms, all en-suite, Open Jan-Dec, B&B per person, double from £25.00.

GUEST HOUSE

The Crags Hotel

101 Main Street, Callander, Perthshire, FK17 8BQ
Tel:01877 330257 Fax:01877 339997
Email:nieto@btinternet.com
Web:www.cragshotel.co.uk

A warm Scottish welcome guaranteed in this personally run small family fully licensed hotel situated on Callander's main street. An ideal base for exploring the Trossachs an area of outstanding natural beauty. Hearty meals using fresh local produce wherever possible.

7 rooms, all en-suite, Open Jan-Dec, B&B per person, single from £32.50, double from £25.00.

GUEST HOUSE

Riverview Guest House

Leny Road, Callander, Perthshire, FK17 8AL
Tel:01877 330635 Fax:01877 339386
Email:drew@visitcallander.co.uk
Web:www.visitcallander.co.uk

Detached stone built Victorian house set in its own garden with private parking. Close to town centre, leisure complex and local amenities. Within easy walking distance of pleasant riverside park and cycle track. Ideal base for exploring the beautiful Trossachs.

5 rooms, all en-suite, Open Mar-Nov, B&B per person, single from £24.00, double from £25.00.

Campbeltown, Argyll

Map Ref: 1D7

SMALL HOTEL

Dellwood Hotel

Drumore, Campbeltown, Argyll, PA28 6HD
Tel/Fax:01586 552465
Email:dellwood@talk21.com
Web:www.smoothhound.com/campbeltown

The Dellwood Hotel, a former manse has been run as a small hotel for the last 35 years (2002) by the same family. Some annexe accommodation and a honeymoon suite available. Plentiful tarmac off-road parking. Among activities which can be enjoyed are golf, genealogy, walking, scenery, cycling, beaches, Springbank Distillery.

12 rooms, some en-suite, Open Jan-Dec excl Xmas/New Year, B&B per person, single £18.00-28.00, double £18.00-23.00.

Important: Prices stated are estimates and may be subject to amendments

Carradale, Argyll

Map Ref: 1E6

SMALL HOTEL

Ashbank Hotel

Carradale, by Campbeltown, Argyll, PA28 6RY
Tel/Fax:01583 431650
Email:ancurrie@btopenworld.com
Web:www.ashbankhotel.com

Comfortable family hotel with compact rooms in small village with views from the rear across the Kilbrannan Sound to Arran and Ailsa Craig. Overlooking Carradale Golf Course and close to safe and sandy beach (10 minutes walk). 25 minutes drive to Campbeltown. Good base for Island hopping, walking, relaxing, touring and visitor attractions.

5 rooms, all en-suite, Open Jan-Dec excl Xmas/New Year, B&B per person, single from £25.00, double from £28.00.

SMALL HOTEL

Carradale Hotel

Carradale, Argyll, PA28 6RY
Tel:01583 431223
Email:carradaleh@aol.com
Web:www.carradalehotel.com

Family run hotel, overlooking Arran. Beautiful scenery, golf, fishing, beaches, mountain bikes, hillwalking and sauna. Taste of Scotland recommended.

9 rooms, all en-suite, Open Jan-Dec, B&B per person, single from £25.00, double from £25.00, BB & Eve.Meal from £44.00.

Colintraive, Argyll

Map Ref: 1F5

SMALL HOTEL

Colintraive Hotel

Colintraive, Argyll, PA22 3AS
Tel:01700 841207
Email:enquiries@colintraivehotel.com

A former hunting lodge, fully refurbished to a high standard with stunning views over the Kyles of Bute. Cosy bar with log fire and excellent bar meals. Elegant a' la carte restaurant using local produce & vegetables from our own garden. Period furniture & big leather chairs in coffee lounge. Beautiful spacious ensuite bedrooms. This family run hotel offers very high standards in relaxed informal surroundings. A great base for walking, sailing, cycling and fishing. Close to Bute ferry.

4 rooms, all en-suite, Open Jan-Dec, B&B per person, single from £45.00, double from £30.00.

Coll, Isle of, Argyll

Map Ref: 1B1

SMALL HOTEL

Coll Hotel

Arinagour, Isle of Coll, Argyll, PA78 6SZ
Tel:01879 230334 Fax:01879 230317
Email:collhotel@aol.com
Web:www.collhotel.com

17c building with panoramic sea views across Mull and the Treshnish Isles. Under 1 mile (2kms) from the ferry terminal. Bar and restaurant meals available, specialising in seafood and using the best of fresh local produce. Taste of Scotland recommended. Winner of Thistle Award 2003 Flavour of Scotland.

6 rooms, all en-suite, Open Jan-Dec excl Xmas/New Year, B&B per person, single from £30.00, double from £30.00.

VAT is shown at 17.5%: changes in this rate may affect prices.

Key to symbols is on back flap.

Crianlarich, Perthshire

Map Ref: 1G2

INN

Ben More Lodge Hotel

Crianlarich, Perthshire, FK20 8QP
Tel:01838 300210 Fax:01838 300218
Email:info@ben-more.co.uk
Web:www.ben-more.co.uk

Pine lodges of a high standard with restaurant and bar adjacent. Ideal base for touring, hillwalking and fishing.

11 rooms, all en-suite, Open Feb-Dec excl Xmas, B&B per person, single from £42.00, double from £26.00.

SMALL HOTEL

Suie Lodge Hotel

Luib, Glen Dochart, Crianlarich, Perthshire, FK20 8QT
Tel:01567 820417 Fax:01567 820040
Email:suielodge@btinternet.com
Web:www.suielodge.co.uk

Family run hotel in former Shooting Lodge, in scenic Glendochart. Offering a relaxed atmosphere, comfortable bedrooms. Many en-suite. Good Scottish food. Excellent centre for touring.

10 rooms, some en-suite, Open Jan-Dec, B&B per person, single from £25.00, double from £27.50.

Dunblane, Perthshire

Map Ref: 2A3

HOTEL

Dunblane Hydro

Perth Road, Dunblane, Perthshire, FK15 0HG
Tel:01786 822551 Fax:01786 825403
Web:www.hilton.com

Hotel with Victorian facade, standing in extensive and attractive grounds. Extensive conference facilities, leisure club and indoor swimming pool.

201 rooms, all en-suite, Open Jan-Dec, BB & Eve.Meal from £59.50.

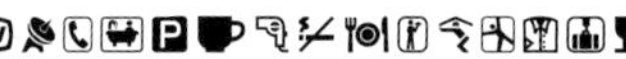

Dunoon, Argyll

Map Ref: 1F5

GUEST HOUSE

The Ardtully Hotel

297 Marine Parade, Hunters Quay, Dunoon, Argyll, PA23 8HN
Tel:01369 702478

Friendly run guest house set in its own grounds in an elevated position offering guests outstanding views of the Clyde Estuary, and the hills and mountains of Scotlands first Natural Park. Visit Dunoon's award winning Castle Museum, explore the many coastal, hill and forest walks. Relax over dinner in comfortable surroundings. Meals prepared using fresh produce. Some chalet bedrooms.

7 rooms, all en-suite, Open Jan-Dec, B&B per person, low season £30.00, high season £35.00. BB & Eve.Meal £54.00-59.00.

Important: Prices stated are estimates and may be subject to amendments

Dunoon, Argyll | **Map Ref: 1F5**

SMALL HOTEL

Enmore Hotel

Marine Parade, Kirn, Dunoon, Argyll, PA23 8HH
Tel:01369 702230 Fax:01369 702148
Email:enmorehotel@btinternet.com
Web:www.enmorehotel.co.uk

Beautifully situated with open sea views. Small, comfortable hotel offering the very best in accommodation, cuisine and hospitality.

10 rooms, all ensuite, Open Jan-Dec, B&B per person, single from £65.00, double from £45.00, family from £60.00. Room Only rates per night, single from £65.00, double from £90.00, family from £120.00.

Falkirk, Stirlingshire | **Map Ref: 2A4**

HOTEL

Best Western Park Hotel

Camelon Road, Falkirk, FK1 5RY
Tel:01324 628331 Fax:01324 611593
Email:office@parkhotelfalkirk.co.uk

An ideal location for touring central Scotland, with easy connections for all major roads/rail links for Glasgow and Edinburgh. This traditional comfortable hotel offers all modern facilities for both commercial and leisure breaks.

55 rooms, all en-suite, Open Jan-Dec excl Xmas/New Year, B&B per person, single from £45.00, double from £30.00.

VAT is shown at 17.5%: changes in this rate may affect prices.

Key to symbols is on back flap.

Fintry, Stirlingshire

Map Ref: 1H4

Culcreuch Castle Hotel and Country Park

Culcreuch Castle, Fintry, Stirlingshire G63 0LW
Tel: 01360 860555 Fax: 01360 860556
e.mail: info@culcreuch.com Web: www.culcreuch.com

Magnificent 1600-acre parkland estate in breathtaking scenery. 700-year-old Culcreuch is a unique opportunity to sample the historic atmosphere of Central Scotland's oldest inhabited castle. Comfortable accommodation, cosy bar, licensed restaurant, free fishing, adjacent squash courts, log fires, warm welcome. Central for all Scotland's attractions, including Edinburgh (55 minutes by road). For free accommodation brochure, free fishing and golf brochures:–

Contact: Laird of Culcreuch, Culcreuch Castle Hotel, Fintry, Stirlingshire G63 0LW.
Tel: (01360) 860555 Fax: (01360) 860556

SMALL HOTEL

Culcreuch Castle Hotel
Fintry, Glasgow, G63 0LW
Tel:01360 860555 Fax:01360 860556
Email:info@culcreuch.com
Web:www.culcreuch.com

14c castle with Dungeon Bar set in 1600 acre estate, with impressive views of Campsie Hills. Good base for touring central Scotland. Golfing, walking and fishing all available locally. Specialising in traditional Scottish Weddings.

14 rooms, all en-suite, Open Jan-Dec, B&B per person, single £70.00-115.00, double £45.00-90.00, BB & Eve.Meal from £74.00-161.00.

Gigha, Isle of, Argyll

Map Ref: 1D6

GIGHA HOTEL & COTTAGES

Isle of Gigha, Argyll PA41 7AA
Tel: 01583 505254 Fax: 01583 505244
e.mail: hotel@gigha.org.uk Web: www.gigha.org.uk

The Isle of Gigha - A secret known to discerning Scots for tranquillity, world renowned gardens, unspoiled sandy beaches, unsurpassed scenery, challenging golf. The hotel has panoramic sea views and a restaurant serving locally caught seafoods and the best of local and Scottish produce. Special Break prices available throughout the year.

SMALL HOTEL

Gigha Hotel & Cottages
Isle of Gigha, Argyll, PA41 7AA
Tel:01583 505254 Fax:01583 505244
Email:hotel@gigha.org.uk
Web:www.gigha.org.uk

Originally an old Inn, the hotel has been thoughtfully and tastefully modernised. Scottish fare, using local produce and seafood.

12 rooms, all en-suite, Open Jan-Dec, B&B per person, single from £35.00, double from £35.00, BB & Eve.Meal from £49.95 per person.

Important: Prices stated are estimates and may be subject to amendments

Grangemouth, Stirlingshire

Map Ref: 2B4

HOTEL

Leapark Hotel

130 Bo'ness Road, Grangemouth, FK3 9BX
Tel:01324 486733 Fax:01324 665412
Email:reception@leapark.com
Web:www.leapark.com

Privately owned family run Hotel in central Scotland. Large function suite ideal for weddings, social functions and conferences. 25 minutes drive from Edinburgh, close to Millenium Wheel in Falkirk, and excellent tourist base for Stirling, Trossachs and Loch Lomond.

51 rooms, all en-suite, Open Jan-Dec, B&B per person, single from £40.00, double from £30.00, BB & Eve.Meal from £50.00.

Helensburgh, Argyll

Map Ref: 1G4

GUEST HOUSE

Sinclair House

91/93 Sinclair Street, Helensburgh, Argyll & Bute, G84 8TR
Tel:0800 1646301
Email:bookings@sinclairhouse.com
Web:www.sinclairhouse.com

Sinclair House is located in Helensburgh town centre with views over the Clyde Estuary from the upper rooms. As such, we are close to numerous restaurants, bars, shops and Helensburgh Central Railway Station. We like to spoil our guests providing mini-fridges, free wireless internet access, freeview receivers and DVD players in all rooms with over 400 free DVD movies available. See our website for full details.

4 rooms, all en-suite, Open Jan-Dec, B&B per person, single from £50.00, double from £25.00.

Inveraray, Argyll

Map Ref: 1F3

HOTEL

Argyll Hotel

Front Street, Inveraray, Argyll, PA32 8XB
Tel:01499 302466 Fax:01499 302389
Email:reception@the-argyll-hotel.co.uk
Web:www.the-argyll-hotel.co.uk

Designed in 1750 by the famous Scottish builder John Adam, The Argyll formed part of the total rebuilding of Inveraray commissioned by the 3rd Duke of Argyll. Originally built to accommodate guests to the Castle, The Argyll today offers standards of hospitality that more than live up to its illustrious past.

31 rooms, all en-suite, Open Jan-Dec, B&B per person, single from £55.00, double from £28.50, BB & Eve.Meal from £59.00.

Iona, Isle of, Argyll

Map Ref: 1B2

HOTEL

St Columba Hotel

Isle of Iona, Argyll, PA76 6SL
Tel:01681 700304 Fax:01681 700688
Email:info@stcolumba-hotel.co.uk
Web:www.stcolumba-hotel.co.uk

A haven for total freedom and relaxation on this exquisite Hebridean island. Close to Abbey. Outstanding views from our sunlounges and dining room, warm welcome, friendly staff, log fire. Our chefs provide imaginative home baking and delicious home-cooked meals using fresh Scottish produce, some from our own organically cultivated garden. Children welcome. Ideal setting for a relaxing holiday for young and old.

27 rooms, all en-suite, Open Mar-Oct, B&B per person, single from £40.00, double from £37.00, BB & Eve.Meal from £52.00.

Port Charlotte, Isle of Islay, Argyll

Map Ref: 1B6

SMALL HOTEL

The Port Charlotte Hotel

Main Street, Port Charlotte, Isle of Islay, PA48 7TU
Tel:01496 850360 Fax:01496 850361
Email:info@portcharlottehotel.co.uk
Web:www.portcharlottehotel.co.uk

Restored Victorian hotel offering all modern facilities in an informal, relaxed atmosphere, situated in this picturesque conservation village on the west shore of Loch Indaal. Fresh local seafood, lamb and beef. Distillery visits, fishing and golfing can be arranged.

10 rooms, all en-suite, Open Jan-Dec, B&B per person, single from £70.00, double from £57.50.

Port Ellen, Isle of Islay, Argyll

Map Ref: 1C6

The Trout Fly Guest House

8 Charlotte Street, Port Ellen, Isle of Islay, PA42 7DF
Tel:01496 302204 Fax:01496 300076

★★ GUEST HOUSE

5 rooms, Open Jan-Dec excl Xmas/New Year, B&B per person, single from £23.00, double from £23.00.

Centrally heated accommodation with TV and Tea/Coffee facilities. Ideal for Distillery tours, golf, walking, birdwatching, diving and fishing. Close to ferry terminal and airport.

Jura, Isle of, Argyll

Map Ref: 1D4

Jura Hotel

Isle of Jura, Argyll, PA60 7XU
Tel:01496 820243 Fax:01496 820249
Email:jurahotel@aol.com
Web:www.jurahotel.co.uk

★★ SMALL HOTEL

17 rooms, 8 ensuite, Open Jan-Dec, B&B per person single from £35.00, double from £35.00.

Family run hotel with gardens, overlooking Small Isles Bay and close to famous distillery. Showers, drying room and laundry facilities for sailors and walkers.

Killin, Perthshire

Map Ref: 1H2

Dall Lodge Country House

Main Street, Killin, Perthshire, FK21 8TN
Tel:01567 820217 Fax:01567 820726
Email:connor@dalllodgehotel.co.uk
Web:www.dalllodgehotel.co.uk

★★★★ GUEST HOUSE

9 rooms, all en-suite, Open Mar-Oct, B&B per person, single from £28.00, double from £25.00.

Country house recently modernised with old world charm retained. On outskirts of picturesque village of Killin overlooking River Lochay with own moorings and spectacular views of mountains. Perfect base for outdoor activities, walking and fishing.

Morenish Lodge Hotel

Morenish, Killin, Perthshire, FK21 8TX
Tel/Fax:01567 820258
Email:thomas@morenishlodgehotel.co.uk
Web:www.morenishlodgehotel.co.uk

★★★ SMALL HOTEL

13 rooms, 12 en-suite, 1 priv.facilities, Open Mar-Nov, B&B per person, single from £38.50, double from £38.50, BB & Eve.Meal from £50.50.

A former shooting lodge in stunning location 3 miles east of the picturesque village of Killin, on the edge of Scotland's first National Park and in an area famed for natural history and outdoor pursuits. Superb views over Loch Tay which is just a short stroll away across the fields. Centrally placed for touring. Peace and tranquillity in comfortable accommodation with freshly-prepared meals featuring, where possible, local produce.

Lochearnhead, Perthshire

Map Ref: 1H2

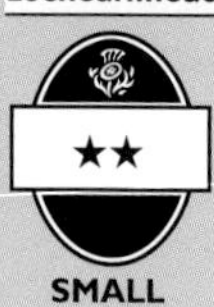

Lochearnhead Hotel

Lochside, Lochearnhead, FK19 8PN
Tel:01567 830229 Fax:01567 830364
Email:info@lochearnhead-hotel.com
Web:www.lochearnhead-hotel.com

★★ SMALL HOTEL

10 rooms, all en-suite, Open Jan-Dec, B&B per person, single from £43.00, double from £33.00.

The Lochearnhead hotel sits in an elevated position overlooking Loch Earn. Water sports centre and sailing facilities adjacent. Ideal centre for touring, golfing, fishing and hillwalking. Off-season special breaks available.

Important: Prices stated are estimates and may be subject to amendments

Luss, Argyll & Bute

Map Ref: 1G4

B&B

Culag Lochside Guest House

Luss, Loch Lomond, G83 8PD
Tel:01436 860248

Set right on the Loch side with spacious patios for sundown's and wonderful views across to Ben Lomond and the Island's. Only 1 mile north of Luss with its restaurants. Ideally placed for day trips to the West Coast, or Stirling and Glasgow. On the cycle path.

8 rooms, all en-suite, Open Jan-Dec excl Xmas/New Year, B&B per person, single from £35.00, double from £30.00.

HOTEL

The Lodge on Loch Lomond

Luss, Alexandria, G83 8PA
Tel:01436 860201 Fax:01436 860203
Email:res@loch-lomond.co.uk
Web:www.loch-lomond.co.uk

Modern pine lodge situated on the serene banks of Loch Lomond close to Luss village. Modern pine panelling character reflects the tranquility of the surrounding scenery. All bedrooms ensuite, some with a sauna. Informal Brasserie style restaurant with magnificent views across Loch Lomond. New leisure facility now open, including a swimming pool. Function and conference facilities available.

59 rooms, all en-suite, Open Jan-Dec, B&B per person, single from £65.00, double from £37.50, BB & Eve.Meal from £45.00.

Bunessan, Isle of Mull, Argyll

Map Ref: 1C3

SMALL HOTEL

Ardachy House Hotel

Uisken, by Bunessan, Isle of Mull, Argyll, PA67 6DS
Tel:01681 700505 Fax:01681 700797
Email:info@ardachy.co.uk
Web:www.ardachy.co.uk

Small, secluded, personally-run hotel, 7 miles (11 kms) from Iona. Safe access to white sands of Ardalanish Beach. Spectacular views to Colonsay, Jura and Islay. 1 room without ensuite. Non-resident dinner available by prior arrangement.

8 rooms, some en-suite, Open Apr-Oct, B&B per person, single from £40.00, double from £40.00, BB & Eve.Meal from £60.00.

Craignure, Isle of Mull, Argyll

Map Ref: 1D2

HOTEL

Isle of Mull Hotel

Craignure, Isle of Mull, Argyll, PA65 6BB
Tel:01680 812351 Fax:01680 812462
Email:isleofmull@british-trust-hotels.com
Web:www.british-trust-hotels.com

Modern hotel set in extensive grounds close to the shore and popular with groups. The hotel has recently been extensively re-furbished and offers two residents' bars. Most bedrooms have view across Firth of Lorne towards Oban. Non-residents are welcome for bar lunch, afernoon tea and dinner etc. The hotel is located only ½ mile (1km) from ferry terminal.

80 rooms, all en-suite, Open Mar-Dec, B&B per person £35.00-48.00, DB&B £46.00-64.00.

Dervaig, Isle of Mull, Argyll

Map Ref: 1C1

SMALL HOTEL

Druimnacroish Hotel

Dervaig, Isle of Mull, PA75 6QW
Tel:01688 400274
Web:www.druimnacroish.co.uk

Converted water mill set on a tranquil and secluded hillside offering a relaxed, friendly atmosphere, spacious accommodation, extensive gardens, good food, home made bread, superb views from every room. Put your feet up by the fire or enjoy the view from the conservatory. Well situated for Mull's many attractions including boat trips, wildlife and walking. Taste of Scotland Award.

6 rooms, all en-suite, Open Apr-Oct, B&B per person, single from £60.00, double from £39.00, BB & Eve.Meal from £59.00.

by Dervaig, Isle of Mull, Argyll

Map Ref: 1C1

SMALL HOTEL

The Calgary Hotel

by Dervaig, Isle of Mull, Argyll, PA75 6QW
Tel:01688 400256
Email:calgary.hotel@virgin.net
Web:www.calgary.co.uk

Converted farm buildings, close to the beautiful white sands of Calgary beach, Cozy, and tastefully decorated friendly small hotel, with much quality local & Scottish produce to be enjoyed in our 'Dovecote Restaurant'. Newly created woodland walk with sculpture combines peace with nature.

9 rooms, all en-suite, Open Easter-Oct (weekends only in Feb, Mar & Nov), B&B from £31.00-48.00. Dinner from £22.00-30.00 for 3x courses a la'carte.

Pennyghael, Isle of Mull, Argyll

Map Ref: 1C2

SMALL HOTEL

Pennyghael Hotel

Pennyghael, Isle of Mull, PA70 6HB
Tel:01681 704288 Fax:01681 704205
Email:enquiries@pennyghaelhotel.com
Web:www.pennyghaelhotel.com

Relax in the peace and quiet of Pennyghael Hotel where we will use every endeavour to make your stay with us all that you would want it to be. The hotel can be used as a base for a family holiday, as a romantic hideaway far removed from the stresses and strains of modern life, as a centre for studying the amazingly diverse flora and fauna on the Ross of Mull and in the loch or just somewhere you want to be to explore all that this corner of Mull has to offer.

6 rooms, all en-suite, Open Jan-Dec, B&B per person, single from £55.00, double from £55.00, BB & Eve.Meal from £80.00.

Tobermory, Isle of Mull, Argyll

Map Ref: 1C1

GUEST HOUSE

Baliscate Guest House

Salen Road, Tobermory, Isle of Mull, Argyll, PA75 6QA
Tel:01688 302048 Fax:01688 302666
Email:bb@baliscate.freeserve.co.uk
Web:www.baliscate.com

Recently refurbished Victorian house set in 1.5 acres of garden and woodland, with magnificent views over The Sound of Mull. 15 minute down hill walk to Tobermory front and all amenities. 'Request' bus stop at bottom of garden.

4 rooms, all en-suite, Open Easter-end Oct, B&B per person, single from £40.00, double from £27.00.

SMALL HOTEL

Highland Cottage

Breadalbane Street, Tobermory, Isle of Mull, PA75 6PD
Tel:01688 302030
Email:davidandjo@highlandcottage.co.uk
Web:www.highlandcottage.co.uk

Family-run 'country house in the town' hotel located in the heart of upper Tobermory in conservation area. Well appointed bedrooms themed after local islands and including 2 with 4 poster beds. Imaginative award-winning cuisine using fresh, local ingredients served in our attractive, homely, dining room. High level of personal attention from resident owners. AA Top 200, AA 2 Rosette, RAC Gold Ribbon.

6 rooms, all en-suite, Open Mar-Nov, B&B per person, single from £95.00, double from £60.00, BB & Eve.Meal from £95.00.

Tobermory, Isle of Mull, Argyll

Map Ref: 1C1

SMALL HOTEL

Tobermory Hotel

Main Street, Tobermory, Isle of Mull, PA75 6NT
Tel:01688 302091 Fax:01688 302254
Email:tobhotel@tinyworld.co.uk
Web:www.thetobermoryhotel.com

This small family-run hotel is superbly sited on the waterfront overlooking the bay. The restaurant (1 AA Rosette) promotes fresh local produce and non-residents are welcome. There are sixteen bedrooms, fifteen of which are en suite, and two are on the ground floor. Ample street parking is available.

16 rooms, all en-suite, Open Jan-Dec excl Xmas, B&B per person, single from £36.00, double from £36.00.

Oban, Argyll

Map Ref: 1E2

INN

Balmoral Inn

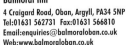

4 Craigard Road, Oban, Argyll, PA34 5NP
Tel:01631 562731 Fax:01631 566810
Email:enquiries@balmoraloban.co.uk
Web:www.balmoraloban.co.uk

Personally run and centrally situated close to shops, ferry and rail terminal.

9 rooms, most en-suite, Open Jan-Dec excl Xmas, B&B per person, single from £35.00, double from £30.00.

GUEST HOUSE

Corriemar House

6 Corran Esplanade, Oban, Argyll, PA34 5AQ
Tel:01631 562476 Fax:01631 564339
Email:corriemar@tinyworld.co.uk
Web:www.corriemarhouse.co.uk

Situated on the seafront, this large Victorian family run Guest House is only 10 minutes walk along the prom to the town centre. Spectacular Oban sunsets looking from the lounge and seaview bedroom over to Kerrara with the hills of Mull beyond. Queen size deluxe rooms and four poster rooms available. One suite room with sea views.

14 rooms, 13 en-suite, 1 priv.facilities, Open Jan-Dec, B&B per person, double £30.00-48.00. Queen sized deluxe rooms and 4 poster room available.

VAT is shown at 17.5%: changes in this rate may affect prices.

Key to symbols is on back flap.

Oban, Argyll **Map Ref: 1E2**

Foxholes Country Hotel

Cologin, Lerags, Oban, Argyll PA34 4SE
Tel: 01631 564982 Fax: 01631 570890
e.mail: shirley.foxholes@tesco.net
Web: www.foxholeshotel.co.uk

Enjoy peace and tranquility at Foxholes, situated in its own grounds in a quiet glen 3 miles south of Oban, with magnificent views of the surrounding countryside. An ideal spot for those who wish to "get away from it all". Enjoy our superb five-course table d'hote menu and large selection of wines and spirits. All bedrooms ensuite, colour TV and tea/coffee-making facilities.
NON-SMOKING HOTEL.
Send for colour brochure and tariff to Mrs S Dowson-Park at the above address.

DB&B from £64 per person per night. B&B from £43 pp per night. Single supplement £17.00 extra per night. OPEN MARCH TO OCTOBER.

SMALL HOTEL

Foxholes Country Hotel

Cologin, Lerags, Oban, Argyll, PA34 4SE
Tel:01631 564982 Fax:01631 570890
Email:shirley.foxholes@tesco.net
Web:www.foxholeshotel.co.uk

7 rooms, all en-suite, Open Mar-Oct, B&B from £43.00 per person per night in double/twin. BB & Eve.Meal from £64.00. Single occupancy £17.00 extra per night.

Peacefully situated in a quiet glen with magnificent views yet a mere 3 miles (5kms) south of Oban. Ideally placed for the ferries for day trips to the islands of the inner Hebrides, Mull and Iona in particular. Many scenic drives including Fort William are within an hour of the Hotel and gardens. Fresh local produce used in our Table D'Hote dinners.

GUEST HOUSE

Glenbervie Guest House

Dalriach Road, Oban, Argyll, PA34 5JD
Tel:01631 564770 Fax:01631 566723

8 rooms, 6 en-suite, Open Feb-Dec excl Xmas/New Year, B&B per person, single from £25.00-30.00, double from £25.00-30.00 pp.

Beautifully situated overlooking Oban Bay, commanding magnificent views. 2 minutes walk from town centre, promenade, harbour and amenities. Evening meal. Ensuite.

GUEST HOUSE

Glenburnie House

Esplanade, Oban, Argyll, PA34 5AQ
Tel/Fax:01631 562089
Email:graeme.strachan@btinternet.com
Web:www.glenburnie.co.uk

16 rooms, 13 en-suite, Open Mar-Nov, B&B per person, single from £30.00, double from £30.00.

Recently refurbished superior rooms with magnificent views of bay and islands, Quiet yet convenient for town centre. Friendly host with attention to detail.

Important: Prices stated are estimates and may be subject to amendments

Oban, Argyll | **Map Ref: 1E2**

Glenrigh Guest House

Corran Esplanade, Oban, Argyll, PA34 5AQ
Tel/Fax:01631 562991
Email:glenrigh@tiscali.co.uk
Web:www.glenrigh.com

Family run Victorian house with excellent views across Oban Bay. Short walk from town centre and all amenities. Ample private parking.

11 rooms, all en-suite, Open Feb-Dec, B&B per person, single from £32.00, double from £30.00.

Great Western Hotel

Corran Esplanade, Oban, Argyll, PA34 5PP
Tel:01942 824824
Email:reservations@WAshearings.com
Web:www.shearingsholidays.com

Situated right on the seafront with fine views over Oban Bay. Entertainment every night.

80 rooms, all en-suite, Open Feb-Dec, B&B per person, double from £30.00.

Greencourt Guest House

Benvoullin Road, Oban, Argyll, PA34 5EF
Tel:01631 563987
Email:relax@greencourt-oban.co.uk
Web:www.greencourt-oban.co.uk

Spacious family run property in quiet situation overlooking outdoor bowling green, a short stroll to town centre and adjacent to leisure centre. Attractive rooms, wholesome breakfasts, private parking. Ideal touring base.

6 rooms, most en-suite, Open Feb-Nov, B&B per person, single £24.00-33.00, double £24.00-33.00.

Hawthornbank Guest House

Dalriach Road, Oban, Argyll, PA34 5JE
Tel/Fax:01631 562041
Email:hawthornbank@aol.com
Web:www.SmoothHound.co.uk/hotels/hawthorn.html

Brian and Valerie look forward to welcoming you to Hawthornbank, a tastefully refurbished Victorian villa set in a quiet location yet only a short stroll from the town centre. Comfortable well equipped rooms some with stunning views over Oban Bay. How can you resist?

7 en-suite rooms, 1 single with priv.fac. Open Jan-Dec excl Xmas, B&B per person, single from £25.00, double from £26.00.

Kathmore Guest House

Soroba Road, Oban, Argyll, PA34 4JF
Tel:01631 562104 Fax:01631 562104/570067
Email:wkathmore@aol.com
Web:www.kathmore.co.uk

Kathmore guest house is just outside Oban Town Centre. A short walk from the bus, train and ferry terminal. Trouble-free parking is assured with our spacious private car park. All rooms are well-furnished and equipped with colour TV's, Tea/Coffee trays, hairdryer etc. Some are ensuite. Within walking distance of many restaurants and pubs.

9 rooms, some en-suite, B&B per person, single £25.00-35.00, double £20.00-25.00.

VAT is shown at 17.5%: changes in this rate may affect prices.

Key to symbols is on back flap.

Oban, Argyll | **Map Ref: 1E2**

The Kimberley Hotel, Bachler's Conservatory

3 Dalriach Road, Oban, Argyll, PA34 5EQ
Tel:01631 571115 Fax:01631 571120
Email:info@kimberley-hotel.com
Web:www.kimberley-hotel.com

Victorian building of character set in an elevated position with open outlook over Oban, harbour and islands. Rooms are furnished in the Victorian style with modern comforts. Excellent dining in conservatory restaurant. 2 minutes from town centre. Truly a choice location.

14 rooms, all en-suite, Open Apr-Oct, B&B per person, single on request, double from £49.00, BB & Eve.Meal a la carte.

Kings Knoll Hotel

Dunollie Road, Oban, PA34 5JH
Tel:01631 562536 Fax:01631 566101
Email:info@kingsknollhotel.co.uk
Web:www.kingsknollhotel.co.uk

Family run hotel overlooking Oban Bay and close to the town centre and sea front. Theme bar and dining room.

15 rooms, some en-suite, Open Feb-Dec, B&B per person, single from £25.00, double from £25.00, double from £50.00 Room Only, BB & Eve.Meal from £34.00.

Manor House

Gallanoch Road, Oban, Argyll, PA34 4LS
Tel:01631 562087 Fax:01631 563053
Email:info@manorhouseoban.com
Web:www.manorhouseoban.com

Georgian house on the foreshore on the south side of Oban with extensive views across the Bay, close to the town centre. AA Rosette for food. Non residents welcome to book for dinner.

11 rooms, all en-suite, Open Jan-Dec excl Xmas, B&B per person, single from £65.00, double from £40.00 (low season).

Oban Bay Hotel

Esplanade, Oban, Argyll, PA34 5AE
Tel:01631 562051 Fax:01631 564006
Email:obanbay@british-trust-hotels.com
Web:www.british-trust-hotels.com

Holiday hotel with modern extension. Refurbished public areas with a sun lounge frontage offering excellent views across Oban Bay. Short walk from town centre and all amenities.

86 rooms, all en-suite, Open Mar-Dec, B&B £25.00-35.00, DB&B £35.00-65.00.

Oban, Argyll

Map Ref: 1E2

HOTEL

The Oban Caledonian Hotel

Waterfront, Oban, Argyll, PA34 5RT
Tel:0871 222 3415 Fax:0871 222 3416
Email:reservations@freedomglen.co.uk
Web:www.obancaledonian.com

Choose Oban's landmark building. Great bedrooms many with ocean views. Warm welcome and friendly service. Good food and comfortable bars.

59 rooms, all en-suite, Open Jan-Dec incl Xmas/New Year, B&B per person, single £52.50-80.00, double £52.50-135.00, BB & Eve.Meal from £52.50-155.00.

GUEST HOUSE

The Old Manse Guest House

Dalriach Road, Oban, Argyll, PA34 5JE
Tel:01631 564886
Email:oldmanse@obanguesthouse.co.uk
Web:www.obanguesthouse.co.uk

Magnificent views over Oban Bay and only minutes walk from the town centre.The Old Manse Guest House offers a superior standard of hospitality and comfort. Enjoy a freshly cooked breakfast from our varied menu. Private parking. Family ensuite available. Discounted 3, 5 and 7 day breaks. All major credit cards accepted.

6 rooms, all en-suite, Open Feb-Nov, B&B per person double from £26.00, family from £24.00, room only double from £52.00, family from £48.00.

by Oban, Argyll

Map Ref: 1E2

★★★★

SMALL HOTEL

Willowburn Hotel

Clachan Seil, by Oban, Argyll, PA34 4TJ
Tel:01852 300276
Email:willowburn.hotel@virgin.net
Web:www.willowburn.co.uk

Personally run, on the shore, in 2 acres of garden, approx. 0.5 miles from famous Atlantic Bridge, on Seil Island. Taste of Scotland recommended. Two AA rosettes. Peaceful, homely atmosphere.

7 rooms, all en-suite, Open Mar-Nov, BB & Eve.Meal from £70.00.

Stirling

Map Ref: 2A4

GUEST HOUSE

Garfield Guesthouse

12 Victoria Square, Stirling, Stirlingshire, FK8 2QZ
Tel/Fax:01786 473730

Family run guest house in traditional stone built Victorian house overlooking quiet square close to the town centre, castle and all local amenities. Ideal base for exploring historic Stirling, Loch Lomond and the Trossachs. Non smoking.

6 rooms, all en-suite, Open Jan-Dec excl Xmas/New Year, B&B per person, double from £24.00.

C V

Stirling

Map Ref: 2A4

SMALL HOTEL

The Park Lodge Country House Hotel

32 Park Terrace, Stirling, FK8 2JS
Tel:01786 474862 Fax:01786 449748
Email:info@parklodge.net
Web:www.parklodge.net

Part Victorian, part Georgian mansion overlooking the park and castle, set amidst landscaped gardens. Antique furnishings including a four poster bed.

10 rooms, all en-suite, Open Jan-Dec excl Xmas/New Year, B&B per person, single from £55.00, double from £47.50.

SMALL HOTEL

The Royal Hotel and Royal Lodge Conference Centre

55 & 103 Henderson Street, Bridge of Allan
Stirlingshire, FK9 4HG
Tel:01786 832284 Fax:01786 834377
Email:stay@royal-stirling.co.uk Web:www.royal-stirling.co.uk

The Royal Hotel offers 32 rooms, all en-suite. The Royal Lodge, 11 en-suite. Both offer unique conference and banqueting facilities. We are ideally located in the centre of Scotland just off the M9 Motorway. Edinburgh and Glasgow are both within 40 minutes drive. Ideal as a touring base, the whole spectrum of Scotland's rich heritage and magnificent scenery is available within 1 hours drive of Bridge of Allan.

Open Jan-Dec, B&B per person, single from £85.00, double from £65.00, BB & Eve.Meal from £95.00.

HOTEL

The Stirling Highland Hotel

Spittal Street, Stirling, FK8 1DU
Tel:01786 272727 Fax:01786 479392
Email:stirling@paramount-hotels.co.uk
Web:www.paramount-hotels.co.uk

Restored, Listed, former High School, converted into very comfortable hotel with full leisure facilities. Friendly, attentive service. In the old town, within walking distance of the castle and other historic attractions. Stirling, an ancient capital of Scotland is now one of its most recent new cities.

96 rooms, all en-suite, Open Jan-Dec, B&B per person.

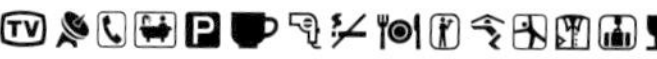

HOTEL

Stirling Management Centre

Stirling University, Stirling, FK9 4LA
Tel:01786 451666 Fax:01786 449940
Email:smc.sales@stir.ac.uk
Web:www.smc.stir.ac.uk

Purpose built conference centre/hotel in peaceful setting on picturesque campus. University leisure facilities available. Ideal touring base.

77 rooms, all en-suite, Open Jan-Dec, B&B per person, single from £82.00, double from £55.50, BB & Eve.Meal from £104.00 pp.

Important: Prices stated are estimates and may be subject to amendments

Strachur, Argyll

Map Ref: 1F3

SMALL HOTEL

The Creggans Inn

Strachur, Argyll, PA27 8BX
Tel:01369 860279 Fax:01369 860637
Email:info@creggans-inn.co.uk Web:www.creggans-inn.co.uk

Country Hotel, steeped in history, with magnificent views of Loch Fyne. An excellent reputation for fine food. 20 miles from Dunoon or Inveraray and only an hour from Glasgow Airport, Creggans is renowned for its food, wine and quality of local produce. Our restaurant overlooking Loch Fyne offers guests the best view in Scotland. Good walking for all abilities.

14 rooms, all en-suite, Open Jan-Dec, B&B per person, single from £60.00, double from £60.00, BB & Eve.Meal from £85.00.

Strathyre, Perthshire

Map Ref: 1H3

RESTAURANT WITH ROOMS

Creagan House Restaurant with Accommodation

Strathyre, Callander, Perthshire, FK18 8ND
Tel:01877 384638 Fax:01877 384319
Email:eatandstay@creaganhouse.co.uk
Web:www.creaganhouse.co.uk

A peaceful little gem of comfort surrounded by beautiful scenery. Five charming bedrooms with many thoughtful extras and a growing collection of antiques, friendly perfection is our aim. The baronial dining hall helps make each evening a special occasion, using meat from Perthshire, fruits and vegetables grown locally, herbs from our garden, all complemented by fine wines. Awarded two AA Rosettes and Red Star, which have been retained for 8 years.

5 rooms, all en-suite, Open Mar-Jan, B&B per person, single from £65.00, double from £55.00, BB & Eve.Meal from £78.50.

Tarbert, Loch Fyne, Argyll

Map Ref: 1E5

SMALL HOTEL

Balinakill Country House Hotel

Clachan, by Tarbet, Kintyre, PA29 6XL
Tel:01880 740206 Fax:01880 740298
Email:info@balinakill.com
Web:www.balinakill.com

Located on the edge of the small hamlet of Clachan, 10 miles south of Tarbrt, Balinakill is a fine family-run country home set within its own grounds offering its guests an excellent home for enjoying the delights of this beautiful and peaceful part of Scotland. Ferries to Ireland, Islay, Jura, Gigha, Arran and Cowal. 'Eat Scotland' and '1 AA Rosette'.

10 rooms, Open Jan-Dec, B&B per person single from £50.00, double from £45.00, family from £45.00.

Tarbet, by Arrochar, Dunbartonshire

Map Ref: 1G3

HOTEL

Tarbet Hotel

Tarbet, Arrochar, Loch Lomond, Argyll & Bute, G83 7DE
Tel:01942 824824
Email:reservations@WAshearings.com
Web:www.shearingsholidays.com

Large touring hotel on the banks of Loch Lomond, central for visiting the Trossachs, the West Coast and West Highlands. Fishing available. Entertainment every night.

73 rooms, all en-suite, Open Feb-Dec, B&B per person, double from £25.00.

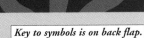

VAT is shown at 17.5%: changes in this rate may affect prices.

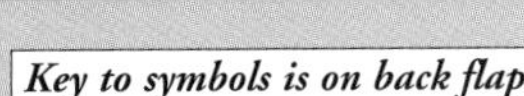
Key to symbols is on back flap.

Welcome to Scotland

Perthshire, Angus & Dundee and the Kingdom of Fife

This is a good place for a break, with a little of everything within easy reach. Lose yourself among the forests of Perthshire, walk the hallowed turf of St Andrews, and marvel at the digital arts of Dundee.

The Old Course at St. Andrews.

Rich soils, scenes and tastes typify the Kingdom of Fife. Begin on the southeast coast among the former herring ports of the East Neuk. Whitewashed walls and hardy fishermen aplenty, Lower Largo provided Daniel Dafoe with inspiration for his novel, *Robinson Crusoe*. More a life than lifestyle, explore the 'old ways' at the Scottish Fisheries Museum in Anstruther.

The coastal road follows around to St. Andrews and the big daddy of golf courses. Yes, the royal golf club lives up to divine reputation, but don't overlook the 40 other golf courses peppering the Kingdom. Survey the majestic ruins of a Cathedral 'redecorated' by John Knox and the Reformation during the 16th century.

Follow the coastal road north of St. Andrews to encounter Dundee, the City of Discovery. Jute and jam were exports in bygone days, but art house and the avant-garde have revamped this industrial port. For a start, Dundee Contemporary Arts have inserted new multi-media facilities within the eroded shell of a former warehouse. The result? Daring exhibitions that blend plastic arts, music, dance and cinema. Verdant Works, named Europe's Top Industrial Museum just a few years ago, weaves the story of Dundee through jute. And "Sensation" is a science centre for hands-on family capers.

Stay in the cultural quarter for good food. Try Howies, The Theatrecafe, Tapas and St Andrews Seafood restaurant. When dinner settles, join the throng of students pouring life into the bars, pubs and clubs. Quench a thirst for live music and affordable rounds at Drouthie Neebors. The Phoenix, Laings, Metro and Basement are also worth a look-in. To begin or end the

Perthshire, Angus & Dundee and the Kingdom of Fife

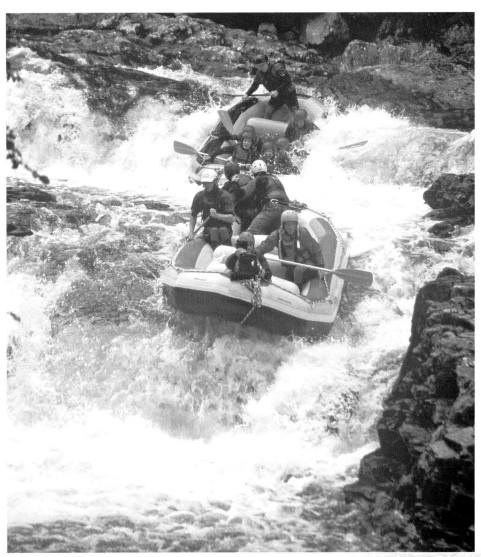

Water rafting down the River Tummel.

The lobster pots of St. Monans, an East Neuk fishing town.

night, swing by Fat Sam's, Mardi Gras or Sessions for some clubbing.

Escape the city limits – and most others - in Dunkeld. 'Nae Limits' organise a variety of hairy activities including Sphere Mania. Strap yourself into a giant 12ft inflatable sphere, point down the hill and relax... The region of Angus chooses to impress with miles of sandy beaches, the untainted beauty of five Glens, and over 2000 carved stones from the 5th century.

Perthshire has the fitting title of 'Big Tree Country', though everything seems epic. Deep forests, vast mountains, and broad rivers provide a playground for walking and adventure sports: white-water rafting, canyoning, cliff jumping, you name it. Even fishing has Olympic prowess – the River Tay holds the UK record for an Atlantic salmon weighing a hefty 64 pounds.

Brimming with specialist shops and cafes, Perth's considerable charm is bound in rich Georgian architecture. Just a stone's throw away, Scone Palace marks the site where early kings were crowned. And if you crave the simple life, consider an Iron Age, Celtic loch-dwelling at the Crannog Centre, Kenmore.

Set deep within the mountains, Pitlochry is a Victorian spa town of natty streets and cheerful bustle. A short trip will take you to the lavish interiors of Blair Castle, or the dramatic river gorge carved by Bruar Falls. Once the visual appetite is sated, get along to the House of Bruar, an emporium of fine Scottish produce. Mmm...

Events

Perthshire, Angus & Dundee and the Kingdom of Fife

16-19 MARCH
STANZA 2006, St Andrews
Scotland's poetry festival.
www.stanzapoetry.org

18-28 MAY
PERTH FESTIVAL OF THE ARTS
Annual arts festival or originality and playfulness.
Tel: 01738 475295
www.perthfestival.co.uk

13 AUGUST
PERTH HIGHLAND GAMES
Traditional Highland games with cycling, running, solo piping, Highland dancing, pipe bands, tug o' war and heavyweight events.
Tel: 01738 627782
www.highlandgames.org.uk

24-27 AUGUST
BOWMORE BLAIR CASTLE HORSE TRIALS, Blair Atholl
International horse trials.
Tel: 01796 481207
www.blairhorsetrials.co.uk

1-3 SEPTEMBER
DUNDEE FLOWER AND FOOD FESTIVAL
Scotland's premier flower and food festival.
Tel: 01382 433815
www.dundeeflowerand foodfestival.com

9 SEPTEMBER
RAF LEUCHARS AIR SHOW
Breathtaking displays of precision flying.
Tel: 01334 839000
www.airshow.co.uk

29 SEPTEMBER - 4 OCTOBER
BLAIRGOWRIE & EAST PERTHSHIRE WALKING FESTIVAL
A four day festival of walking and social events featuring sections of the Cateran Trail, Scotland's newest long distance walk.
Tel: 01738 475255
www.perthshire.co.uk/walkingfest

28-29 OCTOBER
GLENFIDDICH PIPING & FIDDLING CHAMPIONSHIPS, Blair Atholl
International competitions featuring piping on the 28th and fiddling on the 29th.
Tel: 01698 573536
www.glenfiddich.com

23-30 NOVEMBER*
ST ANDREWS WEEK
A week of festivities culminating in St Andrews Day.
Tel: 01334 472021
www.standrewsweek.co.uk

The Kingdom of Fife is a golfer's paradise.

** denotes provisional date, event details are subject to change please check before travelling*

Perthshire, Angus & Dundee and the Kingdom of Fife

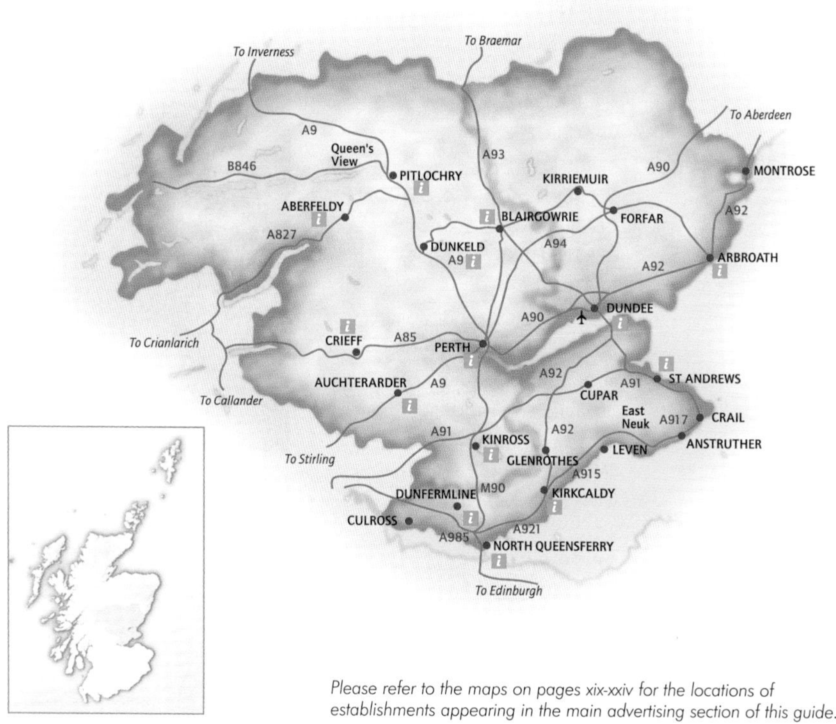

Please refer to the maps on pages xix-xxiv for the locations of establishments appearing in the main advertising section of this guide.

Finding out more...

For practical advice, ideas and information about exploring Scotland and to book your accommodation:

Tel: 0845 22 55 121*
or if calling from outside the UK: +44 (0) 1506 832121

Email: info@visitscotland.com
Web: www.visitscotland.com

* A £3 booking fee applies to telephone bookings of accommodation.

Tourist Information Centres

Perthshire, Angus & Dundee and the Kingdom of Fife

Angus & City of Dundee

Arbroath
Market Place
Tel: (01241) 872609
Jan – Dec

Brechin
Pictavia Centre, Haughmuir
Tel: (01356) 623050
Easter – Sep

Carnoustie
1b High Street
Tel: (01241) 852258
Easter – Sep

Dundee
21 Castle Street
Tel: (01382) 527527
Jan – Dec

Forfar
45 East High Street
Tel: (01307) 467876
Easter – Sep

Kirriemuir
Cumberland Close
Tel: (01575) 574097
Easter – Sep

Montrose
Bridge Street
Tel: (01674) 672000
Easter – Sep

Kingdom of Fife

Anstruther
Scottish Fisheries Museum
Tel: (01333) 311073
Apr – Oct

Crail
Crail Museum
and Heritage Centre
Marketgate
Tel: (01333) 450859
Apr – Oct

Dunfermline
1 High Street
Tel: (01383) 720999
Jan – Dec

Forth Bridges
Queensferry Lodge Hotel
St. Margaret's Head
Tel: (01383) 417759
Jan – Dec

Kirkcaldy
19 Whytescauseway
Tel: (01592) 267775
Jan – Dec

St Andrews
70 Market Street
Tel: (01334) 472021
Jan – Dec

Perthshire

Aberfeldy
The Square
Tel: (01887) 820276
Jan – Dec

Auchterarder
90 High Street
Tel: (01764) 663450
Jan – Dec

Blairgowrie
26 Wellmeadow
Tel: (01250) 872960
Jan – Dec

Crieff
Town Hall
High Street
Tel: (01764) 652578
Jan – Dec

Dunkeld
The Cross
Tel: (01350) 727688
Jan – Dec

Kinross
Heart of Scotland Visitor Centre
Junction 6, M90
Tel: (01577) 863680
Jan – Dec

Perth
Lower City Mills
West Mill Street
Tel: (01738) 450600
Jan – Dec

Pitlochry
22 Atholl Road
Tel: (01796) 472215/472751
Jan – Dec

Aberdour, Fife

Map Ref: 2C4

SMALL HOTEL

Aberdour Hotel

38 High Street, Aberdour, Fife, KY3 0SW
Tel:01383 860325 Fax:01383 860808
Email:reception@aberdourhotel.co.uk
Web:www.aberdourhotel.co.uk

Personally run hotel specialising in traditional cooking and real ales on Fife coast in Conservation village 6 miles (10kms) from Forth Bridges. Convenient for touring and golf. Recently converted stables annexe furnished to a high standard. Non residents welcome.

16 rooms, Open Jan-Dec, B&B per person, single from £40.00, double from £30.00, family from £30.00.

INN

The Cedar Inn

20 Shore Road, Aberdour, Fife, KY3 0TR
Tel:01383 860310 Fax:01383 860004
Email:cedarinnaberdour@supanet.com
Web:www.cedarinn.co.uk

Family run, attractive old Inn, CAMRA listed with 'friendly locals' bar and amiable lounges. Close to golf course, shops and beach. Golfing holidays arranged.

9 rooms, some en-suite, Open Jan-Dec, B&B rates, single from £39.00, double £56.00-80.00, BB & Eve.Meal from £40.00 pp.

SMALL HOTEL

The Woodside Hotel

High Street, Aberdour, Fife, KY3 0SW
Tel:01383 860328 Fax:01383 860920
Email:reception@thewoodsidehotel.co.uk
Web:www.thewoodsidehotel.co.uk

Interesting antiques from 'Orient Line' Vessel routes. Situated 25 minutes by car or train from Edinburgh. Non residents welcome for bar meals. Functions and conferences catered for all year round.

20 rooms, all en-suite, Open Jan-Dec, B&B per person, single from £50.00, double from £35.00.

Aberfeldy, Perthshire

Map Ref: 2A1

Moness House Hotel & Country Club

Crieff Road, Aberfeldy, Perthshire, PH15 2DY
Tel: 0870 443 1460 Fax: 0870 443 1461
Email: info@moness.com
Web: www.moness.com

Set in 35 acres of woodland overlooking the town of Aberfeldy, Moness offers comfortable, quaint rooms, each with its own ensuite. Meals and snacks available daily in our poolside bistro. Guests receive membership of the onsite leisure club, which includes an indoor heated pool.

SMALL HOTEL

The Moness House Hotel & Country Club

Crieff Road, Aberfeldy, Perthshire, PH15 2DY
Tel:0870 4431460 Fax:0870 4431461
Email:info@moness.com
Web:www.moness.com

Former hunting lodge dating from 1758, situated in thirty five acres, on the south side of Aberfeldy. Includes self catering cottages and onsite leisure centre.

12 rooms, all en-suite, Open Jan-Dec, B&B per person, single £41.00-65.00, double £26.00-50.00, BB & Eve.Meal from £41.00-65.00.

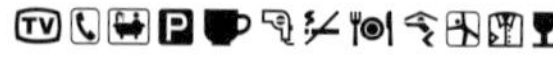

Important: Prices stated are estimates and may be subject to amendments

Aberfeldy, Perthshire

Map Ref: 2A1

★★★★

B&B

Tigh'n Eilean Guest House

Taybridge Drive, Aberfeldy, Perthshire, PH15 2BP
Tel/Fax:01887 820109
Email:info@tighneilean.com
Web:www.tighneilean.com

Elegant Victorian house overlooking the river. Warm and comfortable, home cooking. One room with jacuzzi.

4 rooms (1 grd flr), all en-suite, Open Jan-Dec, B&B per person, single from £30.00, double from £25.00.

Alyth, Perthshire

Map Ref: 2C1

LANDS OF LOYAL HOTEL

Loyal Road, Alyth, Blairgowrie, Perthshire PH11 8JQ
Tel: 01828 633151 Fax: 01828 633313
e.mail: info@landsofloyal.com Web: www.landsofloyal.com

Set on a hillside overlooking the Vale of Strathmore, the "Lands of Loyal" offers the perfect base for exploring the beautiful and historic county of Perthshire. Superb food and wines, the unique ambience, golden oak panelling and log fires create a captivating combination that our guests cherish for many years.

SMALL HOTEL

Lands of Loyal Hotel

Loyal Road, Alyth, Blairgowrie, PH11 8JQ
Tel:01828 633151 Fax:01828 633313
Email:info@landsofloyal.com
Web:www.landsofloyal.com

Country house with magnificent views of surrounding countryside. Central for many sports: walking, fishing, golf. Delicious food, fresh ingredients.

14 rooms, all en-suite, Open Jan-Dec, B&B per person, single from £69.50, double from £49.50, BB & Eve.Meal from £75.50.

Auchterarder, Perthshire

Map Ref: 2B3

Cairn Lodge Hotel

Orchil Road, Auchterarder, PH3 1LX
Tel: 01764 662634/662431 Fax: 01764 664866
e.mail: email@cairnlodge.co.uk & info@cairnlodge.co.uk Web: www.cairnlodge.co.uk

Sitting proudly in beautiful gardens and fronted by Queen Victoria's Commemorative Jubilee Cairn, the Cairn Lodge neighbours the world famous Gleneagles complex on the edge of Auchterarder. Beautiful and luxuriously appointed en-suite accommodation, the elegant 'Capercaille' à la carte restaurant and the new Jubilee Lounge, all add up to Perthshire's premier country house hotel and restaurant. B&B from £60-£95 per person per night. Short breaks 3 nights for the price of 2.

SMALL HOTEL

Cairn Lodge Hotel

Orchil Road, Auchterarder, Perthshire, PH3 1LX
Tel:01764 662634 Fax:01764 664866
Email:email@cairnlodge.co.uk
Web:www.cairnlodge.co.uk

Personally run country house hotel, with large garden and putting green, on outskirts of Auchterarder. Fine dining, prepared from fresh local produce.

10 rooms, all en-suite, B&B per person, single from £75.00, double from £60.00.

Auchterarder, Perthshire

Map Ref: 2B3

INTERNATIONAL RESORT

The Gleneagles Hotel

Auchterarder, Perthshire, PH3 1NF
Tel:01764 662231 Fax:01764 662134
Email:resort.sales@gleneagles.com
Web:www.gleneagles.com

A traditional hotel in the grand style with a wide range of world class sporting and leisure facilities; situated amidst the beautiful countryside of central Perthshire. Choice of several dining venues with different styles.

269 rooms, all en-suite, Open Jan-Dec, B&B per room, double from £355.00.

Blair Atholl, Perthshire

Map Ref: 4C12

GUEST HOUSE

The Firs

St Andrews Crescent, Blair Atholl, by Pitlochry, PH18 5TA
Tel:01796 481256 Fax:01796 481661
Email:kirstie@firs-blairatholl.co.uk
Web:www.firs-blairatholl.co.uk

Friendly country home with half an acre of garden in a tranquil setting. Well situated in Highland Perthshire, close to Blair Castle and ideal as a base for either touring or a relaxing holiday.

4 rooms, all en-suite, Open Jan-Dec, B&B per person, single from £27.50, double from £22.50.

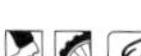

Blairgowrie, Perthshire

Map Ref: 2B1

GUEST HOUSE

Duncraggan

Perth Road, Blairgowrie, Perthshire, PH10 6EJ
Tel:01250 872082 Fax:01250 872098
Email:duncraggan@hotmail.com

Comfortable lovely furnished house with off road parking. An ideal location for tourists, hillwalkers, skiers and golfers alike or relax in our acre gardens with small 9 hole putting green.

3 rooms, all en-suite, Open May-Oct, B&B per person, double from £22.00.

AWAITING INSPECTION

Royal Hotel

53 Allan Street, Blairgowrie, Perthshire, PH10 6AB
Tel:01250 872226 Fax:01250 875905
Email:visit@theroyalhotel.org.uk
Web:www.theroyalhotel.org.uk

27 rooms, all ensuite, Open Jan-Dec, B&B per person, single from £35.00, double from £25.00.Room Only per night, single from £30.00, double from £40.00.

by Blairgowrie, Perthshire

Map Ref: 2B1

SMALL HOTEL

Moorfield House Hotel

Myreriggs Road, Coupar Angus, Perthshire, PH13 9HS
Tel:01828 627303 Fax:01828 627339
Web:www.moorfieldhousehotel.co.uk

Family run, traditional relaxed house hotel of character situated a short distance from Coupar Angus and Blairgowrie. Excellent base for golfing, fishing, shooting or exploring this beautiful area of Scotland; alternatively just come to relax and unwind for a while.

11 rooms, all en-suite, Open Jan-Dec excl Xmas, B&B per person, single from £42.50, double from £85.00 (2 people).

Important: Prices stated are estimates and may be subject to amendments

Burntisland, Fife

Map Ref: 2C4

SMALL HOTEL

Kingswood Hotel

Kinghorn Road, Burntisland, Fife, KY3 9LL
Tel:01592 872329 Fax:01592 873123
Email:rankin@kingswoodhotel.co.uk
Web:www.kingswoodhotel.co.uk

Stunning countryside hotel set in two acres of woodland with beautiful panoramic, balcony views across the Firth of Forth. One of Fife's premier destinations for short breaks, weddings and conferences. Based on the Fife coastal road and ideal for walking, cycling, fishing or golfing breaks. Many rooms with balconies and seaviews. Individual suite and family suite available, and a ground floor bedroom.

13 rooms, all en-suite, Open Jan-Dec excl Xmas/New Year, B&B per person, single from £52.00, double from £38.25.

Carnoustie, Angus

Map Ref: 2D2

SMALL HOTEL

Lochlorian House Hotel

13 Philip Street, Carnoustie, DD7 6ED
Tel:01241 852182 Fax:01241 855440
Email:hotellochlorian@aol.com
Web:www.lochlorian.co.uk

Family run hotel in attractive detached Victorian house with restaurant using the best of Scottish produce. Central location with large south facing garden. Private car parking. Restaurant offers lunches, high teas and suppers. Conveniently situated for Carnoustie's 3 golf courses and within easy travelling distance for St Andrews and other major golf courses.

6 rooms, all en-suite, Open Jan-Dec excl Xmas/New Year, B&B per person, single from £30.00, double from £25.00.

SMALL HOTEL

Station Hotel

Station Road, Carnoustie, Angus, DD7 6AR
Tel:01241 852447 Fax:01241 855605
Email:enquiry@stationhotel.uk.com
Web:www.stationhotel.uk.com

Long established family run hotel, short walk from the beach. 5 minutes walk to world famous championship course and many others within 30 minutes drive.

12 rooms, all en-suite, Open Jan-Dec (closed 25-26 Dec, 1-2 Jan), B&B per person, single from £37.50, twin/double from £30.00.

Comrie, Perthshire

Map Ref: 2A2

SMALL HOTEL

The Royal Hotel

Melville Square, Comrie, Perthshire, PH6 2DN
Tel:01764 679200 Fax:01764 679219
Email:reception@royalhotel.co.uk
Web:www.royalhotel.co.uk

Friendly, family run hotel, offering award winning cuisine and luxurious charming ambience set amidst the stunning Perthshire Highlands.

11 rooms, all en-suite, Open Jan-Dec, B&B per person, single from £75.00, double from £60.00, BB & Eve.Meal from £80.00.

Coupar Angus, Perthshire

Map Ref: 2C1

HOTEL

Red House Hotel

Station Road, Coupar Angus, Blairgowrie, PH13 9AL
Tel:01828 628500 Fax:01828 628574
Email:stay@red-house-hotel.co.uk
Web:www.red-house-hotel.co.uk

Dating back to Victorian times the building was originally the Railway Hotel. Trains have long ceased to run through Coupar Angus and in its place is the vibrant Red House, a magnet for locals, visitors and business traveller. Family owned and managed you can be sure of a friendly team and genuine hospitality. The accommodation has a separate entrance.

20 rooms, all en-suite, Open Jan-Dec excl Xmas/New Year, B&B per person, single from £42.50, double from £75.00 (2 people).

VAT is shown at 17.5%: changes in this rate may affect prices.

Key to symbols is on back flap.

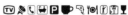

Cowdenbeath, Fife

Map Ref: 2B4

GUEST HOUSE

Struan Bank Hotel

74 Perth Road, Cowdenbeath, Fife, KY4 9BG
Tel/Fax:01383 511057

9 rooms, some en-suite, Open Jan-Dec, B&B per person, single from £25.00, double from £22.50, BB & Eve.Meal from £31.00 pp.

Family run hotel situated in the town centre and convenient for the railway station. Ideal centre for touring. En-suite accommodation available.

Crail, Fife

Map Ref: 2D3

GUEST HOUSE

Caiplie House

53 High Street, Crail, Fife, KY10 3RA
Tel:01333 450564
Email:mail@caipliehouse.com
Web:www.caipliehouse.com

6 rooms, en-suite, Open Mar-Nov, B&B per person, single from £30.00, double from £25.00, BB & Eve.Meal from £35.00.

Very comfortable and friendly guest house renowned for its home cooking, with restricted table licence. On main street of fishing village near coastal path and picturesque harbour. Some rooms with sea views.

SMALL HOTEL

The Golf Hotel

4 High Street, Crail, Fife, KY10 3TD
Tel:01333 450206 Fax:01333 450795
Email:info@thegolfhotelcrail.com
Web:www.thegolfhotelcrail.com

5 rooms, all ensuite, Open Jan-Dec, B&B per person, single from £45.00, double from £30.00.

Family run hotel dating from 1763, in famous fishing village. Convenient for golf, fishing and touring East Neuk of Fife. Only 10 minutes drive to St. Andrews with its famous golf courses and cathedral. The ideal base for touring Fife.

Crieff, Perthshire

Map Ref: 2A2

GUEST HOUSE

Fendoch Guest House

Sma' Glen, Crieff, Perthshire, PH7 3LW
Tel:01764 653446/655619 Fax:01764 653446
Email:bookings@fendoch.co.uk
Web:www.fendoch.co.uk

4 rooms, all en-suite, Open Jan-Dec, B&B per person, single from £23.00, double from £23.00, BB & Eve.Meal from £35.00.

Large modern bungalow with all bedrooms ensuite. Open all year. Evening meals available. Lovely countryside with mountains and hills. Crieff 5 miles. Family run with traditional Highland hospitality. Disabled facilities.

GUEST HOUSE

Galvelbeg House

Perth Road, Crieff, Perthshire, PH7 3EQ
Tel:01764 655061 Fax:01764 650363
Email:mark@philp1984.fsnet.co.uk
Web:www.galvelbeghouse.co.uk

4 rooms en-suite, 1 private facilities, Open Jan-Dec, B&B per person, single from £25.00, double from £20.00.

A warm welcome awaits you at this detached stonebuilt villa, conveniently situated near the town centre with all its amenities. A good base for touring, horseriding and golf, with many local courses. Ample car parking at the rear.

Important: Prices stated are estimates and may be subject to amendments

Crieff, Perthshire

Map Ref: 2A2

★★★

GUEST HOUSE

Kingarth

Perth Road, Crieff, Perthshire, PH7 3EQ
Tel:01764 652060 Fax:01764 655302
Email:info@kingarthguesthouse.com
Web:www.kingarthguesthouse.com

Set in the heart of Scotland, in the bustling town of Crieff, Kingarth is a homely Victorian guest house set in mature gardens, with stunning views overlooking the Strathearn Vale and Ochil Hills. The house has a relaxed, comfortable atmosphere with a cosy residents' lounge, sunny conservatory and dining room. The letting rooms are in the garden wing of the house, and are all ground floor, ensuite and non-smoking. There is ample parking.

6 rooms, all en-suite, Open Jan-Dec, B&B per person, single from £30.00-35.00, double from £25.00.

C V

★★

SMALL HOTEL

Leven House Hotel

Comrie Road, Crieff, PH7 4BA
Tel:01764 652529

Small family run hotel near town centre serving Scottish high teas. Ideally situated for touring and golf. Spacious car park.

10 rooms, Open Feb-Nov, B&B per person single from £25.00, double from £25.00.

Dundee, Angus

Map Ref: 2C2

★★★

GUEST HOUSE

Aberlaw Guest House

230 Broughty Ferry Road, Dundee, Angus, DD4 7JP
Tel/Fax:01382 456929
Email:aberlawguesthouse@btinternet.com
Web:www.aberlawguesthouse.co.uk

Family run Victorian house with private parking. Close to city centre, overlooking River Tay. Five mins on commuter bus to town centre. Ideal for golfing at Carnoustie and St. Andrews. Comfortable lounge available for guests use. All rooms recently upgraded with new ensuite facilities provided.

6 rooms, all en-suite, Open Jan-Dec, B&B per person, single from £30.00, double/twin from £25.00 per person.

C V

Dundee, Angus

Map Ref: 2C2

Apex City Quay Hotel & Spa

1 West Victoria Dock Road, Dundee, DD1 3JP
Tel: 0845 365 0000 Quote VS Fax: 0131 666 5128
e.mail: reservations@apexhotels.co.uk Web:www.apexhotels.co.uk

This contemporary hotel sits on Dundee's quayside, ideally situated for St Andrews and Carnoustie. Fantastic chic bedrooms with wide screen TVs, CD/DVD players, two stunning restaurants (one award winning chef), Yu spa with Japanese hot tubs, sauna, steam room, sanarium, Elemis treatment rooms and gym with the latest Technogym equipment.

★★★★ HOTEL

Apex City Quay Hotel & Spa
1 West Victoria Dock Road, Dundee, DD1 3JP
Tel:0845 365 0000 Fax:0131 666 5128
Email:reservations@apexhotels.co.uk
Web:www.apexhotels.co.uk

Modern hotel in contemporary style situated on Quayside in centre of Dundee. Excellent location for historic attractions. Full conference and leisure facilities.

153 rooms, all en-suite, Open Jan-Dec, B&B per person, single from £70.00, double from £40.00, BB & Eve.Meal from £57.95 pppn.

★★★★ HOTEL

Hilton Dundee
Earl Grey Place, Dundee, DD1 4DE
Tel:01382 229271 Fax:01382 200072
Email:reservations@dundee.stakis.co.uk
Web:www.hilton.com

Modern hotel with leisure facilities situated on the banks of the River Tay with views of the Kingdom of Fife. Easy access by road, rail and air. Conference facilities. Riverside Caffe Cino facility and restaurant and bar with views of the river. 24 hour room service. 90 Car Parking spaces.

129 rooms, all en-suite, Open Jan-Dec, B&B per person, single from £78.00, double from £44.00, BB & Eve.Meal from £59.00 sharing twin/double. Single £95.00.

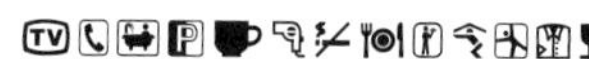

★★★ HOTEL

Invercarse Hotel
371 Perth Road, Dundee, DD2 1PG
Tel:01382 669231
Email:invercarse@bestwestern.co.uk
Web:www.bw-invercarsehotel.co.uk

Quiet residential area with own grounds, near city centre. Ample car parking; conference facilities. Bar meals, a la carte restaurant. Close to Discovery and Heritage Centre.

44 rooms, Open Jan-Dec, B&B per person, single from £55.00, double from £37.00, family subject to availability, room only single from £55.00, double from £74.00, family subject to availability.

★★★ HOTEL

Woodlands Hotel
13 Panmure Terrace, Barnhill, Dundee, DD5 2QL
Tel:01382 480033 Fax:01382 480126
Email:woodlands@bestwestern.co.uk
Web:www.bw-woodlandshotel.co.uk

Woodlands offers a relaxed atmosphere and a very good standard of both comfort and service. Close to excellent beaches and world famous golf courses with the city of Dundee a short drive away with its science centre, contemporary art centre and HMS Discovery, The Woodland Hotel is an ideal base for guests of all ages and the business travellers.

38 rooms, Open Jan-Dec, B&B per person, single from £55.00, double from £37.00, family subject to availability, room only single from £55.00, double from £74.00, family subject to availability.

Important: Prices stated are estimates and may be subject to amendments

Dunfermline, Fife

Map Ref: 2B4

HOTEL

Best Western Keavil House

Crossford, Fife, KY12 8QW
Tel:01383 736258 Fax:01383 621600
Email:sales@keavilhouse.co.uk
Web:www.keavilhouse.co.uk

Historic country house, including extensive leisure facilities, is set in 12 acres of grounds and gardens, making it an ideal location for relaxing. The hotel offers an award winning restaurant. Within easy reach of Edinburgh - only 25 minutes by train.

47 rooms, B&B per person single from £55.00, double from £55.00, family rooms from £65.00 per adult. Four poster rooms from £75.00 per person.

SMALL HOTEL

Davaar House Hotel

126 Grieve Street, Dunfermline, Fife, KY12 8DW
Tel:01383 721886 Fax:01383 623633
Email:enquiries@davaar-house-hotel.com
Web:www.davaar-house-hotel.com

Jim and Doreen extend a warm welcome. Experience Davaar's special atmosphere and enjoy the hospitality comfortable rooms and excellent food. Central location for golfing, walking, touring and enjoying a relaxing break.

10 rooms, all en-suite, Open Jan-Dec excl Xmas/New Year, B&B per person, single from £55.00, double/twin from £45.00.

SMALL HOTEL

Garvock House Hotel

St Johns Drive, Dunfermline, KY12 7TU
Tel:01383 621067 Fax:01383 621168
Email:sales@garvock.co.uk
Web:www.garvock.co.uk

A restored Georgian house set in its own grounds close to Dunfermline town centre. Spacious non-smoking rooms with many thoughtful touches to ensure a comfortable & relaxing stay for all. Comfortable lounges & elegant dining room with good old-fashioned service. Weddings & functions catered for.

12 rooms, all en-suite, Open Jan-Dec, B&B per person, single from £70.00, double from £47.50.

HOTEL

Pitbauchlie House Hotel

Aberdour Road, Dunfermline, KY11 4PB
Tel:01383 722282 Fax:01383 620738
Email:info@pitbauchlie.com
Web:www.pitbauchlie.com

Nestled in wooded and landscaped gardens, this popular hotel is situated 4 miles from the Forth Bridges. 50 En-Suite Bedrooms, an A La Carte Restaurant plus Bar/Bistro Dining areas. An ideal location for discovering Scotland's Ancient and Modern Capitals.

50 rooms, all en-suite, Open Jan-Dec, B&B per person, single from £85.00, double from £51.50.

Dunkeld, Perthshire

Map Ref: 2B1

HOTEL

Royal Dunkeld Hotel

Atholl Street, Dunkeld, PH8 0AR
Tel:01350 727322 Fax:01350 728989
Email:reservations@royaldunkeld.co.uk
Web:www.royaldunkeld.co.uk

Personally run, early 19c coaching inn, situated in centre of historic town of Dunkeld. Golfing breaks and fishing packages a speciality. Some annexe bedrooms.

34 rooms, all en-suite, Open Jan-Dec, B&B per person, single from £45.00, double from £32.00, BB & Eve.Meal from £50.00.

VAT is shown at 17.5%: changes in this rate may affect prices.

Key to symbols is on back flap.

Edzell, Angus

Map Ref: 4F12

SMALL HOTEL

Panmure Arms Hotel

52 High Street, Edzell, Angus, DD9 7TA
Tel:01356 648950 Fax:01356 648000
Email:david@panmurearmshotel.co.uk
Web:www.panmurearmshotel.co.uk

A recently refurbished family run hotel with the emphasis on quality and service. Set in the picturesque village of Edzell with very easy access for golfing, shooting and fishing. A perfect holiday destination for exploring the beautiful Angus glens.

16 rooms, all en-suite, Open Jan-Dec excl Xmas. New Year, B&B per person, single from £47.50, double from £35.00.

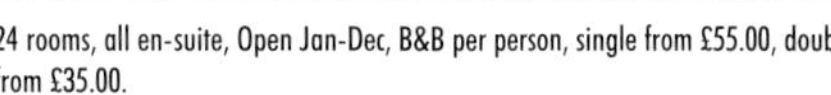

Freuchie, Fife

Map Ref: 2C3

HOTEL

Lomond Hills Hotel and Leisure Centre

Parliament Square, Freuchie, Fife, KY15 7EY
Tel/Fax:01337 857329
Email:reception@lomondhillshotel.com
Web:www.lomondhillshotel.com

Situated at the foot of the Lomond Hills in rolling countryside, The Lomond Hills Hotel has 52 golf courses within 25 miles. With swimming pool, gym, spa and sauna this is the ideal base for golf, leisure or business. Our candlelit restaurant serves fresh local produce. St Andrews 25 mins, Edinburgh Airport 30 mins.

24 rooms, all en-suite, Open Jan-Dec, B&B per person, single from £55.00, double from £35.00.

Glenshee, Perthshire

Map Ref: 4D12

SMALL HOTEL

Dalmunzie

Spittal of Glenshee, Blairgowrie, Perthshire PH10 7QG
Tel:01250 885224 Fax:01250 885225
Email:reservations@dalmunzie.com
Web:www.dalmunzie.com

Dalmunzie is a stunning Highland laird's mansion situated in a gloriously remote location, yet is less than 2 hours from Edinburgh. Golf and tennis on-site.

16 rooms, Open Dec28-Nov30, B&B per person, single from £63.00, double from £45.00, Dinner £30.00.

Kinloch Rannoch, Perthshire

Map Ref: 1H1

HOTEL

Dunalastair Hotel

The Square, Kinloch Rannoch, Perthshire, PH16 5PW
Tel:01882 632218 Fax:01882 632371
Email:stay@dunalastair.co.uk
Web:www.dunalastair.co.uk

Traditional Scottish hotel in picturesque village square. Ideal touring base for the central Highlands.

28 rooms, all en-suite, Open Feb-Dec excl Xmas/New Year, B&B per person, single from £37.50, double from £37.50.

Important: Prices stated are estimates and may be subject to amendments

Kinross, Perthshire | **Map Ref: 2B3**

HOTEL

The Green Hotel

2 The Muirs, Kinross, KY13 8AS
Tel:01577 863467 Fax:01577 863180
Email:reservations@green-hotel.com
Web:www.green-hotel.com

Ideally located in central Scotland. This is one of Scotland's fine independently owned country house hotels. 46 spacious bedrooms equipped to the highest standard. The leisure complex has indoor pool, sauna, exercise facility and squash court plus a four sheet curling rink in season. The hotel has 2 'all weather' tennis courts and 2 '18 hole' golf courses; trout fishing can be arranged on nearby Loch Leven.

46 rooms, all en-suite, Open Jan-Dec, B&B per person, single from £95.00, double/twin from £85.00, BB & Eve.Meal from £75.00 per person sharing a twin/double, min 2 night stay.

RESTAURANT WITH ROOMS

Grouse and Claret Restaurant

Heatheryford, Kinross, KY13 0NQ
Tel:01577 864212 Fax:01577 864920
Email:grouseandclaret@lineone.net
Web:www.grouseandclaret.co.uk

Restaurant featuring fresh local Scottish produce with a hint of oriental flavours. Separate accommodation, all overlooking the trout lochans to the Ochil Hills beyond. Conveniently situated off junction 6 on the M90 motorway. Edinburgh, St Andrews, Perth, Stirling and Glasgow all within an hour's drive.

3 rooms, all en-suite, Open mid Jan-Dec, B&B per person, single from £36.00, double from £32.50.

SMALL HOTEL

Kirklands Hotel

20 High Street, Kinross, Perthshire, KY13 8AN
Tel:01577 863313
Email:pd.fraser@virgin.net
Web:www.thekirklandshotel.com

Friendly service at this former Coaching Inn, all rooms en-suite. Attractively refurbished bar and restaurant with interesting menu choice from award winning chef. Large suite available which is ideal for groups and families.

9 rooms, all en-suite, Open Jan-Dec excl Xmas/New Year, B&B per person, single from £38.00, double/twin from £33.00.

GUEST HOUSE

Roxburghe Guest House

126 High Street, Kinross, KY13 8DA
Tel:01577 862498
Email:guests@roxburgheguesthouse.co.uk
Web:www.roxburgheguesthouse.co.uk

The Roxburghe offers unpretentious Scottish Hospitality with traditional cooking including special diets. Breakfast features continental choices and range of fish dishes, evening meals are cooked to order and the menu includes Highland Beef, Wild Perthshire Venison, Scotch Lamb and Salmon. The Roxburghe is licensed. Lock-up facilities for cycles and drying room for storage of fishing and golf equipment. Listed in The Good Hotel Guide.

4 rooms, Open Jan-Dec, B&B per person, single from £25.00, double from £22.00, BB & Eve.Meal from £34.00.

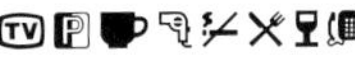

VAT is shown at 17.5%: changes in this rate may affect prices.

Key to symbols is on back flap.

Kinross, Perthshire

Map Ref: 2B3

SMALL HOTEL

The Well Country Inn

Main Street, Scotlandwell, Kinross, KY13 9JA
Tel/Fax:01592 840444
Email:thewellcountryinn@fsbdial.co.uk
Web:www.thewellcountryinn.com

The Well Country Inn is a family run business and is situated in one of the most beautiful areas of Scotland, renowned for its natural beauty and wealth of sporting and leisure interest. Game shooting is a popular sport in this area and our annexe bedrooms are fitted with gun safes and we have kennel facilities.

9 rooms, all en-suite, Open Jan-Dec, B&B per person, double £30.00-35.00.

Kirkcaldy, Fife

Map Ref: 2C4

B&B

Arboretum

20 Southerton Road, Kirkcaldy, Fife, KY2 5NB
Tel:01592 643673

Quietly located adjacent to Beveridge Park and close to the centre of Kirkcaldy. Walking distance from shops and railway station. Private and free on-street parking. Double or twin available both en-suite. Not suitable for children under five years.

3 rooms, all en-suite, Open Jan-Dec, B&B per person, single from £23.00, double from £20.00.

Kirriemuir, Angus

Map Ref: 2C1

SMALL HOTEL

Airlie Arms Hotel

No 4 St. Malcolms Wynd, Kirriemuir, Angus, DD8 4HB
Tel:01575 572847 Fax:01575 573055
Email:info@airliearms-hotel.co.uk
Web:www.airliearms-hotel.co.uk

A delightful family run hotel in the centre of Kirriemuir, the Airlie Arms Hotel has 10 en-suite bedrooms all with bath and shower, Sky TV, telephone, tea/coffee facilities. Enjoy dinner in our award winning restaurant 'The Wynd'. Resident's lounge. Public bar. We can arrange fishing, shooting, golfing and walking packages.

10 rooms, all en-suite, Open Jan-Dec, B&B per person, single from £35.00, double from £30.00.

Leven, Fife

Map Ref: 2C3

GUEST HOUSE

Dunclutha Guest House

16 Victoria Road, Leven, Fife, KY8 4EX
Tel:01333 425515 Fax:01333 422311
Email:pam.leven@dunclutha-accomm.demon.co.uk
Web:www.dunclutha-accomm.demon.co.uk

Victorian former manse. 2 minutes level walk from centre of Leven. Good base for golfing enthusiasts and New Fife Coastal Walk. 50 minutes drive from Edinburgh and 40 minutes from the airport. 7 miles to the nearest railway station. All bedrooms with either ensuite or private facilities.

4 rooms, three en-suite, Open Jan-Dec, B&B per person, single from £30.00, double from £28.00. Non smoking, private parking.

Loch Earn, Perthshire

Map Ref: 1H2

SMALL HOTEL

Achray House Hotel

St Fillans, Perthshire, PH6 2NF
Tel:01764 685231 Fax:01764 685320
Email:info@achray-house.co.uk
Web:www.achray-house.co.uk

Small personally run hotel with fresh homemade produce. Bar and restaurant menus. Picturesque village with stunning views over Loch Earn and self catering lodges.

10 rooms, all en-suite, Open Jan-Dec, BB & Eve.Meal from £50.00 pp.

Important: Prices stated are estimates and may be subject to amendments

Loch Earn, Perthshire

Map Ref: 1H2

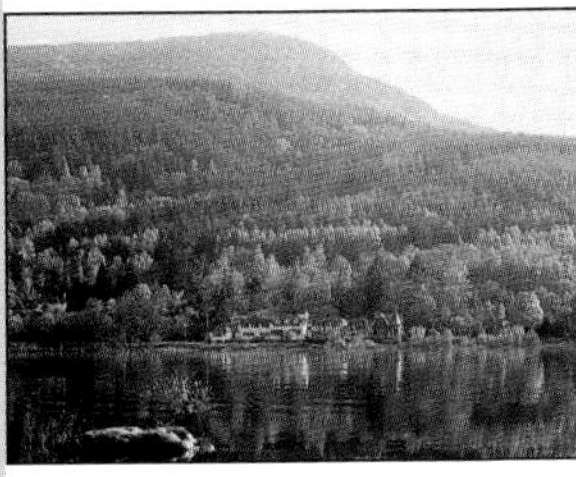

The finest lochside setting in the Southern Highlands

Well placed to enjoy many day trips to include the scenic West Coast, Stirling Castle, Edinburgh, Blair Atholl and the Trossachs. Thirty two golf courses within an hour, scenic lochside walks and Munros to climb. The alternative is to relax in the hotel enjoying the ever changing views down the Loch.

The Four Seasons Hotel

St Fillans, Perthshire PH6 2NF
Tel: 01764 685333
www.thefourseasonshotel.co.uk
email: info@thefourseasonshotel.co.uk

AA ★★★ RAC ★★★ Which Good Hotel Guide

3 for 2 on D,B&B in Spring/Autumn

SMALL HOTEL

The Four Seasons Hotel

St Fillans, Perthshire, PH6 2NF
Tel:01764 685333
info@thefourseasonshotel.co.uk
www.thefourseasonshotel.co.uk

Food glorious food @ The Four Seasons Hotel. Modern European influenced cuisine, with ingredients from Scotland's natural larder, to produce a truly memorable meal. The Fine Dining restaurant includes hand dived Scrabster Scallops, Smoked Duck Breast, Gateau of Scottish Limousin Beef, Rockall Monkfish, Belgian Chocolate Tart, Banana and Date Samosa. Alternatively we can offer freshly prepared bar meals.

18 rooms, all en-suite, Open Mar-Jan, B&B per person, single from £40.00, double from £40.00, BB & Eve.Meal from £66.00.

Markinch, Fife

Map Ref: 2C3

HOTEL

Balbirnie House

Balbirnie Park, Markinch, Fife, KY7 6NE
Tel:01592 610066 Fax:01592 610529
Email:info@balbirnie.co.uk
Web:www.balbirnie.co.uk

Balbirnie is a quite unique multi-award winning Country House Hotel which combines understated luxury with superb service and outstanding value. Many feature breaks available throughout the year. Widely recognised as Scotland's top privately owned hotel 'Conde Nast World Traveller'.

30 rooms, all en-suite, Open Jan-Dec, B&B per person, single from £135.00, double from £97.50, BB & Eve.Meal from £115.00.

Meikleour, by Perth, Perthshire

Map Ref: 2B2

Meikleour Hotel

Meikleour, Perthshire PH2 6EB
Tel: 01250 883206 Fax: 01250 883406
e.mail: visitus@meikleourhotel.co.uk Web: www.meikleourhotel.co.uk

For 180 years Meikleour Hotel has been serving travellers and locals alike. A thriving and almost unique inn, serving bar and dining food to exceptional standards, the same standards being applied to its hotel rooms and very personable service, making it the destination for guests from all walks of life.

INN

Meikleour Hotel

Meikleour, Perthshire, PH2 6EB
Tel:01250 883206 Fax:01250 883406
Email:visitus@meikleourhotel.co.uk
Web:www.meikleourhotel.co.uk

Quality country Inn, situated in the quiet village of Meikleour, near to the famous beech hedge. Meals are available in the dining room or the bar, and fine comfortable bedrooms make the Meikleour Hotel the perfect base for exploring the area, or for fishing, golf or just relaxing.

5 rooms, Open Jan-Dec, B&B per person single from £55.00, double from £55.00.

VAT is shown at 17.5%: changes in this rate may affect prices.

Key to symbols is on back flap.

Montrose, Angus

Map Ref: 4F12

★★★★ HOTEL

Best Western Links Hotel

Midlinks, Montrose, Angus, DD10 8RL
Tel:01674 671000 Fax:01674 672698
Email:reception@linkshotel.com
Web:www.bw-linkshotel.co.uk

A lovely hotel situated on the historic Midlinks. Within easy walking distance of the town centre, beaches and golf courses. Offering an all day 'Koffiehuis' with al-fresco terrace, a restaurant awarded with one AA Rosette and 25 individually designed bedrooms (some with balconies with views of the Midlinks). Enjoy excellent hospitality & a refreshing & relaxing stay.

25 rooms, all en-suite, Open Jan-Dec, B&B £29.00 per person per night sharing.

★★ HOTEL

George Hotel

22 George Street, Montrose, DD10 8EW
Tel:01674 675050 Fax:01674 671153
Email:reception@thegeorge-montrose.co.uk
Web:www.thegeorge-montrose.co.uk

A privately owned stone-built hotel located in the centre of Montrose providing a central base for exploring this interesting part of Eastern Scotland with its championship golf courses, sandy beaches and beautiful glens.

24 rooms, all en-suite, Open Jan-Dec, B&B per person, single from £40.00, double from £25.00.

Perth

Map Ref: 2B2

★★★★ GUEST HOUSE

Achnacarry Guest House

3 Pitcullen Crescent, Perth, PH2 7HT
Tel:01738 621421
Email:info@achnacarry.co.uk
Web:www.achnacarry.co.uk

Victorian dwelling house located a ten minute walk from city centre. We offer warm hospitality in true Scottish tradition, in tastefully decorated surroundings. En suited rooms, including one on ground floor. Ample off street parking. An ideal base for visiting the many attractions in the area, and exploring the Central & Highland areas of Bonnie Scotland. Golfers welcome, clubs available. See Website for seasonal offers.

4 rooms, all en-suite, Open Jan-Dec excl New Year, B&B per person, single £25.00-30.00, double £22.50-27.50.

★★★★ GUEST HOUSE

Ackinnoull Guest House

5 Pitcullen Crescent, Perth, PH2 7HT
Tel:01738 634165
Web:www.ackinnoull.com

Beautifully decorated Victorian semi-villa on the outskirts of town. Private parking on premises. 'Perth in Bloom' winners, as picturesque inside as out. Special rates for bookings of 3 days or more.

4 rooms, all en-suite, Open Jan-Dec, B&B per person, single from £25.00, double from £20.00.

Important: Prices stated are estimates and may be subject to amendments

Perth — **Map Ref: 2B2**

★★★★ GUEST HOUSE

Almond Villa Guest House

51 Dunkeld Road, Perth, PH1 5RP
Tel:01738 629356
Email:enquiries@perth-guesthouse.co.uk
Web:www.perth-guesthouse.co.uk

Elegant Victorian house, close to town. Non-smoking house with cosy lounge and spacious dining room. Teddy bears.

5 rooms, all en-suite, Open Jan-Dec, B&B per person, single from £30.00, double from £27.00. No evening meal.

GUEST HOUSE

Arisaig Guest House

4 Pitcullen Crescent, Perth, PH2 7HT
Tel:01738 628240 Fax:01738 638521
Email:mail@arisaigonline.co.uk
Web:www.arisaigonline.co.uk

Comfortable family run guest house, with off street parking. Close to city's many facilities. Local touring base. Ground floor bedroom.

5 rooms, all en-suite, Open Jan-Dec, B&B per person, single from £25.00-30.00, double £25.00, twin £27.50.

GUEST HOUSE

Beechgrove Guest House

Dundee Road, Perth, PH2 7AQ
Tel/Fax:01738 636147
Email:beechgroveg.h@sol.co.uk
Web:www.smoothhound.co.uk/hotels/beechgr

Listed building, former manse (Rectory) set in extensive grounds. Peaceful, yet only a few minutes walk from the city centre. Non-smoking establishment. Close to local attractions e.g. Scone Palace, Branklyn Gardens, Blackwatch Museum, new Perth Concert Mall just over bridge. Many award winning restaurants close by. GlenTurret Tourism award winner. Non smoking establishment.

8 rooms, all en-suite, Open Jan-Dec, B&B per person, single from £35.00, double from £30.00.

INN

Cherrybank Inn

210 Glasgow Road, Perth, PH2 ONA
Tel:01738 624349 Fax:01738 444962
Email:jackfindlay@kenscott.sagehost.co.uk
Web:www.cherrybankinn.co.uk

Cherrybank Inn is situated on the outskirts of Perth, 1 mile off the motorway, offering accommodation in twin bedded ensuite rooms. Bar meals available. Continental breakfast only served in rooms and full breakfast available.

7 rooms, all en-suite, Open Jan-Dec, B&B per person, single from £32.00, double from £46.00.

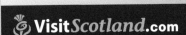

VAT is shown at 17.5%: changes in this rate may affect prices.

Key to symbols is on back flap.

Perth

Map Ref: 2B2

GUEST HOUSE

Clunie Guest House

12 Pitcullen Crescent, Perth, PH2 7HT
Tel:01738 623625
Email:ann@clunieguesthouse.co.uk
Web:www.clunieguesthouse.co.uk

A warm welcome awaits you at Clunie Guest House which is situated on the A94 Coupar Angus road. There is easy access to the city centre with all its amenities including a variety of eating establishments. Alternatively, an evening meal can be provided if it is booked in advance. All rooms ensuite.

7 rooms, all en-suite, Open Jan-Dec, B&B per person, single from £25.00, double from £24.00, Room Only double from £40.00, BB & Eve.Meal from £40.00.

GUEST HOUSE

The Gables

24-26 Dunkeld Road, Perth, PH1 5RW
Tel:01738 624717
Email:gablesguesthouse@btconnect.com
Web:www.thegablesguesthouse.com

Stone built house on main road ½ mile (1km) north of Perth city centre. Close to sports centre, swimming pool and local golf course. Off road parking. Restricted hotel license.

7 rooms, some en-suite, Open Jan-Dec excl Xmas/New Year, B&B per person, single from £25.00, double from £25.00.

GUEST HOUSE

Iona Guest House

2 Pitcullen Crescent, Perth, Perthshire, PH2 7HT
Tel/Fax:01738 627261
Email:daisyandpeter@ionaperth.co.uk
Web:www.ionaperth.co.uk

Traditional friendly Scottish welcome at this comfortable guest house, in a residential area 10 mins walk from the town centre with all its shops and variety of eating establishments. An ideal base for touring, walking and golfing - 30 golf courses within a 30 mile (48 kms) radius.

5 rooms, some en-suite, Open Jan-Dec, B&B per person, single from £20.00, double from £20.00.

SMALL HOTEL

Parklands Hotel

2 St Leonards Bank, Perth, PH2 8EB
Tel:01738 622451 Fax:01738 622046
Email:info@theparklandshotel.com
Web:www.parklandshotel.com

The Parklands Hotel is a classical town house, situated on an elevated position overlooking the South Inch Park. All bedrooms have wireless broadband access, DVD and CD players. Dining options include the informal Bistro, or the more formal Acanthus restaurant. The hotel also has a licence for performing weddings.

14 rooms, all en-suite, Open Jan-Dec, B&B per person, single from £69.00, double from £49.50, BB & Eve.Meal from £57.50.

GUEST HOUSE

Pitcullen Guest House

17 Pitcullen Crescent, Perth, PH2 7HT
Tel:01738 626506
Email:pitcullen.guesthouse@virgin.net

Personally run and conveniently situated on A94 tourist route. Only 5 minutes from City Centre. Private parking. Ideal location for visits to Perth races or Scone Palace.

5 rooms, Open Jan-Dec, B&B per person, single from £22.00, double from £23.00, twin from £23.00, family from £60.00 per room.

Important: Prices stated are estimates and may be subject to amendments

Perth

Map Ref: 2B2

Queens Hotel

Leonard Street, Perth, PH2 8HB
Tel:01738 442222 Fax:01738 638496
Email:email@queensperth.co.uk
Web:www.symphonyhotels.co.uk

Privately owned and family run hotel ideally situated in city centre with ample free car-parking. High quality bedrooms, function and conference facilities. Leisure club including pool, jacuzzi, sauna, steam bath and gym.

50 rooms, all en-suite, Open Jan-Dec excl Xmas/New Year, B&B per person, single from £45.00, double from £35.00.

Westview Bed & Breakfast

49 Dunkeld Road, Perth, PH1 5RP
Tel:01738 627787 Tel/Fax:01738 447790
Email:angiewestview@aol.com

Welcoming Victorian villa with original features reflecting the Victorian theme throughout. Attractive rooms with private facilities and elegant touches including period sitting room and relaxing garden. An enjoyable trip back in time. Ample parking. Smoking area. Scottish High Teas served 5-7pm. Dinner served 7-8.30pm.

4 rooms, 3 en-suite, Open Jan-Dec, B&B per person, single from £25.00, double from £25.00, BB & Eve.Meal from £30.00.

by Perth

Map Ref: 2B2

Ballathie House Hotel

Kinclaven, Stanley, Perthshire, PH1 4QN
Tel:01250 883268 Fax:01250 883396
Email:email@ballathiehousehotel.com
Web:www.ballathiehousehotel.com

Victorian Country House within its own grounds overlooking the River Tay. 12 miles from historic city of Perth. New riverside rooms and suites with balconies overlooking the river.

42 rooms, all en-suite, B&B per person, single from £82.50, double from £82.50. DB&B from £110.00. Special breaks available.

Ballathie House Sportsman's Lodge

Kinclaven, Stanley, Perthshire, PH1 4QN
Tel:01250 883268 Fax:01250 883396
Email:email@ballathiehousehotel.com
Web:www.fishing-shooting-scotland.co.uk

Purpose built Lodge accommodation, situated within the grounds of Ballathie House Hotel, and just a short walk from the hotel. Guests have access to the bar and dining facilities within the hotel, as well as the sporting facilities in the area.

12 rooms, all en-suite, Open Jan-Dec, B&B per person, single from £55.00, double from £40.00, BB & Eve.Meal from £75.00. Special breaks available.

Pitlochry, Perthshire

Map Ref: 2A1

Atholl Palace

Pitlochry, Perthshire, PH16 5LY
Tel:01796 472400 Fax:01796 473036
Email:info@athollpalace.com Web:www.athollpalace.com

At the very heart, where the River Tummel flows to the Tay, sits the historic town of Pitlochry. The Atholl Palace Hotel, the epitome of Scottish Baronial splendour, stands overlooking wooded parkland grounds and the town to the surrounding highlands. Many features of the traditional large country house property have now been recreated, including the traditional Victorian Spa, whilst bedroom facilities and standards often now exceed expectations and complement spacious, relaxing public areas.

90 rooms, all en-suite, Open Jan-Dec, B&B per person £64.00-92.00 single or double. BB & Eve.Meal £79.00-109.00 single or double.

VAT is shown at 17.5%: changes in this rate may affect prices.

Key to symbols is on back flap.

Pitlochry, Perthshire **Map Ref: 2A1**

SMALL HOTEL

Balrobin Hotel

Higher Oakfield, Pitlochry, PH16 5HT
Tel:01796 472901 Fax:01796 474200
Email:info@balrobin.co.uk Web:www.balrobin.co.uk

Situated in residential yet central part of town with most bedrooms (12-4 on ground floor) with superb panaromic views.Traditional home cooked food from a varied choice menu changing daily accompanied by a selection of fine wines. Residents only bar. Our central location affords easy access to 60% of Scotland making it a perfect base for long & short stays. Special short break & advance booking rates.

14 rooms, all en-suite, Open Mar-Oct, B&B per person, single £39.00-43.00, double £33.00-39.00, BB & Eve.Meal from £44.00-52.00.

SMALL HOTEL

Donavourd House Hotel

Pitlochry, Perthshire, PH16 5JS
Tel:01796 472100 Fax:01796 474455
Email:nemckechnie@btconnect.com
Web:www.donavourdhousehotel.co.uk

Traditional country house hotel with 8 acres of ground situated in a peaceful elevated location 1 mile south of Pitlochry. Some rooms with four poster beds. Imaginative Scottish cuisine using fresh local ingredients.

9 rooms, all en-suite, Open Mar-Dec excl Xmas/New Year, B&B per person, single from £55.00, double from £45.00.

HOTEL

Dundarach Hotel

Perth Road, Pitlochry, Perthshire, PH16 5DJ
Tel:01796 472862 Fax:01796 473024
Email:stb@dundarach.co.uk Web:www.dundarach.co.uk

This hotel on the edge of the village is architecturally interesting, inside and out and stands in its own secluded garden but still close to town centre. A warm friendly welcome is assured by the resident owners the Smail family. The hotel offers both traditional and new bedrooms and all are well equipped. The airy comfortable public rooms are attractively decorated in warm colours and give many fine views over the surrounding countryside.

40 rooms, all en-suite, Open Feb-Dec excl Xmas/New Year, B&B per person, single from £30.00, double from £30.00.

GUEST HOUSE

Fasganeoin Country House

Perth Road, Pitlochry, PH16 5DJ
Tel:01796 472387 Fax:01796 474285
Email:sabrina@fasganeoin.freeserve.co.uk
Web:www.fasganeoincountryhouse.co.uk

A long established family run country house with the accent on traditional values of hospitality and service. Dating from the 1870s and set in spacious, secluded gardens, it stands on the edge of town, close to the theatre. Tasty theatre suppers are served between 5-7pm (last orders 6.45), bookings preferred.

8 rooms, 6 en-suite, 2 with priv.facilities, Open Apr-mid Oct, B&B per person, single from £28.00, en-suite double from £32.00, BB & Eve.Meal from £42.50.

HOTEL

The Green Park Hotel

Clunie Bridge Road, Pitlochry, Perthshire, PH16 5JY
Tel:01796 473248 Fax:01796 473520
Email:bookings@thegreenpark.co.uk
Web:www.thegreenpark.co.uk

Family run country house hotel enjoying spectacular views over Loch Faskally. Within strolling distance of the shops and a pleasant walk from the Festival Theatre, the hotel has become a well known landmark of the town. The hotel has a Red Rosette for food, reflecting the emphasis placed on the food served at the Green Park.

51 rooms, all en-suite, Open Jan-Dec, B&B per person, single from £42.00, double from £42.00, BB & Eve.Meal from £58.00.

Important: Prices stated are estimates and may be subject to amendments

Pitlochry, Perthshire Map Ref: 2A1

KNOCKENDARROCH HOUSE

Higher Oakfield, Pitlochry, Perthshire PH16 5HT
Telephone: 01796 473473 Fax: 01796 474068
e.mail: info@knockendarroch.co.uk
web: www.knockendarroch.co.uk

★★★★ SMALL HOTEL

The warmest of welcomes, with first-class food, wines and personal service complement this elegant Victorian mansion. Surrounded by mature oaks and beeches with glorious views over Pitlochry and the Tummel Valley, yet within walking distance of the town centre. Stay at Knockendarroch once and we're confident you'll want to return. AA ★★78% Rosette.

SMALL HOTEL

Knockendarroch House Hotel

Higher Oakfield, Pitlochry, Perthshire, PH16 5HT
Tel:01796 473473 Fax:01796 474068
Email:info@knockendarroch.co.uk
Web:www.knockendarroch.co.uk

An oasis of tranquillity in the heart of the town. Knockendarroch a gracious Victorian mansion, with glorious views over Pitlochry and Tummel valley. Set in it's own grounds surrounded by mature oaks, Knockendarroch with resident proprietors Jane & Tony Ross, combines a relaxed atmosphere, high standards in food, wines and personal attention. Lots to do locally and a perfect base for sightseeing and touring. Non-smoking hotel.

12 rooms, all en-suite, Open Mar-Nov, BB & Eve.Meal from £48.00.

GUEST HOUSE

Macdonald's Restaurant & Guest House

140 Atholl Road, Pitlochry, Perthshire, PH16 5AG
Tel:01796 472170 Fax:01796 474460
Email:macdonalds.pitlochry@usa.net
Web:www.macdonalds-pitlochry.co.uk

We have been welcoming guests since 1959. All rooms ensuite and have LCD televisions. Stay 3 nights or more Sunday-Thursday £20.00 pppn. Double occupancy required.

10 rooms, Open Jan-Dec, B&B per person, single £35.00, double £25.00.

MOULIN HOTEL

11-13 Kirkmichael Road, Moulin, by Pitlochry PH16 5EH
Tel: 01796 472196 Fax: 01796 474098
Email: enquiries@moulinhotel.co.uk Web: www.moulinhotel.co.uk

The Moulin Hotel derives its character from a 305 year old history, a first choice for locals and visitors alike. Open all day, every day, providing fare from, local produce, it's own brewhouse and of course game from the surrounding hills. 18 en-suite rooms complete the package of peace & tranquillity in this ancient village.

INN

Moulin Hotel

11-13 Kirkmichael Road, by Pitlochry, Perthshire, PH16 5EH
Tel:01796 472196 Fax:01796 474098
Email:enquiries@moulinhotel.co.uk
Web:www.moulinhotel.co.uk

Former coaching Inn with wing dating back to 17th C. Quiet village square setting. Home brewed ales served to compliment the local malts. Log fires, extensive use of local fresh produce. 16 routed walks in the area. 6 local golf courses within a ½ hour drive.

18 rooms, Open Jan-Dec, B&B per person, single from £40.00, double from £27.50, family from £25.00, room only from £40.00, double from £55.00, family from £65.00.

Pitlochry, Perthshire

Map Ref: 2A1

SMALL HOTEL

Pine Trees Hotel

Strathview Terrace, Pitlochry, Perthshire, PH16 5QR
Tel:01796 472121 Fax:01796 472460
Email:info@pinetreeshotel.co.uk
Web:www.pinetreeshotel.co.uk

Personally run Victorian country house in elevated position, with 10 acres of garden and woodland yet close to town centre. Walking distance to local golf course. Edradour and Blair Atholl distillery close to village and worth visiting.

20 rooms, all en-suite, Open Jan-Dec, B&B per person, single from £42.00, double from £36.00, BB & Eve.Meal from £56.00.

HOTEL

Pitlochry Hydro Hotel

Knockard Road, Pitlochry, Perthshire, PH16 5JH
Tel:01942 824824
Email:reservations@shearingsholidays.co.uk
Web:www.shearingsholidays.com

The hotel and health club stand in their own grounds overlooking the town. Entertainment every night.

60 rooms, all en-suite, Open Feb-Dec, B&B per person, double from £40.00.

GUEST HOUSE

Torrdarach House

Golf Course Road, Pitlochry, Perthshire, PH16 5AU
Tel:01796 472136
Email:torrdarach@msn.com
Web:www.smoothhound.co.uk/hotels/torrdarach.html

Listed Edwardian country house set in secluded gardens with gorgeous views over Tummel Valley. A highland burn, a family of red squirrels and a variety of wildlife all within its grounds. Located approximately 5 minutes walk from the picturesque town centre and golf course. Douglas and June guarantee a friendly and relaxed atmosphere, hearty breakfasts and a fine selection of wines and malts.

7 rooms, some en-suite, Open Jan-Dec, B&B per person, single from £20.00, double from £20.00.

GUEST HOUSE

The Well House

11 Toberargan Road, Pitlochry, Perthshire, PH16 5HG
Tel/Fax:01796 472239
Email:enquiries@wellhouseandarrochar.co.uk
Web:www.wellhouseandarrochar.co.uk

Personally run, centrally situated in residential area. Easy access to shops, amenities and theatre.

6 rooms, all en-suite, Open Feb-Nov, B&B per person, double from £24.00, BB & Eve.Meal from £42.00.

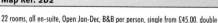

St Andrews, Fife

Map Ref: 2D2

SMALL HOTEL

The Albany Hotel

56 North Street, St Andrews, Fife, KY16 9AH
Tel:01334 477737 Fax:01334 477742
Email:enqu@standrewsalbany.co.uk
Web:www.standrewsalbany.co.uk

Peacefully situated in the heart of St Andrews, close to shops, restaurants, golf courses and historic buildings, this is an elegant Georgian town house, cleverly and sympathetically converted for use as an hotel. With 22 rooms, tastefully decorated, the Albany Hotel is able to maintain high standards in accommodation and service.

22 rooms, all en-suite, Open Jan-Dec, B&B per person, single from £45.00, double from £39.00.

Important: Prices stated are estimates and may be subject to amendments

St Andrews, Fife

Map Ref: 2D2

B&B ★★★★

Bramley House

10 Bonfield Road, Strathkinness, by St Andrews, KY16 9RP
Tel/Fax:01334 850362
Email:heather@bramleyguesthouse.com
Web:www.bramleyguesthouse.com

Beautifully situated 2.5 miles west of St Andrews, this elegant country house is ideal for that special break away. The attractive bedrooms are spacious, well furnished and offer all the expected amenities. Your hostess, Heather McQueen, has a renowned reputation for her relaxed country house atmosphere, enjoyable home cooking and early bird golfing breakfast. Entry in 'Which' Best B&B.

3 rooms, all en-suite, Open Jan-Dec, B&B per person, double from £25.00.

GUEST HOUSE ★★★

Charlesworth House

9 Murray Place, St Andrews, KY16 9AP
Tel/Fax:01334 476528
Email:charlesworth@talk21.com
Web:www.charlesworthstandrews.co.uk

Victorian terraced, family-run guest house in the heart of St Andrews. A few minutes walk from the famous Old Course, beaches, historic buildings and shops. Non-smoking.

5 rooms, Open Jan-Dec, B&B per person, single from £30.00, double from £28.00.

GUEST HOUSE ★★★

Cleveden House

3 Murray Place, St Andrews, Fife, KY16 9AP
Tel/Fax:01334 474212
Email:bookings@clevedenhouse.co.uk
Web:www.clevedenhouse.co.uk

Personally run guest house, five minutes walk from the Old Course, beaches and town centre.

2 double, 3 twin rooms all en-suite, 1 single with priv.facilities, B&B per person from £30.00. Single occupancy from £50.00 pn.

GUEST HOUSE ★★★★

Craigmore Guest House

3 Murray Park, St Andrews, Fife, KY16 9AW
Tel:01334 472142 Fax:01334 477963
Email:enquiries@standrewscraigmore.com
Web:www.standrewscraigmore.com

Victorian stone built guest house in centre of St Andrews. Short walk from town centre, beaches and 'Old Course'. Ground floor room. Non smoking. Relax in the comfortable lounge/dining room after a days golf and sightseeing. Free Internet access.

7 rooms, all en-suite, Open Jan-Dec, B&B per person, single from £45.00, double from £33.00.

GUEST HOUSE ★★★★

Feddinch Mansion Country Guest House

St Andrews, Fife, KY16 8NR
Tel:01334 470888 Fax:01334 477220
Email:enquiries@feddinch-house.com
Web:www.feddinch-house.com

Feddinch House is a Scottish house with a history of 500 years. Recently refurbished by Ken and Lois Wood. Views overlook St Andrews and the Links golf courses. Grass tennis court, pool, billiard room. Private parking.

5 rooms, all en-suite, Open Jan-Dec, B&B per person, double from £30.00.

St Andrews, Fife

Map Ref: 2D2

SMALL HOTEL

Hazelbank Hotel

28 The Scores, St Andrews, Fife, KY16 9AS
Tel/Fax:01334 472466
Email:michael@hazelbank.com
Web:www.hazelbank.com

Refurbished elegant Victorian townhouse. Overlooking St Andrews Bay and golf courses. 200 yards from the 1st tee on The Old Course. 3 minutes walk to University and historic town centre.

10 rooms, all en-suite, Open Jan-Dec excl Xmas/New Year, B&B per person, single from £54.50, double from £39.50.

AWAITING INSPECTION

Macdonald Rusacks Hotel

Pilmour Links, St Andrews, Fife, KY16 9JQ
Tel:0870 4008128 Fax:01334 477896
Email:general.russacks@macdonald-hotels.com
Web:www.macdonald-hotels.com

68 rooms, all en-suite, Open Jan-Dec, B&B per person, single from £60.00, double from £60.00, Dinner B&B from £80.00.

GUEST HOUSE

Montague Guest House

21 Murray Park, St Andrews, Fife, KY16 9AW
Tel:01334 479 287
Email:info@montaguehouse.com
Web:www.montaguehouse.com

Completely refurbished Victorian terraced house with themed rooms, some with hand painted murals, convenient for the town centre, cinema, shops, restaurants and bars. Golf courses, historic buildings, University, seashore all within a few minutes walk. Completely non - smoking house.

6 rooms, all en-suite, Open Jan-Dec excl Xmas/New Year, B&B per person, single from £32.50, double from £32.50.

HOTEL

New Hall, University of St Andrews

North Haugh, St Andrews, Fife, KY16 9XW
Tel:01334 467000 Fax:01334 467001
Email:new.hall@st-andrews.ac.uk
Web:www.escapetotranquillity.com

New Hall offers quality en-suite facilities and excellent standards of food and service in rooms specially upgraded for summer. Within easy walking distance of the beach, golf courses and town centre, it's ideal for golfers, families, short breaks and holidays.

72 rooms, all en-suite, Open Jun-Sep, B&B per person, single from £45.50, double from £34.00, BB & Eve.Meal from £45.25 (based on double occupancy).

Important: Prices stated are estimates and may be subject to amendments

St Andrews, Fife

Map Ref: 2D2

Old Course Hotel, Golf Resort & Spa

St Andrews, Fife, KY16 9SP
Telephone: 01334 474371 Fax: 01334 477668
e.mail: reservations@oldcoursehotel.co.uk
web: www.oldcoursehotel.co.uk

Situated alongside the 17th fairway of the legendary Old Course, this stunning international hotel has five red stars and is a two-minute stroll from the heart of St Andrews and West Sands beach. Offering a luxurious new Spa, the 18 hole championship Duke's Golf Course and an enticing choice of restaurants.

INTERNATIONAL RESORT

Old Course Hotel, Golf Resort & Spa

St Andrews, Fife, KY16 9SP
Tel:01334 474371 Fax:01334 477668
Email:reservations@oldcoursehotel.co.uk
Web:www.oldcoursehotel.co.uk

Overlooking the famous 17th Fairway, the Old Course Hotel, Golf Resort & Spa blends the elegant with the strikingly modern. Enjoy superb cuisine and international atmosphere in the resort's many restaurants and bars. The hotel also boasts its own championship 18 hole course, the Dukes Course, and newly refurbished spa.

146 rooms, all en-suite, Open Jan-Dec, B&B per person, single from £230.00, double from £123.00, BB & Eve.Meal from £163.00 (double).

C £ W V

GUEST HOUSE

The Old Station Country Guest House

Stravithie Bridge, St Andrews, KY16 8LR
Tel:01334 880505 Fax:01334 880622
Email:info@theoldstation.co.uk
Web:www.theoldstation.co.uk

Deluxe accommodation in converted Victorian railway station and train carriage, within 2 acres of peaceful gardens only 2 miles from St Andrews. Roaring log fire, candlelight, fresh flowers make this a luxury home from home.

8 rooms, Open Jan-Dec, B&B per person, single from £50.00, room only single from £50.00, double from £80.00, family from £110.00.

C £ V

GUEST HOUSE

Riverview Guest House

Edenside, St Andrews, Fife, KY16 9SQ
Tel:01334 838009 Fax:01334 839944
Email:admin@riverviewguesthouse.co.uk
Web:www.riverviewguesthouse.co.uk

All rooms ensuite, opening on to courtyard, all extensive views across Eden Estuary. 3 miles (5km) from St Andrews handy for many golf courses. Dining room and 3 bedrooms have level access from car park and are spacious.

7 rooms, Open Jan-Dec, B&B per person single from £40.00, double from £25.00, family from £25.00, room only single from £40.00, double from £50.00, family from £60.00.

C £ V

HOTEL

Rufflets Country House Hotel

Strathkinness Low Road, St Andrews, Fife, KY16 9TX
Tel:01334 472594 Fax:01334 478703
Email:reservations@rufflets.co.uk
Web:www.rufflets.co.uk

Country house with relaxing ambience, set in 10 acres of beautiful gardens. Fresh seasonal produce served in the restaurant. 1.5 miles (3kms) from golf courses and coast. 'Small Luxury Hotels of the World Member'.

25 rooms, all en-suite, Open Jan-Dec, B&B per person, single from £125.00, double from £99.50, BB & Eve.Meal from £127.50.

C £ V

VAT is shown at 17.5%: changes in this rate may affect prices.

Key to symbols is on back flap.

St Andrews, Fife

Map Ref: 2D2

INTERNATIONAL RESORT

St Andrews Bay Golf Resort & Spa

St Andrews, Fife, KY16 8PN
Tel:01334 837000 Fax:01334 471115
Email:info@standrewsbay.com Web:www.standrewsbay.com

It provides an international standard of service and attention to detail in the comfort and convenience of a modern world-class resort. The extensive facilities, including 209 deluxe guest rooms, five restaurants each with their own individual character and style, 36 holes of great golf, a reviving spa offering a wide range of luxurious treatments and an 18 metre indoor pool with sauna, steam-room and Jacuzzi.

209 rooms, all en-suite, Open Jan-Dec, B&B per person, double from £85.00, BB & Eve.Meal from £105.00.

GUEST HOUSE

West Park House

5 St Marys Place, St Andrews, Fife, KY16 9UY
Tel:01334 475933 Fax:01334 476634
Email:rosemary@westparksta.freeserve.co.uk
Web:www.westpark-standrews.co.uk

Beautiful Listed Georgian house c1830 in heart of historic town. Close to Old Course and all amenities. Sandy beaches close by and within easy reach of the pretty East Neuk fishing villages (approx 10 miles).

4 rooms, 3 en-suite, Open Jan-Dec excl Xmas/New Year, B&B per person, single from £45.00, double from £30.00.

GUEST HOUSE

Yorkston Guest House

68-70 Argyle Street, St Andrews, Fife, KY16 9BU
Tel:01334 472019
Email:yorkstonhouse@aol.com
Web:www.yorkstonhouse.co.uk

Privately owned guest house with several spacious family rooms situated close to west port and town centre with easy access to golf course, shops, restaurants and cafe bars.

10 rooms, some en-suite, Open Apr-Nov, B&B per person, single from £36.00, double from £30.00.

by St Andrews, Fife

Map Ref: 2D2

INN

The Inn At Lathones

By Largoward, St Andrews, Fife, KY9 1JE
Tel:01334 840494 Fax:01334 840694
Email:Lathones@theinn.co.uk
Web:www.theinn.co.uk

Charming 400 year old Coaching Inn, just 5 miles from St Andrews. Sympathetically restored and enlarged. Offering modern comfort, great food and friendly people to look after your every need. Award winning chef - two AA rosettes - using freshest of local Scottish produce.

13 rooms, all en-suite, B&B per person, single from £110.00, double from £80.00.

Important: Prices stated are estimates and may be subject to amendments

Stanley, Perthshire

Map Ref: 2B2

SMALL HOTEL

The Tayside Hotel

51 Mill Street, Stanley, Perth, PH1 4NL
Tel:01738 828249 Fax:01738 827216
Email:info@tayside-hotel.co.uk
Web:www.tayside-hotel.co.uk

Edwardian Hotel in historic village of Stanley surrounded by beautiful scenery. Freshly prepared food using local produce and awards for its legendary Tayside Roast. An hour from Edinburgh, ideally located for golfing and fishing.

15 rooms, all en-suite, Open Jan-Dec excl Xmas/New Year, B&B per person, single from £42.00, double from £34.50.

TV P

C £ V

Welcome to Scotland

Aberdeen and Grampian Highlands – Scotland's Castle and Whisky Country

Sure, you'll find Scotland's crème de la crème of fortresses and single malts, but other prizes are for the taking. Aberdeen's nightlife, country towns favoured by the Royal family, and a dreamy coastline...

Balmoral Castle

Aberdeen is a city of tantalising possibilities. One mile is crammed with around 800 shops, the next mile leads to sandy beaches. Above the shopping glitterati of Union Street lies an old world resolutely cast in granite. The eclectic King's college and castellated Citadel at the Castlegate are just two of the architectural treasures to explore. Retrace the city's growth through fishing and offshore oil at the Maritime Museum, or admire the cream of Scottish painters housed in Aberdeen Art Gallery.

Turn to Martha's Bistro, La Bamba restaurant and The Moonfish Café for serious temptation in chilled surroundings. The mood lighting and chic décor continue in the style bars of Neo, Siberia and The Monkey House. Global flavours ensure that live music is never routine at The Lemon Tree, while Café Drummond regularly surprises with newcomers. And retreat to The Ministry, Babylon or The Priory for a dance odyssey.

Moving towards the Cairngorm Mountains, encounter a rich valley prized by the Royal Family. Queen Victoria gave Royal Deeside the thumbs up, acquiring Balmoral as the family's Highland estate. Open to the public in summer, Balmoral is part of the Victorian Heritage trail, encompassing Loch Muick, Crathie Church and Royal Lochnagar Distillery. Ballater, Braemar and other Deeside towns revel in fresh air, fine local foods and a wholesome spirit for adventure. It's a good thing too, because the Cairngorm Mountains are a frontier for mountain walkers who relish the grit of a Munro.

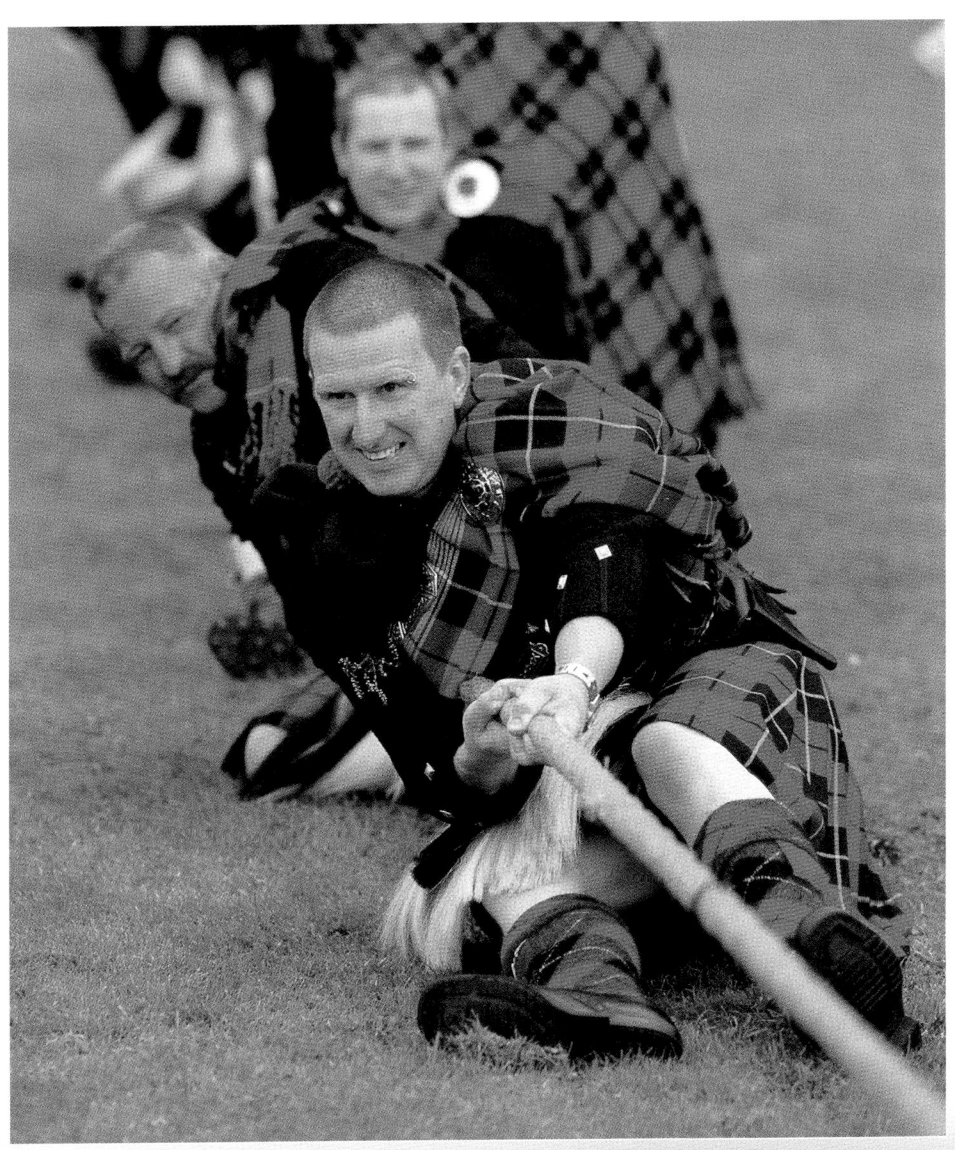

Heave! The clansmen 'Tug of War' competition at the Lonach Highland Games.

Aberdeen and Grampian Highlands – Scotland's Castle and Whisky Country

Sword dancing at the Ballater Highland Games.

Of course, you can't avoid the 350 odd castles in the area, but why would you? Each one has a distinct personality, from the imposing fortress walls of Kildrummy and Dunnottar, to the elegant furnishings of Crathes and Fyvie. Simply follow the signposted trail.

The other trail has become a pilgrimage for travellers throughout the world. Speyside has some sixty or so whisky distilleries within 15 square miles of barley fields and clear spring water. Follow the signposts marking the Malt Whisky trail to visit the famous seven: Benromach, Cardhu, Dallas Dhu (now a distillery museum), Glen Grant, Strathisla, the Glenlivet, and Glenfiddich. Learn how to spot the peat and oak tannins through a wee dram at the end of a distillery tour – or seven.

The narrow and meandering coastline shifts from sand dunes to dramatic cliffs, bonny fishing villages to rich ecosystems. Envy bottle-nosed dolphins leaping through the Moray Firth, or come face-to-beak with an octopus at the Macduff Marine Museum. Perhaps surfing? The waves of Balmedie beach are mesmerising, but then, you can have fun by doing nothing at all.

Events

Aberdeen and Grampian Highlands – Scotland's Castle and Whisky Country

7-12 MARCH
JAZZ ABERDEEN
An international jazz festival with a classy reputation.
Tel: 01224 619770
www.jazzaberdeen.com

27 APRIL-1 MAY
SPIRIT OF SPEYSIDE WHISKY FESTIVAL
A celebration of the "water of life" in whisky country. The festival blends whisky, music, food and fun into an irresistible cocktail with something for everyone.
Tel: 01343 542666
www.spiritofspeyside.com

20-26 MAY
BALLATER ROYAL DEESIDE WALKING WEEK
Annual week-long event on Deeside and the Grampians with 3 graded walks each day to suit all abilities.
Tel: 01339 755467
www.royal-deeside.org.uk

10 JUNE
TASTE OF GRAMPIAN, Inverurie
This food festival celebrates the richness and diversity of Grampians larder.
Tel: 0131 335 6200
www.tasteofgrampian.co.uk

8-9 JULY
SCOTTISH TRADITIONAL BOAT FESTIVAL, Portsoy
One of the largest rallies of traditional sailing craft in the UK plus a full programme of vents.
Tel: 01261 842894
www.scottishtraditionalboat festival.co.uk

2-12 AUGUST
ABERDEEN INTERNATIONAL YOUTH FESTIVAL
International multi arts festival featuring the best in youth talent.
Tel: 01224 213800
www.aiyf.org

26 AUGUST
LONACH GATHERING, Strathdon
Highland gathering including the march of the Lonach Highlanders.
Tel: 01975 651297
www.lonach.org

2 SEPTEMBER
BRAEMAR GATHERING
Grand finale of the Highland games calendar.
Tel: 01339 755377
www.braemargathering.org

28-29 OCTOBER
ARCHAEOLINK EVENTS, Oyne
Go back to the dawn of civilisation with ancient events at this Prehistory Park, including a Wickerman festival.
Tel: 01464 851500
www.archaeolink.co.uk

31 DECEMBER
STONEHAVEN FIREBALL FESTIVAL
Dramatic fireball 'swinging' New Year display.
Tel: 01569 764647
www.stonehavenfireballs.co.uk

** denotes provisional date, event details are subject to change please check before travelling*

The Still Room of Glenfiddich Distillery.

Aberdeen and Grampian Highlands – Scotland's Castle and Whisky Country

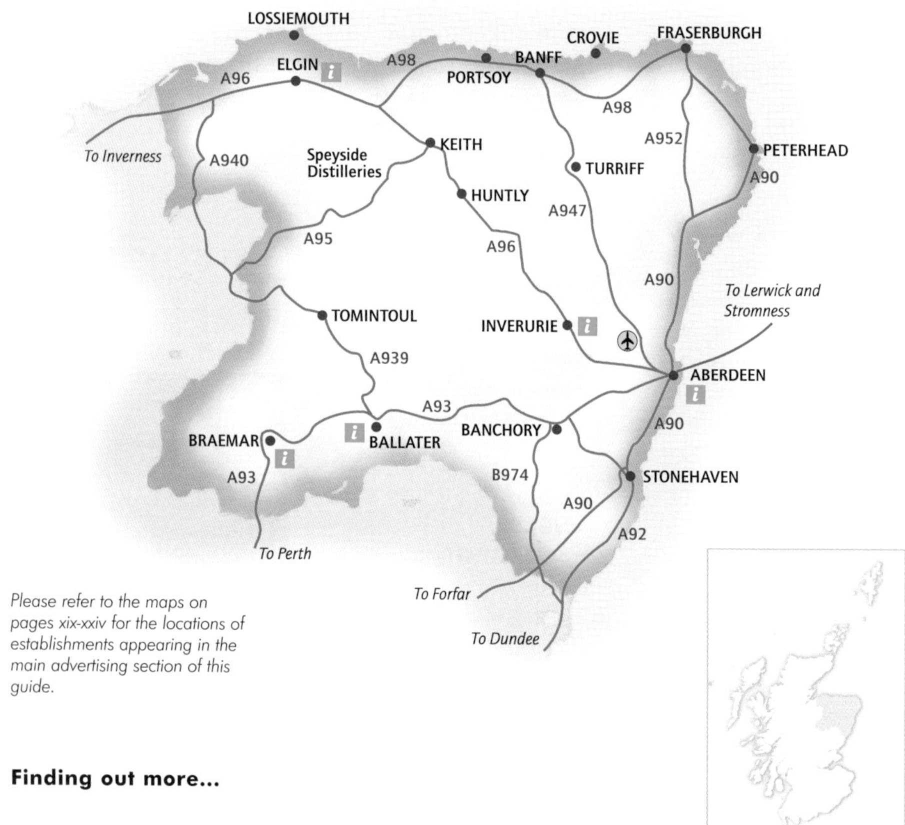

Please refer to the maps on pages xix-xxiv for the locations of establishments appearing in the main advertising section of this guide.

Finding out more...

For practical advice, ideas and information about exploring Scotland and to book your accommodation:

Tel: 0845 22 55 121*
or if calling from outside the UK: +44 (0) 1506 832121

Email: info@visitscotland.com
Web: www.visitscotland.com

* A £3 booking fee applies to telephone bookings of accommodation.

Tourist Information Centres

Aberdeen and Grampian Highlands – Scotland's Castle and Whisky Country

Aberdeen and Grampian

Aberdeen
23 Union Street
Tel: (01224) 288828
Jan – Dec

Alford
Railway Museum
Station Yard
Tel: (01975) 562052
Easter – Oct

Ballater
Albert Hall
Station Square
Tel: (01339) 755306
Jan – Dec

Banchory
Bridge Street
Tel: (01330) 822000
Easter – Oct

Banff
Collie Lodge
Tel: (01261) 812419
Easter – Oct

Braemar
The Mews
Tel: (01339) 741600
Jan – Dec

Crathie
Markethill Car Park
Tel: (01339) 742414
Easter-Oct

Dufftown
Clock Tower
The Square
Tel: (01340) 820501
Easter – Oct

Elgin
17 High Street
Tel: (01343) 542666/543388
Jan – Dec

Forres
116 High Street
Tel: (01309) 672938
Easter – Oct

Fraserburgh
3 Saltoun Square
Tel: (01346) 518315
Easter – Oct

Huntly
9a The Square
Tel: (01466) 792255
Easter – Oct

Inverurie
18 High Street
Tel: (01467) 625800
Jan – Dec

Stonehaven
66 Allardice Street
Tel: (01569) 762806
Easter – Oct

Tomintoul
The Square
Tel: (01807) 580285
Easter – Oct

Aberdeen

Map Ref: 4G10

HOTEL

Aberdeen Northern Hotel

1 Great Northern Road, Aberdeen, AB24 3PS
Tel:01224 483342 Fax:01224 276103
Email:info@aberdeennorthernhotel.com
Web:www.aberdeennorthernhotel.com

Unique grade A listed Art Deco hotel, located near city centre and a short distance from the airport. Ideal for business or pleasure. Conference and seminar facilities available. Choice of dining in the Astoria Restaurant or in Ellington's bar diner.

32 rooms, all en-suite, Open Jan-Dec. Prices on request.

HOTEL

Aberdeen Patio Hotel

Beach Boulevard, Aberdeen, AB24 5EF
Tel:01224 633339 Fax:01224 638833
Email:info@patiohotels.com
Web:www.patiohotels.com

One of Aberdeen's premier hotels located half a mile from the city centre and close to the beach front. Consisting of 90 standard double, 44 deluxe double and 34 premier club double bedrooms, with Atrium bar, full restaurant and conference facilities. In addition, all residents have full use of Breakers Leisure Club, which includes a gymnasium, spa, sauna and swimming pool. Almost 200 car parking spaces available.

168 rooms, all en-suite, B&B per person, single from £46.50, double from £31.50.

GUEST HOUSE

Aberdeen Springdale Guest House

404 Great Western Road, Aberdeen, AB10 6NR
Tel:01224 316561 Fax:01224 316561
Email:jamesestirling@msn.com
Web:www.aberdeenguesthouse.co.uk

Attractive granite house 2 miles (3kms) from city centre. On main bus routes, 5 miles (8kms) from the airport and on route to Royal Deeside. Private car parking at rear.

6 rooms, some en-suite, Open Jan-Dec excl Xmas/New Year, B&B per person, single from £25.00, double from £22.00.

GUEST HOUSE

Adelphi Guest House

8 Whinhill Road, Aberdeen, AB11 7XH
Tel:01224 583078/585434 Fax:01224 585434
Email:stay@adelphiguesthouse.com
Web:www.adelphiguesthouse.com

Family run guest house recently refurbished. Located at the end of Bon Accord Street centrally situated to all city amenities and an ideal base for both the business person and visitor.

5 rooms, some en-suite, Open Jan-Dec excl Xmas/New Year, B&B per person, single from £25.00, double from £17.50.

GUEST HOUSE

Allan Guest House

56 Polmuir Road, Aberdeen, AB11 7RT
Tel:01224 584484 Fax:01224 584484
Email:bookings@theallan.co.uk
Web:www.theallan.co.uk

A Victorian terraced house situated on a bus route to the city centre. A free parking area close to Duthie Park and Winter Gardens. Sociable owners who are keen to offer comfortable accommodation and warm hospitality. Wide choice available at breakfast. Special diets can be catered for.

3 rooms, all en-suite, Open Jan-Dec, B&B per person, single £40.00-45.00, king/double £30.00-35.00.

Aberdeen **Map Ref: 4G10**

GUEST HOUSE ★★

Antrim Guest House

157 Crown Street, Aberdeen, AB11 6HT
Tel/Fax:01224 590987

Situated close to city centre, railway and bus stations. Private parking.

6 rooms, Open Jan-Dec excl Xmas/New Year, B&B per person, single from £25.00, double/trebles from £20.00 pp.

C £ V

HOTEL ★★★★

Atholl Hotel

54 Kings Gate, Aberdeen, AB15 4YN
Tel:01224 323505 Fax:01224 321555
Email:info@atholl-aberdeen.co.uk
Web:www.atholl-aberdeen.com

Privately owned and managed hotel in the West End of Aberdeen, this distinctive building provides comfortable and well appointed accommodation, along with high standards of service, in a friendly and relaxed atmosphere. Extensive menu, bar, conference and function facilities available. Excellent base for exploring the city, and the countryside beyond.

34 rooms, all en-suite, Open Jan-Dec excl 1 Jan, B&B per person, single from £75.00, double from £60.00.

C £ W V

HOTEL ★★★

Brentwood Hotel

101 Crown Street, Aberdeen, AB11 6HH
Tel:01224 595440 Fax:01224 571593
Email:reservations@brentwood-hotel.co.uk
Web:www.brentwood-hotel.co.uk

Centrally situated personally run hotel, and within minutes of the city centre. 'Carriages' Brasserie and Bar with a la carte menu.

65 rooms, all en-suite, Open Jan-Dec excl Xmas/New Year, B&B per person, single £39.00-79.00, double £29.00-45.00.

C £ W V

HOTEL ★★★★

Copthorne Hotel Aberdeen

122 Huntly Street, Aberdeen, AB10 1SU
Tel:01224 630404 Fax:01224 640573
Email:reservations.aberdeen@mill-cop.com
Web:www.millenniumhotels.com

Traditional Aberdeen granite facade in the heart of the city. The Copthorne offers guests all the modern comfort, convenience and facilities both business and leisure visitors expect. Poachers Ocean and Steak Grill and Mac's Cocktail lounge bar.

89 rooms, all en-suite, Open Jan-Dec, B&B per person, single from £69.00, double from £35.00, BB & Eve.Meal from £54.00.

£ V

VAT is shown at 17.5%: changes in this rate may affect prices.

Key to symbols is on back flap.

Aberdeen

Map Ref: 4G10

HOTEL

Craighaar Hotel

Waterton Road, Bucksburn, Aberdeen, AB21 9HS
Tel:01224 712275 Fax:01224 716362
Email:info@craighaar.co.uk
Web:www.craighaarhotel.com

A charming hotel nestling in pleasant surroundings only 5 minutes from the airport and 15 minutes from the city centre. All 55 bedrooms are well appointed, with satellite TV, CD player and trouser press. The restaurant is renowned for quality cuisine and the hotel atmosphere is informal and relaxed. A courtesy bus to the airport is available by arrangement.

55 rooms, all en-suite, Open Jan-Dec excl Xmas/New Year, B&B per person, single from £45.00, double from £32.50.

CAMPUS ACCOMMODATION

Crombie Johnston Hall

University of Aberdeen, Aberdeen, AB24 3TT
Tel:01224 273444 Fax:01224 276246
Email:accommodation@abdn.ac.uk
Web:www.abdn.ac.uk/confevents

Ensuite and standard student accommodation available during summer period. Accommodation is located in historic Old Aberdeen within easy reach of the city centre. Breakfast included.

375 rooms (some en-suite), Open mid Jun-mid Sep, B&B per person from £20.50.

GUEST HOUSE

Crynoch Guest House

164 Bon-Accord Street, Aberdeen, AB10 2TX
Tel/Fax:01224 582743
Email:crynoch@btinternet.com

Crynoch Guest House is a family run Victorian guest house in a quiet residential street close to the city centre. This is a great location in which to explore the city, within walking distance of the main shopping and entertainment centres. Only 5 minutes away from River Dee and Duthie Park. A warm welcome awaits from proprietor Mrs Johnson who will make your stay pleasant and relaxing.

8 rooms, some en-suite, Open Jan-Dec excl Xmas/New Year, B&B per person, single £25.00-40.00, double £20.00-26.00.

SMALL HOTEL

Cults Hotel

328 North Deeside Road, Aberdeen, AB15 9SE
Tel:01224 867632 Fax:01224 867699
Email:info@thecultshotel.co.uk
Web:www.thecultshotel.co.uk

One of Aberdeen's oldest hotels refurbished to modern standards. Warm relaxing atmosphere. On the main road to Royal Deeside.

15 rooms, all en-suite, Open Jan-Dec, B&B per person, single from £50.00-70.00, double from £35.00-45.00 pppn. Special rates for long stay.

GUEST HOUSE

Ellenville Guest House

50 Springbank Terrace, Aberdeen, AB11 6LR
Tel/Fax:01224 213334
Email:ellenvillegh@aol.com
Web:www.ellenvilleguesthouse.co.uk

Terraced house very close to city centre. Convenient for bus/railway station, ferry terminal, theatre and all amenities. Families are very welcome.

7 rooms, 4 en-suite, Open Jan-Dec, B&B per person, single from £25.00, double from £23.00.

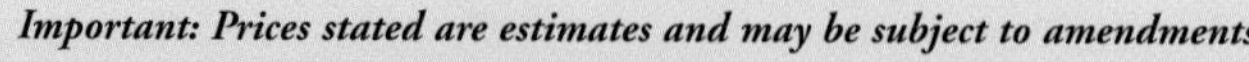

Important: Prices stated are estimates and may be subject to amendments

Aberdeen

Map Ref: 4G10

GUEST HOUSE

Furain Guest House

92 North Deeside Road, Peterculter, Aberdeen, AB14 0QN
Tel:01224 732189 Fax:01224 739070
Email:furain@btinternet.com

8 rooms, all en-suite, Open Jan-Dec excl Xmas/New Year, B&B per person, single from £33.00, double from £23.00.

Late Victorian house built of red granite. Family run. Convenient for town, Royal Deeside and the Castle Trail. Private car parking. Dinner available on Wednesday, Friday and Saturday.

GUEST HOUSE

Greyholme Guest House

35 Springbank Terrace, Aberdeen, AB11 6LR
Tel:01224 587081
Email:greyholme@talk21.com

5 rooms, Open Jan-Dec, B&B per person, single from £27.00, double/twin from £21.00.

Personally run guest house close to city centre and all amenities. Near to main bus routes. Off street parking available.

HOTEL

Maryculter House Hotel

South Deeside Road, Maryculter, Aberdeenshire, AB12 5GB
Tel:01224 732124 Fax:01224 733510
Email:reservations@maryculterhousehotel.com
Web:www.maryculterhousehotel.com

40 rooms, all en-suite, Open Jan-Dec excl Xmas/New Year, B&B per person, single from £45.00, double from £35.00.

Step back in time to days of Lairds, Castles and Clans and experience first hand the lifestyle of Scottish Nobility. Home to Knights Templar, set in acres of woodland and landscaped gardens on the banks of the River Dee. Ideally positioned for over forty quality golf courses with Royal Deeside on the doorstep. Explore the Castle and Whisky trails, maybe even take in some fishing. Traditional hospitality and modern comforts await you in this historic setting.

GUEST HOUSE

Penny Meadow Private Hotel

189 Great Western Road, Aberdeen, AB10 6PS
Tel:01224 588037 Fax:01224 573639
Email:frances@pennymeadow.freeserve.co.uk

3 rooms, all en-suite, Open Jan-Dec, B&B per person, single from £34.00-46.00, double from £25.00-35.00.

A high quality purpose built Guest House with all ensuite bedrooms and off road parking. For the discerning visitor looking for a warm, friendly atmosphere, comfortable accommodation and that little bit extra attention to detail.

HOTEL

The Queen's Hotel

49-53 Queen's Road, Aberdeen, AB15 4YP
Tel:01224 209999 Fax:01224 209009
Email:enquiries@the-queens-hotel.com
Web:www.the-queens-hotel.com

34 rooms, all en-suite, Open Jan-Dec excl Xmas/New Year, B&B per person, single from £45.00, double from £27.50.

Occupying an enviable location in the heart of the West End of Aberdeen, this family run city centre hotel offers modern comforts in the traditional style. All bedrooms have ensuite bath and shower and there is ample parking. A range of function suites and conference facilities.

Aberdeen

Map Ref: 4G10

Royal Hotel

1-3 Bath Street, Aberdeen, AB11 6BJ
Tel:01224 585152 Fax:01224 583900
Email:info@royalhotel.uk.com
Web:www.royalhotel.uk.com

Located right in the centre of Aberdeen and a short walk from the railway station, the Royal Hotel provides friendly atmosphere and comfortable accommodation, (with food served all day). There is a limited amount of private parking available. Good base for the business traveller, or for weekend breaks, to enjoy the city and all its attractions.

42 rooms, all en-suite, Open Jan-Dec, B&B per person, single from £44.00, double from £24.50.

Speedbird Inn

Argyll Road, Aberdeen Airport, Dyce, AB21 0AF
Tel:01224 772883 Fax:01224 772560
Email:reception@speedbirdinns.co.uk
Web:www.speedbirdinns.co.uk

Modern comfortably furnished airport hotel offering facilities expected by todays traveller. 'WiFi' available in public areas and Speedbird Plus rooms. Free 7 channel TV in all rooms. Courtesy transport for surrounding area and airport terminals.

159 rooms, all en-suite, Open Jan-Dec, B&B per person, single from £43.75, double from £23.75.

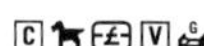

University of Aberdeen, King's Hall

College Bounds, Aberdeen, AB24 3TT
Tel:01224 273444 Fax:01224 276246
Email:accommodation@abdn.ac.uk
Web:www.abdn.ac.uk/confevents

Modern hotel style accommodation located in historic Old Aberdeen. Rooms are available year round, are all ensuite and include a TV, hairdryer, telephone and trouser press. Breakfast is also included within the Zeste restaurant. Guests at King's Hall have access to leisure facilities on the campus during their stay.

65 rooms, all en-suite, Open Jan-Dec excl Xmas/New Year, B&B per room, single from £42.00, twin from £59.00.

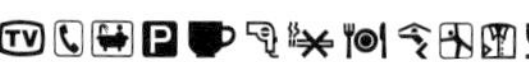

nr Aberdeen

Map Ref: 4G10

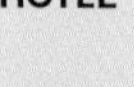

The Belvedere Hotel

41 Evan Street, Stonehaven, Aberdeenshire, AB39 2ET
Tel:01569 762672 Fax:01569 767686
Email:gordonflett@aol.com

The Belvedere is a small hotel a short walk from the town centre, trains and bus station. The hotel offers a comfortable base to explore Dunnatar Castle, the harbour, nearby Aberdeen and Royal Deeside. Beer Garden and full meal service available.

9 rooms, some en-suite, Open Jan-Dec, B&B per person, single from £25.00, double from £25.00, BB & Eve.Meal from £35.00.

Old Mill Inn

South Deeside Road, Maryculter, Aberdeen, AB12 5FX
Tel:01224 733212 Fax:01224 732884
Email:info@oldmillinn.co.uk
Web:www.oldmillinn.co.uk

A friendly and informal family run country inn under the personal attention of the owners Mr Victor Sang and Mr Michael French. Conveniently located only 5 miles from Aberdeen on the edge of the River Dee and well-known for its wholesome dishes using fresh local produce.

7 rooms, all en-suite, Open Jan-Dec, B&B per person, single from £49.00, double from £29.50.

Important: Prices stated are estimates and may be subject to amendments

nr Aberdeen

Map Ref: 4G10

HOTEL ★★★★

Strathburn Hotel

Burghmuir Drive, Inverurie, Aberdeenshire, AB51 4GY
Tel:01467 624422 Fax:01467 625133
Email:strathburn@btconnect.com
Web:www.strathburn-hotel.co.uk

Modern hotel and restaurant with friendly atmosphere, overlooking Strathburn Park in Inverurie. Personally run.

25 rooms, all en-suite, Open 3 Jan-Dec 31, B&B per person, single from £55.00, double from £37.50, BB & Eve.Meal from £57.50.

Ballater, Aberdeenshire

Map Ref: 4E11

RESTAURANT WITH ROOMS

Auld Kirk Hotel & Johnson's Restaurant

Braemar Road, Ballater, Aberdeenshire, AB35 5RQ
Tel/Fax:013397 55762
Email:info@auldkirkhotel.com
Web:www.auldkirkhotel.com

Hotel converted from old church, still retaining many original features. Located in scenic splendour and easy walking distance from village centre. A central location for touring Royal Deeside with an award winning restaurant featuring local Scottish produce.

6 rooms, all en-suite, Open Jan-Dec excl Xmas/New Year, B&B per person, single from £40.00, double from £30.00.

SMALL HOTEL

Cambus O'May Hotel

nr Ballater, Aberdeenshire, AB35 5SE
Tel/Fax:013397 55428
Email:mckechnie@cambusomay.freeserve.co.uk
Web:www.cambusomayhotel.co.uk

Family owned and traditionally run country house hotel dating from the 1870's set amongst its own grounds, 4 miles from Ballater. Very popular with many regular guests. Quality freshly prepared food making use of local produce with the menu changing daily.

12 rooms, all en-suite, Open Jan-Dec, B&B per person, single from £33.00, double from £33.00, BB & Eve.Meal from £51.00.

by Ballater, Aberdeenshire

Map Ref: 4E11

HOTEL

Loch Kinord Hotel

Ballater Road, Dinnet, Royal Deeside, Aberdeenshire, AB34 5JY
Tel:013398 85229 Fax:013398 87007
Email:stay@lochkinord.com Web:www.lochkinord.com

Under the enthusiastic new ownership of Jenny and Andrew Cox the hotel has undergone public areas refurbishment featuring some 4 poster bedrooms with all modern facilities. Situated in the centre of this small village it makes a great base for exploring Royal Deeside, skiing, walking, and playing golf. The hotel is popular in the area for excellent food from their AA rosette restaurant. Non-residents very welcome.

21 rooms, en-suite, Open Jan-Dec, B&B per person, single from £30.00, double from £30.00, BB & Eve.Meal from £49.50.

VAT is shown at 17.5%: changes in this rate may affect prices.

Key to symbols is on back flap.

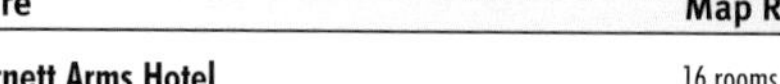

Banchory, Aberdeenshire

Map Ref: 4F11

SMALL HOTEL

The Burnett Arms Hotel

25 High Street, Banchory, Aberdeenshire, AB31 5TD
Tel:01330 824944 Fax:01330 825553
Email:theburnett@btconnect.com
Web:www.burnettarms.co.uk

Former 19c coaching inn situated at the centre of a small, attractive gateway town to Royal Deeside. An ideal base for touring numerous local attractions.

16 rooms, all en-suite, Open Jan-Dec, B&B per person, single £44.00-69.00, double £32.00-48.00.

HOTEL

Raemoir House Hotel

Banchory, Aberdeenshire, AB31 4ED
Tel:01330 824884 Fax:01330 822171
Email:relax@raemoir.com
Web:www.raemoir.com

Dating from 16c, country house on a 3,500 acre estate. We offer shooting, salmon fishing by prior arrangement, tennis, and 9 hole mini-golf. Tranquility, health and beauty salon.

20 rooms, all en-suite, Open Jan-Dec, B&B per person, single from £76.00, double from £50.00.

Banff

Map Ref: 4F7

SMALL HOTEL

Carmelite House Hotel

Low Street, Banff, AB45 1AY
Tel/Fax:01261 812152
Email:carmelitehoho@aol.com
Web:www.northeastscotlandhotels.com

Family run Georgian town house in central location. Convenient for golf and all amenities. Evening meals available. Cosy residents bar. Private parking.

9 rooms, most en-suite, Open Jan-Dec, B&B per person, single from £25.00, double/twin from £22.50.

Braemar, Aberdeenshire

Map Ref: 4D11

GUEST HOUSE

Callater Lodge Guest House

9 Glenshee Road, Braemar, Aberdeenshire, AB35 5YQ
Tel:013397 41275 Fax:013397 41345
Email:laura2@hotel-braemar.co.uk
Web:www.hotel-braemar.co.uk

A warm welcome awaits you at this pleasant Victorian house in its own spacious grounds. Ideal centre for touring and walking. Close to village centre. 8 miles to Balmoral Castle and Glenshee Ski Centre. Take advantage of our snack menu and enjoy the benefits of our residents lounge.

6 rooms, all en-suite, Open Jan-Oct, B&B per person, single from £28.00, double from £26.00.

Important: Prices stated are estimates and may be subject to amendments

Braemar, Aberdeenshire

Map Ref: 4D11

GUEST HOUSE

Clunie Lodge Guest House

Cluniebank Road, Braemar, Aberdeenshire, AB35 5ZP
Tel:013397 41330
Email:karen@clunielodge.com
Web:www.clunielodge.com

Victorian former manse house peacefully located close to village centre and short drive to golf course. Ideal base for walking, touring and golfing & ski-ing.

5 rooms with en-suite/private facilities, Open Jan-Dec, B&B per person, single from £26.00, double from £23.00.

HOTEL

Invercauld Arms

Main Street, Braemar, Aberdeenshire, AB35 5YR
Tel:01942 824824
Email:reservations@WAshearings.com
Web:www.shearingsholidays.com

This famous and historic building in Royal Deeside is furnished to provide traditional Scottish hospitality in sumptuous surroundings.

66 rooms, all en-suite, Open Feb-Dec, B&B per person, single from £35.00, double from £35.00, BB & Eve.Meal from £45.00.

GUEST HOUSE

Schiehallion House

10 Glenshee Road, Braemar, Aberdeenshire, AB35 5YQ
Tel:013397 41679
Email:bookings@schiehallionhouse.com
Web:www.schiehallionhouse.com

Comfortable, tastefully decorated, Victorian house with attractive garden at gateway to Royal Deeside. Offering personal service and log fires. One ground floor annexe room. All nationalities welcome.

9 rooms, some en-suite, Open Jan-Oct, B&B per person, single from £25.00, double from £21.00.

Cruden Bay, Aberdeenshire

Map Ref: 4H9

SMALL HOTEL

Kilmarnock Arms Hotel

Bridge Street, Cruden Bay, by Peterhead, AB42 0HD
Tel:01779 812213 Fax:01779 812153
Email:reception@kilmarnockarms.com
Web:www.kilmarnockarms.com

Traditional Victorian village hotel, providing comfortable and recently upgraded accommodation for business travellers, golfers and families. Many activities available in the area - walking, birdwatching, historic houses and much more.

14 rooms, all en-suite, Open Jan-Dec excl Xmas/New Year, B&B per person, single from £40.00, double from £30.00.

VAT is shown at 17.5%: changes in this rate may affect prices.

Key to symbols is on back flap.

Cullen, Moray

Map Ref: 4E7

The Seafield Hotel

Seafield Street, Cullen AB56 4SG
Tel: 01542 840791 Fax: 01542 840736
e.mail: stay@theseafieldhotel.com Web: www.theseafieldhotel.com

The Seafield renowned for its fresh seafood, game, wines and collection of malt whiskies, comfortable surroundings and friendly service, the ideal place to relax and let the world go by. Situated in the village of Cullen, overlooking the Moray coast, beaches, golf, the castle trail and the famous whisky trail. AA ★★★

★★★ HOTEL

The Seafield Hotel

Seafield Street, Cullen, Banffshire, AB56 4SG
Tel:01542 840791 Fax:01542 840736
Email:stay@theseafieldhotel.com
Web:www.theseafieldhotel.com

A warm friendly welcome at this family run hotel in the centre of a small town on the Moray coast. Ideal location for golfing, walking and exploring the whisky trail. Midway between Inverness and Aberdeen. AA 3 stars One Rosette. Hospitality assured.

19 rooms, all en-suite, Open Jan-Dec, B&B per person, single from £50.00, double from £40.00.

Elgin, Moray

Map Ref: 4D8

★★★ GUEST HOUSE

Auchmillan Guest House

12 Reidhaven Street, Elgin, IV30 1QG
Tel:01343 549077 Fax:01343 569164
Email:auchmillan@hotmail.co.uk

Victorian villa with garden in conservation area of Elgin, quietly situated yet close to town centre and all amenities.

8 rooms, all en-suite, Open Jan-Dec excl Xmas/New Year, B&B per person, single from £30.00, double from £23.00.

★★★ HOTEL

Eight Acres Hotel & Leisure Club

Morriston Road, Elgin, Moray, IV30 6UL
Tel:01343 543077 Fax:01343 540001
Email:enquiries@eightacreshotel.com
Web:www.eightacreshotel.com

Modern hotel set in landscaped grounds on the western approach to Elgin. Swimming pool, sauna, squash courts, spa bath and games room.

53 rooms, all en-suite, Open Jan-Dec excl Xmas, B&B per person, single from £45.00, double from £40.00.

★★★ HOTEL

Sunninghill Hotel

Hay Street, Elgin, Moray, IV30 1NH
Tel:01343 547799 Fax:01343 547872
Email:wross@sunninghillhotel.com
Web:www.sunninghillhotel.com

Victorian house, modern extension with annexe accommodation. Near centre of historic Cathedral town. Many golf courses. Sandy beaches 5 miles (8kms).

21 rooms, all en-suite, Open Jan-Dec, B&B per person, single from £40.00, double from £32.50.

Important: Prices stated are estimates and may be subject to amendments

Elgin, Moray

Map Ref: 4D8

GUEST HOUSE

West End Guest House

282 High Street, Elgin, IV30 1AQ
Tel:01343 549629
Email:westend.house@virgin.net

Traditional Victorian villa with garden, close to A96. 10 minute walk from city centre and all amenities.

6 rooms, some en-suite, Open Jan-Dec, B&B per person, single £25.00-35.00, double £25.00-27.00.

Forres, Moray

Map Ref: 4C8

B&B

April Rise

16 Forbes Road, Forres, Moray, IV36 1HP
Tel:01309 674066

Traditional Scottish hospitality in friendly family home. 2 rooms ensuite. Short walk to town and all amenities. Ideal base for the castle and whisky trails, and the coastal villages.

3 rooms, some en-suite, Open Jan-Dec excl Xmas/New Year, B&B per person, single from £25.00, double from £22.50.

★★★★

SMALL HOTEL

Knockomie Hotel

Grantown Road, Forres, Moray, IV36 2SG
Tel:01309 673146 Fax:01309 673290
Email:stay@knockomie.co.uk
Web:www.knockomie.co.uk

A 'B' listed country house c1914, built in an arts and crafts style. Extended and created to a high standard, retaining much warmth and character.

15 rooms, all en-suite, Open Jan-Dec excl Xmas, B&B per person, single £108.00-135.00, double £71.50-93.00.

B&B

Morven

Caroline Street, Forres, Moray, IV36 1AN
Tel/Fax:01309 673788
Email:morven2@globalnet.co.uk
Web:www.golfgreenfees.com/morven/

Victorian house offering bed and breakfast in a warm friendly atmosphere, with all conveniences. Town centre location. En-suite bedrooms. Off-street parking. Ideal location for exploring the Whisky Trail, castles and Moray coast.

2 ensuite, 1 standard room, Bed&Breakfast per person, ensuite twin £22.00, ensuite single £30.00, standard double £20.00, single £27.00.

HOTEL

Ramnee Hotel

Victoria Road, Forres, Moray, IV36 3BN
Tel:01309 672410 Fax:01309 673392
Email:info@ramneehotel.com
Web:www.ramneehotel.com

Charming Edwardian Mansion in mature gardens close to town centre and golf course offering delightful accommodation, friendly service and superb cuisine.

19 rooms, all en-suite, Open Jan-Dec excl Xmas/New Year, B&B per person, single from £70.00, double from £47.50.

Kildrummy, Aberdeenshire

Map Ref: 4E10

HOTEL

Kildrummy Castle Hotel

Kildrummy, Alford, Aberdeenshire, AB33 8RA
Tel:019755 71288 Fax:019755 71345
Email:bookings@kildrummycastlehotel.co.uk
Web:www.kildrummycastlehotel.co.uk

Traditional Scottish mansion house set amidst acres of gardens and woodland overlooking the original 13th century castle ruins. Tastefully furnished and decorated retaining original features. A la carte restaurant using finest local ingredients.

16 rooms, all en-suite, Open Feb-Dec, B&B per person, single from £80.00, double from £75.00, BB & Eve.Meal from £77.00. (Low season rate for a stay of 2 or more nights.)

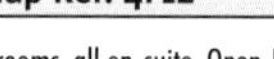

Laurencekirk, Kincardineshire

Map Ref: 4F12

INN

Marykirk Hotel

Main Street, Marykirk, Laurencekirk, Aberdeenshire, AB30 1UT
Tel:01674 840239
Email:marykirkhotel@tesco.net
Web:www.marykirkhotel.com

Small village hotel restaurant/lounge bar, village bar, breakfast room, beer garden, large car park at rear.

4 rooms, all en-suite, Open Jan-Dec excl Xmas/New Year, B&B per person, single from £30.00, double from £28.00.

Macduff, Aberdeenshire

Map Ref: 4F7

HOTEL

The Highland Haven

Shore Street, Macduff, Aberdeenshire, AB44 1UB
Tel:01261 832408 Fax:01261 833652
Email:highlandhaven@surfrer.co.uk
Web:www.highlandhaven.co.uk

Well appointed family run 40 bedroom hotel overlooking the Moray Firth. All bedrooms ensuite with satellite TV. etc. Golf, river and loch fishing, sea angling, Duff House (stately house and art gallery), Deep sea Aquarium, Aden Country Park, castle, coastal and whisky trails, nearby.

40 rooms, all en-suite, Open Jan-Dec, B&B per person, single from £35.00, double from £25.00, BB & Eve.Meal from £35.00.

Oldmeldrum, Aberdeenshire

Map Ref: 4G9

INN

The Redgarth

Kirk Brae, Oldmeldrum, Aberdeenshire, AB51 0DJ
Tel:01651 872353

Quality family run inn enjoying outstanding views of surrounding countryside. Our menu is home cooked using local produce and includes two vegetarian options. A selection of cask conditioned ales available.

3 rooms, all en-suite, Open Jan-Dec excl Xmas/New Year, B&B per person, single from £50.00, double from £35.00.

Peterhead, Aberdeenshire

Map Ref: 4H8

GUEST HOUSE

Carrick Guest House

16 Merchant Street, Peterhead, Aberdeenshire, AB42 1DU
Tel/Fax:01779 470610

Comfortable accommodation, centrally situated for all amenities. Two minutes walk from main shopping centre, harbour and beach. Convenient for maritime museum, lighthouse museum and several nearby golf courses.

6 rooms, all en-suite, Open Jan-Dec excl Xmas/New Year, B&B per person, single from £22.00, double from £22.00.

Important: Prices stated are estimates and may be subject to amendments

Portsoy, Banffshire

Map Ref: 4F7

SMALL HOTEL

The Boyne Hotel Portsoy

2 North High Street, Portsoy, Aberdeenshire, AB45 2PA
Tel/Fax:01261 842242
Email:enquiries@boynehotel.co.uk
Web:www.boynehotel.co.uk

Refurbished 18c building on Square in seaside town, close to harbour and sandy seaside. Home cooking. Under personal supervision.

12 rooms, all en-suite, Open Jan-Dec, B&B per person, single £20.00-25.00, double £20.00-25.00, BB & Eve.Meal from £27.50-35.00.

SMALL HOTEL

The Station Hotel Portsoy

Seafield Street, Portsoy, Aberdeenshire, AB45 2QT
Tel:01261 842327 Fax:01261 842975
Email:enquiries@stationhotelportsoy.co.uk
Web:www.stationhotelportsoy.co.uk

Friendly, family-run hotel with a fine restaurant using the freshest, local produce, situated in the beautiful town of Portsoy on the Grampian coastal trail. Great location for golf, walking, dolphin watching etc. Golf parties welcome.

11 rooms, all en-suite including 4 family rooms, Open Jan-Dec, B&B per person, single from £30.00, double from £30.00 pp, BB & Eve.Meal from £40.00.

Rothienorman, Aberdeenshire

Map Ref: 4F9

INN

Rothie Inn

Main Street, Rothienorman, Aberdeenshire, AB51 8UD
Tel:01651 821206
Email:rothieinn@accom90.freeserve.co.uk

Family run 19c stone built inn located in the centre of the village, with own garden. 10 miles (16kms) north of Inverurie, situated on Castle Trail. Home cooking in a cosy lounge. Cosy ensuite bedrooms.

2 rooms, all en-suite, Open Jan-Dec excl Xmas/New Year, B&B per person, single from £30.00, double from £25.00.

Welcome to Scotland

The Highlands and Skye

Once, the Highlands weren't just separated from the Lowlands by rugged mountains, but through a different language and culture too. Now you'll find their influence worldwide, from caber tossing in outback Australia, to the Highland songs of Nepalese Gurkhas.

Mountain bikes and adrenalin race at the Nevis Range, Fort William.

The Highlands continue to inspire people throughout the world. To some, the turbulent past is a role model for strength of character. For others, the epic wilderness denotes a simpler way of life. And some just like the whisky.

Inverness is dubbed 'capital of the Highlands' for a good reason: intense shopping, nightlife and activities are condensed into a city ideally situated to nearby wilderness. Fresh vegetables, leanest venison, seafood straight from the harbour and scotch beef are exemplified by the Highlands, including this city. The Mustard seed, Riva, Rocpool and Zanzibar are a few ideas for eating out. Hootenany offers live music of a Gaelic lilt; Bar Pivo and Barbazzas are softly lit style bars; and traditional pub fare is found at The Waterfront or picturesque Dores Inn. Johnny Foxes comes alive after dark, while Bakoo and Gs attract the clubbing crowd. When Sunday arrives, unwind on the sandy beaches of Nairn.

A short drive from Inverness will take you to the seminal battlefield of Culloden, where Bonnie Prince and the Jacobites faced-off with the Duke of Cumberland. A real turning point, clan authority was undermined and the Highland Clearances followed. Pursue the trail of history through a series of stunning castles: Urquhart's ancient ruins are perched on Loch

The Highlands and Skye

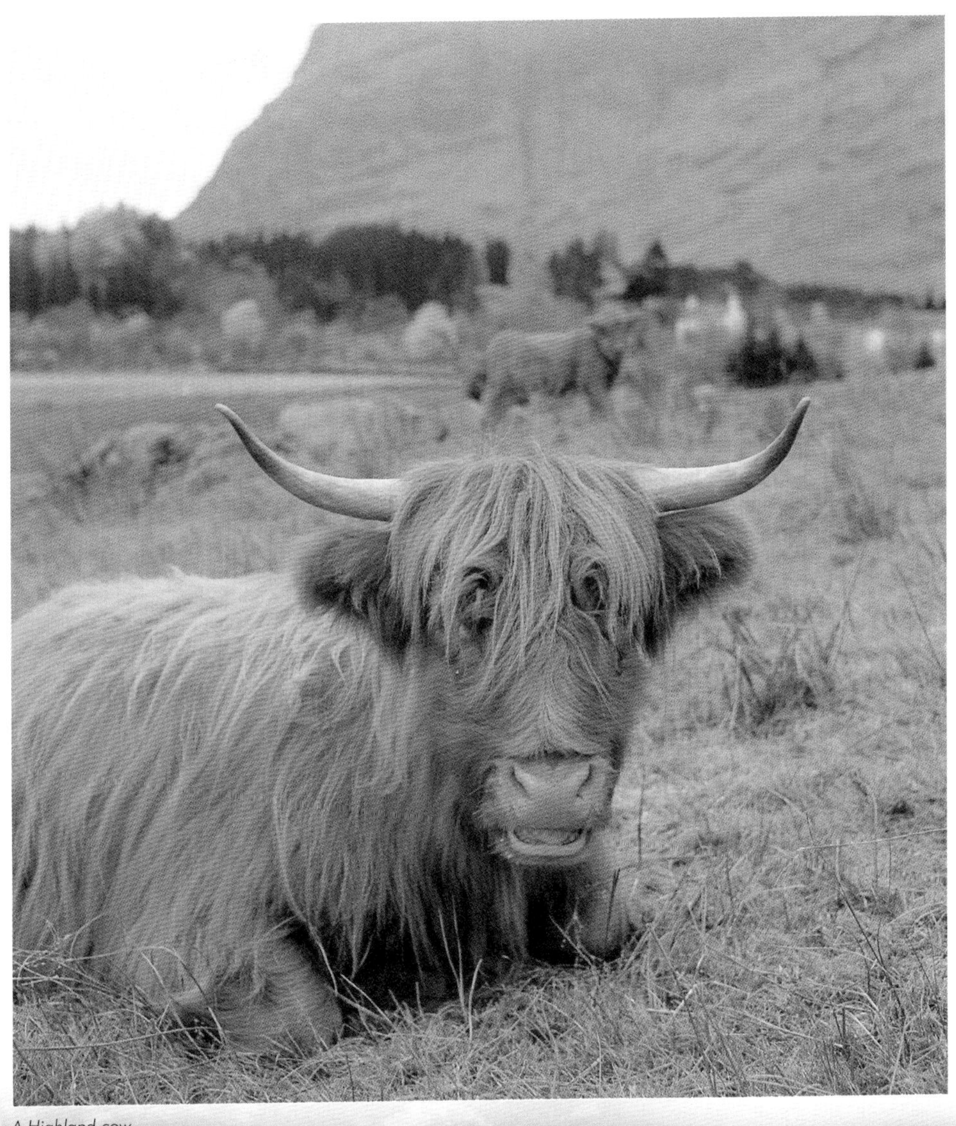

A Highland cow.

The Highlands and Skye

Red deer in the wilderness.

Ness; Eilean Donan draws photographers to the west coast; and Dunrobin espouses French grandeur in the shire of Sutherland.

Craving some action? Described as the outdoor capital of the UK, Fort William's reputation is founded on The Nevis Range. A gondola effortlessly lifts you to 2150ft on the north face of Aonach Mor, catching views of the Great Glen and towering Ben Nevis. Mountain biking, climbing and skiing are first-rate experiences. Moving east, Aviemore is another action town noted for skiing on the Cairngorm Mountains, plus rollicking nightlife.

Of course, The Highlands are regarded as Europe's last great wilderness. The Cairngorm Mountain National Park, Glencoe, Ardnamurchan and Glen Affric are intimidating or liberating – from different points of view. Vast skies and Scotch pines are a backdrop to wildlife, from birds of prey and red deer to wildcats and red squirrels. Signposted walks can range from a sedate meander to the 73 miles of the Great Glen Way, stretching from Fort William to Inverness.

It's not all mountains, there are character-rich towns to explore: Dornoch with its cathedral and famous championship golf course, and the Glenmorangie Distillery of Tain are just two examples. Continue north to encounter the flat lands of the Flow Country in Caithness and Sutherland.

Soft accents, gentle manners and the craggy ridges of the Cuillin Hills have made the Isle of Skye a dream getaway. While climbers and campers stake the hills, a trip to Dunvegan Castle and the Aros Experience will reveal the island's startling history.

Events

The Highlands and Skye

10-18 FEBRUARY
FORT WILLIAM FILM FESTIVAL
Delivers a world of celluloid through international film, lectures and activities.
www.mountainfilmfestival.co.uk

20 FEBRUARY-11 MARCH
INVERNESS MUSIC FESTIVAL
Instrumental and vocal performers compete in this major musical event.
Tel: 01463 716616

6-14 MAY
AVIEMORE WALKING FESTIVAL
A wide choice of guided walks from easy strolls in the forest floor to strenuous days out on the highest mountains, complimented by a full programme of entertainment.
www.aviemorewalking.com

13-21 MAY
CAITHNESS WALKING FESTIVAL
A variety of high and low level walks in the UK's most northerly county with superb wildlife watching and spectacular scenery.
Tel: 01847 851991
www.walkcaithness.com

20 MAY-4 JUNE
HIGHLAND WILD ENCOUNTERS, Caithness and Sutherland
An unrivalled opportunity to experience the wildlife of these unique islands through talks and walks.
Tel: 01847 821531
www.highlandwildencounters.com

3-4 JUNE*
MOUNTAIN BIKE WORLD CUP, Fort William
The world's best mountain bikers take part in the most gruelling mountain biking in the world.
Tel: 01397 705825
www.fortwilliamworldcup.co.uk

3-5 JUNE
GLEN AFFRIC WALKING FESTIVAL
Over 20 walks for all abilities centred around 2 National Nature Reserves and one bird reserve.
Tel: 01456 476363
www.glenaffric.info

JULY-SEPTEMBER
TALISKER SUMMER SESSIONS, Isle of Skye
Pubs and various venues jump with live bands and traditional melodies through summer months.
Tel: 01478 614003
www.skyemusic.org

2 SEPTEMBER
BEN NEVIS RACE, Fort William
Compete or just watch as the annual race up and down Britain's highest mountain unfolds.
www.bennevis.race.co.uk

** denotes provisional date, event details are subject to change please check before travelling.*

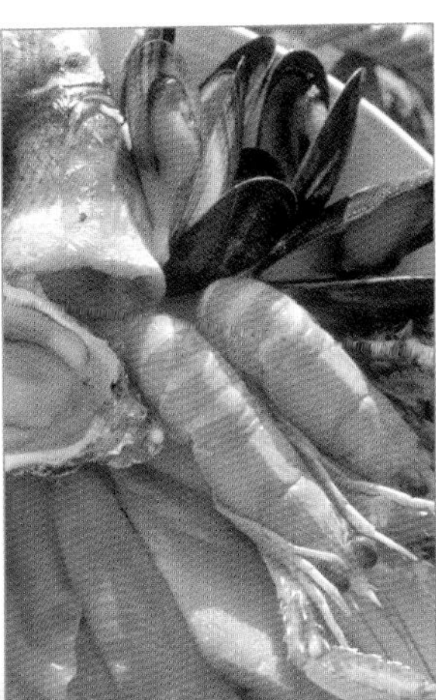

For seafood straight off the boat: Crannog Restaurant, Fort William.

The Highlands and Skye

Please refer to the maps on pages xix-xxiv for the locations of establishments appearing in the main advertising section of this guide.

Finding out more...

For practical advice, ideas and information about exploring Scotland and to book your accommodation:

Tel: 0845 22 55 121*
or if calling from outside the UK: +44 (0) 1506 832121

Email: info@visitscotland.com
Web: www.visitscotland.com

* A £3 booking fee applies to telephone bookings of accommodation.

Tourist Information Centres

The Highlands and Skye

The Highlands of Scotland

Aviemore
Grampian Road
Tel: (0845) 22 55 121
Jan – Dec

Daviot Wood
Picnic Area, A9
Tel: (0845) 22 55 121
Apr – Oct

Dornoch
The Square
Tel: (0845) 22 55 121
Jan – Dec

Drumnadrochit
The Car Park
Tel: (0845) 22 55 121
Easter – Oct

Dunvegan
2 Lochside
Tel: (0845) 22 55 121
Easter – Oct

Durness
Durine
Tel: (0845) 22 55 121
Easter – Oct

Fort Augustus
Car Park
Tel: (0845) 22 55 121
Apr – Oct

Fort William
Cameron Centre
Tel: (0845) 22 55 121
Jan – Dec

Grantown-on-Spey
54 High Street
Tel: (0845) 22 55 121
Jan – Dec

Inverness
Castle Wynd
Tel: (0845) 22 55 121
Jan – Dec

John O'Groats
County Road
Tel: (0845) 22 55 121
Apr – Oct

Kilchoan
Pier Road
Tel: (0845) 22 55 121
Apr – Oct

Lochinver
Kirk Lane
Tel: (0845) 22 55 121
Apr – Oct

Mallaig
Tel: (0845) 22 55 121
Apr – Oct. Oct-March (limited opening)

North Kessock
Picnic Site
Tel: (0845) 22 55 121
Apr – Sept

Portree
Bayfield House
Tel: (0845) 22 55 121
Jan – Dec

Strontian
Tel: (0845) 22 55 121
Apr – Oct

Thurso
Riverside
Tel: (0845) 22 55 121
Apr – Oct

Ullapool
Argylle Street
Tel: (0845) 22 55 121
Jan – Dec

Aultbea, Ross-shire

Map Ref: 3F6

SMALL HOTEL

Aultbea Hotel

Aultbea, Ross-shire, IV22 2HX
Tel:01445 731201
Email:aultbeahotel@btconnect.com
Web:www.aultbeahotel.co.uk

Comfortable hotel situated on the shore of Loch Ewe with magnificent views. Fishing available. Inverewe Gardens, 5 miles (9kms). Food served in our Waterside Bistro, lounge bar & Zetland Restaurant.

8 rooms, all en-suite, Open Jan-Dec, B&B per person, single from £30.00, double from £30.00.

Aviemore, Inverness-shire

Map Ref: 4C10

HOTEL

Cairngorm Hotel

Grampian Road, Aviemore, PH22 1PE
Tel:01479 810233 Fax:01479 810791
Email:reception@cairngorm.com
Web:www.cairngorm.com

Independent hotel providing 3 star accommodation with that friendly, caring service only a privately run hotel can offer.

31 rooms, all en-suite, Open Jan-Dec, B&B per person, single from £45.00, double from £35.00.

GUEST HOUSE

Cairngorm Guest House

Grampian Road, Aviemore, Inverness-shire, PH22 1RP
Tel:01479 810630
Email:conns@lineone.net
Web:www.cairngormguesthouse.com

Peter and Gail welcome you to our lovely Victorian House, 5 min walk from centre of Aviemore. Relax by the open fire in the guest lounge and enjoy home baking. Hearty breakfasts with vegetarian option. En-suite rooms some on ground floor. King sized beds with TV and VCR also available. Drying/storage facilities and private parking.

12 rooms, all en-suite, Open Jan-Dec, B&B per person, single from £30.00, double from £25.00.

GUEST HOUSE

Ravenscraig Guest House

Grampian Road, Aviemore, Inverness-shire, PH22 1RP
Tel:01479 810278 Fax:01479 810210
Email:info@aviemoreonline.com
Web:www.aviemoreonline.com

Ravenscraig is centrally located in the village and an ideal base for touring the Highlands. Popular with birdwatchers, golfers, walkers & cyclists are our quiet ground floor garden rooms with their own front doors allowing easy access as well as privacy. We also offer family rooms, a comfortable guest lounge with local information, drying facilities, ski/golf locker, plentiful parking and legendary breakfasts!

12 rooms, all en-suite, Open Jan-Dec, B&B per person, single from £22.00, double from £22.00.

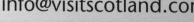

Important: Prices stated are estimates and may be subject to amendments

Ballachulish, Argyll **Map Ref: 1F1**

The Ballachulish Hotel and Bùlas Bar & Bistro

Ballachulish, Near Fort William, The Scottish Highlands PH49 4JY
Tel: 0871 222 3415 Fax: 0871 222 3416
e.mail: reservations@freedomglen.co.uk web: www.ballachulishhotel.com

Make yourself at Home at one of Scotland's most famous lochside Hotels: The Ballachulish Hotel featuring **Bùlas Bar & Bistro**. Perfect venue for great escapes, exploring the west coast or use of nearby Leisure Centre. Fantastic contemporary eating at Bùlas with signature dishes served in the bùlas, a traditional Highland pot!

HOTEL

Ballachulish Hotel & Bùlas Bar & Bistro
Ballachulish, nr Fort William, Argyll, PH49 4JY
Tel:0871 222 3415 Fax:0871 222 3416
Email:reservations@freedomglen.co.uk
Web:www.ballachulishhotel.com

Make yourself at home in one in one of Scotland's most famous lochside hotels: The Ballachulish Hotel featuring Bùlas Bar and Bistro. Perfect venue for great escapes and exploring the West Coast. Use of nearby leisure centre.

54 rooms, all en-suite, Open Feb-Dec incl Xmas/New Year.

C £ V

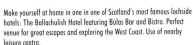

GUEST HOUSE

Craiglinnhe House
Lettermore, Ballachulish, Argyll, PH49 4JD
Tel:01855 811270
Email:info@craiglinnhe.co.uk
Web:www.craiglinnhe.co.uk

Lochside Victorian villa amid spectacular mountain scenery offering period charm with modern comfort. Warm, friendly atmosphere, good food and wine. Ideal base for exploring the Western Highlands.

5 rooms, all en-suite, Open Feb-Dec, B&B per person, double from £28.00, BB & Eve.Meal from £45.50.

£ W

Fern Villa Guest House

Loan Fern, Ballachulish, Glencoe, PH49 4JE
Tel: 01855 811393 Fax: 01855 811727
e.mail: fernctg@aol.com
web: www.fernvilla.com

All rooms ensuite - Comfortable guest lounge. A warm drink welcomes you each time you return from your day's activity. Homemade Natural Cooking of Scotland dinner menus using fresh local ingredients. **AA-✦✦✦✦ Perfect for the Great Outdoors** – walking, climbing, skiing, touring or just relaxing in beautiful surroundings. Short stay rates available. Non smoking throughout.

GUEST HOUSE

Fern Villa Guest House
Loanfern, Ballachulish, PH49 4JE
Tel:01855 811393 Fax:01855 811727
Email:fernctg@aol.com
Web:www.fernvilla.com

A warm welcome awaits you in this fine Victorian granite built house in the lochside village amidst spectacular scenery. One mile from Glencoe, convenient for Fort William. Home baking and Natural Cook of Scotland features on our dinner menu. Table licence. The perfect base for walking, climbing or touring in the West Highlands. Private parking.

5 rooms, all en-suite, Open Jan-Dec, B&B per person, double from £25.00, BB & Eve.Meal from £39.00.

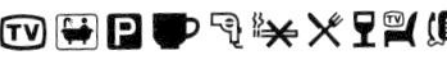

£ W V

Ballachulish, Argyll

Map Ref: 1F1

HOTEL

Isles of Glencoe Hotel & Leisure Centre

Ballachulish, nr Fort William, Argyll, PH49 4HL
Tel:0871 222 3415 Fax:0871 222 3416
Email:reservations@freedomglen.co.uk
Web:www.islesofglencoe.com

Almost afloat, nestling on the lochside, this friendly, family hotel offers everything for which you dream on holiday: spacious loch and mountain-view bedrooms and a relaxed, convivial ambience. Luxuriate in the Leisure Centre - heated pool, sauna, steam room, jacuzzi, exercise room and solarium. Enjoy the casual lochside conservatory restaurant. Special breaks.

59 rooms, all en-suite, Open Jan-Dec incl Xmas+New Year.

GUEST HOUSE

Lyn Leven Guest House

Ballachulish, Argyll, PH49 4JP
Tel:01855 811392 Fax:01855 811600
Web:www.lynleven.co.uk

A very warm Highland welcome awaits you at this RAC award winning establishment. Situated within attractive, well cared for gardens overlooking Loch Leven in the heart of some of Scotland's most spectacular scenery. Traditional home cooking. Ample parking. Glencoe only 1 mile. Ideal base for skiing, walking, climbing and fishing.

8 rooms, all en-suite, Open Jan-Dec excl Xmas, B&B per person, double from £25.00.

Boat of Garten, Inverness-shire

Map Ref: 4C10

The Boat

The Boat, Deshar Road, Boat of Garten, Inverness-shire PH24 3BH
Tel: 01479 831258 Fax: 01479 831414
e.mail: info@boathotel.co.uk Web: www.boathotel.co.uk

Relax and enjoy log fires, lovely comfortable individually decorated rooms, superb 2 AA Rosette cuisine, golf, fishing, lochs, mountains and activities in the Cairngorms National Park in this privately owned Victorian country hotel overlooking an 18 hole golf course and the River Spey.

HOTEL

The Boat Hotel

Boat of Garten, Inverness-shire, PH24 3BH
Tel:01479 831258 Fax:01479 831414
Email:info@boathotel.co.uk
Web:www.boathotel.co.uk

Privately owned Victorian hotel recently refurbished to a very high standard, overlooking the 18 hole championship golf course. Award winning '2 AA Rosette' cuisine in 'The Capercaillie' restaurant. Individual in style with friendly personalised service. Golf and fishing packages arranged.

26 rooms, all en-suite, Open Feb-5 Jan, B&B per person, single from £84.50, double from £64.50, BB & Eve.Meal from £89.50.

Important: Prices stated are estimates and may be subject to amendments

Boat of Garten, Inverness-shire **Map Ref: 4C10**

GUEST HOUSE

Moorfield House

Deshar Road, Boat of Garten, Inverness-shire, PH24 3BN
Tel:01479 831646
Email:enquiries@moorfieldhouse.com
Web:www.moorfieldhouse.com

Informality is the key to this luxuriously furnished Victorian house. Ideally suited to those seeking relaxed and peaceful surroundings. A friendly welcome, comfortable beds and a hearty breakfast await. Fully non smoking. Evening meal by arrangement.

6 rooms, all en-suite, Open Dec-Nov excl Xmas, B&B per person, single from £40.00, double from £33.00.

Brackla, Loch Ness-side, Inverness-shire **Map Ref: 4A9**

HOTEL

Loch Ness Clansman Hotel

Brackla, Loch Ness Side, Inverness-shire, IV3 8LA
Tel:01456 450326 Fax:01456 450845
Email:lochnessclansman@aol.com
Web:www.lochnessview.com

Family run hotel situated on the west shores of Loch Ness. 9 miles from Inverness, and 4 miles from Drumnadrochit. Wheelchair access to all public areas. Many attractions within 90 minutes drive, including the Isle of Skye and the Whisky Trail. Historic Sites such as Culloden Battlefield and Cawdor Castle, plus numerous Golf courses. Short break packages available, whether you are travelling by plane, train or by car.

23 rooms, all en-suite, Open Jan-Dec excl Xmas/New Year, B&B per person, single from £45.00, double from £34.50.

Carrbridge, Inverness-shire **Map Ref: 4C9**

INN

The Cairn Hotel

Main Road, Carrbridge, Inverness-shire, PH23 3AS
Tel:01479 841212 Fax:01479 841362
Email:info@cairnhotel.co.uk
Web:www.cairnhotel.co.uk

Enjoy the country pub atmosphere, log fire, malt whiskies, real ales and affordable food in this family owned village centre hotel. Close to the historic bridge. A perfect base for touring the Cairngorms, Whisky Trail and Loch Ness.

7 rooms, most en-suite, Open Jan-Dec, B&B per person from £24.00.

Carrbridge, Inverness-shire | Map Ref: 4C9

Dalrachney Lodge Hotel

CARRBRIDGE, INVERNESS-SHIRE PH23 3AT
Tel: 01479 841252 Fax: 01479 841383
e.mail: dalrachney@aol.com Web: www.dalrachney.co.uk

A lovingly refurbished Victorian Sporting Lodge in the heart of the Scottish Highlands, Dalrachney is an ideal base for a memorable holiday. Enjoy the breathtaking scenery, abundant wildlife and numerous outdoor activities of the Cairngorm National Park. Spacious well-appointed rooms. Emphasis on good food and wines served in a relaxed and friendly setting.

SMALL HOTEL

Dalrachney Lodge Hotel

Carrbridge, Inverness-shire, PH23 3AT
Tel: 01479 841252 Fax: 01479 841383
Email: dalrachney@aol.com
Web: www.dalrachney.co.uk

Victorian former hunting lodge, with many antique and period furnishings, set in 16 acres of peaceful surroundings. Cuisine using local produce.

10 rooms, 9 en-suite, 1 priv.facilities, Open Jan-Dec, B&B per person, single from £50.00, double from £35.00, BB & Eve.Meal from £45.00.

TV P C V

Cromarty, Ross-shire | Map Ref: 4B7

★★★

SMALL HOTEL

Royal Hotel

Marine Terrace, Cromarty, Ross-shire, IV11 8YN
Tel:01381 600217 Fax:01381 600813
Email:info@royalcromartyhotel.co.uk
Web:www.royalcromartyhotel.co.uk

Family run hotel overlooking harbour and beach with fine views over Cromarty Firth. Specialising in food using good local produce. Situated in the historic conservation village of Cromarty. Dolphin watching, museums, good walks or just quiet relaxation.

10 rooms, some en-suite, Open Jan-Dec, B&B per person, single from £35.00, double from £30.00, BB & Eve.Meal from £45.00.

TV P C W V

nr Cromarty, Ross-shire | Map Ref: 4B7

Braelangwell House

Balblair, Ross-shire IV7 8LT
Tel: 01381 610353 Fax: 01381 610467
e.mail: braelangwell@btinternet.com
Web: www.braelangwell.co.uk

Beautiful 18th Century Georgian country house set in its own private, ancient wooded estate. Four-poster bed, richly furnished dining room, log fires. Play billiards, croquet or relax in the conservatory, enjoy the peace and tranquillity of Braelangwell and our abundant wildlife. Ideal base for Inverness and touring the Highlands.

B&B

Braelangwell House

Balblair, Ross-shire, IV7 8LT
Tel:01381 610353 Fax:01381 610467
Email:braelangwell@btinternet.com
Web:www.braelangwell.co.uk

Fine Georgian house dating from the late 18th Century, situated in 5 acres of garden and 50 acres of woodland. 7 miles from Cromarty. Convenient for road and air links from the south. Ideal base for exploring the northern Highlands.

3 rooms, Open Mar-Dec, B&B per person, single from £60.00, double from £40.00, room only single £60.00-80.00, double £80.00-100.00.

TV P

Important: Prices stated are estimates and may be subject to amendments

Dalwhinnie, Inverness-shire

Map Ref: 4B11

INN ★

The Inn at Loch Ericht

Dalwhinnie, Inverness-shire, PH19 1AG
Tel:01528 522257 Fax:01528 522270
Email:reservations@priory-hotel.com
Web:www.priory-hotel.com

Friendly hotel in small Highland village. All rooms with ensuite facilities. Meals served all day. Walkers and Cyclists welcome.

27 rooms, all en-suite, Open Jan-Dec, B&B per person, single from £27.50, double from £24.50, BB & Eve.Meal from £37.50.

Dornie, by Kyle of Lochalsh, Ross-shire

Map Ref: 3G9

SMALL HOTEL ★★★

Dornie Hotel

Francis Street, Dornie, Ross-shire, IV40 8DT
Tel:01599 555205 Fax:01599 555429
Email:dornie@madasafish.com
Web:www.dornie-hotel.co.uk

Occupying one of the most scenic areas in Scotland, this family run 13 bedroom hotel is situated in the village of Dornie & is only a short walk from the magnificent Eilean Donan Castle. Rooms are well equipped & the hotel offers an excellent selection of modern cuisine specialising in local seafood. Castle weddings attractively catered for. We look forward to welcoming you to a relaxing & peaceful stay.

13 rooms, some en-suite, Open Jan-Dec, B&B per person, single £25.00-35.00, double £25.00-35.00.

GUEST HOUSE ★★★

Eilean A-Cheo

Dornie, by Kyle of Lochalsh, Ross-shire, IV40 8DY
Tel:01599 555485
Email:stay@scothighland.com
Web:www.scothighland.com

Situated on a quiet side road just a few minutes walk from the picturesque Eilean Donan Castle and overlooking the loch. Easy access to the Isle of Skye, Plockton with its famous palm trees and the wonderful countryside round about. Excellent hospitality and a true Gaelic welcome.

5 rooms, some en-suite, Open Jan-Dec, B&B per person, single from £26.00, double from £18.00.

Dornoch, Sutherland

Map Ref: 4B6

HOTEL ★★

Dornoch Hotel

Grange Road, Dornoch, IV25 3LD
Tel:01942 824824
Email:reservations@WAshearings.com
Web:www.shearingsholidays.com

Close to famous golf course and overlooking Dornoch Firth, this hotel offers comfortable accommodation and entertainment every night, and a pitch and putt on front lawn.

110 rooms, all en-suite, Open Feb-Dec, B&B per person, double from £25.00.

Drumnadrochit, Inverness-shire

Map Ref: 4A9

HOTEL ★★★

Loch Ness Lodge Hotel

Drumnadrochit, Inverness-shire, IV63 6TU
Tel:01456 450342 Fax:01456 450429
Email:info@lochness-hotel.com
Web:www.lochness-hotel.com

Traditional country lodge hotel dating back to 1740 set within 8 acres of woodland and attractive grounds with lawns. Renowned 'Piobrach Restaurant', for superb Scottish food using local ingredients, and hospitality. Loch Ness, Nessie and Great Glen Way close by. Visitors centre, shops, Loch Ness cruises, in the complex. Friendly and welcoming staff. Quality assured award. Fine wine list and malt whiskies. Cafè Bar Bistro.

50 rooms, all en-suite, Open 1Mar-mid Jan (closed Feb), B&B per person, single from £49.00, double from £39.50, BB & Eve.Meal from £65.00.

Dulnain Bridge, by Grantown-on-Spey, Inverness-shire

Map Ref: 4C9

SMALL HOTEL

Muckrach Lodge Hotel & Restaurant

Dulnain Bridge, Grantown on Spey, Inverness-shire, PH26 3LY
Tel:01479 851257 Fax:01479 851325
Email:info@muckrach.co.uk
Web:www.muckrach.co.uk

An ideal touring base for Royal Deeside, Loch Ness and the Malt Whisky Trail, this comfortable and welcoming country house in 10 acres of landscaped grounds is surrounded by glorious scenery of the Cairngorms National Park. Enjoy golf, walking, wildlife and much more. Lovely rooms, log fires, 2 AA Rosette dining and excellent cellar.

10 rooms, all en-suite, Open Jan-Dec excl Xmas, B&B per person, single from £40.00, double from £40.00.

Fort Augustus, Inverness-shire

Map Ref: 4A10

SMALL HOTEL

Caledonian Hotel

Fort Augustus, Inverness-shire, PH32 4BQ
Tel:01320 366256 Fax:08701 602708
Email:hotel@thecaledonianhotel.com
Web:www.thecaledonianhotel.com

This 100 year old Highland hotel is set within its own grounds with 2 rink bowling and 9 hole putting green. Peaceful and spacious reception room and lounge. Ideal rates for half board short breaks. In addition to the hotel facilities there is golfing, boat cruises, exhibitions and fishing available within the village area. Fort Augustus's central position is suitable for exploring the rest of the Highlands.

11 rooms, 10 en-suite, 1 priv.facilities, Open Easter-Nov, B&B per person, single from £45.00, double from £33.00, BB & Eve.Meal from £44.50.

Fort William, Inverness-shire

Map Ref: 3H12

HOTEL

Alexandra Hotel

The Parade, Fort William, PH33 6AZ
Tel:01397 702241
Email:salesalexandra@strathmorehotels.com
Web:www.strathmorehotels.com

Large traditional hotel fully modernised, situated in town centre. Some rooms with views of the surrounding hills and lochside.

94 rooms, all en-suite, Open Jan-Dec, B&B per person, single from £59.00, double from £44.50.

HOTEL

Ben Nevis Hotel & Leisure Club

North Road, Fort William, Inverness-shire, PH33 6TG
Tel:01397 702331 Fax:01786 469400
Email:salesmilton@strathmorehotels.com
Web:www.strathmorehotels.com

On the A82 facing Ben Nevis, this hotel with its own grounds and leisure club with new beauty salon is about 1ml (2km) from the town centre.

119 rooms, all en-suite, Open Jan-Dec, B&B per person, single from £59.00, double from £69.00, BB & Eve.Meal from £79.00.

HOTEL

Caledonian Hotel

Achintore Road, Fort William, Inverness-shire, PH33 6RW
Tel:01942 824824
Email:reservations@WAshearings.com
Web:www.shearingsholidays.com

Modern hotel situated on the edge of the town with extensive views across Loch Linnhe.

68 rooms, all en-suite, Open Feb-Dec, B&B per person, single from £30.00, double from £30.00, BB & Eve.Meal from £40.00.

Fort William, Inverness-shire Map Ref: 3H12

HOTEL

Clan MacDuff Hotel

Achintore Road, Fort William, Inverness-shire, PH33 6RW
Tel:01397 702341 Fax:01397 706174
Email:reception@clanmacduff.co.uk
Web:www.clanmacduff.co.uk

This family run hotel overlooks Loch Linnhe, 2 miles south of Fort William. The hotel is situated in its own grounds with large car park. Enjoy the highland scenery from the conservatory or patio. All public rooms have magnificent views of the Loch and the mountains beyond. Dinner is a traditional menu with varied choice. We offer the comfort and freedom of a hotel at economic prices. Brochure on request.

42 rooms, all en-suite, Open Apr-Nov, B&B per person, single from £34.00, double from £25.50, BB & Eve.Meal from £39.50.

HOTEL

Cruachan Hotel

Achintore Road, Fort William, Inverness-shire, PH33 6RQ
Tel:01397 702022 Fax:01397 702239
Email:reservations@cruachan-hotel.co.uk
Web:www.cruachan-hotel.co.uk

Victorian villa, modern wing attached, standing in own grounds overlooking Loch Linnhe and only 400 yards from Fort William's main shopping street.

57 rooms, Open Jan-Dec, B&B per person, single from £25.00, double from £22.00 per person.

GUEST HOUSE

Distillery Guest House

Nevis Bridge, Fort William, Inverness-shire, PH33 6LR
Tel:01397 700103 Fax:01397 702980
Email:disthouse@aol.com
Web:www.stayinfortwilliam.co.uk

Distillery house at old Glenlochy Distillery in Fort William beside A82, Road to the Isles. Situated at the entrance to Glen Nevis short distance from the town centre. Distillery House has been upgraded to high standards. Set in the extensive grounds of the Glenlochy Distillery with views over the River Nevis. All bedrooms are ensuite with TV, and hospitality tray. Non smoking establishment. Complimentary whisky upon arrival.

8 rooms, all en-suite, Open Jan-Dec, B&B per person, single from £22.50, double from £22.50.

Fort William, Inverness-shire Map Ref: 3H12

★★★ GUEST HOUSE

Glenlochy Guest House
Nevis Bridge, Fort William, Inverness-shire, PH33 6LP
Tel:01397 702909
Email:glenlochy1@aol.com
Web:www.glenlochy.co.uk

Detached house with garden situated at Nevis Bridge, midway between Ben Nevis and the town centre. 0.5 miles (1km) to railway station. 2 annexe rooms.

10 rooms, some en-suite, Open Jan-Dec, B&B per person, single £20.00-50.00, double £20.00-35.00.

★★★ HOTEL

Grand Hotel
Gordon Square, Fort William, Inverness-shire, PH33 6DX
Tel/Fax:01397 702928
Email:grandhotel.scotland@virgin.net
Web:www.grandhotel-scotland.co.uk

Conveniently located in the town centre, our family run hotel offers good food and accommodation at competitive prices. Excellent base from which to explore the scenic West Highlands by car or by foot. Children welcome. Baby listening service as well as highchairs and cots. Our chef is happy to assist with all your dietary requests.

30 rooms, all en-suite, Open Feb-Dec excl Xmas/New Year, B&B per person, single from £39.50, double from £29.50.

★★★ SMALL HOTEL

The Inn at Ardgour
Ardgour, by Fort William, Inverness-shire, PH33 7AA
Tel:01855 841225 Fax:01855 841214
Email:theinn@ardgour.biz
Web:www.ardgour.biz

A traditional Highland inn with spectacular views up Loch Linnhe. Family run, offering warm hospitality, traditional Scottish food and a good selection of malt whiskies.

10 rooms, all en-suite, Open Jan-Dec, B&B per person, single from £40.00, double from £30.00, BB & Eve.Meal from £40.00.

★★★ GUEST HOUSE

Mansefield Guest House
Corpach, Fort William, Inverness-shire, PH33 7LT
Tel:01397 772262
Email:mansefield@btopenworld.com
Web:www.fortwilliamaccommodation.com

This traditional Scottish guest house is situated on the 'Road to the Isles' and set in mature gardens with views of the surrounding mountains. We specialise in relaxation, comfort and home cuisine. Being small and select the ambience is special and attention personal and friendly. Sorry we are unable to accommodate children under 12 years of age.

6 rooms, all en-suite, Open Jan-Dec, B&B per person, single from £21.00, double from £21.00, BB & Eve.Meal from £34.00.

Important: Prices stated are estimates and may be subject to amendments

Fort William, Inverness-shire

Map Ref: 3H12

★★★★

HOTEL

Moorings Hotel

Banavie, Fort William, PH33 7LY
Tel:01397 772797 Fax:01397 772441
Email:reservations@moorings-fortwilliam.co.uk
Web:www.moorings-fortwilliam.co.uk

Privately owned hotel situated beside the Caledonian Canal and Neptune's Staircase. Many rooms have views of the Ben Nevis mountain range and canal locks. Meals are served in the restaurant, or in the Upper Deck, providing a good range of dining options, both formal and informal. Ten superior mountain view rooms with extra sized beds.

28 rooms, all en-suite, Open Jan-Dec excl Xmas, B&B per person, single from £48.00, double from £40.00.

C 🐕 £ V

★★★

GUEST HOUSE

The Neuk

Corpach, Fort William, Inverness-shire, PH33 7LR
Tel:01397 772244
Email:norma.mccallum@theneuk.fsbusiness.co.uk

A warm friendly welcome awaits you at this detached villa on Mallaig road (A830) with panoramic views over the Mamore Mountains, Ben Nevis and Loch Linnhe. Within few mins walk of Canal Bank and Neptunes Staircase. Evening meals by arrangement. Ideal base for touring surrounding area or walking, cycling and skiing. Featured in Scotland's essential guide to the high roads.

4 rooms, all en-suite, Open Jan-Dec excl Xmas/New Year, B&B per person, single from £35.00, double from £22.00.

C 🐕 W V

★★

HOTEL

Nevis Bank Hotel

Belford Road, Fort William, Inverness-shire, PH33 6BY
Tel:01397 705721 Fax:01397 706275
Email:info@nevisbankhotel.co.uk
Web:www.nevisbankhotel.co.uk

Privately owned hotel situated on A82 at Glen Nevis access road. Ideally situated for touring and business. Walkers and cyclists welcome (limited cycle storage space).

35 rooms, all en-suite, Open Jan-Dec, B&B per person, single from £25.00, double from £24.00, BB & Eve.Meal from £35.00.

C £ W V

VAT is shown at 17.5%: changes in this rate may affect prices.

Key to symbols is on back flap.

Fort William, Inverness-shire **Map Ref: 3H12**

HOTEL

West End Hotel
Achintore Road, Fort William, PH33 6ED
Tel:01397 702614 Fax:01397 706279
Email:welcome@westend-hotel.co.uk
Web:www.westend-hotel.co.uk

Family run hotel in the centre of Fort William overlooking Loch Linnhe. Ideal base for touring the West Highlands.

51 rooms, all en-suite, Open Feb-Dec excl Xmas/New Year, B&B per person, single from £35.00, double from £25.00.

C £ V

by Fort William, Inverness-shire **Map Ref: 3H12**

★★★★
SMALL HOTEL

Old Pines Hotel & Restaurant
Spean Bridge, by Fort William, PH34 4EG
Tel:01397 712324
Email:enquiries@oldpines.co.uk
Web:www.oldpines.co.uk

A unique blend of relaxed informality and excellent food. All rooms ensuite with T.V. Light lunches and five course evening meals. Children welcome.

8 rooms, all en-suite, Open Jan-Dec excl Xmas.

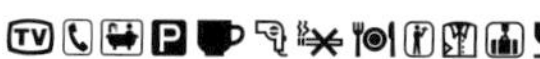

C £ W V

nr Fort William, Inverness-shire **Map Ref: 3H12**

★★
INN

The Tailrace Inn
Riverside Road, Kinlochleven, Argyll, PH50 4QH
Tel:01855 831777 Fax:01855 831291
Email:tailrace@btconnect.com
Web:www.tailraceinn.co.uk

The Tailrace Inn is situated in the centre of the scenic village of Kinlochleven. Surrounded by the Mamore Mountains midway between Glencoe and Ben-Nevis. An ideal stopover for walkers, climbers or those who enjoy the outdoors. Excellent drying room facilities. Lively, atmospheric bar with wide-screen satellite TV. All rooms comfortably furnished with TV's and tea trays.

6 rooms, all en-suite, Open Jan-Dec, B&B per person, single from £38.00, double from £30.00.

C £ V

Gairloch, Ross-shire **Map Ref: 3F7**

HOTEL

Gairloch Hotel
Gairloch, Highland Region, IV21 2BL
Tel:01942 824824
Email:reservations@WAshearings.com
Web:www.shearingsholidays.com

Victorian hotel overlooking the Gair Loch. Recently refurbished throughout. Ideal centre for touring west coast. Golf and sailing nearby.

72 rooms, all en-suite, Open Mar-Nov, B&B per person, double from £25.00.

£ W V

Important: Prices stated are estimates and may be subject to amendments

Gairloch, Ross-shire Map Ref: 3F7

MYRTLE BANK HOTEL

Low Road, Gairloch, Ross-shire IV21 2BS
Telephone: 01445 712004 Fax: 01445 712214
e.mail: myrtlebankhotel@msn.com
Web: www.myrtlebankhotel.com

Privately owned hotel enjoying panoramic views to the Isle of Skye with Inverewe Garden nearby. Widely recommended restaurant specialises in local produce and seafood. Golf, sailing, sandy beaches within easy reach.

SMALL HOTEL

Myrtle Bank Hotel
Low Road, Gairloch, Ross-shire, IV21 2BS
Tel:01445 712004 Fax:01445 712214
Email:myrtlebank@msn.com
Web:www.myrtlebankhotel.com

This privately run hotel, recently refurbished and extended is situated on waterfront with views over Gairloch towards Isle of Skye. Restaurant and bar meals available, using fresh local produce.

12 rooms, all en-suite, Open Jan-Dec, B&B per person, single from £36.00, double from £36.00.

THE OLD INN

FLOWERDALE GLEN, GAIRLOCH, ROSS-SHIRE IV21 2BD
TEL: 01445 712006 FAX: 01445 712044
E.MAIL: info@theoldinn.net WEB: www.theoldinn.net

AA PUB OF THE YEAR FOR SCOTLAND & N.I. 2003
AA BEST SEAFOOD PUB OF THE YEAR FOR SCOTLAND 2005/6
CAMRA SCOTTISH HIGHLAND PUB OF THE YEAR 2004/5
ABBOT ALE PERFECT PUB FOR SCOTLAND AWARD 2005/2006

A must visit for seafood lovers (langoustine, scallops, mussels). Renowned for the range and quality of real ales, fine malts and wines. 14 well-appointed rooms. Ideal base for outdoor enthusiasts.

INN

The Old Inn
Gairloch, Ross-shire, IV21 2BD
Tel:01445 712006 Fax:01445 712044
Email:info@theoldinn.net
Web:www.theoldinn.net

18c coaching Inn in picturesque harbour location. Renowned for selection of seafood, real ales, and friendly atmosphere. 'AA' Pub of the Year for Scotland and N.I. for 2003. CAMRA Highland Pub of the Year 2004/5. Abbot Ale Perfect Pub for Scotland 2005/6. AA Best Seafood Pub of the Year for Scotland 2005/6.

14 rooms, all en-suite, Open Feb-Dec excl Xmas/New Year, B&B per person, single from £35.00, double from £27.50.

Glencoe, Argyll

Map Ref: 1F1

INN

Clachaig Inn

Glencoe, Argyll, PH49 4HX
Tel:01855 811252 Fax:01855 812030
Email:inn@clachaig.com
Web:www.clachaig.com

Located in the heart of Glencoe with stunning mountain views and a great Highland atmosphere. The Inn offers upgraded ensuite accommodation, an imaginative all day menu and an unrivalled selection of cask ales and malt whiskies. Recent winners Best Pub in Scotland. An Outdoor Inn for Outdoor Folk. Open all Year.

23 en-suite bedrooms, B&B from £34.00-40.00 per person per night.

SMALL HOTEL

MacDonald Hotel

Fort William Road, Kinlochleven, Argyll, PH50 4QL
Tel:01855 831539 Fax:01855 831416
Email:enquiries@macdonaldhotel.co.uk
Web:www.macdonaldhotel.co.uk

A modern, yet traditional, hotel set beside a tidal creek at the head of Loch Leven. Mid-way between Glen Nevis and Glencoe at the foot of the Mamores, the Macdonald Hotel is the perfect base to enjoy the best of west Highland walking or touring. Personally managed by John, Lynn and team who pride themselves on providing a relaxed, informal, environment and the very best of Highland foods from fresh local produce.

10 rooms, all en-suite, Open Jan-Dec, B&B per person, single from £40.00, double from £28.00, BB & Eve.Meal from £40.00.

Glencoe, Argyll

Map Ref: 1F1

GUEST HOUSE

Scorrybreac Guest House

Glencoe, Argyll, PH49 4HT
Tel:01855 811354 Fax:01855 811024
Email:info@scorrybreac.co.uk
Web:www.scorrybreac.co.uk

Scorrybreac sits on the edge of Glencoe village in an elevated forested location amidst some of the most dramatic scenery Scotland has to offer. The house has 6 well appointed bedrooms all with en-suite or private facilities. The lounge and dining room have excellent views across Loch Leven and to the mountains beyond, where guests talk enthusiastically to one another about their daily activities.

6 rooms, some en-suite, Open Jan-Dec, B&B per person, single from £25.00, double from £20.00, BB & Eve.Meal from £34.00.

GUEST HOUSE

Strathassynt Guest House

Loan Fern, Ballachulish, Argyll, PH49 4JB
Tel:01855 811261 Fax:01855 811914
Email:info@strathassynt.com
Web:www.strathassynt.com

Beautiful village location near Glencoe. All rooms are ensuite with TV/DVD and tea/coffee facilities. Drying room. Secure bike store. Access to leisure facilities including swimming, jacuzzi and sauna. Family room with discounts for children. Garden. Take an evening stroll beside the Loch or relax with a drink in our guest lounge. Always be assured of the warmest welcome. 10% discount for stays of 3 nights or longer.

6 rooms, all en-suite, Open Jan-Dec, B&B per person, single from £23.00, double from £18.00.

Glenfinnan, Inverness-shire

Map Ref: 3G12

SMALL HOTEL

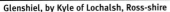

The Princes' House Hotel

Glenfinnan, Inverness-shire, PH37 4LT
Tel:01397 722246 Fax:01397 722323
Email:princeshouse@glenfinnan.co.uk
Web:www.glenfinnan.co.uk

Set amidst stunning West Highland scenery, this family run former coaching inn, with its award winning restaurant offers an excellent base for touring historic Bonnie Prince Charlie country along the romantic 'Road to the Isles'. 2 AA Rosettes for dining room.

9 rooms, all en-suite, Open Mar-Dec excl Xmas and 1wk Oct, B&B per person, single from £49.00, double from £37.00.

Glenshiel, by Kyle of Lochalsh, Ross-shire

Map Ref: 3G10

SMALL HOTEL

Kintail Lodge Hotel

Glenshiel, Ross-shire, IV40 8HL
Tel:01599 511275 Fax:01599 511226
Email:reception@kintaillodgehotel.co.uk
Web:www.kintaillodgehotel.co.uk

Converted well appointed former shooting lodge on the shores of Loch Duich near Eilean Donan Castle and the Five Sisters of Kintail. Ideal touring and hill walking centre. Conservatory Restaurant and Bar open to non-residents.

12 rooms, all en-suite, Open Jan-Dec, B&B per person, single from £32.50, double from £32.50, BB & Eve.Meal from £58.00.

Glen Urquhart, Inverness-shire

Map Ref: 4A9

SMALL HOTEL

Glenurquhart House

Glenurquhart, Drumnadrochit, Inverness-shire, IV63 6TJ
Tel:01456 476234 Fax:01456 476286
Email:carol@glenurquhartlodges.co.uk
Web:www.glenurquhart-house-hotel.co.uk

Situated in a scenic location overlooking Loch Meiklie. Attractions nearby include Loch Ness, Glen Affric for hill-walking, loch and river fishing, and pony trekking. Restaurant using freshly prepared produce. At the end of your day relax in our comfortable lounge by the log fires.

6 rooms, en-suite, Open Mar-Nov, B&B per person, single from £30.00, double from £35.00, BB & Eve.Meal from £49.50.

Grantown-on-Spey, Moray Map Ref: 4C9

GUEST HOUSE

An Cala Guest House

Woodlands Terrace, Grantown on Spey, Moray, PH26 3JU
Tel/Fax:01479 873293
Email:ancala@globalnet.co.uk
Web:www.ancala.info

AA 5 diamond rating. A lovely large Victorian house set in ½ an acre with on-site parking, overlooking woods yet within easy walking distance of Grantown centre. Doubles are kingsize, including a magnificent mahogany 4 poster bed from Castle Grant; all rooms en-suite. We aim to make you feel welcome, relaxed and comfortable.

4 rooms, Open Jan-Dec, B&B per person single from £40.00, double from £26.00, family from £25.00, room rate, single from £40.00, double from £52.00, triple from £75.00.

GUEST HOUSE

Dunallan House

Woodside Avenue, Grantown-on-Spey, Moray, PH26 3JN
Tel/Fax:01479 872140
Email:dunallan@cwcom.net
Web:www.dunallan.mcmail.com

Dunallan is a splendid example of Victorian elegance oozing with the charm of a bygone era. Original period fireplaces are in the residents lounge and dining room, giving extra warmth to cheer you on those cooler evenings. Elegant bedrooms, featuring Victorian room and Honeymoon Suite with Victorian bathroom. We have a ground floor bedroom.

7 rooms, all en-suite, Open Jan-Dec, B&B per person, single £28.00-35.00, double £22.00-30.00.

GUEST HOUSE

Firhall Guest House

Grant Road, Grantown-on-Spey, Moray, PH26 3LD
Tel/Fax:01479 873097
Email:info@firhall.com
Web:www.firhall.com

Firhall is a fine example of Victorian elegance, retaining much of the original character of this period. Particular features include the beautifully preserved pitched pine woodwork, ornate cornices and marble fireplaces. Home cooking. Family run.

6 rooms, 3 en suite, Open Jan-Dec excl Xmas, B&B per person single from £18.00, double from £19.00, family from £18.00.

GUEST HOUSE

Garden Park Guest House

Woodside Avenue, Grantown-on-Spey, Moray, PH26 3JN
Tel:01479 873235
Email:gardenpark@waitrose.com
Web:www.garden-park.co.uk

Victorian, stone built house set in own colourful garden, quietly located a short walk from the centre of Grantown on Spey. Guests' lounge with log-burning stove; home cooked breakfast made with fresh produce served in the dining room with its individual tables. A short selection of malt whiskies are available. Five ensuite rooms, one 4 poster, one on the ground floor. A friendly and relaxing base for exploring the area.

5 rooms, all en-suite, Open Jan-Dec, B&B per person, single from £30.00, double from £25.00.

GUEST HOUSE

Kinross House

Woodside Avenue, Grantown-on-Spey, Moray, PH26 3JR
Tel:01479 872042 Fax:01479 873504
Web:www.kinrosshouse.co.uk

Attractive Victorian villa in peaceful residential area. Welcoming and relaxed atmosphere with open fires. Traditional home-cooking using fresh local produce. Fine selection of Speyside malts. Small gym and sauna. Free use of mountain bikes. No-smoking house. Laptop and internet access available.

6 rooms, some en-suite, Open Mar-Oct, B&B per person, single from £25.00, double from £27.00, BB & Eve.Meal from £42.50.

Important: Prices stated are estimates and may be subject to amendments

Grantown-on-Spey, Moray

Map Ref: 4C9

GUEST HOUSE

Rosegrove Guesthouse

Skye of Curr, Dulnain Bridge, Grantown on Spey
Inverness-shire, PH26 3PA
Tel/Fax:01479 851335
Email:info@rosegroveguesthouse.com
Web:www.rosegroveguesthouse.com

Traditional, family run guesthouse, home cooking. A short distance from Dulnain Bridge.

6 rooms, some en-suite, Open Jan-Dec, B&B per person, single from £18.00, double from £20.00, BB & Eve.Meal from £30.00.

C V

★★★★

GUEST HOUSE

Rossmor Guest House

Woodlands Terrace, Grantown on Spey, Moray, PH26 3JU
Tel/Fax:01479 872201
Email:johnsteward.rossmor@lineone.net
Web:www.rossmor.co.uk

Spacious Victorian detached house with original features and large garden. A warm welcome. Parking. Panoramic views. No smoking throughout. Tudor style four poster bed, iron and trouser press facility available.

6 rooms, all en-suite, Open Jan-Dec, B&B per person, single from £26.00, double from £26.00.

TV P

W V

Invergarry, Inverness-shire

Map Ref: 3H11

Glengarry Castle Hotel

Invergarry, Inverness-shire PH35 4HW
Tel: 01809 501254 Fax: 01809 501207
e.mail: castle@glengarry.net
Web: www.glengarry.net

Country House Hotel privately owned and personally run by the MacCallum family for over 40 years. Situated in the heart of the Great Glen, this is a perfect centre for touring both the West Coast and Inverness/Loch Ness area. Magnificently situated in 60 acres of wooded grounds overlooking Loch Oich. Recently refurbished, 5 rooms with 4-poster beds, all rooms have ensuite bathrooms, TV, radio and telephone. Private tennis court, trout and pike fishing in Loch Oich. Children and dogs welcome.

For brochure please contact Mr D MacCallum.

HOTEL

Glengarry Castle Hotel

Invergarry, Inverness-shire, PH35 4HW
Tel:01809 501254 Fax:01809 501207
Email:castle@glengarry.net
Web:www.glengarry.net

Privately owned country mansion, some rooms with four-poster beds. Extensive wooded grounds to loch with impressive hill and forest views.

26 rooms, some en-suite, Open mid Mar-early Nov, B&B per person, single from £63.00, double from £49.00.

TV P

C W V

Invergordon, Ross-shire **Map Ref: 4B7**

Kincraig House Hotel

Invergordon, Ross-shire IV18 0LF
Tel: 01349 852587 Fax: 01349 852193
e.mail: info@kincraig-house-hotel.co.uk
Web: www.kincraig-house-hotel.co.uk

Set in its own grounds overlooking the Cromarty Firth, the recently refurbished Kincraig House Hotel offers a choice of individually designed Premier/Executive rooms or Standard rooms.

Enjoy fine dining in the superb restaurant, or a meal in the bar, both overlooking the extensive gardens and relax after dinner in the spacious oak panelled lounge. Kincraig House is over 200 years old and retains many of the original features.

The hotel's private drive leads off the A9, about 20 minutes drive north from Inverness, offering easy access to some of Scotland's best golf courses and the Scottish Highlands.

AA ★★★ STB ★★★★

HOTEL

Kincraig House Hotel
Invergordon, Ross-shire, IV18 0LF
Tel:01349 852587 Fax:01349 852193
Email:info@kincraig-house-hotel.co.uk
Web:www.kincraig-house-hotel.co.uk

Kincraig House Hotel offers 15 en-suite rooms, a number of which are newly created Premier and Executive rooms, A refurbished a'la Carte Restaurant and bar and a spacious oak panelled lounge offer superb character and comfort.

15 rooms, all en-suite, Open Jan-Dec, B&B per person, single from £55.00, double from £45.00, BB & Eve.Meal from £68.00.

Inverness **Map Ref: 4B8**

★★★★

GUEST HOUSE

Avalon Guest House
79 Glenurquhart Road, Inverness, IV3 5PB
Tel:01463 239075 Fax:01463 709827
Email:avalonhouse79@hotmail.com

Family run Guest House, situated on A82 road to Loch Ness and Fort William. A 10 minute walk takes you into the town centre and all its amenities such as restaurants, Eden Court Theatre, cinemas and many more. Close to Sports Centre and Aquadome. Ideal base for touring the Highlands.

6 rooms, 5 en-suite, 1 priv.facilities, Open Feb-Dec, B&B per person, single £40.00-45.00, double/twin £28.00-32.00.

Important: Prices stated are estimates and may be subject to amendments

Inverness

Map Ref: 4B8

HOTEL

Best Western Inverness Palace Hotel & Spa
Ness Walk, Inverness, IV3 5NG
Tel:01463 223243 Fax:01463 236865
Email:palace@miltonhotels.com
Web:www.miltonhotels.com

Modernised Victorian hotel on banks of the River Ness opposite the castle. Many rooms recently refurbished. Milton Leisure Club features 50ft swimming pool. Close to town centre and Eden Court Theatre. Some parking at the hotel, plus valet parking available.

88 rooms, all en-suite, Open Jan-Dec, B&B per person, single from £69.00, double from £44.95, BB & Eve.Meal from £61.95.

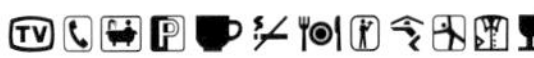

SMALL HOTEL

Bunchrew House Hotel
Bunchrew, Inverness, IV3 8TA
Tel:01463 234917 Fax:01463 710620
Email:welcome@bunchrew-inverness.co.uk
Web:www.bunchrew-inverness.co.uk

Bunchrew House is more than just another Country House Hotel. Steeped in history and lovingly restored, the house has an incredibly warm and welcoming atmosphere. It lies in 20 acres of lawns and magnificent woodlands and is rightfully known as 'the hotel on the shore' standing as it does only yards from the sea. Yet this fabulous house is only 3 miles from the Highland Capital - the City of Inverness and right in the heart of some of the most spectacular scenery in the world.

16 rooms, all en-suite, Open Jan-Dec excl Xmas, B&B per person, single from £95.00 pp, double from £70.00 pp.

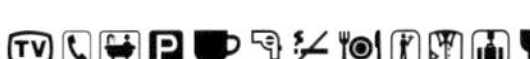

GUEST HOUSE

Cedar Villa Guest House
33 Kenneth Street, Inverness, IV3 5DH
Tel/Fax:01463 230477
Email:enquiries@guesthouseinverness.co.uk
Web:www.guesthouseinverness.co.uk

Centrally situated with easy access to theatre, bus and railway.

6 rooms, some en-suite, Open Jan-Dec excl Xmas, B&B per person, single from £25.00, double from £20.00.

HOTEL

Drumossie Hotel
Old Perth Road, Inverness, IV2 5BE
Tel:01463 236451 Fax:01463 712858
Email:stay@drumossiehotel.co.uk
Web:www.drumossiehotel.co.uk

Luxury hotel standing in its own grounds 3 miles (5kms) South of Inverness with easy access to A9. Ideal for touring. Facilities for meetings and conferences. 44 Newly refurbished bedrooms all ensuite.

44 rooms, all en-suite, Open Jan-Dec, B&B per person, double from £85.00.

VAT is shown at 17.5%: changes in this rate may affect prices.

Key to symbols is on back flap.

Inverness Map Ref: 4B8

GUEST HOUSE

Fraser House

49 Huntly Street, Inverness, IV3 5HS
Tel/Fax:01463 716488
Email:fraserlea@btopenworld.com
Web:www.fraserhouse.co.uk

Fraser House built in 1821, a listed building, has been sympathetically refurbished to offer comfortable accommodation. All rooms are ensuite with river views. City centre and all amenities only 5 minutes walk. AA◆◆◆

5 rooms, all en-suite, Open Jan-Dec, B&B per person, single from £30.00, double from £25.00.

SMALL HOTEL

Glendruidh House Hotel

Old Edinburgh Road South, Inverness, IV2 6AR
Tel:01463 226499 Fax:01463 710745
Email:welcome@cozzee-nessie-bed.co.uk
Web:www.cozzee-nessie-bed.co.uk

Mainly 19th century house set amongst large grounds consisting of woods and rolling lawns. Unique circular drawing room and elegant dining room serving excellent traditional cuisine prepared from the very best local produce. With a superb wine list and an excellent selection of malt whiskies you can be sure of a very pleasant stay. A wonderful base for many activity holidays, touring or just taking things easy. No smoking throughout.

5 rooms, all en-suite, Open Jan-23 Dec excl Xmas, B&B per person, single from £69.00, double/twin from £49.50, king-size double suite from £65.00.

HOTEL

Glen Mhor Hotel & Restaurant

8-13 Ness Bank, Inverness, IV2 4SG
Tel:01463 234308 Fax:01463 713170
Email:glenmhorhotel@btconnect.com
Web:www.glen-mhor.com

Traditional stone built house in quiet residential area, overlooking River Ness. Only 5 minutes walk to town centre and Eden Court Theatre on opposite side of river. Adjacent cottage/annexe accommodation. Choice of restaurant and Nicos Bistro.

42 rooms, some en-suite, Open Jan-Dec excl New Year, B&B per person, single from £59.00, double from £45.00.

Important: Prices stated are estimates and may be subject to amendments

Inverness

Map Ref: 4B8

HOTEL

Inverness Marriott Hotel

Culcabock Road, Inverness, IV2 3LP
Tel:01463 237166 Fax:01463 225208
Email:events.inverness@marriotthotels.co.uk
Web:www.marriotthotels.co.uk/invkm

Original manor house dating back to the 18th century set in 4 acres of gardens. Leisure club with indoor swimming pool, jacuzzi, sauna, steam room, exercise room, hairdresser, beauty treatments. Choice of 2 restaurants. 1 mile (2kms) from city centre, 7 miles (11kms) from airport.

82 rooms, all en-suite, Open Jan-Dec, B&B per person, single from £75.00, double from £55.00, BB & Eve.Meal from £75.00.

GUEST HOUSE

Larchfield House

15 Ness Bank, Inverness, IV2 4SF
Tel:01463 233874 Fax:01463 711600
Email:info@larchfieldhouse.com
Web:www.larchfieldhouse.com

Peacefully situated on the banks of the River Ness and yet within five minutes pleasant walk to the city centre, rail and coach terminals. Larchfield House offers quality accommodation at a reasonable price. All rooms are fully ensuite and prices include a traditional cooked breakfast. All produce is sourced locally. Internet access is also available.

6 rooms, all en-suite, Open Jan-Dec excl Xmas/New Year, B&B per person, single from £30.00, double from £30.00.

HOTEL

Loch Ness House Hotel

Glenurquhart Road, Inverness, IV3 8JL
Tel:01463 231248 Fax:01463 239327
Email:LNHHCHRIS@aol.com
Web:www.smoothhound.co.uk/hotels/lochness.html

Privately owned, overlooking the Torvean Golf Course and Caledonian Canal. 20 minutes walk to town centre. Restaurant specialising in seafood and Scottish dishes.

22 rooms, all en-suite, Open Jan-Dec, B&B per person, single from £50.00, double from £50.00, BB & Eve.Meal from £60.00.

GUEST HOUSE

Moray Park House

Island Bank Road, Inverness, IV2 4SX
Tel/Fax:01463 233528
Email:info@morayparkhotel.co.uk
Web:www.morayparkhotel.co.uk

Run by owners and pleasantly situated with open outlook over gardens and river, yet close to town centre and all its amenities. Private car park.

8 rooms, all en-suite, Open Jan-Dec excl Xmas, B&B per person, single from £27.00, double from £22.00.

HOTEL

The Priory Hotel

The Square, Beauly, Inverness-shire, IV4 7BX
Tel:01463 782309 Fax:01463 782531
Email:reservations@priory-hotel.com
Web:www.priory-hotel.com

Situated in the attractive village square of Beauly, this privately run hotel offers excellent facilities, coupled with friendly, efficient informal service. Enjoy the flexibility of early check-in's, late check out's, food available all day and best of all - breakfast available till lunchtime.

34 rooms, all en-suite, Open Jan-Dec, B&B per person, single from £42.50, double from £35.00, BB & Eve.Meal from £45.00.

VAT is shown at 17.5%: changes in this rate may affect prices.

Key to symbols is on back flap.

Inverness

Map Ref: 4B8

HOTEL

The Royal Highland Hotel, Ash Restaurant

Station Square, 18 Academy Street, Inverness, IV1 1LG
Tel:01463 231926 Fax:01463 710705
Email:info@royalhighlandhotel.co.uk
Web:www.royalhighlandhotel.co.uk

Traditional Victorian hotel with modern facilities offering Highland hospitality. Centrally situated for shops and local attractions. Ideal base for touring Loch Ness and the northern Highlands.

70 rooms, all en-suite, Open Jan-Dec excl Xmas, B&B per person, single from £89.00, double from £129.00.

GUEST HOUSE

St Ann's House

37 Harrowden Road, Inverness, IV3 5QN
Tel:01463 236157 Fax:01463 236157
Email:stannshous@aol.com
Web:www.hotelinverness.co.uk

19C traditional stone built house in quiet residential area. Small comfortable family run, assuring a friendly welcome. Tranquil, well planted garden available for guests enjoyment.

6 rooms, some en-suite, Open all year, B&B per person, single from £27.00, double from £26.00.

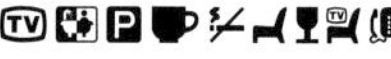

John o'Groats, Caithness

Map Ref: 4E2

GUEST HOUSE

Caber Feidh Guest House

John O'Groats, Wick, Caithness, KW1 4YR
Tel:01955 611219

Centrally situated in John O' Groats and 2 miles (3kms) from Duncansby Head. It is well situated for exploring the north east, including the north coast of Sutherland, the inland Flow Country, and more. Day trips to Orkney are a popular choice and the Castle of Mey 6 miles West.

14 rooms, some en-suite, Open Jan-Dec, B&B per person, single from £18.00, double from £17.00.

SMALL HOTEL

Seaview Hotel

John O'Groats, Caithness, KW1 4YR
Tel/Fax:01955 611220
Email:seaviewhotel@barbox.net
Web:www.johnogroats-seaviewhotel.co.uk

Comfortable range of accommodation, situated 300 yds from Orkney Passenger Ferry. Secure facilities for bikes/cycles. Internet access available. Off-road parking. John 'O' Groats Visitor/Craft Centre, Stacks of Duncansby, cliff walks and puffins, fine views of the sea and nearby Orkney.

10 rooms, 9 en-suite, Open Jan-Dec, B&B per person, single from £30.00, double from £20.00, BB & Eve.Meal from £35.00.

Kingussie, Inverness-shire

Map Ref: 4B11

GUEST HOUSE

The Hermitage Guest House

Spey Street, Kingussie, Inverness-shire, PH21 1HN
Tel:01540 662137 Fax:01540 662177
Email:thehermitage@clara.net
Web:www.thehermitage-scotland.com

Enjoy the splendour of the Highlands and make Kingussie your base. Let us help you plan your daily itinerary. Wonderful walking and mountain bike trails. In easy reach of skiing, fishing, birdwatching, Heritage centres and whisky trail. A warm welcome awaits you at the Hermitage.

5 rooms, all en-suite, Open Jan-Dec, B&B per person, single from £29.00, double from £25.00, BB & Eve.Meal from £39.00.

Important: Prices stated are estimates and may be subject to amendments

Kingussie, Inverness-shire | Map Ref: 4B11

AWAITING INSPECTION

The Osprey Hotel
Ruthven Road, Kingussie, Inverness-shire, PH21 1EN
Tel/Fax:01540 661510
Email:aileen@ospreyhotel.co.uk
Web:www.ospreyhotel.co.uk

8 rooms, all en-suite, Open Jan-Dec, B&B per person, single from £27.00, double from £27.00, BB & Eve.Meal from £45.00.

Kinlochleven, Argyll | Map Ref: 3H12

GUEST HOUSE

Tigh-Na-Cheo Guest House
Garbhein Road, Kinlochleven, PH50 4SE
Tel/Fax:01855 831434
Web:www.tigh-na-cheo.co.uk

Under new management and newly refurbished. Tigh-Na-Cheo is in a village location with views of the Mamore Hills. Drying facilities and bike store. All rooms ensuite with baths, TV, hairdryer and tea/coffee making facilities.

9 rooms, Open All Year, B&B per person, single from £25.00, double from £25.00, BB & Eve.Meal from £35.00.

Laggan Bridge, by Newtonmore, Inverness-shire

Map Ref: 4B11

SMALL HOTEL

Monadhliath Hotel

Laggan Bridge, nr Newtonmore, Inverness-shire PH20 1BT
Tel/Fax:01528 544276
Email:monadhliath@lagganbridge.com
Web:www.lagganbridge.com

Family run hotel in secluded area but close to main Spey Valley tourist resorts and on main road from Newtonmore to Fort William/Isle of Skye.

8 rooms, all en-suite, Open Feb-Dec, B&B per person, single from £20.00, double from £20.00, BB & Eve.Meal from £29.50.

Lairg, Sutherland

Map Ref: 4A6

SMALL HOTEL

The Nip Inn

Main Street, Lairg, Sutherland, IV27 4DB
Tel:01549 402243 Fax:01549 402593
Email:info@nipinn.co.uk
Web:www.nipinn.co.uk

Allow us to look after you while you explore the far Northern Highlands and all they have to offer. Golf, fishing, hillwalking, cycling, birdwatching, touring rugged and untamed countryside with panoramic views and scenery. Base yourself at The Nip Inn, a small family run inn, relax in warm welcoming accommodation and enjoy our home cooking, all fresh produce where possible. At The Nip Inn our priority is your comfort.

6 rooms, all en-suite, Open Jan-Dec excl Xmas/New Year, B&B per person, single £23.00-30.00, double £23.00-30.00.

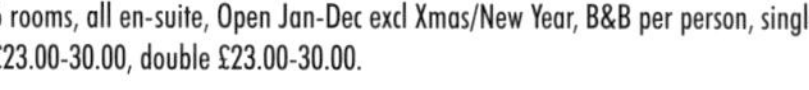

by Lairg, Sutherland

Map Ref: 4A6

SMALL HOTEL

The Overscaig House Hotel

Loch Shin, Sutherland, IV27 4NY
Tel:01549 431203 Fax:01549 431210
Email:visits@overscaig.com
Web:www.overscaig.com

Located on the banks of Loch Shin, the Overscaig is an ideal base to explore all the attractions of the Northern Highlands. Hill walking, bird watching, fishing available. A warm Highland welcome awaits.

8 rooms, all ensuite, Open Mar-Oct, B&B per person, single from £34.00, double from £34.00, family from £34.00. Room only per night, single from £34.00, double from £68.00, family from £102.00.

Lochinver, Sutherland **Map Ref: 3G5**

HOTEL

Inver Lodge Hotel

Lochinver, Sutherland, IV27 4LU
Tel:01571 844496 Fax:01571 844395
Email:stay@inverlodge.com
Web:www.inverlodge.com

Modern hotel with accent on comfort and friendliness. Restaurant and all bedrooms can enjoy sea-scape and setting sun over Lochinver harbour.

20 rooms, all en-suite, Open Apr-Nov, B&B per person, single from £80.00, double from £75.00, BB & Eve.Meal from £100.00.

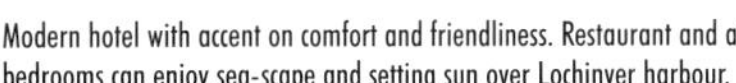

SMALL HOTEL

Kylesku Hotel

Kylesku, by Lochinver, Sutherland, IV27 4HW
Tel:01971 502231 Fax:01971 502313
Email:info@kyleskuhotel.co.uk
Web:www.kyleskuhotel.co.uk

This former ferry hotel in NW Highlands has stunning views of Loch Glendhu and the mountains beyond from the restaurant, bar and most bedrooms. The chef uses local produce wherever possible and seafood (particularly langoustine) and game are a speciality. Many photo's sample menus and local attractions and activities can be found on our website.

8 rooms, 6 en-suite, Open Mar-Oct, B&B per person, single from £40.00, double from £35.00.

GUEST HOUSE

Polcraig Guest House

Lochinver, Sutherland, IV27 4LD
Tel/Fax:01571 844429
Email:cathelmac@aol.com
Web:www.smoothhound.co.uk/hotels/polcraig.html

A warm, friendly welcome awaits you here at Polcraig. Ideally situated in a quiet location with views across Lochinver Bay & Harbour. A short walk takes you to a choice of places for eating out. Your hosts Jean and Cathel will provide you with a hearty breakfast before you set out for your day. Explore the Highlands, taking in the spectacular views and an abundance of wildlife.

5 rooms, all en-suite, Open Jan-Dec, B&B per person, single from £25.00, double from £25.00.

C V

Loch Ness, Inverness-shire | **Map Ref: 4A10**

SMALL HOTEL

Craigdarroch House Hotel

Foyers, South Loch Ness, Inverness-shire, IV2 6XU
Tel:01456 486400 Fax:01456 486444
Email:munro@hotel-loch-ness.co.uk
Web:www.hotel-loch-ness.co.uk

Traditional Highland country house with panoramic views over Loch Ness. Roaring log fires. Excellence in food and service.

14 rooms, all en-suite, Open Jan-Dec excl Xmas/New Year, B&B per person, single from £60.00, double from £60.00.

GUEST HOUSE

Foyers Bay House

Lower Foyers, Inverness, IV2 6YB
Tel:01456 486624 Fax:01456 486337
Email:carol@foyersbay.co.uk
Web:www.foyersbay.co.uk

Set in its own 4 acres of wooded pine slopes, rhododendrons and apple orchard, Foyers Bay House offers 6 rooms all with ensuite facilities. Just 500 yards from the famous Falls of Foyers and situated just by Loch Ness, home of the famous monster.

6 rooms, all en-suite, Open Jan-Dec, B&B per person, single from £33.00, double from £27.00, BB & Eve.Meal from £37.00.

SMALL HOTEL

Whitebridge Hotel

Whitebridge, Inverness-shire, IV2 6UN
Tel:01456 486226 Fax:01456 486413
Email:info@whitebridgehotel.co.uk
Web:www.whitebridgehotel.co.uk

Personally run hotel nestling in foothills of Monadliath Mountains. Beside the quiet B862 on the East side of Loch Ness and 24 miles South of Inverness.

12 rooms, all en-suite, Open Jan-Dec, B&B per person, single from £35.00, double from £27.00, BB & Eve.Meal from £42.00.

Lybster, Caithness | **Map Ref: 4D4**

SMALL HOTEL

Swallow Portland Arms Hotel

Lybster, Caithness, KW3 6BS
Tel:01593 721721 Fax:01593 721722
Email:info@portlandarms.co.uk
Web:www.portlandarms.co.uk

Former staging inn, some rooms with four poster beds or half testers. Local 9 hole golf course. Fishing available. Courtesy transport to/from airport. Convenient stopover en-route to Orkney. Ideal base for touring Caithness.

22 rooms, all en-suite, Open Jan-Dec, B&B per person, single from £55.00, double from £40.00.

Important: Prices stated are estimates and may be subject to amendments

Mallaig, Inverness-shire Map Ref: 3F11

HOTEL

Morar Hotel

Morar, nr Mallaig, PH40 4PA
Tel:01687 462346 Fax:01687 462212
Email:info@morarhotel.com
Web:www.morarhotel.co.uk

Family run hotel, now under new ownership with magnificent views over Silver Sands of Morar and islands of Rhum and Eigg. Only 3 miles from Mallaig and car ferry to Isle of Skye.

28 rooms, all en-suite, Open Jan-Dec, B&B per person, single from £35.00, double from £30.00, family from £30.00.

C V

GUEST HOUSE

Seaview

Main Street, Mallaig, Inverness-shire, PH41 4QS
Tel:01687 462059 Fax:01687 462768
Email:seaviewmallaig@talk21.com

Situated in the centre of the village overlooking the harbour. Convenient for railway station and ferry terminal, for Skye, Small Isles and Knoydart. Family run with great Scottish breakfasts.

4 rooms, some en-suite, Open Mar-Oct, B&B per person, double £20.00-30.00.

V

GUEST HOUSE

Western Isles

East Bay, Mallaig, Inverness-shire, PH41 4QG
Tel/Fax:01687 462320
Email:westernisles@aol.com

Modern house overlooking the harbour and fishing boats, well situated for ferries to the islands. 4 miles (6kms) from renowned Morar sands, 10mins from ferry to Skye, Eigg, Rhum, Canna & the Knoydart Peninsula.

4 rooms, ensuite, Open Mar-Oct, B&B per person, single £28.00, double £25.00-30.00.

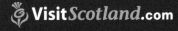

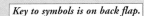

V

Mallaig, Inverness-shire

Map Ref: 3F11

★★★ HOTEL

West Highland Hotel

Mallaig, Inverness-shire, PH41 4QZ
Tel:01687 462210 Fax:01687 462130
Email:westhighland.hotel@virgin.net
Web:www.westhighlandhotel.co.uk

40 rooms, all en-suite, Open Apr-Nov, B&B per person, single from £40.00, double from £35.00, BB & Eve.Meal from £50.00.

Hotel with recent conservatory extension. Stands above the village of Mallaig with views over the harbour to the Isle of Skye beyond. All public areas recently upgraded to high standard. Bar meals served and non-residents welcome. 4 annexe bedrooms.

Muir of Ord, Ross-shire

Map Ref: 4A8

★★ SMALL HOTEL

Ord House Hotel

Muir of Ord, Ross-shire, IV6 7UH
Tel/Fax:01463 870492
Email:admin@ord-house.co.uk
Web:www.ord-house.co.uk

10 rooms, all en-suite, Open May-Oct, single B&B per person from £40.00, BB & Eve.Meal from £66.00.

Country house dating from 1637, set in extensive grounds of both formal garden and park and woodland. Taste of Scotland with emphasis on fresh food. Friendly and informal service in comfortable surroundings - a relaxing environment. 'AA' rosette.

Nairn

Map Ref: 4C8

★★ SMALL HOTEL

Braeval Hotel

Crescent Road, Nairn, IV12 4NB
Tel/Fax:01667 452341
Email:ian@braeval-hotel.co.uk
Web:www.braeval-hotel.co.uk

7 rooms, all en-suite, Open Jan-Dec, B&B per person, single from £35.00.

A small family run hotel, a Scottish experience with traditional Scottish fayre in a relaxed and friendly atmosphere.

★★★★ SMALL HOTEL

Claymore House Hotel

Seabank Road, Nairn, IV12 4EY
Tel:01667 453731 Fax:01667 455290
Email:claymorehouse@btconnect.com
Web:www.claymorehousehotel.com

13 rooms, all en-suite, Open Jan-Dec, B&B per person, single from £47.50, double from £47.50, BB & Eve.Meal from £59.50.

Family run hotel with the emphasis on friendliness, traditional food and flexibility and customer care.

Important: Prices stated are estimates and may be subject to amendments

Nairn

Map Ref: 4C8

GUEST HOUSE

Invernairne Guest House

Thurlow Road, Nairn, Inverness-shire, IV12 4EZ
Tel:01667 452039 Fax:01667 456760
Email:info@invernairne.com
Web:www.invernairne.com

Elegant, comfortable and family run, the stately Invernairne has magnificent views over the Moray Firth and garden path down to the sandy beach and promenade. The friendly wood-panelled lounge bar serves real ale and malt whiskies. Accommodation all en-suite. Ground floor bedroom available. Nearby restaurants and local amenities. The perfect base for touring, golf, cycling and total relaxation.

9 rooms, all en-suite, Open Jan-Dec, B&B per person, single from £33.00, double from £33.00.

SMALL HOTEL

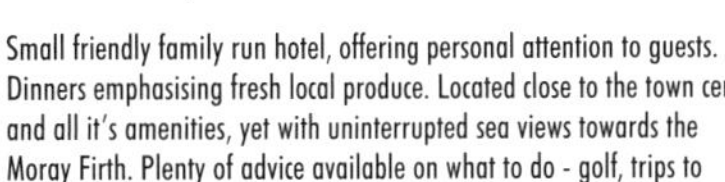

Sunny Brae Hotel

Marine Road, Nairn, IV12 4EA
Tel:01667 452309 Fax:01667 454860
Email:wsag@sunnybraehotel.com
Web:www.sunnybraehotel.com

Small friendly family run hotel, offering personal attention to guests. Dinners emphasising fresh local produce. Located close to the town centre and all it's amenities, yet with uninterrupted sea views towards the Moray Firth. Plenty of advice available on what to do - golf, trips to Speyside, the Moray Coast or over to the West Coast and the Far North.

8 rooms, all en-suite, Open Jan-Dec, B&B per person, single from £59.00, double from £45.00, BB & Eve.Meal from £68.00.

HOTEL

Windsor Hotel

Albert Street, Nairn, IV12 4HP
Tel:01667 453108 Fax:01667 456108
Email:windsornairnscot@btconnect.com
Web:www.windsor-hotel.co.uk

Set within residential area of Nairn and within 3 mins walk of town centre, close to the beach, many sporting activities, including the town's two championship golf courses. It has retained much of its character, whilst being sympathetically refurbished in line with the owners commitment to a continual upgrade. Ideal base for touring the Inverness Highlands. Fort George, Culloden Battlefield, Cawdor and Brodie Castles and Loch Ness.

52 rooms, all en-suite, Open Jan-Dec, B&B per person, single from £45.00, double from £45.00.

Newtonmore, Inverness-shire

Map Ref: 4B11

SMALL HOTEL

Alvey House Hotel

Golf Course Road, Newtonmore, Inverness-shire, PH20 1AT
Tel:01540 673260 Fax:01540 673003
Email:enquiries@alveyhouse.co.uk
Web:www.alveyhouse.co.uk

In the heart of Monarch of the Glen country, a friendly small hotel with spectacular mountain views. Perfect base for exploring Scotland with walking, cycling, horse riding, watersports and golf on our doorstep. Home cooking and a true Scottish welcome make this a memorable place to stay.

6 rooms, all en-suite, Open Jan-Dec, single from £22.50, double from £22.50, BB & Eve.Meal from £40.00.

GUEST HOUSE

Crubenbeg House

Falls of Truim, By Newtonmore, PH20 1BE
Tel:01540 673300
Email:enquiries@crubenbeghouse.com
Web:www.crubenbeghouse.com

Set amid stunning scenery, Crubenbeg House offers comfortable, spacious bedrooms, a delightful lounge with open fire, marvellous home-cooked breakfasts and a friendly, informal, relaxed atmosphere.

4 rooms, 3 en-suite, 1 priv.facilities, Open Jan-Dec, B&B per person, single from £30.00, double from £25.00.

VAT is shown at 17.5%: changes in this rate may affect prices.

Key to symbols is on back flap.

Onich, by Fort William, Inverness-shire

Map Ref: 3G12

SMALL HOTEL

Lodge on the Loch Hotel

Onich, nr Fort William, Inverness-shire, PH33 6RY
Tel:01855 821237 Fax:01855 821190
Email:info@lodgeontheloch.com
Web:www.lodgeontheloch.com

Discover seclusion and serenity - enjoy one of the West Coast's finest panoramas. The lodge is a perfect Highland retreat. Relax in peaceful lounges. Savour memorable evenings in the charming loch view Taste of Scotland restaurant - renowned for the freshest produce. Choice of individually designed rooms available with many personal touches.

15 rooms, all en-suite, Open all year. B&B per person per night, double from £50.00-£100.00 (double occupancy). BB & Eve. meal from £70.00-£120.00 per person per night (double occupancy).

HOTEL

Onich Hotel

Onich, by Fort William, PH33 6RY
Tel:01855 821214 Fax:01855 821484
Email:enquiries@onich-fortwilliam.co.uk
Web:www.onich-fortwilliam.co.uk

Personally run hotel with gardens extending down to the lochside. Superb all season views across Loch Linnhe to the mountains beyond. Imaginative dinners are served in the restaurant using quality local produce; alternatively, freshly prepared bar meals are available all day.

26 rooms, all en-suite, Open Jan-Dec excl Xmas, B&B per person, single from £48.00, double from £40.00.

Poolewe, Ross-shire

Map Ref: 3F7

SMALL HOTEL

Poolewe Hotel

Main Street, Poolewe, IV22 2JX
Tel:01445 781241
Email:info@poolewehotel.co.uk
Web:www.poolewehotel.co.uk

Former inn dating in part from 18C. Now a family run hotel recently refurbished. Situated in village and close to Inverewe Gardens. Excellent restaurant - real ale bar.

9 rooms, all en-suite, Open Jan-Dec, B&B per person, single from £27.50, double from £25.00, BB & Eve.Meal from £41.50.

Rhiconich, Sutherland

Map Ref: 3H3

SMALL HOTEL

Rhiconich Hotel

Rhiconich, Sutherland, IV27 4RN
Tel:01971 521224 Fax:01971 521732
Email:rhiconichhotel@aol.com
Web:www.rhiconichhotel.co.uk

Imagine a place where beauty, peace & tranquility are the order of the day, where your every need is looked after by the friendliest staff, where you can Salmon & Trout fish, walk, climb, birdwatch, beachcomb or just amaze at the finest mountain & Loch scenery in the Highlands, a place specializing in fresh seafood, vension, beef, lamb, halibut & sole and proud of its malt whisky selection and open log fire. No need to imagine it any longer.

11 rooms, en-suite, Open Jan-Dec closed Xmas/New Year, B&B per person, single from £40.00, double from £39.50.

Important: Prices stated are estimates and may be subject to amendments

Scourie, Sutherland — Map Ref: 3H4

★★★ SMALL HOTEL

Eddrachilles Hotel

Badcall Bay, Scourie, Sutherland, IV27 4TH
Tel:01971 502080 Fax:01971 502477
Email:enq@eddrachilles.com
Web:www.eddrachilles.com

Magnificently situated overlooking the islands of Eddrachilles Bay, this 200 year old building has been carefully refurbished, providing modern comfortable bedrooms but retaining the charm and character of older times. Fully licensed with an extensive wine list, cooking concentrates on traditional style benefiting from high quality local produce, commended by Taste of Scotland. Close to Handa Island bird sanctuary. Deer, seals, otters and badgers can be seen in and around the hotel grounds.

11 rooms, all en-suite, Open Mar-Oct.

SMALL HOTEL

Scourie Hotel

Scourie, Sutherland, IV27 4SX
Tel:01971 502396 Fax:01971 502423
Email:patrick@scourie-hotel.co.uk
Web:www.scourie-hotel.co.uk

Personally run, ideally situated for touring this rugged area of North West Scotland. Hotel specialises in fishing for brown trout and salmon. Some boats available. Four course dinner with local produce.

20 rooms, 19 en-suite, Open Apr-Oct, B&B per person, single from £37.00, double from £32.00 per person.

Dunvegan, Isle of Skye, Inverness-shire — Map Ref: 3D9

SMALL HOTEL

Atholl House Hotel

Dunvegan, Isle of Skye, IV55 8WA
Tel:01470 521219
Email:info@athollhotel.co.uk
Web:www.athollhotel.co.uk

A delightful family run hotel. Newly refurbished to a high standard, to which you will want to return time and time again to experience Highland hospitality at its best, and enjoy the freshly prepared home cooking. A perfect base from which to explore the Isle of Skye.

6 rooms, Open Mar-Oct, B&B per person double from £40.00, family from £45.00.

Portree, Isle of Skye, Inverness-shire Map Ref: 3E9

HOTEL

Cuillin Hills Hotel

Portree, Isle of Skye, IV51 9QU
Tel:01478 612003 Fax:01478 613092
Email:info@cuillinhills-hotel-skye.co.uk
Web:www.cuillinhills-hotel-skye.co.uk

19th Century former hunting lodge, set in 15 acres of grounds overlooking Portree Bay, with views towards the Cuillin Hills. Friendly staff, and an emphasis on good food, with a choice of formal or informal dining. Facilities available for conferences, functions and weddings. Open all year.

27 rooms, all en-suite, Open Jan-Dec, B&B per person, single from £55.00, double from £55.00, BB & Eve.Meal from £89.00.

C £ W V

HOTEL

Rosedale Hotel

Beaumont Crescent, Portree, Isle of Skye, IV51 9DB
Tel:01478 613131 Fax:01478 612531
Email:rosedalehotelsky@aol.com
Web:www.rosedalehotelskye.co.uk

Very comfortable and unusual hotel imaginatively created from former fishermens houses dating back to the reign of William IV. Award winning cuisine in an outstanding waterside location. Described by leading food critic as 'Portree's best kept secret'. AA Rosette.

18 rooms, all en-suite, Open Mar-Nov, B&B per person, single from £30.00, double from £30.00, BB & Eve.Meal from £52.00.

TV P

C £ V

Portree, Isle of Skye, Inverness-shire **Map Ref: 3E9**

★★★ SMALL HOTEL

Viewfield House Hotel

Portree, Isle of Skye, IV51 9EU
Tel:01478 612217 Fax:01478 613517
Email:info@viewfieldhouse.com
Web:www.viewfieldhouse.com

12 rooms, most en-suite, Open mid Apr-mid Oct, B&B per person, single from £40.00, double from £40.00, BB & Eve.Meal from £65.00.

A magnificent Georgian listed building set in spacious policies. Still under original family ownership and kept in as authentic a manner as possible, the house contains mostly antique furnishings and an outstanding collection of trophies and memorabilia.

Skeabost, Isle of Skye, Inverness-shire **Map Ref: 3D8**

★★★ HOTEL

Skeabost Country House Hotel

Skeabost Bridge, Isle of Skye, IV51 9NP
Tel:01470 532202 Fax:01470 532454
Email:reception@skeabostcountryhouse.com
Web:www.skeabostcountryhouse.com

19 rooms, all en-suite, Open Jan-Dec, B&B pppn from £69.00, BB & Eve.Meal pppn from £89.00.

Historic country house with 9 hole, 18 tee parkland golf course (par 62) and 8 miles (13 kms) salmon and trout fishing on River Snizort. Extensive landscaped gardens. Fine dining restaurant. Ghillie service.

Sleat, Isle of Skye, Inverness-shire **Map Ref: 3F10**

★★★ SMALL HOTEL

Hotel Eilean Iarmain

Sleat, Isle of Skye, IV43 8QR
Tel:01471 833332 Fax:01471 833275
Email:hotel@eilean-iarmain.co.uk
Web:www.eileaniarmain.co.uk

16 rooms, all en-suite, Open Jan-Dec, B&B per person, single from £90.00, double from £60.00.

Over 100 years old with many original antiques Eilean Iarmain is idyllically located overlooking the picturesque Isle Ornsay harbour, having a unique character, being traditional, hospitable and homely. Award winning restaurant with menus featuring the very best of local seafood and game. Superior suites alongside the hotel, all with mini bars.

★★★★ SMALL HOTEL

Kinloch Lodge

Sleat, Isle of Skye, IV43 8QY
Tel:01471 833214 Fax:01471 833277
Email:bookings@kinloch-lodge.co.uk
Web:www.kinloch-lodge.co.uk

16 rooms, all en-suite, Open Jan-Dec excl Xmas, B&B per person, single from £50.00, double from £50.00.

Ancestral home of Lord and Lady MacDonald in secluded lochside setting with panoramic views throughout the year. Unique demonstration cooking residential breaks are presented by Lady Macdonald.

Sleat, Isle of Skye, Inverness-shire

Map Ref: 3F10

Toravaig House Hotel & Iona Restaurant

Knock Bay, Sleat, Isle of Skye IV44 8RE
Tel: 01471 833231/01471 820200
e.mail: info@skyehotel.co.uk
Web: www.skyehotel.co.uk

Scottish Island Hotel of the Year 2005. (Hotel Review Scotland) Charming 9 bedroom Country House Hotel, totally refurbished, beautifully decorated, with open fire in drawing room. Personally run by Ken and Anne. Set in large garden, enjoying fine views over the sea and surrounding countryside. Parking. Beautiful ensuite bedrooms, most having bath & shower, feature beds, Sky TV, direct dial telephones, and delightful restaurant. Enjoy the selection of wines and malt whiskies. New for 2006 – daily yacht trips exclusively for residents. Walk by the shore or climb in the Cuillin Mountains. Real luxury...really affordable! B&B £59.50-£69.50 pppn.

SMALL HOTEL

Toravaig House Hotel & Iona Restaurant
Knock Bay, Sleat, Isle of Skye, IV44 8RE
Tel:01471 833231/820200
Email:info@skyehotel.co.uk
Web:www.skyehotel.co.uk

Scottish Island Hotel of the Year 2005 - Toravaig is situated on the Sleat Peninsula. Personally-run by the owners Toravaig is enjoying a growing reputation for quality food and a high standard of accommodation and service. New for 2006 - daily yacht trips for residents.

9 rooms, all en-suite, Open Jan-Dec, B&B per person, single from £69.50, double from £59.50.

Staffin, Isle of Skye, Inverness-shire

Map Ref: 3E8

FLODIGARRY COUNTRY HOUSE HOTEL

Staffin, Isle of Skye IV51 9HZ Tel: 01470 552203 Fax: 01470 552301
e.mail: info@flodigarry.co.uk Web: www.flodigarry.co.uk

BEST LOVED HOTELS

Fine historic mansion in secluded grounds - home of Flora MacDonald with breathtaking sea and mountain views. Award winning country house hotel - informal, family and pet friendly. Guided mountain and wildlife walks, sea fishing and traditional music evenings - much log fire relaxation and gourmet food in restaurant, bar and conservatory. Open all year. Special low season unwind luxury breaks from £40 B&B pppn. Fun 2 night weekends from £160 DBB pp.
Contact: Robbie Cairns. ★★★★

SMALL HOTEL

Flodigarry Country House Hotel
Staffin, Isle of Skye, IV51 9HZ
Tel:01470 552203 Fax:01470 552301
Email:info@flodigarry.co.uk
Web:www.flodigarry.co.uk

Family-run Victorian house with strong Jacobite connections. Superb sea and mountain views, private grounds. Award winning food and accommodation. Relaxed and informal. Sea fishing and guided walks.

18 rooms, all en-suite, Open Jan-Dec, B&B per person, double from £50.00, BB & Eve.Meal from £80.00-125.00.

Important: Prices stated are estimates and may be subject to amendments

Waternish, Isle of Skye, Inverness-shire

Map Ref: 3D8

★★★
INN

Stein Inn

Macleod's Terrace, Waternish
Isle of Skye, Inverness-shire, IV55 8GA
Tel:01470 592362
Email:angus.teresa@steininn.co.uk
Web:www.steininn.co.uk

Set in a beautiful lochside position, this historic village Inn C1790 offers traditional hospitality. Comfortable rooms, good food and a warm welcome. Excellent base for touring.

7 rooms, all en-suite, Open Jan-Dec excl Xmas/New Year, B&B per person, single from £25.00, double from £25.00.

Spean Bridge, Inverness-shire

Map Ref: 3H12

Corriegour Lodge Hotel

Loch Lochy, by Spean Bridge,
Lochaber, Inverness-shire PH34 4EA
Tel: +44 (0)1397 712685 Fax: +44 (0)1397 712696
E.mail: info@corriegour-lodge-hotel.com
Web: www.corriegour-lodge-hotel.com

"Better food than the top London restaurants, and a view to die for" - The Mirror.

This former Victorian hunting lodge enjoys the very finest setting in "The Great Glen". Dine in our Loch View Conservatory, enjoying the very best Scottish cuisine, fresh seafood, Aberdeen Angus, homemade breads and puddings, extensive selection of wines and malt whiskies. Our emphasis is on your total relaxation and comfort. Log fires and big comfy sofas. Come and be cushioned from the stresses of everyday life. Walking, scenery, skiing, history. Private beach and fishing school. Special spring/autumn breaks available.

Corriegour Lodge Hotel

Loch Lochy, by Spean Bridge, Inverness-shire PH34 4EA
Tel:01397 712685 Fax:01397 712696
Email:info@corriegour-lodge-hotel.com
Web:www.corriegour-lodge-hotel.com

Corriegour Lodge Hotel, a former hunting lodge, is set in nine acres of mature woodland and garden with open views over Loch Lochy. Seventeen miles North of Fort William on the road to Skye, many of Scotland's attractions are in easy reach. Local activities include walking, cycling, climbing, pony trekking or fishing from the hotel jetty.

12 rooms, all en-suite, Open Feb-Nov & New Year, B&B per person, single £59.50-69.50, double £59.50-69.50, BB & Eve.Meal from £75.00-105.50.

Inverour Guest House

Roy Bridge Road, Spean Bridge, Inverness-shire PH34 4EU
Tel/Fax:01397 712218
Email:enquiries@inverourguesthouse.co.uk
Web:www.inverourguesthouse.co.uk

Comfortable guest house located centrally in the village of Spean Bridge. Ideal base for touring the West Highlands of Scotland.

8 rooms, some en-suite, Open Jan-Dec, B&B per person, single from £20.00, double from £22.50. Family room from £70.00. Evening meals by pre-order. Packed lunches by arrangement. Drying facilities.

Spean Bridge, Inverness-shire

Map Ref: 3H12

SMALL HOTEL

Letterfinlay Lodge Hotel

Loch Lochy, Spean Bridge, Inverness-shire PH34 4DZ
Tel:01397 712622
Email:info@letterfinlaylodgehotel.com
Web:www.letterfinlaylodgehotel.com

Originally a Victorian shooting lodge this hotel stands on an enchanting site overlooking beautiful Loch Lochy in romantic Lochaber. Family run and owned by the Forsyth family for over 40 years. Popular for bar lunches and suppers. Ideal centre for touring the Highlands. Fishing and shooting by arrangement.

13 rooms, some en-suite, Open Apr-Oct, B&B per person, single from £35.00, double from £35.00, BB & Eve.Meal from £55.00.

by Strathcarron, Ross-shire

Map Ref: 3G9

SMALL HOTEL

Tigh an Eilean Hotel

Shieldaig, by Strathcarron, Ross-shire, IV54 8XN
Tel:01520 755251 Fax:01520 755321
Email:tighaneileanhotel@shieldaig.fsnet.co.uk

Personally run, small loch front hotel in charming village. All rooms en suite, most with sea views. Fresh produce, local seafood.

11 rooms, Open Mar-Nov, B&B per person, from £62.50 single, £65.00 double, £65.00 family. Room only rate per night from £62.50 single, £130.00 double, £130.00 family.

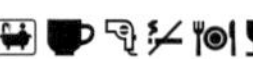

Strathpeffer, Ross-shire

Map Ref: 4A8

HOTEL

Ben Wyvis Hotel

Strathpeffer, Ross-shire, IV14 9DN
Tel:01997 421323 Fax:01997 421228
Email:benwyvis@british-trust-hotels.com
Web:www.british-trust-hotels.com

Beautifully restored Victorian hotel standing in 6 acres of garden in spa town. Hotel facilities include cinema and putting green. The perfect Highland setting offering peace and tranquility, 17 miles (29kms) west of Inverness.

92 rooms, all en-suite, Open Feb-Dec, B&B £35.00-45.00, DB&B £45.00-65.00.

SMALL HOTEL

Brunstane Lodge Hotel

Golf Road, Strathpeffer, Ross-shire, IV14 9AT
Tel:01997 421261 Fax:01997 421272
Email:chris@guichot.freeserve.co.uk
Web:www.brunstanelodge.com

Family run hotel set in its own mature garden in residential area and close to golf course. All rooms with ensuite facilities. Conveniently situated for touring Northern Highlands. Fresh local produce prepared and served by French chef/patron Chris Guichot and Paul Mackay.

10 rooms, all en-suite, Open all year, B&B per person, single from £42.00, double from £35.00. No dogs.

HOTEL

Coul House Hotel

Contin, by Strathpeffer, Ross-shire, IV14 9ES
Tel:01997 421487 Fax:01997 421945
Email:stay@coulhousehotel.com
Web:www.coulhousehotel.com

Secluded country house with forest walks and pitch & putt course in the grounds. The hotel is enjoying a growing reputation for quality food and exceptional hospitality.

20 rooms, all en-suite, Open Jan-Dec, B&B per person, single from £55.00, double from £40.00, BB & Eve.Meal from £65.00.

Important: Prices stated are estimates and may be subject to amendments

Strathpeffer, Ross-shire

Map Ref: 4A8

HOTEL

Highland Hotel

Strathpeffer, Highland Region, IV14 9AN
Tel:01942 824824
Email:reservations@WAshearings.com
Web:www.shearingsholidays.com

Large Victorian Hotel with oak panelled public areas. Hotel overlooks village square and pump room. Entertainment every night.

132 rooms, all en-suite, Open Feb-Dec, B&B per person, double from £25.00.

Strontian, Argyll

Map Ref: 1E1

SMALL HOTEL

The Strontian Hotel

Strontian, Acharacle, Argyll, PH36 4HZ
Tel:01967 402029 Fax:01967 402314
Email:strontianhotel@supanet.com
Web:www.strontianhotel.supanet.com

Family run hotel in superb location at the head of Loch Sunart. Ideal for fishing, bird watching, walking and good centre for touring the area.

6 rooms, all en-suite, Open Jan-Dec, B&B per person, single from £35.00, double from £27.50, BB & Eve.Meal from £40.00.

Tain, Ross-shire

Map Ref: 4B7

★★★★

SMALL HOTEL

Glenmorangie Highland Home at Cadboll

Fearn, by Tain, Ross-shire, IV20 1XP
Tel:01862 871671 Fax:01862 871625
Email:relax@glenmorangie.co.uk
Web:www.glenmorangie.com

Small and exclusive, a must on the list of those with a passion for malt whisky. This is the whisky world's equivalent of a French Chateau. The relaxed style and informality belies a serious and total dedication to your well being, with cuisine to match. Cottage suites close to the house are available and are simpler in style.

9 rooms, all en-suite, Open Feb-Dec, BB & Eve.Meal from £140.00.

Thurso, Caithness

Map Ref: 4D3

SMALL HOTEL

Forss House Hotel

Forss, by Thurso, Caithness, KW14 7XY
Tel:01847 861201 Fax:01847 861301
Email:anne@forsshousehotel.co.uk
Web:www.forsshousehotel.co.uk

Country house hotel set in 25 acres of woodland and gardens, with the River Forss and waterfall only 200 yards away. Excellent cuisine, fine wines and 300 malt whiskies await. An ideal base for visiting the Orkney Islands or the Castle of Mey, the late Queen Mother's Highland Home.

13 rooms, Open Jan-Dec, B&B per person, single from £65.00, double from £47.50, family from £43.33.

Thurso, Caithness — **Map Ref: 4D3**

SMALL HOTEL

Park Hotel

Thurso, KW14 8RE
Tel:01847 893251 Fax:01847 804044
Email:reception@parkhotelthurso.co.uk
Web:www.parkhotelthurso.co.uk

Comfortable and friendly family run hotel fully licenced with 21 well appointed ensuite bedrooms all with TV, hairdryer, tea and coffee etc. All meals served. Conservatory lounge and dining room. Large private car park. Gold Green Tourism Award.

21 rooms, all en-suite, Open Jan-Dec excl New Year, B&B per person, single from £45.00, double from £35.00. Reduced rates off season.

HOTEL

Weigh Inn Hotel

Burnside, Thurso, KW14 7UG
Tel:01847 893722 Fax:01847 892112
Email:reception@weighinn.co.uk
Web:www.weighinn.co.uk

Recently built sixteen bedroom hotel, situated a short distance from the harbour, and ideal for travellers catching the Orkney ferry. The hotel also makes an excellent base for the business traveller or for the winter visitor wanting to explore the county of Caithness, and the north Sutherland coastline.

16 rooms, all en-suite, Open Jan-Dec excl Xmas/New Year, B&B per person, single from £60.00, double from £40.00.

Tongue, Sutherland — **Map Ref: 4A3**

SMALL HOTEL

Ben Loyal Hotel

Main Street, Tongue, Sutherland, IV27 4XE
Tel:01847 611216 Fax:01847 611212
Email:benloyalhotel@btinternet.com
Web:www.benloyal.co.uk

Stone built hotel with fine views of Ben Loyal and Kyle of Tongue. Friendly atmosphere. Fishing available. AA ★★ AA.

11 rooms, all en-suite, Open Mar-Dec, B&B per person, single from £35.00, double from £25.00.

Important: Prices stated are estimates and may be subject to amendments

Tongue, Sutherland

Map Ref: 4A3

TONGUE HOTEL

Tongue, By Lairg, Sutherland IV27 4XD
Tel: 01847 611206 Fax: 01847 611345
e.mail: info@tonguehotel.co.uk Web: www.scottish-selection.co.uk

Amid spectacular seacliffs, beaches and a dramatic mountain backdrop this Victorian Highland Hotel enjoys panoramic views over the Kyle of Tongue. An ideal base for hillwalkers, birdwatching and fishing. While still retaining its original style and charm the hotel provides enhanced modern comforts and facilities. Menus offer excellent Scottish fayre.

SMALL HOTEL

Tongue Hotel

Tongue, by Lairg, Sutherland, IV27 4XD
Tel:01847 611206 Fax:01847 611345
Email:info@tonguehotel.co.uk
Web:www.scottish-selection.co.uk

A traditional Victorian Highland hotel retaining original style and charm. Panoramic views over Kyle of Tongue, ideal base for nature enthusiasts.

19 rooms, all en-suite, Open Mar-Oct, B&B per person, single from £45.00, double from £40.00, BB & Eve.Meal from £65.00.

Ullapool, Ross-shire

Map Ref: 3G6

GUEST HOUSE

Dromnan Guest House

Garve Road, Ullapool, Ross-shire, IV26 2SX
Tel:01854 612333
Email:info@dromnan.com
Web:www.dromnan.com

Modern family run guest house overlooking Lochbroom. Ideally situated, excellent facilities and stunning views. Sumptuous buffet breakfasts served in our newly built conservatory.
"All in All – First Class Accommodation" – AA ◆◆◆◆◆.

7 rooms, all en-suite, Open Jan-Dec, B&B per person, single £28.00-38.00, double £26.00-29.00.

GUEST HOUSE

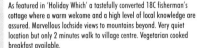

Point Cottage Guest House

22 West Shore Street, Ullapool, Ross-shire IV26 2UR
Tel:01854 612494
Email:macrae@pointcottage.co.uk
Web:www.pointcottage.co.uk

As featured in 'Holiday Which' a tastefully converted 18C fisherman's cottage where a warm welcome and a high level of local knowledge are assured. Marvellous lochside views to mountains beyond. Very quiet location but only 2 minutes walk to village centre. Vegetarian cooked breakfast available.

3 rooms, all en-suite, Open Feb-Nov, B&B per person, single £25.00-45.00, double £22.00-28.00.

GUEST HOUSE

Strathmore House

Morefield, Ullapool, Ross-shire, IV26 2TH
Tel:01854 612423 Fax:01854 613485
Email:murdo_urquhart1957@msn.com

Guest house enjoying panoramic views over Loch Broom and Ullapool. Ideal touring base for north west coast. Comfortable TV lounge and reading room.

5 rooms, all en-suite, Open Easter-Sep, B&B per person, double from £23.00.

Welcome to Scotland

The Outer Islands: Outer Hebrides, Orkney, Shetland

Villages older than time. Accordians. Viking longships on fire. Standing stones. Cheese with bite. Birds. More birds. Holidays heat up under a midnight sun...

The Old Man of Hoy is a sea stack rising 449 feet off the Isle of Hoy, Orkney.

For a spot of meditation, seriously ponder the Outer Hebrides. Stretching for 130 miles, the islands indulge your thoughts - and fantasies – with oodles of quiet space. Sea kayaking along the coastline reveals inlets of seabirds and wildlife. Dreamy beaches await you on Harris, including Luskentyre and Scarista.

And the people? Charismatic, warm and Gaelic to their last breath. Pubs ignite with the toe-tapping lilt of poetry and fiddles embracing the Gaelic creed, 'ceud mile failte' - a hundred thousand welcomes. A rich source of island life, Stornoway is the main town of Lewis. Contact an operator to join a boat, trawl the Lewis coast and heave in a lobster creel. Catch up on 3000 years of prehistory in the Calanais Standing Stones, or 1000 years of croft domestics in the preserved Black House of Arnol.

Orkney has the mythical appeal of a Tolkien novel. Fiery sunsets, ancient ruins, lyrical and vibrant people. These islands defy backwater expectations with headline-grabbing festivals on the summer's bounty, music, even science.

Skara Brae is simply the best-preserved Stone Age village in Western Europe; farmsteads at Papa Westray predate the Pyramids, and some cheeky Vikings got to the Ring of Brodgar with graffiti - 900 years ago. Scuba divers are drawn to the ghostly depths of Scapa Flow where the German fleet was scuttled at the end of the First World War. Skip to the Second World War for a unique chapel built from scrap materials and the ingenuity of 500 Italian prisoners. And follow the scent of peat to Kirkwall, a frisky hub of Orkney life, especially under a

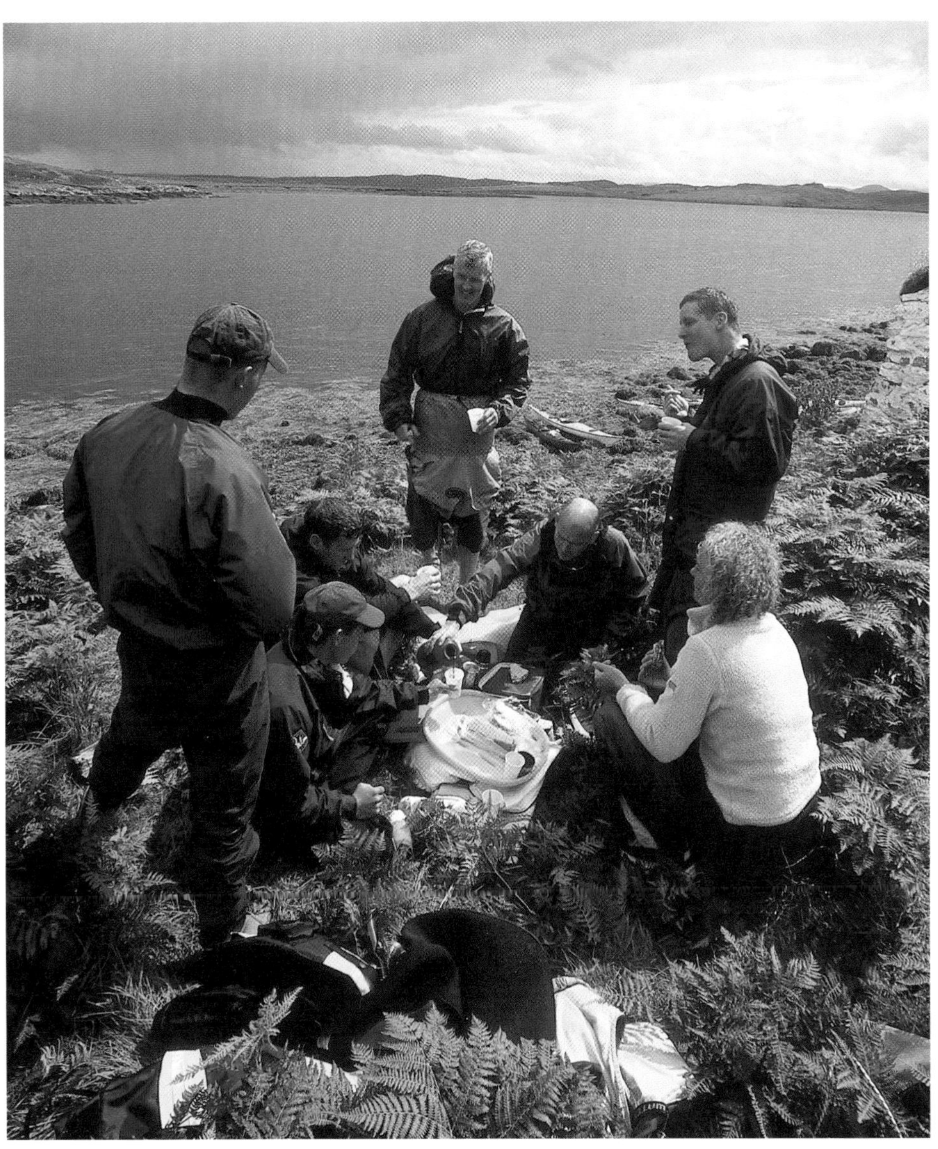

A group of kayakers take time out in the Outer Hebrides

Shetland's unmistakable fire festival, Up Helly Aa.

midnight sun. Don't overlook the jewellery shops opposite St. Magnus Cathedral; the smoky charm of Highland Park Distillery, or melting tang of Orkney cheese.

Shetland was a Viking playground, so plenty of axe waving and pathological tendencies here. Why don't you join in? A jolly good time is reserved for the world's biggest fire festival, Up Helly Aa. Held in January, a torchlit procession drags a Viking longboat through streets, sets it on fire, and retreats to the local halls for revelry. Old habits die hard in a land once home to the ancient Viking parliament of Althing and still influenced by Norse Udal law. The people have a gift for music, whether plucking the fiddle in a pub or wooing crowds, accordian style, at the October music festival.

Climb the stairs of Mousa Broch, an ancient stone tower guarding an island uninhabited for over 2000 years. The remains of 120 brochs inhabit the islands, and there are 100 or so islands to explore. And the wildlife is stunning. Puffins, arctic skuas and the rare phalaropes contribute to a bird haven, while some 1200 playful otters scour the island waters for dinner. Cue the Northern Lights, sigh, and enjoy the show...

Events

The Outer Islands: Outer Hebrides, Orkney, Shetland

OUTER HEBRIDES

19-23 JUNE
SEO SEINN
A Gaelic singing competition of lyrical beauty.
Tel: 01851 703088
www.visithebrides.com/seoseinn

MID JULY
HEBRIDEAN CELTIC FESTIVAL
Festival of Celtic music showcasing local and international talent.
Tel: 07001 878787
www.hebceltfest.com

LATE JULY
BARRA MUSIC FESTIVAL
Traditional live music festival in the beautiful setting of Barra.
Tel: 01871 810 579

Event details are subject to change please check before travelling.

ORKNEY

14-17 APRIL
ORKNEY DANCE FESTIVAL
Lively music and people will have you on the dance floor, learning new moves and old.
Tel: 01478 613104
www.orkneydancefestival.co.uk

25-28 MAY
ORKNEY FOLK FESTIVAL
Traditional music festival focused in the town of Stromness with events also staged in rural areas and smaller Islands.
Tel: 01856 851331
www.orkneyfolkfestival.com

16-21 JUNE
ST MAGNUS FESTIVAL
World-class performances and the magic of Orkney at midsummer combine to stage musical events, drama, dance, literature and the visual arts.
Tel: 01856 871445
www.stmagnusfestival.com

Event details are subject to change please check before travelling.

SHETLAND

31 JANUARY
UP HELLY AA
Viking fire festival.
Tel: 01595 693434
www.visitshetland.com

27 APRIL-30 APRIL
SHETLAND FOLK FESTIVAL
26th anniversary celebrations of this folk music festival featuring international musicians and home grown talent.
Tel: 01595 694757
www.shetlandfolkfestival.com

26 AUGUST-2 SEPTEMBER
NATWEST ISLAND GAMES XI
Lead with your feet, and your heart, in this remarkable corner of the world.
Tel: 01595 693434
www.visitshetland.com

Event details are subject to change please check before travelling.

The Outer Islands: Outer Hebrides, Orkney, Shetland

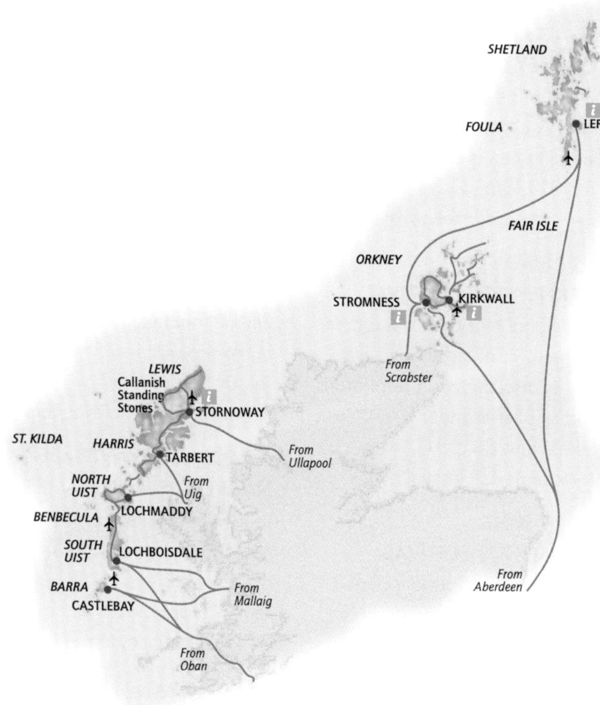

Please refer to the maps on pages xix-xxiv for the locations of establishments appearing in the main advertising section of this guide.

Finding out more...

For practical advice, ideas and information about exploring Scotland and to book your accommodation:

Tel: 0845 22 55 121*
or if calling from outside the UK: +44 (0) 1506 832121

Email: info@visitscotland.com
Web: www.visitscotland.com

* A £3 booking fee applies to telephone bookings of accommodation.

Tourist Information Centres

The Outer Islands: Outer Hebrides, Orkney, Shetland

Outer Hebrides

Castlebay
Main Street
Tel: (01871) 810336
Easter – Oct

Lochboisdale
Pier Road
Tel: (01878) 700286
Easter – Oct

Lochmaddy
Pier Road
Tel: (01876) 500321
Easter – Oct

Stornoway
26 Cromwell Street
Tel: (01851) 703088
Jan – Dec

Tarbert (Harris)
Pier Road
Tel: (01859) 502011
Jan – Dec

Orkney

Kirkwall
6 Broad Street
Tel: (01856) 872856
Jan – Dec

Stromness
Ferry Terminal Building
Tel: (01856) 850716
Jan – Dec

Shetland

Kirkwall
The Market Cross
Tel: (08701) 999440
Jan – Dec

Castlebay, Isle of Barra, Outer Hebrides

Map Ref: 3A11

SMALL HOTEL

Castlebay Hotel

Castlebay, Isle of Barra, HS9 5XD
Tel:01871 810223 Fax:01871 810455
Email:castlebayhotel@aol.com
Web:www.castlebay-hotel.co.uk

Elevated position, overlooking bay, pier and Kisimul Castle. Central location, easy access to ferry terminal. All rooms ensuite. Some rooms on ground floor level.

10 rooms, all en-suite, Open Jan-Dec excl Xmas/New Year.

Tangasdale, Isle of Barra, Outer Hebrides

Map Ref: 3A11

HOTEL

Isle of Barra Hotel

Tangasdale Beach, Isle of Barra, Western Isles, HS9 5XW
Tel:01871 810383 Fax:01871 810385
Email:barrahotel@aol.com
Web:www.isleofbarra.com/iob.html

Family run hotel, with friendly local staff, specialising in fresh local seafood, Aberdeen Angus beef and fine wines. Superbly situated overlooking beautiful white sandy bay washed by the Atlantic Ocean.

32 rooms, all en-suite, Open Easter-begn Oct, B&B per person, single £50.00, double £44.00, BB & Eve.Meal £62.00.

Creagorry, Isle of Benbecula, Outer Hebrides

Map Ref: 3B9

HOTEL

Creagorry Hotel

Creagorry, Isle of Benbecula, Western Isles, HS7 5PG
Tel:01870 602024 Fax:01870 603108
Email:reservations@iobhh.co.uk

Long established hotel (over 100 years) with popular local bar and regular entertainment. Bar lunches and suppers available, non-residents very welcome. Hotel has fishing rights over 16 Lochs and some sea-pools.

16 rooms, all en-suite, Open Jan-Dec, B&B per person, single from £58.00, double from £44.00, BB & Eve.Meal from £77.00.

Liniclate, Isle of Benbecula, Outer Hebrides

Map Ref: 3B8

HOTEL

Dark Island Hotel

Liniclate, Isle of Benbecula, Western Isles, HS7 5PJ
Tel:01870 603030 Fax:01870 602347
Email:reception@darkislandhotel.co.uk

Modern hotel in centre of Benbecula, near sandy beaches, about 4 miles (7kms) from airport. Free golf and trout fishing available.

42 rooms, all en-suite, Open Jan-Dec, B&B per person, single from £69.00, double from £48.50, BB & Eve.Meal from £90.00.

Ardhasaig, Isle of Harris, Outer Hebrides

Map Ref: 3C6

SMALL HOTEL

Ardhasaig House

Ardhasaig, Isle of Harris, HS3 3AJ
Tel:0185950 2066/2500 Fax:01859 502077
Email:accommodation@ardhasaig.co.uk
Web:www.ardhasaig.co.uk

The Good Hotel Guide. Scottish Hotel Breakfast of the Year Runner Up 2005. Scottish Island Hotel of the Year Runner Up 2005.

6 rooms, all en-suite, Open Jan-Dec, B&B per person, single from £55.00, double from £55.00, BB & Eve.Meal from £85.00.

Important: Prices stated are estimates and may be subject to amendments

Tarbert, Isle of Harris, Outer Hebrides

Map Ref: 3C6

INN

MacLeod Motel

Pier Road, Tarbert, Isle of Harris, HS3 3DG
Tel:01859 502364 Fax:01859 502578
Email:angus@macleodmotel.com
Web:www.macleodmotel.com

Friendly welcome, good food and lively lounge bar situated directly beside ferry and bus terminals.

15 rooms, some en-suite, Open Jan-Dec, B&B per person, single from £30.00, twin from £25.00, double from £35.00.

Callanish, Isle of Lewis, Outer Hebrides

Map Ref: 3D4

GUEST HOUSE

Eshcol Guest House

Breasclete, Callanish, Isle of Lewis, HS2 9ED
Tel/Fax:01851 621357
Email:neil@eshcol.com
Web:www.eshcol.com

Modern detached house quietly situated in the crofting village of Breasclete, with an open outlook over Loch Roag towards the Uig hills. Good base to explore Lewis, or just to relax. Only 2 miles to the Callanish Standing Stones. All bedrooms non-smoking. Local produce used where possible in our highly recommended evening meals. B.Y.O.B.

3 rooms, 2 en-suite, 1 with priv.bath, Open Mar-Oct, B&B per person, single from £33.00, double from £33.00, BB & Eve.Meal from £55.00.

Stornoway, Isle of Lewis, Outer Hebrides

Map Ref: 3D4

HOTEL

Caladh Inn

James Street, Stornoway, Isle of Lewis, HS1 2QN
Tel:01851 702604 Fax:01851 703158
Email:caladhinn@calahotels.com
Web:www.calahotels.com

Modern hotel, the largest on the island, situated in the centre of Stornoway, within walking distance of the ferry terminal. Local leisure and fitness centre is just across the road. The hotel makes an excellent base for exploring Lewis and Harris.

68 rooms, Open all year, B&B per person, single from £32.00, double/twin from £24.50.

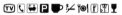

Carinish, Isle of North Uist, Outer Hebrides

Map Ref: 3B8

SMALL HOTEL

Temple View Hotel

Carinish, Isle of North Uist, Western Isles, HS6 5EJ
Tel:01876 580676 Fax:01876 580682
Email:templeviewhotel@aol.com
Web:www.templeviewhotel.co.uk

Warm and friendly family run small hotel traditionally furnished to high standards offering comfort and style with contemporary quality facilities.

10 rooms, Open Jan-Dec, room only single from £45.00, double from £85.00, family from £95.00.

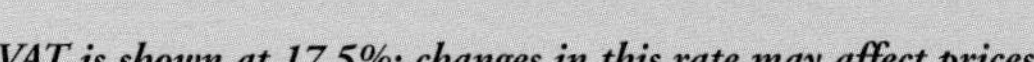

Key to symbols is on back flap.

Locheport, Isle of North Uist, Outer Hebrides — Map Ref: 3B8

★★★

SMALL HOTEL

Langass Lodge

Locheport, North Uist, Western Isles, HS6 5HA
Tel:01876 580285 Fax:01876 580385
Email:langasslodge@btconnect.com
Web:www.langasslodge.co.uk

7 rooms, all en-suite, Open Jan-Dec, B&B per room, single from £60.00, double from £90.00.

Traditional Hotel, set in splendid isolation, overlooking Loch Eport and about 8 miles (13kms) from Lochmaddy ferry terminal. Popular retreat for anglers, ornithologists and lovers of the outdoors. Fishing available on all of the North Uists renowned lochs.

C £ W V

Kirkwall, Orkney — Map Ref: 5B12

★★

GUEST HOUSE

Sanderlay Guest House

2 Viewfield Drive, Kirkwall, Orkney, KW15 1RB
Tel:01856 875587 Fax:01856 876350
Email:enquiries@sanderlay.co.uk

7 rooms, some en-suite, Open Jan-Dec excl Xmas, New Year, B&B per person, single £20.00-26.00, double £18.00-24.00.

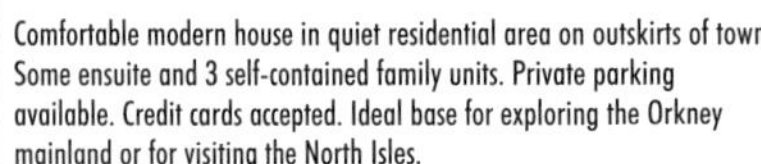

Comfortable modern house in quiet residential area on outskirts of town. Some ensuite and 3 self-contained family units. Private parking available. Credit cards accepted. Ideal base for exploring the Orkney mainland or for visiting the North Isles.

C £ W V

★★★

GUEST HOUSE

St Ola Hotel

Harbour Street, Kirkwall, Orkney, KW15 1LE
Tel/Fax:01856 875090
Email:enquiries@stolahotel.co.uk
Web:www.stolahotel.co.uk

6 rooms, all en-suite, Open Jan-Dec excl Xmas/New Year, B&B per person, single from £37.00, double/twin from £27.00.

Friendly, family run, harbour front hotel. All rooms have ensuite facilities. Convenient for North Isles ferries.

Stromness, Orkney — Map Ref: 5B12

★★★

HOTEL

Stromness Hotel

The Pier Head, Stromness, Orkney, KW16 3AA
Tel:01856 850298 Fax:01856 850610
Email:info@stromnesshotel.com
Web:www.stromnesshotel.com

40 rooms, all en-suite, Open Jan-Dec excl Xmas/New Year, B&B pppn Off-season from £29.00. Peak-season from £50.00.

Traditional hotel, situated in the heart of the fishing port of Stromness. Overlooking the harbour, with views out towards Scapa Flow. Much to see and do locally, plus all of Orkney's famous archaeological sites. Fishing, golf, birdwatching are all available.

C £ V

Important: Prices stated are estimates and may be subject to amendments

VisitScotland, in conjunction with the English Tourism Council and Wales Tourist Board operates a national accessible scheme that identifies, acknowledges and promotes those accommodation establishments that meet the needs of visitors with disabilities.

The three categories of accessibility, drawn up in close consultation with specialist organisations concerned with the needs of people with disabilities are:

Category 1

Unassisted wheelchair access for residents

Category 2

Assisted wheelchair access for residents

Category 3

Access for residents with mobility difficulties

Category 1

ABERDEEN
Aberdeen Patio Hotel
Beach Boulevard
Aberdeen
Aberdeenshire
AB24 5EF
Tel: 01224 633339

Copthorne Hotel
122 Huntly Street
Aberdeen
AB10 1SU
Tel: 01224 630404

Crynoch
164 Bon-Accord Street
Aberdeen
Scotland
AB10 2TX
Tel: 01224 582743

Express by Holiday Inn
Chapel Street
Aberdeen
AB10 1SQ
Tel: 01224 623500

Kings Hall
University of Aberdeen
Aberdeen
AB24 3FX
Tel: 01224 272660

Thistle Aberdeen Airport Hotel
Argyll Road
Aberdeen
Aberdeenshire
AB21 0AF
Tel: 01224 640233

ABERNETHY
Gattaway Farm
Abernethy
Perthshire
PH2 9LQ
Tel: 01738 850746

ABINGTON
Days Inn
Welcome Break M74/A7
Abington
Lanarkshire
ML12 6RG
Tel: 01864 502782

ACHNASHEEN
Loch Torridon Hotel
Torridon
Achnasheen
Ross-shire
IV22 2EY
Tel: 01445 791242

ALEXANDRIA
De Vere Cameron House
Loch Lomond
Alexandria
Dunbartonshire
G83 8QZ
Tel: 01389 755565

ALTENS, ABERDEEN
Thistle Aberdeen Altens
Soutarhead Road
Altens, Aberdeen
Aberdeenshire
AB12 3LF
Tel: 01224 723101

AUCHENCAIRN, BY CASTLE DOUGLAS
Balcary Bay Hotel
Auchencairn, By Castle Douglas
Kirkcudbrightshire
DG7 1QZ
Tel: 01556 640217

AUCHTERARDER
The Gleneagles Hotel
Auchterarder
Perthshire
PH3 1NF
Tel: 01764 662231

AULDEARN
Covenanters' Inn
High Street
Auldearn
Nairn
IV12 5TG
Tel: 01667 452456

BALLACHULISH
Isles of Glencoe Hotel & Leisure Centre
Ballachulish
Argyll PH49 4HL
Tel: 01855 821582

BALLATER
Glenernan
37 Braemar Road
Ballater
Aberdeenshire
AB35 5RQ
Tel: 013397 53111

ISLE OF BARRA
Northbay House
Balnabodach
Isle of Barra
Outer Hebrides HS9 5UT
Tel: 01871 890255

BRAEMAR
The Invercauld Arms Hotel
Invercauld Road
Braemar
Aberdeenshire
AB35 5YR

BROUGHTON, BY BIGGAR
The Glenholm Centre
Broughton, by Biggar
Lanarkshire
ML12 6JF
Tel: 01899 830408

BROUGHTY FERRY, DUNDEE
The Fishermans Tavern Hotel
10-16 Fort Street
Broughty Ferry, Dundee
Angus
DD5 2AD
Tel: 01382 775941

BURNTISLAND
Kingswood Hotel
Kinghorn Road
Burntisland
Fife
KY3 9LL
Tel: 01592 872329

CARRADALE
Dunvalanree
Portrigh Bay
Carradale
Argyll
PA28 6SE
Tel: 01583 431226

CASTLE DOUGLAS
Douglas House B&B
63 Queen Street
Castle Douglas
Dumfries
DG7 1HS
Tel: 01556 503262

CLYDEBANK
Beardmore Hotel
Beardmore Street
Clydebank
Greater Glasgow
G81 4SA
Tel: 0141 951 6000

CONNEL, BY OBAN
Wide Mouthed Frog
Dunstaffnage Marina
Connel, by Oban
Argyll
PA37 1PX
Tel: 01631 567005

COYLTON
Finlayson Arms Hotel
24 Hillhead
Coylton
Ayrshire
KA6 6JT
Tel: 01292 570298

DAVIOT
The Lodge at Daviot Mains
Daviot
By Inverness
IV2 5ER
Tel: 01463 772215

DUNDEE
Days Inn Dundee
296a Strathmore Avenue
Dundee
DD3 6SP
Tel: 01382 826000

West Park Centre
319 Perth Road
Dundee
Angus
DD2 1NN
Tel: 01382 573050

DUNOON
Dhailling Lodge
155 Alexandra Parade
Dunoon
Argyll
PA23 8AW
Tel: 01369 701253

EDINBURGH
Ardgarth Guest House
1 St Mary's Place, Portobello
Edinburgh
EH15 2QF
Tel: 0131 669 3021

Best Western Edinburgh City Hotel
79 Lauriston Place
Edinburgh
EH3 9HZ
Tel: 0131 622 7979

Brae Lodge Guest House
30 Liberton Brae
Edinburgh
Lothian
EH16 6AF
Tel: 0131 672 2876

Express By Holiday Inn
16-22 Picardy Place
Edinburgh
Lothian EH1 3JT
Tel: 0131 5582300

Jurys Inn Edinburgh
43 Jeffrey Street
Edinburgh
Lothian
EH1 1DH
Tel: 0131 200 3300

Melville Guest House
2 Duddingston Crescent
Edinburgh
Lothian
EH15 3AS
Tel: 0131 669 7856

Novotel Edinburgh Centre
80 Lauriston Place
Edinburgh
Lothian
EH3 9DE
Tel: 0131 656 3500

Premier Travel Inn Metro
1 Morrison Link
Edinburgh
EH3 8DN
Tel: 0870 238 3319

Ramada Mount Royal Hotel
53 Princes Street
Edinburgh
EH2 2DG
Tel: 0131 225 7161

Thistle Edinburgh
107 Leith Street
Edinburgh
EH1 3SW
Tel: 0141 332 3311

Toby Carvery & Innkeepers Lodge
114-116 St Johns Road
Edinburgh
EH12 8AX
Tel: 0131 334 8235

FALLS OF TRUIM
Crubenbeg House
Falls of Truim
By Newtonmore
PH20 1BE
Tel: 01540 673300

FINSTOWN
Lynwood
Maitland Place
Finstown
Orkney
KW17 2EQ
Tel: 01856 761786

FORGANDENNY
Battledown Bed & Breakfast
Off Station Road
Forgandenny
Perthshire
PH2 9EL
Tel: 01738 812471

FORT WILLIAM
Cuil-Na-Sithe
Lochyside
Fort William
Inverness-shire
PH33 7NX
Tel: 01397 702 267

GAILES
The Gailes Lodge
Marine Drive
Gailes
Irvine
KA11 5AE
Tel: 01294 204040

GLASGOW
Carlton George Hotel
44 West George Street
Glasgow
G2 1DH
Tel: 0141 353 6373

Glasgow Hilton
1 William Street
Glasgow
G3 8HT
Tel: 0141 204 5555

Glasgow Marriott
500 Argyle Street
Glasgow
G3 8RR
Tel: 0141 226 5577

Holiday Inn
161 West Nile Street
Glasgow
G1 2RL
Tel: 0141 352 8300

Holiday Inn Glasgow City West
Bothwell Street
Glasgow
G2 7EN
0870 400 9032

Jurys Inn Glasgow
Jamaica Street
Glasgow
G1 4QE
Tel: 0141 334 8161

Tulip Inn Glasgow
80 Ballater Street
Glasgow
G5 0TW
Tel: 0141 429 4233

GREENOCK
Express by Holiday Inn
Cartsburn
Greenock PA15 4RT
Tel: 01475 786666

James Watt College
Waterfront Campus,
Customhouse Way
Greenock
Renfrewshire
PA15 1EN
Tel: 01475 731360

GRETNA
The Garden House Hotel
Sarkfoot Road
Gretna
Dumfriesshire
DG16 5EP
Tel: 01461 337621

GRETNA GREEN
Days Inn
Welcome Break Service Area,
M74
Gretna Green
Dumfriesshire
DG16 5HQ
Tel: 01461 337566

HADDINGTON
Maitlandfield House Hotel
24 Sidegate
Haddington
East Lothian
EH41 4BZ
Tel: 01620 826513

INVERALMOND, PERTH
Express by Holiday Inn
200 Dunkeld Road
Inveralmond, Perth
Perthshire
PH1 3AQ
Tel: 01738 636666

INVERGORDON
Delny House
Delny
Invergordon
Ross-shire
IV18 0NP
Tel: 01862 842678

INVERKIP
The Foresters
Station Road
Inverkip
Renfrewshire
PA16 0AY
Tel: 01475 521433

INVERNESS
Inverness Marriott
Culcabock Road
Inverness
Inverness-shire
IV2 3LP
Tel: 01463 237166

Silverwells Guest House
28 Ness Bank
Inverness
IV2 4SF
Tel: 01463 232113

IRVINE
Thistle Irvine
46 Annick Road
Irvine
Ayrshire
KA11 4LD
Tel: 0141 332 3311

KILMARNOCK
Park Hotel
Rugby Park
Kilmarnock
Ayrshire
KA1 2DP
Tel: 01563 545999

KINLOCHLEVEN
Tigh-Na-Cheo
Garbien Road
Kinlochleven
Argyll PH50 4SE
Tel: 01855 831434

KIRKWALL
Lav'rockha Guest House
Inganess Road
Kirkwall
Orkney KW15 1SP
Tel: 01856 876103

LAIRG
Lochview
Lochside
Lairg
Sutherland
IV27 4EH
Tel: 01549 402578

LERWICK
Shetland Hotel
Holmsgarth Road
Lerwick
Shetland
ZE1 OPW
Tel: 01595 695515

LEUCHARS, BY ST ANDREWS
Drumoig Hotel & Golf Resort
Drumoig
Leuchars, by St Andrews
Fife
KY16 0BE
Tel: 01382 541800

LEWIS
Western Isles Cross Inn
Cross Ness
Lewis, Western Isles
HS2 0SN
Tel: 01851 810152

LIVINGSTON
Ramada Jarvis Livingston
Almondview
Livingston
West Lothian EH54 6QB
Tel: 01506 431222

LOCHMABEN
The Crown Hotel
8 Bruce Street
Lochmaben
Dumfriesshire
DG11 1PD
Tel: 01387 811750

LOSSIEMOUTH
Ceilidh B&B
34 Clifton Road
Lossiemouth
Moray IV31 6DP
Tel: 01343 815848

MOFFAT
Lochhouse Farm Retreat Centre
Beattock
Moffat
Dumfries & Galloway
DG10 9SG
Tel: 01683 300451

MOTHERWELL
Express By Holiday Inn
Strathclyde Park M74 Jct 5
Motherwell
Lanarkshire ML1 3RB
Tel: 01698 858585

Motherwell College
Stewart Hall
Dalzell Drive
Motherwell
Lanarkshire
ML1 2DD
Tel: 01698 261890

NAIRN
Claymore House Hotel
45 Seabank Road
Nairn
Inverness-shire
IV12 4EY
Tel: 01667 453731

Windsor Hotel
16 Albert Street
Nairn
Inverness-shire
IV12 4HP
Tel: 01667 453108

PAISLEY
Express by Holiday Inn Glasgow Airport
St Andrews Drive
Paisley PA3 2TJ
Tel: 0131 553 4422

Travelodge Glasgow Airport
Marchburn Drive
Paisley
Glasgow PA3 2AR
Tel: 0141 848 1359

PEEBLES
Cringletie House Hotel
Edinburgh Road
Peebles
Peeblesshire
EH45 8PL
Tel: 01721 725750

PETERHEAD
Invernettie Guest House
South Road
Peterhead
Aberdeenshire
AB42 0YX
Tel: 01779 473530

PITFODELS, ABERDEEN
Marcliffe at Pitfodels
North Deeside Road
Pitfodels, Aberdeen
AB15 9YA
Tel: 01224 861000

PITLOCHRY
Atholl Villa Guest House
29/31 Atholl Road
Pitlochry
Perthshire
PH16 5BX
Tel: 01796 473820

POINT
Dolly's B&B
33 Aignish
Point
Lewis, Western Isles
HS2 0PB
Tel: 01851 870755

PORTREE
Cuillin Hills Hotel
Portree
Isle of Skye
IV51 9QU
Tel: 01478 612003

Viewfield House Hotel
Portree
Isle of Skye
IV51 9EU
Tel: 01478 612217

PRESTWICK
Golf View Hotel
17 Links Road
Prestwick
Ayrshire
KA9 1QG
Tel: 01292 671234

ROTHESAY
The Boat House
15 Battery Place
Rothesay
Argyll & Bute
PA20 9DP
Tel: 01700 502696

SALEN
Ard Mhor House
Pier Road
Salen
Isle of Mull PA72 6JL
Tel: 01680 300255

SOUTH UIST
Crossroads
Stoneybridge
South Uist
Western Isles
HS8 5SD
Tel: 01870 620321

BY SPEAN BRIDGE
Old Pines Hotel and Restaurant
Gairlochy Road
By Spean Bridge
Inverness-shire
PH34 4EG
Tel: 01397 712324

ST ANDREWS
The Old Station, Country House
Stratvithie Bridge
St Andrews
Fife KY16 8LR
Tel: 01334 880505

ST BOSWELLS, MELROSE
Dryburgh Abbey Hotel
St Boswells, Melrose
Scottish Borders
TD6 0RQ
Tel: 01835 822261

STIRLING
Express by Holiday Inn - Stirling
Springkerse Business Park
Stirling
Stirlingshire
FK7 7XH
Tel: 01786 449922

Stirling Management Centre
University of Stirling
Stirling
FK9 4LA
Tel: 01786 451666

STONEHOUSE
Thorndale Guest House
Manse Road
Stonehouse
Lanarkshire
ML9 3NX
Tel: 01698 791133

TOBERMORY
Highland Cottage
Breadalbane Street
Tobermory
Isle of Mull
PA75 6PD
Tel: 01688 302030

TURNBERRY
The Westin Turnberry Resort
Turnberry
Ayrshire
KA26 9LT
Tel: 01655 331000

WALLS
Burrastow House
Walls
Shetland
ZE2 9PD
Tel: 01595 809307

Category 2

ABBOTSINCH
Ramada Glasgow Airport
Marchburn Drive
Abbotsinch
Paisley
PA3 2SJ
Tel: 0141 8402200

ABERDEEN
Aberdeen Marriott Hotel
Riverview Drive
Farburn, Dyce
Aberdeenshire
AB21 7AZ
Tel: 0870 400 7291

Crombie Johnston
University of Aberdeen
Aberdeen
AB24 3TS
Tel: 01224 272660

ABERFELDY
Tomvale
Tom of Cluny
Aberfeldy
Perthshire PH15 2JT
Tel: 01887 820171

ABERFOYLE
Crannaig House
Trossachs Road
Aberfoyle
Stirlingshire
FK8 3SR
Tel: 01877 382276

BY ABERFOYLE
Forest Hills Hotel
Kinlochard
By Aberfoyle
Stirlingshire
FK8 3TL
Tel: 01877 387277

AVIEMORE
MacDonald Academy
Aviemore Highland Resort
Aviemore
Inverness-shire
PH22 1PF
Tel: 01479 810781

AYR
Horizon Hotel
Esplanade
Ayr
Ayrshire
KA7 1DT
Tel: 01292 264384

BY AYR
Alt-Na-Craig
Hollybush
By Ayr KA6 7EB
Tel: 01292 560555

AYRSHIRE
Glenapp Castle
Ballantrae
Ayrshire
KA26 0NZ
Tel: 01465 831212

BALLACHULISH
The Ballachulish Hotel
Ballachulish
Argyll
PH49 4JY
Tel: 01855 811606

BALTASOUND, UNST
The Baltasound Hotel
Baltasound, Unst
Shetland ZE2 9DS
Tel: 01957 711334

BLACK ISLE
Autumn Gold
Blablair
Black Isle
Ross & Cromarty
IV7 8LR
Tel: 01381 622315

BRIDGE OF ALLAN
The Queen's Hotel
24 Henderson Street
Bridge of Allan
Stirlingshire
FK9 4HP
Tel: 01786 833268

BRODICK
Auchrannie Country House Hotel
Brodick
Isle of Arran
KA27 8BZ
Tel: 01770 302234

BRORA
Glenaveron
Golf Road
Brora
Sutherland
KW9 6QS
Tel: 01408 621 601

CARRUTHERSTOWN
Hetland Hall Hotel
Carrutherstown
Dumfriesshire
DG1 4JX
Tel: 01387 840201

CRIEFF
Comely Bank Guest House
32 Burrell Street
Crieff
Perthshire PH7 4DT
Tel: 01764 653409

Murraypark Hotel
Connaught Terrace
Crieff
Perthshire
PH7 3DJ
Tel: 01764 653731

CUMBERNAULD
Red Deer & Innkeeper's Lodge
1 Auchenkilns Park
Cumbernauld
North Lanarkshire
G68 9AZ
Tel: 01236 795 861

DRUMNADROCHIT
Clunebeg Lodge Guest House
Clunebeg Estate
Drumnadrochit
Inverness-shire
IV63 6US
Tel: 01456 450387

Woodlands
East Lewiston
Drumnadrochit
Inverness-shire
IV63 6UW
Tel: 01456 450356

DUNFERMLINE
Best Western
Keavil House Hotel
Crossford
Dunfermline
Fife KY12 8QW
Tel: 01383 736258

Garvock House Hotel
St John's Drive, Transy
Dunfermline
Fife KY12 7TU
Tel: 01383 621067

Rooms at 29 Bruce Street
29-35 Bruce Street
Dunfermline
Fife
KY12 7AG
Tel: 01383 840041

DYCE
Dyce Skean Dhu Hotel
Farburn Terrace
Dyce
Aberdeenshire
AB21 7DW
Tel: 01224 723101

Speedbird Inn
Argyll Road
Dyce, Aberdeen
Aberdeenshire
AB21 0AF
Tel: 01224 772884

EDINBURGH
Edinburgh First
Chancellor Court, Pollock Halls
18 Holyrood Park Road
Edinburgh
EH10 5AY
Tel: 0131 651 2011

EDINBURGH
Aalpha Laurels
320 Gilmerton Road
Edinburgh
Midlothian
EH17 7PR
Tel: 0131 666 2229

Caledonian Hilton Hotel
Princes Street
Edinburgh
EH1 2AB
Tel: 0131 222 8888

Edinburgh Marriott
111 Glasgow Road
Edinburgh
EH12 8NF
0870 400 7293

Hilton Edinburgh Airport
Edinburgh International Airport
Edinburgh
EH28 8LL
Tel: 0131 519 4400

Hilton Edinburgh Grosvenor
7-21 Grosvenor Street
Edinburgh
EH12 5EF
Tel: 0131 226 6001

Holiday Inn Edinburgh
Corstorphine Road
Edinburgh
EH12 6UA
Tel: 0870 400 9026

Holiday Inn Edinburgh-North
107 Queensferry Road
Edinburgh
EH4 3HL
Tel: 0131-332-2442

Queen Margaret College
36 Clerwood Terrace
Edinburgh
EH12 8TS
Tel: 0131 317 3317/3314

FORT WILLIAM
Clan MacDuff Hotel
Achintore Road
Fort William
Inverness-shire
PH33 6RW
Tel: 01397 702341

GLASGOW
Bewleys Hotel Glasgow
110 Bath Street
Glasgow
G2 2EN
Tel: 0141 353 0800

Campanile Glasgow
Tunnel Street
Glasgow
Scotland
G3 8HL
Tel: 0141 2877700

Glasgow Moat House
Congress Road
Glasgow
G3 8QT
Tel: 0141 306 9988

Ibis Hotel Glasgow
220 West Regent Street
Glasgow
G2 4DQ
Tel: 0141 225 6000

Wolfson Hall
Kelvin Campus,
West Scotland Science Park
Maryhill Road
Glasgow
G20 0TH
Tel: 0141 330 3110

Milton Hotel & Spa, Glasgow
27 Washington Street
Glasgow
G3 8AZ
Tel: 0141 222 2929

Novotel Glasgow Centre
181 Pitt Street
Glasgow
G2 4DT
Tel: 0141 222 2775

Queen Margaret Hall
55 Bellshaugh Road
Glasgow
G12 0SQ
Tel: 0141 330 3110

The Millennium, Glasgow Hotel
George Square
Glasgow
G2 1DS
Tel: 0141 332 6711

GOREBRIDGE
Ivory House
14 Vogrie Road
Gorebridge
Midlothian
EH23 4HH
Tel: 01875 820755

GRANGEMOUTH
Leapark Hotel
130 Bo'ness Road
Grangemouth
Stirlingshire
FK3 9BX
Tel: 01324 486733

GRANTOWN-ON-SPEY
Muckrach Lodge Hotel
Dulnain Bridge
Grantown-on-spey
Moray PH26 3LY
Tel: 01479 851257

GRETNA
The Willows
Loanwath Road
Gretna
Dumfriesshire
DG16 5ES
Tel: 01461 337996

HAWICK
Whitchester Guest House
Hawick
Roxburghshire
TD9 7LN
Tel: 01450 377477

HOY
Stromabank
Hoy
Orkney
KW16 3PA
Tel: 01856 701494

INVERARAY
Loch Fyne Hotel
Newtown
Inveraray
Argyll PA32 8XJ
Tel: 0131 554 7173

INVERNESS
Ramada Jarvis Inverness
Church Street
Inverness
Inverness-shire
IV1 1DX
Tel: 01463 235181

ISLE OF MULL
Seilisdeir
Lochdon
Isle of Mull
PA64 6AP
Tel: 01680 812465

KELSO
Ingleston House
Abbey Row
Kelso
Roxburghshire
TD5 7HQ
Tel: 01573 225800/225315

KINGUSSIE
Arden House
Newtonmore Road
Kingussie
Inverness-shire
PH21 1HE
Tel: 01540 661369

KINLOCH RANNOCH
Dunalastair Hotel
The Square
Kinloch Rannoch
Perthshire
PH16 5PW
Tel: 01882 632323

KIRKMICHAEL, BLAIRGOWRIE
The Log Cabin Hotel
Glen Derby
Kirkmichael, Blairgowrie
Perthshire
PH10 7NA
Tel: 01250 881288

KIRKPATRICK FLEMING, BY LOCKERBIE
The Mill
Grahamshill
Kirkpatrick Fleming, by Lockerbie
Dumfriesshire
DG11 3BQ
Tel: 01461 800344

KIRKWALL
Eastbank House
East Road
Kirkwall
Orkney
KW15 1LX
Tel: 01856 870179

LEDAIG
Isle of Eriska Hotel
Ledaig
Argyll
PA37 1SD
Tel: 01631 720371

LOCHGILPHEAD
Empire Travel Lodge
Union Street
Lochgilphead
Argyll
PA31 8JS
Tel: 01546 602381

LOCKERBIE
Dryfesdale Country House Hotel
Dryfebridge
Lockerbie
Dumfriesshire
DG11 2SF
Tel: 01576 202427

MARKINCH, BY GLENROTHES
Balbirnie House Hotel
Balbirnie Park
Markinch, by Glenrothes
Fife
KY7 6NE
Tel: 01592 610066

MILLPORT
The Cathedral of the Isles
The College
Millport
Isle of Cumbrae
KA28 0HE
Tel: 01475 530353

MINARD
Minard Castle
Minard
Argyll
PA32 8YB
Tel: 01546 886272

MOTHERWELL
Moorings Hotel
114 Hamilton Road
Motherwell
Lanarkshire
ML1 3DG
Tel: 01698 258131

The Alona Hotel
Strathclyde Country Park
Motherwell
North Lanarkshire
ML1 3RT
Tel: 01698 333777

NETHYBRIDGE
Nethybridge Hotel
Nethybridge
Inverness-shire
PH25 3DP
Tel: 01479 821203

NEW LANARK
New Lanark Mill Hotel
New Lanark
Lanarkshire
ML11 9DB
Tel: 01555 667200

NORTH RONALDSAY
Observatory Guest House
North Ronaldsay
Orkney
KW17 2BE
Tel: 011857 633200

PEEBLES
Glentress Hotel
Innerleithen Road
Peebles
Peebles-shire
EH45 8NB
Tel: 01721 720100

PERTH
Huntingtower Hotel
Crieff Road
Perth
Perthshire
PH1 3JT
Tel: 01738 583771

PITLOCHRY
Cuil-an-Daraich
2 Cuil-an-Daraich, Logierait
Pitlochry
Perthshire
PH9 0LH
Tel: 01796 482750

PLOCKTON
Plockton Hotel
Harbour Street
Plockton
Ross-shire
IV52 8TN
Tel: 01599 544274

POLMONT
Inchyra Grange Hotel
Grange Road
Polmont
Stirlingshire
FK2 0YB
Tel: 01324 711911

PRESTWICK
Parkstone Hotel
Esplanade
Prestwick
Ayrshire
KA9 1QN
Tel: 01292 477286

ROY BRIDGE
The Stronlossit Inn
Roy Bridge
Inverness-shire
PH31 4AG
Tel: 0800 015 5321

SANQUHAR
Newark
Sanquhar
Dumfriesshire
DG4 6HN
Tel: 01659 50263

SCONE
Perth Airport Skylodge
Norwell Drive, Perth Airport
Scone
Perthshire PH2 6PL
Tel: 01738 555700

ST ANDREWS
Rufflets Country House Hotel
Strathkinness Low Road
St Andrews
Fife
KY16 9TX
Tel: 01334 472594

BY TAYNUILT
Roineabhal Country House
Kilchrenan
by Taynuilt
Argyll PA35 1HD
Tel: 01866 833207

THURSO
Weigh Inn Hotel
Burnside
Thurso
Caithness
KW14 7UG
Tel: 01847 893722

TROON
South Beach Hotel
South Beach
Troon
Ayrshire
KA10 6EG
Tel: 01292 312033

TUMMEL BRIDGE
Kynachan Loch Tummel Hotel
Tummel Bridge
Perthshire
PH16 5SB
Tel: 01389 713713

WESTHILL
Copperfield
Culloden Road
Westhill
Inverness
IV2 5BP
Tel: 01463 792251

WHITBURN
Hilcroft Hotel
East Main Street
Whitburn
West Lothian
EH47 0JU
Tel: 01501 740818

Category 3

ABERDEEN
Britannia Hotel
Malcolm Road
Aberdeen
Grampian
AB21 9LN
Tel: 01224 409988

Northern Hotel
1 Great Northern Road
Aberdeen
AB24 3PS
Tel: 01224 483342

ABERDOUR
Aberdour Hotel
38 High Street
Aberdour
Fife
KY3 0SW
Tel: 01383 860325

ABERFOYLE
Rob Roy Hotel
Aberfoyle
Stirlingshire
FK8 3UX
Tel: 01877 382245

ABERUTHVEN
Kilrymont
8 Loanfoot Park
Aberuthven
Perthshire PH3 1JF
Tel: 01764 662660

ABOYNE
Chesterton House
Formaston Park
Aboyne
Aberdeenshire AB34 5HF
Tel: 013398 86740

BY ACHMORE
Soluis Mu Thuath
Braeintra
by Achmore
Lochalsh
IV53 8UP
Tel: 01599 577219

ARDFERN,BY LOCHGILPHEAD
Galley of Lorne Inn
Main Street
Ardfern,by Lochgilphead
Argyll
PA31 8QN
Tel: 01852 500284

ARROCHAR
Village Inn
Main Street
Arrochar
Dunbartonshire
G83 7AX
Tel: 01301 702279

AUCHTERARDER
Greystanes
Western Road
Auchterarder
Perthshire PH3 1SS
Tel: 01764 664239

AVIEMORE
Ravenscraig Guest House
141 Grampian Road
Aviemore
Inverness-shire
PH22 1RP
Tel: 01479 810278

Waverley
35 Strathspey Avenue
Aviemore
Inverness-shire
PH22 1SN
Tel: 01479 811226

AVOCH
Inverleod
Toll Road
Avoch
Ross-shire
IV9 8PR
Tel: 01381 621595

AYR
Fairfield House Hotel
12 Fairfield Road
Ayr
Ayrshire
KA7 2AR
Tel: 01292 267461

Miller House
36 Miller Road
Ayr
Ayrshire KA7 2AY
Tel: 01292 282016

BY AYR
Enterkine Country House
Annbank
By Ayr
Ayrshire KA6 5AL
Tel: 01292 521608

BALLATER
Darroch Learg Hotel
Braemar Road
Ballater
Aberdeenshire
AB35 5UX
Tel: 01339 755443

Moorside Guest House
26 Braemar Road
Ballater
Aberdeenshire
AB35 5RL
Tel: 01339 755492

BALLOCH
Anchorage Guest House
31 Balloch Road
Balloch
Dunbartonshire
G83 8SS
Tel: 01389 753336

BELLOCHANTUY, BY CAMPBELTOWN
Argyll Hotel
Bellochantuy,
by Campbeltown
Argyll
PA28 6QE
Tel: 01583 421212

BELLSHILL
Hilton Strathclyde
Pheonix Crescent
Bellshill
North Lanarkshire
ML4 3JQ
Tel: 01698 395500

BENDERLOCH, OBAN
Island Home
12 Pony Park, Letterwalton
Benderloch, Oban
Argyll
PA37 1SA
Tel: 01631 720078

BIGGAR
Cormiston Cottage
Cormiston Road
Biggar
Lanarkshire
ML12 6NS
Tel: 01899 220200

BISHOPTON
Mar Hall
Mar Estate
Bishopton
Renfrewshire
PA7 5PU
Tel: 0141 812 9999

BLACKFORD
Blackford Hotel
Moray Street
Blackford
Perthshire
PH4 1QF
Tel: 01764 682497

BLAIRGOWRIE
Holmrigg
Wester Essendy
Blairgowrie
Perthshire
PH10 6RD
Tel: 01250 884309

BRIDGE OF ALLAN
Lynedoch
7 Mayne Avenue
Bridge of Allan
Stirlingshire
FK9 4QU
Tel: 01786 832178

BRIDGE OF CALLY
Bridge of Cally Hotel
Bridge of Cally
Perthshire PH10 7JJ
Tel: 01250 886231

Glen Albyn
Bridge of Cally
Perthshire
PH10 7JL
Tel: 01250 886352

BROADFORD
Seaview
Main Street
Broadford
Isle of Skye
IV49 9AB
Tel: 01471 820308

BRODICK
Belvedere Guest House
Alma Road
Brodick
Isle of Arran
KA27 8AZ
Tel: 01770 302397

Strathwhillan House
Brodick
Isle of Arran
KA27 8BQ
Tel: 01770 302331

BUCKIE
The Bungalow
81 High Street
Buckie
Banffshire
AB56 1BB
Tel: 01542 832367

CALLANDER
Roman Camp Hotel
Main Street
Callander
Perthshire
FK17 8BG
Tel: 01877 330003

The Crags Hotel
101 Main Street
Callander
Perthshire
FK17 8BQ
Tel: 01877 330257

The Knowe
Ancaster Road
Callander
Perthshire
FK17 8EL
Tel: 01877 330076

The Old Rectory Guest House
Leny Road
Callander
Perthshire
FK17 8AL
Tel: 01877 339215

CANDERSIDE TOLL, BY LARKHALL
Shawlands Hotel
Ayr Road
Canderside Toll, by Larkhall
Lanarkshire
ML9 2TZ
Tel: 01698 791111

COLDINGHAM
Dunlaverock
Coldingham Bay
Coldingham
Berwickshire
TD14 5PA
Tel: 01890 771450

COLVEND, DALBEATTIE
Clonyard House Hotel
Colvend, Dalbeattie
Kircudbrightshire
DG5 4QW
Tel: 01556 630372

COMRIE
Drumearn Cottage
The Ross
Comrie
Perthshire
PH6 2JU
Tel: 01764 670030

CONTIN
Hideaway
Craigdarroch Drive
Contin
Ross-shire
IV14 9EL
Tel: 01997 421127

COUPAR ANGUS
Red House Hotel
Station Road
Coupar Angus
Perthshire
PH13 9AL
Tel: 01828 628500

CRIEFF
Achray House Hotel
St Fillans
Crieff
Perthshire
PH6 2NF
Tel: 01764 685 231

Ardo Howe
31 Burrell Street
Crieff
Perthshire
PH7 4DT
Tel: 01764 652825

Crieff Hydro Hotel
Crieff
Perthshire
PH7 3LQ
Tel: 01764 655555

Fendoch Guest House
Sma' Glen
Crieff
Perthshire
PH7 3LW
Tel: 01764 653446

Tuchethill House
Dollerie
Crieff
Perthshire
PH7 3NX
Tel: 01764 653188

DALBEATTIE
Bellevue B&B
Port Road
Dalbeattie
DG5 4AZ
Tel: 01556 611833

DALMALLY
Glenorchy Lodge Hotel
Dalmally
Argyll
PA33 1AA
Tel: 018382 00312

DALRYMPLE
Kirkton Inn
1 Main Street
Dalrymple
Ayrshire
KA6 6DF
Tel: 01292 560241

DIRLETON
Station House
Station Road
Dirleton
North Berwick
EH39 5LR
Tel: 01620 890512

DORNOCH
Dornoch Castle Hotel
Castle Street
Dornoch
Sutherland
IV25 3SD
Tel: 01862 810216

DUFFTOWN
Braehead Villa
Braehead Terrace
Dufftown
Keith, Banffshire
AB55 4AN
Tel: 01340 320461

DUMFRIES
Hazeldean Guest House
4 Moffat Road
Dumfries DG1 1NJ
Tel: 01387 266178

Netherfield
Lochanhead
Dumfries
Dumfries & Galloway
DG2 8JE
Tel: 01387 730217

Torbay Lodge
31 Lovers Walk
Dumfries
DG1 1LR
Tel: 01387 253922

Wallamhill House
Kirkton
Dumfries
Dumfriesshire
DG1 1SL
Tel: 01387 248249

DUNBAR
Goldenstones Hotel
Queens Road
Dunbar
East Lothian
EH42 1LG
Tel: 01368 862356

DUNDEE
Hilton Dundee
Earl Grey Place
Dundee
Angus
DD1 4DE
Tel: 01382 229271

DUNFERMLINE
Clarke Cottage Guest House
139 Halbeath Road
Dunfermline
Fife
KY11 4LA
Tel: 01383 735935

Pitbauchlie House Hotel
Aberdour Road
Dunfermline
Fife
KY11 4PB
Tel: 01383 722282

DUNTOCHER
West Park Hotel
Great Western Road
Duntocher
Clydebank G81 6DB
Tel: 01389 872333

EDINBURGH
Abbey Lodge Hotel
137 Drum Street, Gilmerton
Edinburgh EH17 8RJ
Tel: 0131 664 9548

Express By Holiday Inn
Britannia Way, Ocean Drive
Edinburgh
Lothian
EH6 6LA
Tel: 0131 555 4422

Holland House
18 Holyrood Park Road
Edinburgh
EH16 5AY
Tel: 0131 651 2011

Holyrood Hotel
Holyrood Road
Edinburgh
EH8 6AE
Tel: 0131 550 4500

Hotel Ceilidh-Donia
14-16 Marchhall Crescent
Edinburgh
EH16 5HL
Tel: 0131 667 2743

International Guest House
37 Mayfield Gardens
Edinburgh
EH9 2BX
Tel: 0131 667 2511

Kelly's Guest House
3 Hillhouse Road
Edinburgh
Lothian
EH4 3QP
Tel: 0131 332 3894

Kings Manor Hotel
100 Milton Road East
Edinburgh
EH15 2NP
Tel: 0131 669 0444

Lindsay Guest House
108 Polwarth Terrace
Edinburgh
Midlothian
EH11 1NN
Tel: 0131 337 1580

Masson House
18 Holyrood Park Road
Edinburgh
EH16 5AY
Tel: 0131 651 2011

Roxburghe Hotel
38 Charlotte Square
Edinburgh
EH2 4HG
Tel: 0131 240 5500

Western Manor House Hotel
92 Corstorphine Road
Edinburgh
EH12 6JG
Tel: 0131 538 7490

EDZELL
Kelvingrove
Dunlappie Road
Edzell
Angus
DD9 7UB
Tel: 01356 648316

ERSKINE
Erskine Bridge Hotel
Erskine
Renfrewshire
PA8 6AN

ESKBANK
Glenarch House
Melville Road
Eskbank
Dalkeith
EH22 3NJ
Tel: 0131 663 1478

FINTRY
Culcreuch Castle
Culcreuch Castle Country Park
Fintry
Stirlingshire
G63 0LW
Tel: 01360 860555

FORT WILLIAM
Craig Nevis West
Belford Road
Fort William
Inverness-shire
PH33 6BU
Tel: 01397 702023

Lochan Cottage Guest House
Lochyside
Fort William
Inverness-shire
PH33 7NX
Tel: 01397 702695

BY FORT WILLIAM
The Inn at Ardgour
Ardgour
by Fort William
Inverness-shire
PH33 7AA
Tel: 01855 841225

GAIRLOCH
Dunedin
42 Strath
Gairloch
Ross-shire
IV21 2DB
Tel: 01445 712050

GALASHIELS
Ettrickvale
33 Abbotsford Road
Galashiels
Selkirkshire
TD1 3HW
Tel: 01896 755224

GLASGOW
The Knowes
32 Riddrie Knowes
Glasgow
G33 2QH
Tel: 0141 770 5213

GOUROCK
Spinnaker Hotel
121 Albert Road
Gourock
Renfrewshire
PA19 1BU
Tel: 01475 633107

GRANTOWN ON SPEY
Holmhill House
Woodside Avenue
Grantown on Spey
Morayshire
PH26 3JR
Tel: 01479 873977

Dunallan House
Woodside Avenue
Grantown-on-Spey
Moray
PH26 3JN
Tel: 01479 872140

Kinross Guest House
Woodside Avenue
Grantown-on-Spey
Moray
PH26 3JR
Tel: 01479 872042

GREENOCK
Tontine Hotel
6 Ardgowan Square
Greenock
Renfrewshire
PA16 8NG
Tel: 01475 723316

GRETNA
The Gables Hotel
1 Annan Road
Gretna
Dumfriesshire
DG16 5DQ
Tel: 01461 338300

GULBERWICK
Virdafjell
Shurton Brae
Gulberwick
Shetland ZE2 9TX
Tel: 01595 694336

ISLE OF HARRIS
Ardhasaig House
9 Ardhasaig
Isle of Harris
HS3 3AJ
Tel: 01859 502066

Carminish House
1 A Strond
Isle of Harris
HS5 3UB
Tel: 01859 520400

HELENSBURGH
RSR Braeholm
31 East Montrose Street
Helensburgh
Argyll & Bute
G84 7HR
Tel: 01436 671880

HELMSDALE
Kindale House
5 Lilleshall Street
Helmsdale
Sutherland
KW8 6JF
Tel: 01431 821415

INVERGOWRIE, DUNDEE
Swallow Hotel
Kingsway West
Invergowrie, Dundee
Angus
DD2 5JT
Tel: 01382 641122

INVERNESS
Avalon Guest House
79 Glenurquhart Road
Inverness
Inverness-shire
IV3 5PB
Tel: 01463 239075

Drumossie Park Cottage
Drumossie Brae
Inverness
Inverness-shire
IV2 5BB
Tel: 01463 224127

Express by Holiday Inn
Stoneyfield
Inverness
IV2 7PA
Tel: 01463 732700

Glen Mhor Hotel
9-12 Ness Bank
Inverness
Inverness-shire
IV2 4SG
Tel: 01463 234308

INVERURIE
Strathburn Hotel
Burghmuir Drive
Inverurie
Aberdeenshire
AB51 4GY
Tel: 01467 624422

ISLE OF IONA
Finlay Ross (Iona) Ltd
Martyr's Bay
Isle of Iona
Argyll
PA76 6SP
Tel: 01505 704000

JEDBURGH
Allerton House
Oxnam Road
Jedburgh
Roxburghshire
TD8 6QQ
Tel: 01835 869633

Crailing Old School
Jedburgh
Roxburghshire
TD8 6TL
Tel: 01835 850382

KELSO
Craignethan House
Jedburgh Road
Kelso
Roxburghshire
TD5 8AZ
Tel: 01573 224818

Cross Keys Hotel
36-37 The Square
Kelso
Roxburghshire
TD5 7HL
Tel: 01573 223303

Edenmouth Farm
Kelso
Roxburghshire
TD5 7QB
Tel: 01890 830391

KILLIN
Breadalbane House
Main Street
Killin
Perthshire
FK21 8UT
Tel: 01567 820134

BY KILMARNOCK
Fenwick Hotel
Fenwick
by Kilmarnock
Ayrshire KA3 6AU
Tel: 01560 600 478

KINCLAVEN, BY STANLEY
Ballathie House Hotel
Kinclaven, by Stanley
Perthshire
PH1 4QN
Tel: 01250 883268

KINGUSSIE
The Hermitage Guest House
Spey Street
Kingussie
Inverness-shire
PH21 1HN
Tel: 01540 662137

KINTYRE
Hunting Lodge Hotel
Bellochantuy
Kintyre
Argyll PA28 6QE
Tel: 01583 421323

KIRKCALDY
Scotties B&B
213 Nicol Street
Kirkcaldy
Fife
KY1 1PF
Tel: 01592 268596

KIRKLISTON
Crannog
New Liston Road
Kirkliston
Edinburgh
EH29 9EA
Tel: 0131 333 4621

KYLE OF LOCHALSH
Isle of Raasay Hotel
Raasay
Kyle of Lochalsh
Ross-shire
IV40 8PB
Tel: 01478 660222

LAMLASH
Lilybank
Shore Road
Lamlash
Isle of Arran
KA27 8LS
Tel: 01770 600230

LERWICK
Glen Orchy Guest House
20 Knab Road
Lerwick
Shetland
ZE1 0AX
Tel: 01595 692031

LINLITHGOW
Arden House
Belsyde
Linlithgow
West Lothian
EH49 6QE
Tel: 01506 670172

LOANHEAD
Aaron Glen Guest House
7 Nivensknowe Road
Loanhead
Midlothian
EH20 9AU
Tel: 0131 440 1293

LOCH LOMOND
Culag Lochside Guest House
Luss
Loch Lomond
Argyll and Bute
G83 8PD
Tel: 01436 860248

LOCHMABEN
Ardbeg Cottage
19 Castle Street
Lochmaben
Dumfries-shire
DG11 1NY
Tel: 01387 811855

LOCKERBIE
Carik Cottage
Waterbeck
Lockerbie
Dumfriesshire
DG11 3EU
Tel: 01461 600 652

LUSS
Blairglas
Luss
Dunbartonshire
G83 8RG
Tel: 01389 850278

MELROSE
Easter Cottage
Lilliesleaf
Melrose
Roxburghshire
TD6 9JD
Tel: 01835 870281

MILTON
Milton Inn
Dumbarton Road
Milton
Dunbartonshire
G82 2DT
Tel: 01389 761401

MOFFAT
Black Bull Hotel
Churchgate
Moffat
Dumfriesshire
DG10 9EG
Tel: 01683 220206

MONIFIETH
Panmure Hotel
Tay Street
Monifieth
Angus
DD5 4AX
Tel: 01382 532911

MONTROSE
Best Western Links Hotel
Mid Links
Montrose
Angus
DD10 8RL
Tel: 01674 671000

MUIR-OF-ORD
Hillview Park
Muir-of-Ord
Ross-shire
IV6 7TU
Tel: 01463 870787

ISLE OF MULL
Birchgrove
Lochdon
Isle of Mull
PA64 4AP
Tel: 01680 812364

MUSSELBURGH
Carberry Conference Centre
Carberry Tower
Musselburgh
East Lothian
EH21 8PY
Tel: 0131 665 3135

NAIRN
Napier
60 Seabank Road
Nairn
IV12 4HA
Tel: 01667 453330

NEWTON STEWART
East Culkae Farm House
Sorbie
Newton Stewart
Wigtownshire
DG8 8AS
Tel: 01988 850214

NORTHBAY
Airds Guest House
244 Bruernish
Northbay
Isle of Barra
HS9 5UT
Tel: 01871 890720

ISLE OF NORTH UIST
Redburn House
Lochmaddy
Isle of North Uist
Western Isles
HS6 5AA
Tel: 0208 6927271

OBAN
The Caledonian Hotel
Station Square
Oban
Argyll PA34 5RT
Tel: 01631 563133

The Kimberley Hotel
Dalriach Road
Oban
Argyll
PA34 5EQ
Tel: 01631 571115

BY OBAN
Falls of Lora Hotel
Connel Ferry
by Oban
Argyll
PA37 1PB
Tel: 01631 710483

ORPHIR
Houton Bay Lodge
Houton Bay
Orphir
Orkney
KW17 2RD
Tel: 01856 811320

PAISLEY
Ardgowan Town House Hotel
94 Renfrew Road
Paisley
Renfrewshire
PA3 4BJ
Tel: 0141 889 4763

PERTH
Arisaig Guest House
4 Pitcullen Crescent
Perth
PH2 7HT
Tel: 01738 628240

Cherrybank Inn
210 Glasgow Road
Perth
PH2 ONA
Tel: 01738 624349

Petra's B&B
4 Albany Terrace
Perth
Perthshire
PH1 2BD
Tel: 01738 563050

Sunbank House Hotel
50 Dundee Road
Perth
Perthshire
PH2 7BA
Tel: 01738 624882

BY PETERHEAD
Greenbrae Farmhouse
Longside
By Peterhead
Aberdeenshire
AB42 4JX
Tel: 01779 821051

PIRNHALL, STIRLING
Barn Lodge
Croftside
Pirnhall, Stirling
Stirlingshire
FK7 8EX
Tel: 01786 813591

PITLOCHRY
Craigatin House & Courtyard
165 Atholl Road
Pitlochry
Perthshire
PH16 5QL
Tel: 01796 472478

Craigvrack Hotel
38 West Moulin Road
Pitlochry
Perthshire
PH16 5EQ
Tel: 01796 472399

Fishers Hotel
75-79 Atholl Road
Pitlochry
Perthshire
PH16 5BN
Tel: 0131 554 7173

Green Park Hotel
Clunie Bridge Road
Pitlochry
Perthshire
PH16 5JY
Tel: 01796 473248

The Poplars
27 Lower Oakfield
Pitlochry
Perthshire
PH16 5DS
Tel: 01796 472129

The Well House
11 Toberargan Road
Pitlochry
Perthshire PH16 5HG
Tel: 01796 472239

BY PITLOCHRY
East Haugh House Country
Hotel & Res
East Haugh
by Pitlochry
Perthshire PH16 5JS
Tel: 01796 473121

PORTPATRICK
Braefield Guest House
Braefield Road
Portpatrick
Wigtownshire DG9 8TA
Tel: 01776 810255

Portpatrick Hotel
Heugh Road
Portpatrick
Wigtownshire
DG9 8TQ
Tel: 01776 810333

The Fernhill Hotel
Heugh Road
Portpatrick
Wigtownshire
DG9 8TD
Tel: 01776 810220

SOUTH QUEENSFERRY
Priory Lodge
8 The Loan
South Queensferry
West Lothian
EH30 9NS
Tel: 0131 331 4345

SOUTH RONALDSAY
Taftshurie B&B
Grimness
South Ronaldsay
Orkney
KW17 2TH
Tel: 01856 831323

SPEAN BRIDGE
Distant Hills Guest House
Roybridge Road
Spean Bridge
Inverness-shire
PH34 4EU
Tel: 01397 712452

The Heathers
Invergloy Halt
Spean Bridge
Inverness-shire PH34 4DY
Tel: 01397 712077

BY SPEAN BRIDGE
Dreamweavers
Mucomir
By Spean Bridge
Inverness-shire
PH34 4EQ
Tel: 01397 712 548

ST ANDREWS
Pitmilly West Lodge
Kingsbarns
St Andrews
Fife KY16 8QA
Tel: 01334 880581

STAFFIN
Gairloch View
3 Digg
Staffin
Isle of Skye
IV51 9LA
Tel: 01470 562718

STEIN, WATERNISH
Stein Inn
MacLeods Terrace
Stein, Waternish
Isle of Skye, Inverness-shire
IV55 8GA
Tel: 01470 592362

STIRLING
Cambria Guest House
141 Bannockburn Road
Stirling FK7 OEP
Tel: 01786 814603

BY STRANRAER
Corsewall Lighthouse Hotel
Kirkcolm
by Stranraer
Wigtownshire
DG9 0QG
Tel: 01776 853220

STRATHAVEN
Springvale Hotel
18 Lethame Road
Strathaven
Lanarkshire
ML10 6AD
Tel: 01357 521131

BY THURSO
Creag-Na-Mara
East Mey
by Thurso
Caithness
KW14 8XL
Tel: 01847 851850

Forss House Hotel
Forss
by Thurso
Caithness
KW14 7XY
Tel: 01847 861201

TOBERMORY
Tobermory House
Dervaig
Tobermory
Isle of Mull
PA75 6QW
Tel: 01688 400345

Tobermory Hotel
53 Main Street
Tobermory
Isle of Mull
PA75 6NT
Tel: 01688 302091

TROON
Piersland House Hotel
15 Craigend Road
Troon
Ayrshire
KA10 6HD
Tel: 01292 314747

ULLAPOOL
Dromnan Guest House
Garve Road
Ullapool
Ross-shire
IV26 2SX
Tel: 01854 612333

SOUTH OF SCOTLAND

Ayrshire and Arran, Dumfries & Galloway, Scottish Borders

ALLOWAY

Belleisle Country House Hotel
Belleisle Park, Doonfoot, Ayr, Ayrshire, KA7 4DU
Tel: 01292 442331
Small Hotel

ANNAN

The Old Rectory Guest House
12 St Johns Road, Annan, Dumfriesshire, DG12 6AW
Tel: 01461 202029
★★★ Guest House

Warmanbie House Hotel
Annan, Dumfriesshire, DG12 5LL
Tel: 01461 204015
Awaiting Inspection

ANNBANK

Enterkine Country House
Annbank, by Ayr, Ayrshire, KA6 5AL
Tel: 01292 521608
★★★★★ Small Hotel

BLACKWATERFOOT

Blackwaterfoot Lodge
Blackwaterfoot, Isle of Arran, KA27 8EU
Tel: 01770 860202
★★ Small Hotel

Kinloch Hotel
Blackwaterfoot, Isle of Arran, KA27 8ET
Tel: 01770 860444
★★★ Hotel

BRODICK, ISLE OF ARRAN

Allandale House
Corriegills Road, Brodick, Isle of Arran, KA27 8BJ
Tel: 01770 302278
★★★ Guest House

Auchrannie Country House Hotel
Brodick, Isle of Arran, KA27 8BZ
Tel: 01770 302234
★★★★ Hotel

Belvedere Guest House
Alma Road, Brodick, Isle of Arran, KA27 8AZ
Tel: 01770 302397
★★★ Guest House

Carrick Lodge
Pier Lodge, Brodick, Isle of Arran, KA27 8BH
Tel: 01770 302550
★★★ Guest House

Dunvegan House
Shore Road, Brodick, Isle of Arran, KA27 8AJ
Tel: 01770 302811
★★★★ Guest House

Glenartney Hotel
Mayish Road, Brodick, Isle of Arran, KA27 8BX
Tel: 01770 302220
★★★ Small Hotel

Glencloy Farm Guest House
Glen Cloy Road, Brodick, Isle of Arran, KA27 8DA
Tel: 01770 302351
★★★ Guest House

Glenfloral
Shore Road, Brodick, Isle of Arran, KA27 8AJ
Tel: 01770 302707
★★ Guest House

Invercloy Hotel
Shore Road, Brodick, Isle of Arran, KA27 8AJ
Tel: 01770 302225
★★★ Guest House

Kilmichael Country House Hotel
Brodick, Isle of Arran, KA27 8BY
Tel: 01770 302219
★★★★★ Small Hotel

Ormidale Hotel
Brodick, Isle of Arran, KA27 8BY
Tel: 01770 302293
★★ Small Hotel

Strathwhillan House
Brodick, Isle of Arran, KA27 8BQ
Tel: 01770 302331
★★★ Guest House

KILDONAN, ISLE OF ARRAN

Breadalbane Hotel
Kildonan, Isle of Arran, KA27 8SE
Tel: 01770 820284
★★★ Inn

Kildonan Hotel
Kildonan, Isle of Arran, KA27 8SE
Tel: 01770 820207
★★★ Small Hotel

LAGG, ISLE OF ARRAN

Lagg Hotel
Lagg, Kilmory, Isle of Arran, KA27 8PQ
Tel: 01770 870255
★★ Small Hotel

LAMLASH, ISLE OF ARRAN

Glenisle Hotel
Shore Road, Lamlash, Isle of Arran, KA27 8LY
Tel: 01770 600559
★★★ Small Hotel

Lilybank
Shore Road, Lamlash, Isle of Arran, KA27 8LS
Tel: 01770 600230
★★★★ Guest House

Marine House Hotel
Shore Road, Lamlash, Isle of Arran, KA27 8JZ
Tel: 01770 600298
★★★ Guest House

LOCHRANZA, ISLE OF ARRAN

Apple Lodge
Lochranza, Isle of Arran, KA27 8HJ
Tel: 01770 830229
★★★★ Guest House

Lochranza Hotel
Shore Road, Lochranza, Isle of Arran, KA27 8HL
Tel: 01770 830223
★★★ Small Hotel

SANNOX, ISLE OF ARRAN

Sannox Bay Hotel
Main Road, Sannox, Isle of Arran, KA27 8JD
Tel: 01770 810225
★★★ Small Hotel

WHITING BAY, ISLE OF ARRAN

Burlington Hotel
Shore Road, Whiting Bay, Isle of Arran, KA27 8PZ
Tel: 01770 700255
★★★ Small Hotel

Eden Lodge
Whiting Bay, Isle of Arran, KA27 8QH
Tel: 01770 700357
★★★ Small Hotel

The Royal Arran
Whiting Bay, Isle of Arran, KA27 8PZ
Tel: 01770 700286
★★★★ Guest House

View Bank House
Golf Course Road, Whiting Bay, Isle of Arran, KA27 8QT
Tel: 01770 700326
★★★ Guest House

AUCHENCAIRN, BY CASTLE DOUGLAS

The Old Smugglers Inn
Main Street, Auchencairn, Dumfries & Galloway, DG7 1QU
Tel: 01556 640331
★★ Inn

AULDGIRTH

Friars Carse Hotel
Auldgirth, Dumfriesshire, DG2 0SA
Tel: 01387 740388
★★ Hotel

AYR

Abbotsford Hotel
14 Corsehill Road, Ayr, Ayrshire, KA7 2ST
Tel: 01292 261506
★★★ Small Hotel

ESTABLISHMENTS PRINTED IN RED HAVE A DETAILED ENTRY IN THIS GUIDE.

Directory of all VisitScotland Quality Assured Serviced Establishments

Arrandale Hotel
2-4 Cassillis Street, Ayr, Ayrshire, KA7 1DW
Tel: 01292 289959
★★★ Small Hotel

Ayrshire & Galloway Hotel
1 Killoch Place, Ayr, Ayrshire, KA7 2EA
Tel: 01292 262626
★★★ Hotel

Belmont Guest House
15 Park Circus, Ayr, KA7 2DJ
Tel: 01292 265588
★★ Guest House

Bethshan Cottage
125A Prestwick Road, Ayr, Ayrshire, KA8 8NJ
Tel: 01292 285373
Awaiting Inspection

Brig O' Doon Hotel
Alloway, Ayr, Ayrshire, KA7 4PQ
Tel: 01292 442466
★★★★ Small Hotel

Burnbank Hotel
49 Maybole Road, Ayr, Ayrshire, KA7 4SF
Tel: 01292 441986
★★ Small Hotel

The Cariston Hotel
11 Miller Road, Ayr, Ayrshire, KA7 2AX
Tel: 01292 262474
★★★ Small Hotel

Carrick Lodge Hotel
Carrick Road, Ayr, Ayrshire, KA7 2RE
Tel: 01292 262846
★★★ Small Hotel

The Chestnuts Hotel
52 Racecourse Road, Ayr, Ayrshire, KA7 2UZ
Tel: 01292 264393
★★ Small Hotel

Coila Guest House
10 Holmston Road, Ayr, Ayrshire, KA7 3BB
Tel: 01292 262642
★★★★ Guest House

Craggallan Guest House
8 Queens Terrace, Ayr, Ayrshire, KA7 1DU
Tel: 01292 264998
★★★★ Guest House

Daviot House
12 Queen's Terrace, Ayr, Ayrshire, KA7 1DU
Tel: 01292 269678
★★★ Guest House

Dunlay House
1 Ailsa Place, Ayr, Ayrshire, KA7 1JG
Tel: 01292 610230
★★★★ Guest House

Eglinton Guest House
23 Eglinton Terrace, Ayr, Ayrshire, KA7 1JJ
Tel: 01292 264623
★★ Guest House

Elms Court Hotel
21-23 Miller Road, Ayr, Ayrshire, KA7 2AX
Tel: 01292 264191
★★★ Small Hotel

Fairfield House Hotel
12 Fairfield Road, Ayr, Ayrshire, KA7 2AR
Tel: 01292 267461
★★★★ Hotel

Glenmore Guest House
35 Bellevue Crescent, Ayr, Ayrshire, KA7 2DP
Tel: 01292 269830
★★★ Guest House

Horizon Hotel
Esplanade, Ayr, KA7 1DT
Tel: 01292 264384
★★★ Hotel

The Jarvis Caledonian Hotel
Dalblair Road, Ayr, Ayrshire, KA7 1UG
Tel: 01292 269331
★★★ Hotel

Langley Bank Guest House
39 Carrick Road, Ayr, Ayrshire, KA7 2RD
Tel: 01292 264246
★★★★ Guest House

Miller House
36 Miller Road, Ayr, Ayrshire, KA7 2AY
Tel: 01292 282016
★★★ Guest House

Old Racecourse Hotel
2 Victoria Park, Ayr, South Ayrshire, KA7 2TR
Tel: 01292 262873
★★★ Small Hotel

The Richmond
38 Park Circus, Ayr, KA7 2DL
Tel: 01292 265153
★★★ Guest House

St Andrews Hotel
7 Prestwick Road, Ayr, KA8 8LD
Tel: 01292 263211
★★ Small Hotel

Savoy Park Hotel
16 Racecourse Road, Ayr, KA7 2UT
Tel: 01292 266112
★★★ Small Hotel

Swallow Station Hotel Ayr
Burns Statue Square, Ayr, Ayrshire, KA7 3AT
Tel: 01292 263268
★★ Hotel

Western House Hotel & Western Lodge
2 Whitletts Road, Ayr, Ayrshire, KA9 2TA
Tel: 0870 8505666
★★★★ Hotel

Windsor Hotel
6 Alloway Place, Ayr, Ayrshire, KA7 2AA
Tel: 01292 264689
★★ Guest House

BALLANTRAE

Glenapp Castle
Ballantrae, Ayrshire, KA26 0NZ
Tel: 01465 831212
★★★★★ Hotel

Kings Arms Hotel
40 Main Street, Ballantrae, Ayrshire, KA26 0NB
Tel: 01465 831202
Awaiting Inspection

BEATTOCK

Marchbankwood House
Beattock, Moffat, Dumfries & Galloway, DG10 9RG
Tel: 01683 300118
★★★ Guest House

BERWICK ON TWEED

Banrach
Tweedhill, Berwick-upon-Tweed, Berwickshire, TD15 1XQ
Tel: 01289 386851
Awaiting Inspection

BROUGHTON, BY BIGGAR

The Glenholm Centre
Broughton, by Biggar, Lanarkshire, ML12 6JF
Tel: 01899 830408
★★★ Guest House

Over Tweed
Near Broughton, Biggar, Lanarkshire, ML12 6QH
Tel: 01899 830455
Awaiting Inspection

BURNHOUSE, BY BEITH

The Burnhouse Manor Hotel
Burnhouse, by Beith, Ayrshire, KA15 1LJ
Tel: 01560 484006
★★★ Hotel

CANONBIE

Cross Keys Hotel
Canonbie, Dumfriesshire, DG14 0SY
Tel: 013873 71205
★★★ Small Hotel

CASTLE DOUGLAS

Balcary Bay Hotel
Shore Road, Auchencairn, by Castle Douglas, Kirkcudbrightshire, DG7 1QZ
Tel: 01556 640217
★★★★ Hotel

Crown Hotel
King Street, Castle Douglas, Kirkcudbrightshire, DG7 1AA
Tel: 01556 502031
★★★ Small Hotel

Douglas Arms Hotel
King Street, Castle Douglas, DG7 1DB
Tel: 01556 502231
★★ Hotel

The Imperial Hotel
35 King Street, Castle Douglas, DG7 1AA
Tel: 01556 502086
★★★ Small Hotel

Kings Arms Hotel
St Andrew Street, Castle Douglas, Kirkcudbrightshire, DG7 1EL
Tel: 01556 502626
★★ Small Hotel

Market Inn Hotel
6/7 Queen Street, Castle Douglas, Kirkcudbrightshire, DG7 1HX
Tel: 01556 502105
★★ Small Hotel

Station Hotel
1 Queen Street, Castle Douglas, Kirkcudbrightshire, DG7 1HX
Tel: 01556 502152
★★★ Small Hotel

The Urr Valley Hotel
Ernespie Road, Castle Douglas, Kirkcudbrightshire, DG7 3JG
Tel: 01556 502188
★★ Small Hotel

CHIRNSIDE, BY DUNS

Chirnside Hall Hotel
Chirnside, By Duns, Berwickshire, TD11 3LD
Tel: 01890 818219
★★★★ Small Hotel

COLVEND

Clonyard House Hotel
Colvend, Dalbeattie, Kircudbrightshire, DG5 4QW
Tel: 01556 630372
★★ Small Hotel

CREETOWN

Ellangowan Hotel
St John Street, Creetown, Wigtownshire, DG8 7JF
Tel: 01671 820201
★★ Hotel

CROCKETFORD, DUMFRIES

Galloway Arms Hotel
Crocketford, nr Dumfries, Dumfries & Galloway, DG2 8RA
Tel: 01556 690248
★★ Small Hotel

MILLPORT, ISLE OF CUMBRAE

The Millerston
29 West Bay Road, Millport, Isle of Cumbrae, KA28 0HA
Tel: 01475 530480
★★★ Small Hotel

The Cathedral of the Isles
The College, Millport, Isle of Cumbrae, KA28 0HE
Tel: 01475 530353
★★★ Guest House

DALRY, BY CASTLE DOUGLAS

The Lochinvar Hotel
3 Main Street, St Johns Town of Dalry, Dumfriesshire, DG7 3UP
Tel: 01644 430210
★★ Small Hotel

DALRYMPLE

The Kirkton Inn
1 Main Street, Dalrymple, Ayrshire, KA6 6DF
Tel: 01292 560241
★★ Inn

DUMFRIES

Aberdour Hotel
16-20 Newall Terrace, Dumfries, Dumfries-shire, DG1 1LW
Tel: 01387 252060
★★★ Small Hotel

Cairndale Hotel & Leisure Club
English Street, Dumfries, DG1 2DF
Tel: 01387 254111
★★★ Hotel

Dalston House Hotel
5 Laurieknowe, Dumfries, Dumfrieshire, DG2 7AH
Tel: 01387 254422
★★★ Small Hotel

Edenbank Hotel
17 Laurieknowe, Dumfries, DG2 7AH
Tel: 01387 252759
★★★ Small Hotel

Fulwood Hotel
30 Lovers Walk, Dumfries, DG1 1LX
Tel: 01387 252262
★★★ Guest House

Glenlossie Guest House
75 Annan Road, Dumfries, Dumfries-shire, DG1 3EG
Tel: 01387 254305
★★★★ Guest House

Hazeldean Guest House
4 Moffat Road, Dumfries, DG1 1NJ
Tel: 01387 266178
★★★★ Guest House

Huntingdon House Hotel
18 St Marys Street, Dumfries, DG1 1LZ
Tel: 01387 254 893
★★★ Small Hotel

Moreig Hotel
67 Annan Road, Dumfries, DG1 3EG
Tel: 01387 255524
★★★ Small Hotel

Redbank House
New Abbey Road, Dumfries, Dumfriesshire, DG2 8EW
Tel: 01387 266220/247034
★★★★ Guest House

Station Hotel
49 Lovers Walk, Dumfries, Dumfries-shire, DG1 1LT
Tel: 01387 254316
★★★ Hotel

Torbay Lodge
31 Lovers Walk, Dumfries, DG1 1LR
Tel: 01387 253922
★★★★ Guest House

Woodland House Hotel
Newbridge, Dumfries, Dumfriesshire, DG2 OHZ
Tel: 01387 720233
★ Small Hotel

BY DUMFRIES

Comlongon Castle
Clarencefield, Dumfriesshire, DG1 4NA
Tel: 01387 870283
★★★ Small Hotel

Hetland Hall Hotel
Carrutherstown, Dumfriesshire, DG1 4JX
Tel: 01387 840201
★★★ Hotel

Kirklands Hotel
Ruthwell, Dumfriesshire, DG1 4NP
Tel: 01387 250677
★★ Small Hotel

Nith Hotel
Glencaple, Dumfriesshire, DG1 4RE
Tel: 01387 770213
★★ Small Hotel

DUNURE, BY AYR

The Jaggy Thistle
19 Castle Road, Dunure, Ayrshire, KA7 4LW
Tel: 01292 500545
Awaiting Inspection

EARLSTON

Broomfield House
10 Thorn Street, Earlston, Berwickshire, TD4 6DR
Tel: 01896 848084
★★★ Guest House

ECCLEFECHAN

Cressfield Country House Hotel
Townfoot, Ecclefechan, Dumfriesshire, DG11 3DR
Tel: 01576 300281
★★★ Small Hotel

Swallow Kirkconnel Hall
Ecclefechan, By Lockerbie, Dumfriesshire, DG11 3JH
Tel: 01576 300277
★★★ Small Hotel

ESKDALEMUIR

Hart Manor
Eskdalemuir, Langholm, Dumfriesshire, DG13 0QQ
Tel: 01387 373217
★★★★ Small Hotel

ETTRICKBRIDGE, BY SELKIRK

Ettrickshaws Country House Hotel
Ettrick Bridge, by Selkirk, TD7 5HW
Tel: 01750 52229
★★★★ Small Hotel

EYEMOUTH

The Dolphin Hotel
North Street, Eyemouth, Berwickshire, TD14 5ES
Tel: 01890 750280
Awaiting Inspection

FENWICK, BY KILMARNOCK

Fenwick Hotel
Fenwick, by Kilmarnock, Ayrshire, KA3 6AU
Tel: 01560 600478
★★★ Hotel

GALASHIELS

Kings Hotel
56 Market Street, Galashiels, Selkirkshire, TD1 3AN
Tel: 01896 755497
★★ Small Hotel

Kingsknowes Hotel
Selkirk Road, Galashiels, Selkirkshire, TD1 3HY
Tel: 01896 758375
★★★ Small Hotel

Monorene
23 Stirling Street, Galashiels, Selkirkshire, TD1 1BY
Tel: 01896 753073
★★ Guest House

Morven Guest House
12 Sime Place, Galashiels, Selkirkshire, TD1 1ST
Tel: 01896 756255
★ Guest House

Watson Lodge Guest House
15/16 Bridge Street, Galashiels, Selkirkshire, TD1 1SW
Tel: 01896 750551
★★★ Guest House

GATEHOUSE OF FLEET

The Bank of Fleet Hotel
47 High Street, Gatehouse of Fleet, Kirkcudbrightshire, DG7 2HR
Tel: 01557 814302
★★★ Small Hotel

Bobbin Guest House
36 High Street, Gatehouse-of-Fleet, Kirkcudbrightshire, DG7 2HP
Tel: 01557 814229
★★★ Guest House

Cally Palace Hotel
Gatehouse of Fleet, Kirkcudbrightshire, DG7 2DL
Tel: 01557 814341
★★★★ Hotel

Murray Arms Hotel
High Street, Gatehouse of Fleet, Castle Douglas, DG7 2HY
Tel: 01557 814207
★★★ Small Hotel

GIRVAN

Southfield Hotel
The Avenue, Girvan, Ayrshire, KA26 9DS
Tel: 01465 714222
Awaiting Inspection

Westcliffe Hotel
15-17 Louisa Drive, Girvan, KA26 9AH
Tel: 01465 712128
★★ Hotel

GLENLUCE

The Kelvin House Hotel
53 Main Street, Glenluce, Wigtownshire, DG8 0PP
Tel: 01581 300303
★★★ Small Hotel

GRETNA

The Gables Hotel
1 Annan Road, Gretna, Dumfriesshire, DG16 5DQ
Tel: 01461 338300
★★★★ Hotel

The Garden House Hotel
Sarkfoot Road, Gretna, Dumfriesshire, DG16 5EP
Tel: 01461 337621
★★★ Hotel

Hunters Lodge Hotel
Annan Road, Gretna, Dumfriesshire, DG16 5DL
Tel: 01461 338214
★★★ Small Hotel

GRETNA GREEN

Gretna Hall Hotel
Gretna Green, Dumfriesshire, DG16 5DY
Tel: 01461 338257
★★★ Hotel

Hazeldene Hotel
Gretna Green, Gretna, Dumfriesshire, DG16 5EA
Tel: 01461 338292
★★ Small Hotel

Kirkcroft
Glasgow Road, Gretna Green, Dumfriesshire, DG16 5DU
Tel: 01461 337403
★★ Guest House

The Mill
Grahamshill, Kirkpatrick Fleming, Lockerbie, DG11 3BQ
Tel: 01461 800344
★★★ Lodge

Smiths @ Gretna Green
Gretna Green, Dumfries & Galloway, DG16 5EA
Tel: 0845 3676768
Awaiting Inspection

HAWICK

Bridge House
Sandbed, Hawick, Roxburghshire, TD9 0HE
Tel: 01450 370701
★★ Guest House

Elm House Hotel
17 North Bridge Street, Hawick, Roxburghshire, TD9 9BD
Tel: 01450 372866
★★ Small Hotel

Mansfield House Hotel
Weensland Road, Hawick, Roxburghshire, TD9 8LB
★★★ Small Hotel

BY HAWICK

Glenteviot Park Hotel
Hassendeanburn, by Hawick, Roxburghshire, TD9 8RU
Tel: 01450 870660
★★★★ Small Hotel

Whitchester Guest House
Hawick, Roxburghshire, TD9 7LN
Tel: 01450 377477
★★★ Guest House

INNERLEITHEN

Caddon View Hotel
14 Pirn Road, Innerleithen, Peeblesshire, EH44 6HH
Tel: 01896 830208
★★★★ Small Hotel

Traquair Arms Hotel
Traquair Road, Innerleithen, Peeblesshire, EH44 6PD
Tel: 01896 830229
★★ Small Hotel

IRVINE

Annfield House Hotel
6 Castle Street, Irvine, Ayrshire, KA12 8RJ
Tel: 01294 278903
★★★ Small Hotel

The Gailes Lodge
Marine Drive, Gailes, Irvine, KA11 5AE
Tel: 01294 204040
★★★ Hotel

The Golf Hotel
18 Kilwinning Road, Irvine, Ayrshire, KA12 8RU
Tel: 01294 278 633
★★ Small Hotel

Harbourside Hotel
86 Montgomery Street, Irvine, Ayrshire, KA12 8PW
Tel: 01294 275515
★ Guest House

Laurelbank Guest House
3 Kilwinning Road, Irvine, Ayrshire, KA12 8RR
Tel: 01294 277153
★★★ Guest House

Thistle Irvine
46 Annick Road, Irvine, Ayrshire, KA11 4LD
Tel: 01294 274272
★★★ Hotel

NR IRVINE

Montgreenan Mansion House Hotel
Montgreenan Estate, Kilwinning, Ayrshire, KA13 7QZ
Tel: 01294 850005
★★★ Hotel

ISLE OF WHITHORN

Steam Packet Inn
Harbour Row, Isle of Whithorn, Wigtownshire, DG8 8LL
Tel: 01988 500334
★ Inn

JEDBURGH

Allerton House
Oxnam Road, Jedburgh, Roxburghshire, TD8 6QQ
Tel: 01835 869633
★★★★ Guest House

Glenbank House Hotel
Castlegate, Jedburgh, Roxburghshire, TD8 6BD
Tel: 01835 862258
★ Small Hotel

Glenfriars House
The Friars, Jedburgh, Roxburghshire, TD8 6BN
Tel: 01835 862000
★★ Guest House

Jedforest Hotel
Camptown, Jedburgh, Roxburghshire, TD8 6PJ
Tel: 01835 840222
★★★★ Small Hotel

Meadhon House
48 Castlegate, Jedburgh, Roxburghshire, TD8 6BB
Tel: 01835 862504
★★★ Guest House

Spread Eagle Hotel
20 High Street, Jedburgh, Roxburghshire, TD8 6AG
Tel: 01835 862870
★ Small Hotel

BY JEDBURGH

Ferniehirst Mill Lodge
Jedburgh, Roxburghshire, TD8 6PQ
Tel: 01835 863279
★ Guest House

JOHNSTONE BRIDGE

Dinwoodie Lodge Hotel
Johnstone Bridge, by Lockerbie, Dumfriesshire, DG11 2SL
Tel: 01576 470289
★★ Small Hotel

KELSO

Bellevue House
Bowmont Street, Kelso, TD5 7DZ
Tel: 01573 224588
★★★ Guest House

Cross Keys Hotel
36-37 The Square, Kelso, TD5 7HL
Tel: 01573 223303
★★★ Hotel

Ednam House Hotel
Bridge Street, Kelso, Roxburghshire, TD5 7HT
Tel: 01573 224168
★★★ Hotel

Ingleston House
Abbey Row, Kelso, Roxburghshire, TD5 7HQ
Tel: 01573 225800
★★★ Guest House

Queens Head Hotel
Bridge Street, Kelso, Roxburghshire, TD5 7JD
0870 2424453
★★★ Small Hotel

BY KELSO

Roxburghe Hotel and Golf Course
Heiton, Kelso, Roxburghshire, TD5 8JZ
Tel: 01573 450331
★★★★ Hotel

KILMARNOCK

Dean Park Guest House
27 Wellington Street, Kilmarnock, Ayrshire, KA3 1DZ
Tel: 01563 572 794
★★★ Guest House

Howard Park Hotel
136 Glasgow Road, Kilmarnock, Ayrshire, KA3 1UT
Tel: 01563 312111
★★ Hotel

Millhouse Hotel
6/8 Dean Street, Stewarton, Kilmarnock, Ayrshire, KA3 5EQ
Tel: 01560 482255
Awaiting Inspection

Nether Underwood
Symington, by Kilmarnock, Ayrshire, KA1 5NG
Tel: 01563 830666
★★★★★ Guest House

Park Hotel
Rugby Park, Kilmarnock, Ayrshire, KA1 2DP
Tel: 01563 545999
★★★★ Hotel

KIPPFORD, BY DALBEATTIE

Rosemount
Kippford, Dalbeattie, Kirkcudbrightshire, DG5 4LN
Tel: 01556 620214
Awaiting Inspection

Roughfirth House
Roughfirth, Kippford, Dumfries & Galloway, DG5 4LJ
Awaiting Inspection

KIRKBEAN

Cavens
Kirkbean,by Dumfries, By Dumfries, DG2 8AA
Tel: 01387 880234
★★★★ Small Hotel

KIRKCUDBRIGHT

Dee Cottage
Tongland, Kirkcudbright, Dumfries & Galloway, DG6 4LT
Tel: 01557 330338
Awaiting Inspection

Gladstone House
48 High Street, Kirkcudbright, DG6 4JX
Tel: 01557 331734
★★★★ Guest House

Gordon House Hotel
116 High Street, Kirkcudbright, Kirkcudbrightshire, DG6 4JQ
Tel: 01557 330670
★★★ Small Hotel

Royal Hotel
50 St Cuthbert Street, Kirkcudbright, DG6 4DY
Tel: 01557 331213
★★ Small Hotel

Selkirk Arms Hotel
High Street, Kirkcudbright, Kirkcudbrightshire, DG6 4JG
Tel: 01557 330402
★★★★ Small Hotel

LANGHOLM

Whitecroft Hotel
81 High Street, Langholm, Dumfries & Galloway, DG13 0DJ
Tel: 01387 381343
★★★ Small Hotel

LARGS

Burnlea Hotel
Burnlea Road, Largs, Ayrshire, KA30 8BX
Tel: 01475 687235
★★ Hotel

Haylie Hotel
108 Irvine Road, Largs, Ayrshire, KA30 8EY
Tel: 01475 673207
★★ Small Hotel

Lea-Mar Guest House
20 Douglas Street, Largs, Ayrshire, KA30 8PS
Tel: 01475 672447
★★★ Guest House

Lilac Holm Guest House
14 Noddleburn Road, Largs, Ayrshire, KA30 8PY
Tel: 01475 672020
★★★ Guest House

Nixons Hotel
2 Barr Crescent, Largs, Ayrshire, KA30 8PX
Tel: 01475 673381
★★★ Small Hotel

Tigh An Struan
29 Gogo Street, Largs, North Ayrshire, KA30 8BU
Tel: 01475 670668
Awaiting Inspection

Tigh-Na-Ligh
104 Brisbane Road, Largs, Ayrshire, KA30 8NN
Tel: 01475 673975
★★★ Guest House

Whin-Park Guest House
16 Douglas Street, Largs, Ayrshire, KA30 8PS
Tel: 01475 673437
★★★★ Guest House

Willowbank Hotel
96 Greenock Road, Largs, North Ayrshire, KA30 8PG
Tel: 01475 672311
★★★ Hotel

LOCKERBIE

Dryfesdale Country House Hotel
Dryfebridge, Lockerbie, Dumfriesshire, DG11 2SF
Tel: 01576 202427
★★★★ Small Hotel

Kings Arms Hotel
29 High Street, Lockerbie, Dumfriesshire, DG11 2JL
Tel: 01576 202410
★★★ Small Hotel

Lockerbie Manor
Boreland Road, Lockerbie, Dumfriesshire, DG11 2RG
Tel: 01576 202610
★★ Hotel

Queens Hotel
Annan Road, Lockerbie, Dumfriesshire, DG11 2RB
Tel: 01576 202415
★★★ Hotel

Ravenshill House Hotel
12 Dumfries Road, Lockerbie, Dumfriesshire, DG11 2EF
Tel: 01576 202882
★★ Small Hotel

Rosehill Guest House
Carlisle Road, Lockerbie, Dumfriesshire, DG11 2DR
Tel: 01576 202378
★★★ Guest House

Somerton House Hotel
35 Carlisle Road, Lockerbie, Dumfries-shire, DG11 2DR
Tel: 01576 202583
★★★ Small Hotel

MAINSRIDDLE

Manse House
Mainsriddle, Dumfries and Galloway, DG2 8AG
Tel: 01387 780270
Awaiting Inspection

MELROSE

Burts Hotel
Market Square, Melrose, Roxburghshire, TD6 9PL
Tel: 01896 822285
★★★★ Small Hotel

Dryburgh Abbey Hotel
St Boswells, Melrose, Scottish Borders, TD6 0RQ
Tel: 01835 822261
★★★★ Hotel

George & Abbotsford Hotel
High Street, Melrose, Roxburghshire, TD6 9PD
Tel: 01896 822308
★★ Hotel

Station Hotel
Market Square, Melrose, Roxburghshire, TD6 9PT
Tel: 0870 2424453
Awaiting Inspection

The Townhouse Hotel
Market Square, Melrose, Roxburghshire, TD6 9PQ
Tel: 01896 822645
★★★ Small Hotel

Waverley Castle Hotel
Skirmish Hill, Waverley Road, Melrose, TD6 9AA
Tel: 01942 824824
★★★ Hotel

BY MELROSE

Clint Lodge Country House
Clinthill, St Boswells, Melrose, Roxburghshire, TD6 0DZ
Tel: 01835 822027
★★★★ Guest House

Whitehouse
St Boswells, Roxburghshire, TD6 OED
Tel: 01573 460343
★★★★★ Bed & Breakfast

MOFFAT

Annandale Arms Hotel
High Street, Moffat, Dumfriesshire, DG10 9HF
Tel: 01683 220013
★★★ Small Hotel

Barnhill Springs Country Guest House
Moffat, Dumfries & Galloway, DG10 9QS
Tel: 01683 220580
★★ Guest House

Black Bull Hotel
Churchgate, Moffat, Dumfriesshire, DG10 9EG
Tel: 01683 220206
★★★ Small Hotel

Bridge House
Well Road, Moffat, Dumfrieshire, DG10 9JT
Tel: 01683 220558
★★★ Guest House

Buccleuch Arms Hotel
High Street, Moffat, Dumfriesshire, DG10 9ET
Tel: 01683 220003
★★★ Small Hotel

Buchan Guest House
Beechgrove, Moffat, Dumfriesshire, DG10 9RS
Tel: 01683 220378
★★ Guest House

The Famous Star Hotel
44 High Street, Moffat, DG10 9EF
Tel: 01683 220156
★★ Small Hotel

Hartfell House
Hartfell Crescent, Moffat, Dumfriesshire, DG10 9AL
Tel: 01683 220153
★★★ Guest House

Marvig Guest House
Academy Road, Moffat, Dumfriesshire, DG10 9HW
Tel: 01683 220628
★★★ Guest House

Moffat House Hotel
High Street, Moffat, DG10 9HL
Tel: 01683 220039
★★★ Small Hotel

Rockhill Guest House
14 Beechgrove, Moffat, Dumfriesshire, DG10 9RS
Tel: 01683 220283
★★ Guest House

Well View Hotel
Ballplay Road, Moffat, Dumfriesshire, DG10 9JU
Tel: 01683 220184
★★★★ Small Hotel

BY MOFFAT

Auchen Castle Hotel
Beattock, Moffat, Dumfriesshire, DG10 9SH
Tel: 01683 300407
★★★ Hotel

MONKTON, BY PRESTWICK

Adamton House Hotel
Tarbolton Road, Monkton, Ayrshire, KA9 2SQ
Tel: 01292 470722
★★ Hotel

NEWCASTLETON

Liddesdale Hotel
Douglas Square, Newcastleton, Roxburghshire, TD9 OSB
Tel: 01387 375255
★★ Small Hotel

NR NEW CUMNOCK

Lochside House Hotel
New Cumnock, Ayrshire, KA18 4PN
Tel: 01290 333000
★★★ Small Hotel

NEW GALLOWAY

Leamington Hotel
High Street, New Galloway, Kirkcudbrightshire, DG7 3RN
Tel: 01644 420327
★★ Guest House

NEWTON STEWART

The Bruce Arms
88 Queen Street, Newton Stewart, Wigtownshire, DG8 6JL
Tel: 01671 402294
★★★ Small Hotel

Creebridge House Hotel
Newton Stewart, Wigtownshire, DG8 6NP
Tel: 01671 402121
★★★ Small Hotel

Flowerbank Guest House
Millcroft Road, Minnigaff, Newton Stewart, DG8 6PJ
Tel: 01671 402629
★★★ Guest House

Galloway Arms Hotel
Victoria Street, Newton Stewart, Wigtownshire, DG8 6DB
Tel: 01671 402653
★★ Small Hotel

Kirroughtree House
Newton Stewart, Wigtownshire, DG8 6AN
Tel: 01671 402141
★★★★ Small Hotel

Rowallan House
Corsbie Road, Newton Stewart, Wigtownshire, DG8 6JB
Tel: 01671 402520
★★★ Guest House

Stables Guest House
Corsbie Road, Newton Stewart, Wigtownshire, DG8 6JB
Tel: 01671 402157
★★★ Guest House

PEEBLES

Castle Venlaw Hotel
Edinburgh Road, Peebles, Peeblesshire, EH45 8QG
Tel: 01721 720384
★★★★ Small Hotel

Cross Keys Hotel
24 Northgate, Peebles, EH45 8RS
Tel: 01721 724222
★★ Inn

Green Tree Hotel
41 Eastgate, Peebles, Peeblesshire, EH45 8AD
Tel: 01721 720582
★★ Small Hotel

Park Hotel
Innerleithen Road, Peebles, EH45 8BA
Tel: 01721 720451
★★★ Hotel

Peebles Hotel Hydro
Innerleithen Road, Peebles, Peebles-shire, EH45 8LX
Tel: 01721 720602
★★★★ Hotel

Tontine Hotel
High Street, Peebles, Peeblesshire, EH45 8AJ
Tel: 01721 720892
★★★ Hotel

BY PEEBLES

Barony Castle
Eddleston, Peebleshire, EH45 8QW
Tel: 01721 730395
Awaiting Inspection

Cringletie House Hotel
Edinburgh Road, Peebles, Peeblesshire, EH45 8PL
Tel: 01721 725750
★★★★ Small Hotel

Glentress Hotel
Innerleithen Road, Peebles, Peebles-shire, EH45 8NB
Tel: 01721 720100
★★ Small Hotel

Cardrona Hotel Golf & Country Club
Cardrona, Peebles, EH45 6LZ
Tel: 01896 833600
★★★★ Hotel

PORTPATRICK

Blinkbonnie Guest House
School Brae, Portpatrick, Wigtownshire, DG9 8LG
Tel: 01776 810282
★★★ Guest House

Braefield Guest House
Braefield Road, Portpatrick, Wigtownshire, DG9 8TA
Tel: 01776 810255
★★ Guest House

Dunskey Golf Hotel
Heugh Road, Portpatrick, Wigtownshire, DG9 8TD
Tel: 01776 810241
★★ Small Hotel

The Fernhill Hotel
Heugh Road, Portpatrick, Wigtownshire, DG9 8TD
Tel: 01776 810220
★★★★ Hotel

Knockinaam Lodge
Portpatrick, Wigtownshire, DG9 9AD
Tel: 01776 810471
★★★★ Small Hotel

The Knowe
1 North Crescent, Portpatrick, Wigtownshire, DG9 8SX
Tel: 01776 810441
★★★ Guest House

Mount Stewart Hotel
South Crescent, Portpatrick, Wigtownshire, DG9 8LE
Tel: 01776 810291
Awaiting Inspection

Portpatrick Hotel
Heugh Road, Portpatrick, Wigtownshire, DG9 8TQ
Tel: 01776 810333
★★★ Hotel

Rickwood House Hotel
Heugh Road, Portpatrick, Wigtownshire, DG9 8TD
Tel: 01776 810270
★★★ Guest House

Torrs Warren Hotel
Stoneykirk, Stranraer, Dumfries & Galloway, DG9 9DH
1776830204
★★★ Small Hotel

The Waterfront Hotel
7 North Crescent, Portpatrick, Wigtownshire, DG9 8SX
Tel: 01776 810800
★★★ Small Hotel

POWFOOT, BY ANNAN

Powfoot Golf Hotel
Links Avenue, Powfoot, Dumfriesshire, DG12 5PN
Tel: 01461 700254
★★ Hotel

PRESTWICK

The Carlton Hotel
187 Ayr Road, Prestwick, Ayrshire, KA9 1TP
Tel: 01292 476811
★ Hotel

Fernbank Guest House
213 Main Street, Prestwick, Ayrshire, KA9 1LH
Tel: 01292 475027
★★★ Guest House

Golf View Hotel
17 Links Road, Prestwick, Ayrshire, KA9 1QG
Tel: 01292 671234
★★★★ Guest House

Kincraig Private Hotel
39 Ayr Road, Prestwick, Ayrshire, KA9 1SY
Tel: 01292 479480
★★★ Guest House

North Beach Hotel
5-7 Link's Road, Prestwick, Ayrshire, KA9 1QG
Tel: 01292 479069
★★★ Small Hotel

Parkstone Hotel
Central Esplanade, Prestwick, Ayrshire, KA9 1QN
Tel: 01292 477286
★★★ Hotel

Prestwick Old Course Hotel
13 Links Road, Prestwick, KA9 1QG
Tel: 01292 477446
Awaiting Inspection

ROCKCLIFFE, BY DALBEATTIE

Baron's Craig Hotel
Rockcliffe, by Dalbeattie, Kirkcudbrightshire, DG5 4QF
Tel: 01556 630225
★★ Hotel

ST ABBS

Castle Rock
Murrayfield, St Abbs, Berwickshire, TD14 5PP
Tel: 01890 771715
★★★ Guest House

ST BOSWELLS

Buccleuch Arms Hotel
The Green, St Boswells, Roxburghshire, TD6 OEW
Tel: 01835 822243
★★★ Small Hotel

SANDYHILLS, BY DALBEATTIE

Cairngill House
Sandyhills, Dalbeattie, Kirkcudbrightshire, DG5 4NZ
Tel: 01387 780681
★★★★ Guest House

Craigbittern House
Sandyhills, Dalbeattie, Kirkcudbrightshire, DG5 4NZ
Tel: 0138778 247
★★★★ Guest House

SANQUHAR

Blackaddie House Hotel
Blackaddie Road, Sanquhar, Dumfriesshire, DG4 6JJ
Tel: 01659 50270
★★★ Small Hotel

SEAMILL

Seamill Hydro
39 Ardrossan Road, Seamill, Ayrshire, KA23 9NB
Tel: 01294 822217
★★★ Hotel

SELKIRK

The County Hotel
Market Square, 3-5 High Street, Selkirk, TD7 4BZ
Tel: 01750 21233
★★★ Small Hotel

The Glen Hotel
Yarrow Terrace, Selkirk, Selkirkshire, TD7 5AS
Tel: 01750 20259
★★★ Small Hotel

Heatherlie House Hotel
Heatherlie Park, Selkirk, Selkirkshire, TD7 5AL
Tel: 01750 721200
★★★ Small Hotel

Philipburn Country House Hotel and Restaurant
Selkirk, Selkirkshire, TD7 5LS
Tel: 01750 20747
★★★★ Small Hotel

Tower Street Guest House
29 Tower Street, Selkirk, Scottsh Borders, TD7 4LR
Tel: 01750 23222
★★★ Guest House

BY SKIRLING, BY BIGGAR

Skirling House
Skirling, by Biggar, Lanarkshire, ML12 6HD
★★★★★ Guest House

STRANRAER

George Hotel
49 George Street, Stranraer, Wigtownshire, DG9 7RJ
Tel: 01776 702487
★ Hotel

Harbour Guest House
11 Market Street, Stranraer, Wigtownshire, DG9 7RF
Tel: 01776 704626
★★★ Guest House

Hartforth Guest House
33 London Road, Stranraer, Wigtownshire, DG9 8AF
Tel: 01776 704832
★★ Guest House

Ivy House & Ferry Link
London Road, Stranraer, Wigtownshire, DG9 8ER
Tel: 01776 704176
★★ Guest House

Lakeview Guest House
19 Agnew Crescent, Stranraer, Wigtownshire, DG9 7JY
Tel: 01776 703472
★★★ Guest House

Marine House Hotel
23 Agnew Crescent, Stranraer, Wigtownshire, DG9 7JZ
Tel: 01776 703370
★★★ Small Hotel

Neptunes Rest Guest House
25 Agnew Crescent, Stranraer, Wigtownshire, DG9
Tel: 01776 704729
★★ Guest House

North West Castle Hotel
Royal Crescent, Stranraer, Wigtownshire, DG9 8EH
Tel: 01776 704413
★★★★ Hotel

NR STRANRAER

Corsewall Lighthouse Hotel
Kirkcolm, Stranraer, DG9 0QG
Tel: 01776 853220
★★★★ Small Hotel

SWINTON

The Wheatsheaf
Swinton, Berwickshire, TD11 3JJ
Tel: 01890 860257
★★★★ Restaurant with Rooms

THORNHILL

Buccleuch & Queensferry Hotel
112 Drumlanrig Street, Thornhill, Dumfriesshire, DG3 5LU
Tel: 01848 330215
★★ Small Hotel

Gillbank House
8 East Morton Street, Thornhill, Dumfriesshire, DG3 5LZ
Tel: 01848 330597
★★★★ Guest House

The Thornhill Inn
103-106 Drumlanrig Street, Thornhill, Dumfriesshire, DG3 5LU
Tel: 01848 330326
★★★ Small Hotel

BY THORNHILL

Trigony House Hotel
Closeburn, Thornhill, Dumfriesshire, DG3 5EZ
Tel: 01848 331211
★★★★ Small Hotel

TROON

Ardneil Hotel
St Meddans Street, Troon, Ayrshire, KA10 6NU
Tel: 01292 311611
★★ Small Hotel

Lochgreen House
Monktonhill Road, Troon, Ayrshire, KA10 7EN
Tel: 01292 313343
★★★★★ Hotel

Marine Hotel
Crosbie Road, Troon, Ayrshire, KA10 6HE
Tel: 01292 314444
★★★★ Hotel

Piersland House Hotel
15 Craigend Road, Troon, Ayrshire, KA10 6HD
Tel: 01292 314747
★★★★ Hotel

South Beach Hotel
South Beach, Troon, Ayrshire, KA10 6EG
Tel: 01292 312033
★★★ Hotel

TURNBERRY

Malin Court
Turnberry, Ayrshire, KA26 9PB
Tel: 01655 331457
★★★★ Small Hotel

The Westin Turnberry Resort
Turnberry, Ayrshire, KA26 9LT
Tel: 01655 331000
★★★★★ International Resort

TWEEDSMUIR

Victoria Lodge
Tweedsmuir, Peeblesshire, ML12 6QP
Tel: 01899 880293
Awaiting Inspection

WALKERBURN

The George Hotel
29 Galashiels Road, Walkerburn, Peebleshire, EH43 6AF
Tel: 01896 870336
★★ Small Hotel

WATERBECK, BY LOCKERBIE

Torbeckhill Bungalow
Waterbeck, Lockerbie, Dumfriesshire, DG11 3EX
Tel: 01461 600683
Awaiting Inspection

WIGTOWN

Hillcrest House
Maidland Place, Station Road, Wigtown, Wigtownshire, DG8 9EU
Tel: 01988 402018
★★★ Guest House

EDINBURGH AND LOTHIANS

ABERLADY

Kilspindie House Hotel
High Street, Aberlady, Longniddry, EH32 0RE
Tel: 01875 870682
Hotel

BATHGATE

The Cairn Hotel
Blackburn Road, Bathgate, West Lothian, EH48 2EL
Tel: 01506 633366
★★★ Hotel

BONNYRIGG

The Retreat Castle
Cockpen Road, Bonnyrigg, Midlothian, EH19 3HS
Tel: 0131 660 3200
★★ Small Hotel

BROXBURN

Bankhead Farm
Dechmont, Broxburn, West Lothian, EH52 6NB
Tel: 01506 811209
★★★★ Guest House

CURRIE

Riccarton Arms
198 Lanark Road West, Currie, Edinburgh, EH14 5NX
Tel: 0131 449 2230
Awaiting Inspection

DALKEITH

The County Hotel
152 High Street, Dalkeith, Midlothian, EH22
Tel: 0131 663 3495
★★★ Hotel

The Guesthouse@Eskbank
Rathan, 45 Eskbank Road, Eskbank, Dalkeith, EH22 3BH
Tel: 0131 663 3291
★★★ Guest House

Glenarch House
Melville Road, Eskbank, Dalkeith, EH22 3NJ
Tel: 0131 663 1478
★★★ Guest House

DIRLETON

Open Arms Hotel
Dirleton, East Lothian, EH39 5EG
Tel: 01620 850241
★★★★ Small Hotel

DUNBAR

The Barns Ness Hotel
Station Road, Dunbar, East Lothian, EH42 1JY
Tel: 01368 863231
★★★ Small Hotel

Goldenstones Hotel
Queens Road, Dunbar, East Lothian, EH42 1LG
Tel: 01368 862356
★★ Small Hotel

Hillside Hotel
3 Queens Road, Dunbar, East Lothian, EH42 1LA
Tel: 01368 862071
★ Small Hotel

Muirfield
40 Belhaven Road, Dunbar, East Lothian, EH42 1NF
Tel: 01368 862289
Awaiting Inspection

Springfield Guest House
Belhaven Road, Dunbar, East Lothian, EH42 1NH
Tel: 01368 862502
★★ Guest House

EAST CALDER

Ashcroft Farmhouse
East Calder, Nr Edinburgh, EH53 0ET
Tel: 01506 881810
★★★★ Guest House

EAST LINTON

Bridgend Hotel
3 Bridgend, East Linton, East Lothian, EH40 3AF
Tel: 01620 860202
★ Small Hotel

EDINBURGH

A'Abide'an'Abode
18 Moat Place, Edinburgh, EH14 1PP
Tel: 0131 443 5668
★★★ Guest House

Aalpha Laurels
320 Gilmerton Road, Edinburgh, Midlothian, EH17 7PR
Tel: 0131 666 2229
★★★ Guest House

Aarajura Guest House
14 Granville Terrace, Edinburgh, EH10 4PQ
Tel: 0870 7668232
★★★ Guest House

Aaran Lodge Guest House
30 Milton Road East, Edinburgh, Midlothian, EH15 2NW
Tel: 0131 657 5615
★★★★ Guest House

Abbey Lodge Hotel
137 Drum Street, Gilmerton, Edinburgh, EH17 8RJ
Tel: 0131 664 9548
★★ Guest House

Abbotsford Guest House
36 Pilrig Street, Edinburgh, EH6 5AL
Tel: 0131 554 2706
★★★ Guest House

Abcorn Guest House
4 Mayfield Gardens, Edinburgh, EH9 2BU
Tel: 0131 667 6548
★★★ Guest House

Directory of all VisitScotland Quality Assured Serviced Establishments

Abercorn Guest House
1 Abercorn Terrace, Edinburgh,
East Lothian, EH15 2DD
Tel: 0131 669 6139
★★★★ Guest House

Acer Lodge Guest house
425 Queensferry Road,
Edinburgh, Midlothian, EH4 7NB
Tel: 0131 336 2554
★★★★ Guest House

Acorn Guest House
70 Pilrig Street, Edinburgh,
EH6 5AS
Tel: 0131 554 2187
★★★★ Guest House

The Acorn Lodge
26 Pilrig Street, Edinburgh,
EH6 5AJ
Tel: 0131 555 1557
★★ Guest House

Adam Drysdale House
42 Gilmore Place, Edinburgh,
Midlothian, EH3 9NQ
Tel: 0131 2288952
Awaiting Inspection

Addison Hotel
2 Murrayfield Avenue,
Edinburgh, Lothian, EH12 6AX
Tel: 0131 337 4060
★★★ Guest House

Adria Hotel
11-12 Royal Terrace, Edinburgh,
EH7 5AB
Tel: 0131 556 7875
★★★ Guest House

Aeon-Kirklands Guest House
128 Old Dalkeith Road,
Edinburgh, EH16 4SD
Tel: 0131 664 2755
★★★ Guest House

Afton Guest House
1 Hartington Gardens,
Edinburgh, EH10 4LD
Tel: 0131 229 1019
★★★ Guest House

Afton Town House
6 Grosvenor Crescent,
Edinburgh, EH12 5EP
Tel: 0131 225 7033
★★★ Guest House

A Haven Townhouse
180 Ferry Road, Edinburgh,
EH6 4NS
Tel: 0131 554 6559
★★★ Small Hotel

Ailsa Craig Hotel
24 Royal Terrace, Edinburgh,
EH7 5AH
Tel: 0131 556 6055
★★★ Small Hotel

Airdenair Guest House
29 Kilmaurs Road, Edinburgh,
EH16 5DB
Tel: 0131 668 2336
★★★ Guest House

Airlie Guest House
29 Minto Street, Edinburgh,
EH9 1SB
Tel: 0131 667 3562
★★★ Guest House

Albany Hotel
39/43 Albany Street, Edinburgh,
EH1 3QY
Tel: 0131 556 0397
★★★★ Hotel

Alexander Guest House
35 Mayfield Gardens,
Edinburgh, EH9 2BX
Tel: 0131 258 4028
★★★★ Guest House

Allison House
17 Mayfield Gardens,
Edinburgh, EH9 2AX
Tel: 0131 667 8049
★★★ Small Hotel

Alloway Guest House
96 Pilrig Street, Edinburgh,
EH6 5AY
Tel: 0131 554 1786
★★★ Guest House

Amaragua Guest House
10 Kilmaurs Terrace, Edinburgh,
Lothian, EH16 5DR
Tel: 0131 667 6775
★★★★ Guest House

Amaryllis Guest House
21 Upper Gilmore PLace,
Edinburgh, EH3 9NL
Tel: 0131 229 3293
★★ Guest House

Aonach Mor Guesthouse
14 Kilmaurs Terrace, Edinburgh,
EH16 5DR
Tel: 0131 667 8694
★★★ Guest House

Apex City Hotel
61 Grassmarket, Edinburgh,
EH1 2JF
Tel: 0845 608 3456
★★★★ Hotel

Apex European Hotel
90 Haymarket Terrace,
Edinburgh, EH12 5LQ
Tel: 0845 6083456
★★★★ Hotel

Apex International Hotel
31/35 Grassmarket, Edinburgh,
EH1 2HS
Tel: 0845 365 0000
★★★★ Hotel

Appin House
4 Queens Crescent, Edinburgh,
Midlothian, EH9 2AZ
Tel: 0131 668 2947
★★ Guest House

Ardenlee Guest House
9 Eyre Place, Edinburgh,
EH3 5ES
Tel: 0131 556 2838
★★★ Guest House

Ardgarth Guest House
1 St Mary's Place, Portobello,
Edinburgh, EH15 2QF
Tel: 0131 669 3021
★★★ Guest House

Ardgowan House
1 Lady Road, Edinburgh,
EH16 5PA
Tel: 0131 667 7774
★★ Guest House

Ardleigh Guest House
260 Ferry Road, Edinburgh,
EH5 3AN
Tel: 0131 552 1833
★★★ Guest House

Ardmillan Hotel
9-10 Ardmillan Terrace,
Edinburgh, EH11 2JW
Tel: 0131 337 9588
★★ Small Hotel

Ardmor House
74 Pilrig Street, Edinburgh,
Lothians, EH6 5AS
Tel: 0131 554 4944
★★★★ Guest House

Ard-Na-Said
5 Priestfield Road, Edinburgh,
Lothian, EH16 5HH
Tel: 0131 667 8754
★★★★ Guest House

The Armadillo Guest House
12 Gilmore Place, Edinburgh,
EH3 9NQ
Tel: 0131 229 6457
★★★ Guest House

Arrandale Guest House
28 Mayfield Gardens,
Edinburgh, Lothian, EH9 2BZ
Tel: 0131 622 2232
★★★ Guest House

Ascot Guest House
98 Dalkeith Road, Edinburgh,
EH16 5AF
Tel: 0131 667 1500
★ Guest House

Ashdene House
23 Fountainhall Road,
Edinburgh, EH9 2LN
Tel: 0131 667 6026
★★★★ Guest House

Ashgrove House
12 Osborne Terrace, Edinburgh, EH12 5HG
Tel: 0131 337 5014
★★★ Guest House

Ashlyn Guest House
42 Inverleith Row, Edinburgh, EH3 5PY
Tel: 0131 552 2954
★★★★ Guest House

Auld Reekie Guest House
16 Mayfield Gardens, Edinburgh, EH9 2BZ
Tel: 0131 667 6177
★★★ Guest House

Aynetree Guest House
12 Duddingston Crescent, Milton Road, Edinburgh, Midlothian, EH15 3AS
Tel: 0131 657 5039
★★ Guest House

Ballantrae Hotel
8 York Place, Edinburgh, EH1 3EP
Tel: 0131 478 4748
★★★ Small Hotel

Ballarat Guest House
14 Gilmore Place, Edinburgh, EH3 9NQ
Tel: 0131 228 9413
Awaiting Inspection

The Balmoral
1 Princes Street, Edinburgh, EH2 2EQ
Tel: 0870 460 7040
★★★★★ Hotel

Balmoral Guest House
32 Pilrig Street, Edinburgh, EH6 5AL
Tel: 0131 554 1857
★★★ Guest House

Barony House
23 Mayfield Gardens, Edinburgh, EH9 2BX
Tel: 0131 667 5806
★★★★ Guest House

Barossa Guest House
21 Pilrig Street, Edinburgh, EH6 5AN
Tel: 0131 554 3700
★★ Guest House

Beechcroft House
46 Murrayfield Avenue, Edinburgh, Lothian, EH12 6AY
Tel: 0131 337 4009
★★★★ Guest House

Belford Guest House
13 Blacket Avenue, Edinburgh, EH9 1RR
Tel: 0131 667 2422
★★ Guest House

11 Belford Place
Edinburgh, Midlothian, EH4 3DH
Tel: 0131 332 9704
Awaiting Inspection

Bellerose Guest House
36 Minto Street, Edinburgh, EH9 2BS
Tel: 0131 667 8933
★★ Guest House

Ben Craig House
3 Craigmillar Park, Edinburgh, EH16 5PG
Tel: 0131 667 2593
★★★ Guest House

Ben Doran
11 Mayfield Gardens, Edinburgh, EH9 2AX
Tel: 0131 667 8488
★★★★ Guest House

Beresford Hotel
32 Coates Gardens, Edinburgh, EH12 5LE
Tel: 0131 337 0850
★★★ Guest House

Best Western Bruntsfield Hotel
69 Bruntsfield Place, Edinburgh, EH10 4HH
Tel: 0131 229 1393
★★★★ Hotel

Best Western Edinburgh City Hotel
79 Lauriston Place, Edinburgh, EH3 9HZ
Tel: 0131 622 7979
★★★★ Hotel

The Beverley
40 Murrayfield Avenue, Edinburgh, EH12 6AY
Tel: 0131 337 1128
★★★★ Bed & Breakfast

Blossom House
8 Minto Street, Edinburgh, EH9 1RG
Tel: 0131 667 5353
★ Guest House

Boisdale Hotel
9 Coates Gardens, Edinburgh, EH12 5LG
Tel: 0131 337 1134
★★★ Guest House

The Bonham
35 Drumsheugh Gardens, Edinburgh, EH3 7RN
Tel: 0131 274 7400
★★★★ Hotel

Bonnington Guest House
202 Ferry Road, Edinburgh, EH6 4NW
Tel: 0131 554 7610
★★★★ Guest House

Borough
72-80 Causewayside, Edinburgh, EH9 1PY
Tel: 0131 668 2255
★★★ Small Hotel

Botanic House Hotel
27 Inverleith Row, Edinburgh, Lothians, EH3 5QH
Tel: 0131 552 2563
★★★ Small Hotel

Brae Guest House
119 Willowbrae Road, Edinburgh, EH8 7HN
Tel: 0131 661 0170
★★★ Guest House

Brae Lodge Guest House
30 Liberton Brae, Edinburgh, Lothian, EH16 6AF
Tel: 0131 672 2876
★★★ Guest House

Braid Hills Hotel
134 Braid Road, Edinburgh, EH10 6JD
Tel: 0131 447 8888
★★★ Hotel

Braveheart Guest House
26 Gilmore Place, Edinburgh, EH3 9NQ
Tel: 0131 221 9192
★★ Guest House

Briggend Guest House
19 Old Dalkeith Road, Edinburgh, EH16 4TE
Tel: 0131 258 0810
★★★ Guest House

Brig O'Doon Guest House
262 Ferry Road, Edinburgh, EH5 3AN
Tel: 0131 552 3953
★★★ Guest House

Brothaigh House
18 Craigmillar Park, Edinburgh, EH16 5PS
Tel: 0131 667 2202
★★★ Guest House

The Broughton Hotel
37 Broughton Place, Edinburgh, Lothian, EH1 3RR
Tel: 0131 558 9792
★★★ Guest House

Buchan & Haymarket Hotel
1-3 Coates Gardens, Edinburgh, Lothian, EH12 5LG
Tel: 0131 337 1045
★★★ Small Hotel

Caledonian Hilton Hotel
Princes Street, Edinburgh, EH1 2AB
Tel: 0131 222 8888
★★★★★ Hotel

Capital Guest House
7 Mayfield Road, Newington, Edinburgh, EH9 2NG
Tel: 0131 466 0717
★★★ Guest House

Directory of all VisitScotland Quality Assured Serviced Establishments

Capital Guest House
2 St Catherines Gardens, Edinburgh, EH12 7AZ
Tel: 0131 334 6159
★★ Guest House

Caravel Guest House
30 London Street, Edinburgh, EH3 6NA
Tel: 0131 556 4444
★★ Guest House

Carlton Hotel
North Bridge, Edinburgh, EH1 1SD
Tel: 0131 472 3001
★★★★ Hotel

Carlton House
15 Mayfield Gardens, Edinburgh, Midlothian, EH9 2AX
Tel: 0131 667 2400
★ Guest House

Carrington Guest House
38 Pilrig Street, Edinburgh, EH6 5AL
Tel: 0131 554 4769
★★★ Guest House

Casa Buzzo Guest House
8 Kilmaurs Road, Edinburgh, EH16 5DA
Tel: 0131 667 8998
★★★ Guest House

Castle Guest House
38 North Castle Street, Edinburgh, EH2 3BN
Tel: 0131 225 1975
★★★ Guest House

47 Castle Street
47 Castle Street (N), Edinburgh, Lothian, EH2 3BG
Tel: 0131 225 7796
Awaiting Inspection

Castle View
30 Castle Street, Edinburgh, Lothian, EH2 3HT
Tel: 0131 226 5784
★★★★ Guest House

Channings
12-16 South Learmonth Gardens, Edinburgh, EH4 1EZ
Tel: 0131 274 7401
★★★★ Hotel

Cherry Tree Villa
9 East Mayfield, Edinburgh, Midlothian, EH9 1SD
Tel: 0131 258 0009
★★★ Guest House

Christopher North House Hotel
6 Gloucester Place, Edinburgh, EH3 6EF
Tel: 0131 225 2720
★★★ Small Hotel

Clan Campbell Hotel
11 Brunswick Street, Edinburgh, EH7 5JB
Tel: 0131 557 6910
★★★ Small Hotel

Claremont Hotel
14a/15 Claremont Crescent, Edinburgh, EH7 4HX
Tel: 0131 556 1487
★ Small Hotel

Classic Guest House
50 Mayfield Road, Edinburgh, EH9 2NH
Tel: 0131 667 5847
★★★ Guest House

Claymore Guest House
68 Pilrig Street, Edinburgh, EH6 5AS
Tel: 0131 554 2500
★★ Guest House

Cluaran House
47 Leamington Terrace, Edinburgh, EH10 4JS
Tel: 0131 221 0047
★★★★ Guest House

The Corstorphine House
188 St Johns Road, Edinburgh, EH12 8SG
Tel: 0131 539 4237
★★★ Guest House

Corstorphine Lodge Hotel
186 St Johns Road, Edinburgh, EH12 8SG
Tel: 0131 476 7116
★★★ Small Hotel

Craigelachie Hotel
21 Murrayfield Avenue, Edinburgh, EH12 6AU
Tel: 0131 337 4076
★★★★ Guest House

Craigmoss Guest House
62 Pilrig Street, Edinburgh, EH6 4HS
Tel: 0131 554 3885
★★★ Guest House

Crioch Guest House
23 East Hermitage Place, Leith Links, Edinburgh, EH6 8AD
Tel: 0131 554 5494
★★★ Guest House

Cruachan Guest House
53 Gilmore Place, Edinburgh, Midlothian, EH3 9NT
Tel: 0131 229 6219
★★★ Guest House

Cumberland Hotel
1-2 West Coates, Edinburgh, EH12 5JQ
Tel: 0131 337 1198
★★★ Small Hotel

Davenport House
58 Great King Street, Edinburgh, Lothian, EH3 6QY
Tel: 0131 558 8495
★★★★ Guest House

Dean Hotel
10 Clarendon Crescent, Edinburgh, EH4 1PT
Tel: 0131 332 0308
★ Small Hotel

Dene Guest House
7 Eyre Place, off Dundas Street, Edinburgh, EH3 5ES
Tel: 0131 556 2700
★★★ Guest House

Dorstan House
7 Priestfield Road, Edinburgh, EH16 5HJ
Tel: 0131 667 6721
★★★ Guest House

Duke's of Windsor Street
17 Windsor Street, Edinburgh, EH7 5LA
Tel: 0131 556 6046
★★★ Small Hotel

Dunedin Guest House
8 Priestfield Road, Edinburgh, Lothian, EH16 5HH
Tel: 0131 668 1949
Awaiting Inspection

Dunstane House Hotel
4 West Coates, Haymarket, Edinburgh, EH12 5JQ
Tel: 0131 337 6169
★★★★ Small Hotel

Duthus Lodge
5 West Coates, Edinburgh, EH12 5JG
Tel: 0131 337 6876
★★★ Guest House

Ecosse International
15 MacDonald Road, Edinburgh, EH7 4LX
Tel: 0131 556 4967
★★★ Guest House

Edinburgh Agenda Hotel
92 St John's Road, Edinburgh, EH12 8AT
Tel: 0131 316 4466
★★★ Hotel

Edinburgh Brunswick Hotel
7 Brunswick Street, Edinburgh, EH7 5JB
Tel: 0131 556 1238
★★★ Guest House

Edinburgh Capital Hotel
187 Clermiston Road, Edinburgh, EH12 6UG
Tel: 0131 535 9988
★★★ Hotel

Directory of all VisitScotland Quality Assured Serviced Establishments

Edinburgh House
11 McDonald Road, Edinburgh, EH7 4LX
Tel: 0131 556 3434
★★★ Guest House

Edinburgh Marriott Hotel
111 Glasgow Road, Edinburgh, EH12 8NF
Tel: 0131 334 9191
★★★★ Hotel

The Edinburgh Residence
7 Rothesay Terrace, Edinburgh, EH3 7RY
Tel: 0131 274 7403
★★★★★ Hotel

Eglinton Hotel
29 Eglinton Crescent, Edinburgh, EH12 5BY
Tel: 0131 337 2641
★★★ Small Hotel

Elas Guest House
10 Claremont Crescent, Edinburgh, EH7 4HX
Tel: 0131 556 1929
★ Guest House

Elder York Guest House
38 Elder Street, Edinburgh, EH1 3DX
Tel: 0131 556 1926
★★★ Guest House

Ellersly House Hotel
Ellersly Road, Edinburgh, EH12 6HZ
Tel: 0131 337 6888
★★ Hotel

Ellesmere Guest House
11 Glengyle Terrace, Edinburgh, EH3 9LN
Tel: 0131 229 4823
★★★★ Guest House

Emerald Guest House
3 Drum Street, Gilmerton, Edinburgh, EH17 8GG
Tel: 0131 664 5918
Awaiting Inspection

Express By Holiday Inn
16-22 Picardy Place, Edinburgh, Lothian, EH1 3JT
Tel: 0131 5582300
★★★ Hotel

Express By Holiday Inn
Britannia Way, Ocean Drive, Edinburgh, Lothian, EH6 6LA
Tel: 0131 555 4422
★★★ Hotel

Failte Guest House
117 Willowbrae Road, Edinburgh, EH8 7HN
Tel: 0131 661 3629
★★★ Guest House

Fairholme
13 Moston Terrace, Edinburgh, EH9 2DE
Tel: 0131 667 8645
★★★ Guest House

Falcon Crest Guest House
70 South Trinity Road, Edinburgh, EH5 3NX
Tel: 0131 552 5294
★ Guest House

Fountain Court Apartments
123 Grove Street, Edinburgh, EH3 8AA
Tel: 0131 622 6677
★★★★ Serviced Apartments

Fountain Court Apartments
123 Grove Street, Edinburgh, EH3 8AA
Tel: 0131 622 6677
★★★★★ Serviced Apartments

Fountainhall Guest House
40 Fountainhall Road, Edinburgh, EH9 2LW
Tel: 0131 667 2544
★ Guest House

Four Twenty Guest House
420 Ferry Road, Edinburgh, EH5 2AD
Tel: 0131 552 2167
★ Guest House

Frederick House Hotel
42 Frederick Street, Edinburgh, EH2 1EX
Tel: 0131 226 1999
★★★ Lodge

Galloway Guest House
22 Dean Park Crescent, Edinburgh, EH4 1PH
Tel: 0131 332 3672
★★★ Guest House

Garfield Guest House
264 Ferry Road, Edinburgh, EH5 3AN
Tel: 0131 552 2369
★★ Guest House

Garlands Guest House
48 Pilrig Street, Edinburgh, EH6 5AL
Tel: 0131 554 4205
★★★ Guest House

The George Hotel
19-21 George Street, Edinburgh, EH2 2PB
Tel: 0131 225 1251
★★★★ Hotel

Gifford House
103 Dalkeith Road, Edinburgh, EH16 5AJ
Tel: 0131 667 4688
★★★★ Guest House

Gildun Guest House
9 Spence Street, Edinburgh, EH16 5AG
Tel: 0131 667 1368
★★★★ Guest House

Gilmore Guest House
51 Gilmore Place, Edinburgh, EH3 9NT
Tel: 0131 229 5008
★★ Guest House

34 Gilmore Place
Edinburgh, Lothian, EH3 9NQ
Tel: 0131 221 1331
★★★★ Guest House

Gladstone Guest House
90 Dalkeith Road, Edinburgh, EH16 5AF
Tel: 0131 667 4708
★★★ Guest House

The Glasshouse
2 Greenside Place, Edinburgh, EH1 3AA
Tel: 0131 525 8200
Awaiting Inspection

Glenallan Guest House
19 Mayfield Road, Edinburgh, EH9 2NG
Tel: 0131 667 1667
★★★★ Guest House

Glenalmond Guest House
25 Mayfield Gardens, Edinburgh, EH9 2BX
Tel: 0131 668 2392
★★★★ Guest House

Glenora Hotel
14 Rosebery Crescent, Edinburgh, EH12 5JY
Tel: 0131 337 1186
★★★★ Guest House

Granville Guest House
13 Granville Terrace, Edinburgh, EH10 4PQ
Tel: 0131 229 1676
★★ Guest House

Greens Hotel
24 Eglinton Crescent, Edinburgh, EH12 5BY
Tel: 0131 337 1565
★★★ Hotel

Greenside Hotel
9 Royal Terrace, Edinburgh, EH7 5AH
Tel: 0131 557 0022
★★★ Small Hotel

Grosvenor Gardens Hotel
1 Grosvenor Gardens, Edinburgh, Midlothian, EH12 5JU
Tel: 0131 313 3415
Awaiting Inspection

Halcyon Hotel
8 Royal Terrace, Edinburgh, EH7 5AB
Tel: 0131 556 1033
★ Guest House

Hampton Hotel
14 Corstorphine Road, Edinburgh, EH12 6HN
Tel: 0131 337 1130
★★★ Small Hotel

Directory of all VisitScotland Quality Assured Serviced Establishments

Hanover House Hotel
26 Windsor Street, Edinburgh, EH7 5JR
Tel: 0131 556 1325
★★★ Guest House

B&B Harrison
58 Buckstone Terrace, Edinburgh, Lothian, EH10 6RQ
Tel: 0131 445 1430
Awaiting Inspection

Harvest Guest House
33 Straiton Place, Edinburgh, EH15 2BA
Tel: 0131 657 3160
★ Guest House

Heatherlea Guest House
13 Mayfield Gardens, Edinburgh, EH9 2AX
Tel: 0131 667 3958
★ Guest House

Herald House Hotel
70 Grove Street, Edinburgh, EH3 8AP
Tel: 0131 228 2323
★★ Hotel

Heriott Park Guest House
254/256 Ferry Road, Edinburgh, EH5 3AN
Tel: 0131 552 3456
★★★ Guest House

Highfield Guest House
83 Mayfield Road, Edinburgh, EH9 3AE
Tel: 0131 667 8717
★★★★ Guest House

Hilton Edinburgh Airport
Edinburgh International Airport, Edinburgh, EH28 8LL
Tel: 0131 519 4400
★★★★ Hotel

Hilton Edinburgh Grosvenor
7-21 Grosvenor Street, Edinburgh, EH12 5EF
Tel: 0131 226 6001
★★★ Hotel

Holiday Inn Edinburgh
Corstorphine Road, Edinburgh, EH12 6UA
Tel; 0870 400 9026
★★★★ Hotel

Holiday Inn Edinburgh-North
107 Queensferry Road, Edinburgh, EH4 3HL
Tel: 0131 332 2442
★★★ Hotel

Holyrood Hotel
Holyrood Road, Edinburgh, EH8 6AE
Tel: 0131 550 4500
★★★★ Hotel

Hotel Ceilidh-Donia
14-16 Marchhall Crescent, Edinburgh, EH16 5HL
Tel: 0131 667 2743
★★★ Small Hotel

Hotel Ibis Edinburgh
6 Hunter Square, Edinburgh, EH1 1QW
Tel: 0131 240 7000
★★ Hotel

Fraoch House
66 Pilrig Street, Edinburgh, Midlothian, EH6 5AS
Tel: 0131 554 1353
★★★ Guest House

The Howard
34 Great King Street, Edinburgh, EH3 6QH
Tel: 0131 274 7402
★★★★★ Small Hotel

The Inverleith Hotel
5 Inverleith Terrace, Edinburgh, EH3 5NS
Tel: 0131 556 2745
★★★ Small Hotel

Ivy Guest House
7 Mayfield Gardens, Edinburgh, EH9 2AX
Tel: 0131 667 3411
★★★ Guest House

Jocks Lodgings
8 Magdal Crescent, Edinburgh, Lothian, EH12 5BE
Tel: 0131 3371043
Awaiting Inspection

Joppa Turrets Guest House
1 Lower Joppa (at Beach end of Morton St), Edinburgh, EH15 2ER
Tel: 0131 669 5806
★★★ Guest House

Jurys Inn Edinburgh
43 Jeffrey Street, Edinburgh, Lothian, EH1 1DH
Tel: 0131 200 3300
★★★ Hotel

Kaimes Guest House
12 Granville Terrace, Edinburgh, EH10 4PQ
Tel: 0131 229 3401
★★ Guest House

Kariba Guest House
10 Granville Terrace, Edinburgh, EH10 4PQ
Tel: 0131 229 3773
★★★ Guest House

Kelly's Guest House
3 Hillhouse Road, Edinburgh, Lothian, EH4 3QP
Tel: 0131 3323894
★★★ Guest House

Kenvie Guest House
16 Kilmaurs Road, Edinburgh, EH16 5DA
Tel: 0131 668 1964
★★★ Guest House

Kew House
1 Kew Terrace, Murrayfield, Edinburgh, EH12 5JE
Tel: 0131 313 0700
★★★★ Small Hotel

Kildonan Lodge Hotel
27 Craigmillar Park, Edinburgh, EH16 5PE
Tel: 0131 667 2793
★★★★ Small Hotel

Kilmaurs House
9 Kilmaurs Road, Edinburgh, EH16 5DA
Tel: 0131 667 8315
★★★ Guest House

Kingsburgh House
2 Corstorphine Road, Edinburgh, Midlothian, EH12 6HN
Tel: 0131 313 1679
★★★★★ Guest House

Kingsley Guest House
30 Craigmillar Park, Edinburgh, EH16 5PS
Tel: 0131 667 3177
★★★ Guest House

Best Western Kings Manor Hotel
100 Milton Road East, Edinburgh, EH15 2NP
Tel: 0131 468 8003
★★★ Hotel

Kingsview Guest House
28 Gilmore Place, Edinburgh, EH3 9NQ
Tel: 0131 229 8004
★★ Guest House

Kingsway Guest House
5 East Mayfield, Edinburgh, EH9 1SD
Tel: 0131 667 5029
★★★ Guest House

Kirklea Guest House
11 Harrison Road, Edinburgh, EH11 1EG
Tel: 0131 337 1129
★★★ Guest House

The Knight Residence
12 Lauriston Street Edinburgh, Lothian, EH3 9DJ
Tel: 0131 622 8120
★★★★★ Serviced Apartments

The Lairg
11 Coates Gardens, Edinburgh, EH12 5LG
Tel: 0131 3371050
Awaiting Inspection

Lauderville House
52 Mayfield Road, Edinburgh, EH9 2NH
Tel: 0131 667 7788
★★★★ Guest House

Learmonth Hotel
18-20 Learmonth Terrace, Edinburgh, EH4 1PW
Tel: 0131 343 2671
★ Hotel

Lindsay Guest House
108 Polwarth Terrace, Edinburgh, Midlothian, EH11 1NN
Tel: 0131 337 1580
★★★ Guest House

Links Hotel and Bar
4 Alvanley Terrace, Whitehouse Loan, Edinburgh, Lothian, EH9 1DU
Tel: 0131 622 6800
★★ Hotel

The Lodge Hotel
6 Hampton Terrace, Edinburgh, EH12 5JD
Tel: 0131 337 3682
★★★★ Small Hotel

McDonald Guest House
5 McDonald Road, Edinburgh, EH7 4LX
Tel: 0131 557 5935
★★★ Guest House

Mackenzie Guest House
2 East Hermitage Place, Edinburgh, EH6 8AA
Tel: 0131 554 3763
★★★★ Guest House

Clarendon Hotel
25-33 Shandwick Place, Edinburgh, EH2 4RG
Tel: 0131 229 1467
★★★ Hotel

Malmaison Hotel et Brasserie
1 Tower Place, Leith, Edinburgh, EH6 7DB
Tel: 0131 468 5000
★★★★ Hotel

Mardale Guest House
11 Hartington Place, Edinburgh, EH10 4LF
Tel: 0131 229 2693
★★★ Guest House

Mayfield Lodge
75 Mayfield Road, Edinburgh, EH9 3AA
Tel: 0131 662 8899
★★★ Guest House

Mayville Guest House
5 Minto Street, Edinburgh, EH9 1RG
Tel: 0131 667 6103
★★★ Guest House

Melville Castle Hotel
Melville Gate, Gilmerton Road, Midlothian, EH18 1AP
Tel: 0131 654 0088
★★★★ Hotel

Melville Guest House
2 Duddingston Crescent, Edinburgh, Lothian, EH15 3AS
Tel: 0131 669 7856
★★★ Guest House

Melvin House Hotel
3 Rothesay Terrace, Edinburgh, EH3 7RY
Tel: 0131 225 5084
★★★ Hotel

Menzies Belford Hotel
69 Belford Road, Edinburgh, EH4 3DG
Tel: 0131 332 2545
★★★★ Hotel

Menzies Guest House
33 Leamington Terrace, Edinburgh, EH10 4JS
Tel: 0131 229 4629
★★ Guest House

Merlin Guest House
14 Hartington Place, Edinburgh, EH10 4LE
Tel: 0131 229 3864
★★ Guest House

Mingalar
2 East Claremont Street, Edinburgh, Midlothian, EH7 4JP
Tel: 0131 556 7000
★★★ Guest House

The Morningside Guest House
7 Hermitage Terrace, Edinburgh, EH10 4RP
Tel: 0131 447 4089
★★★ Guest House

Murrayfield Hotel
18 Corstorphine Road, Edinburgh, EH12 6HN
Tel: 0131 337 1844
★ Hotel

Murrayfield Park Hotel
89 Corstorphine Road, Edinburgh, EH12 5QE
Tel: 0131 337 5370
★★★ Guest House

MW Guesthouse
94 Dalkeith Road, Edinburgh, Mid Lothian, EH16 5AF
Tel: 0131 662 9265
★★★★ Guest House

MW Town House
11 Spence Street, Edinburgh, Mid Lothian, EH16 5AG
Tel: 0131 662 9265
★★★★ Guest House

Alness Guest House
27 Pilrig Street, Edinburgh, EH6 5AN
Tel: 0131 554 1187
★★ Guest House

Newington Guest House
18 Newington Road, Edinburgh, EH9 1QS
Tel: 0131 667 3356
★★ Guest House

Northumberland Hotel
31-33 Craigmillar Park, Edinburgh, EH16 5PE
Tel: 0131 668 3131
★★ Small Hotel

Norton House Hotel
Ingliston, Edinburgh, EH28 8LX
Tel: 0131 333 1275
★★★★ Hotel

Novotel Edinburgh Centre
80 Lauriston Place, Edinburgh, Lothian, EH3 9DE
Tel: 0131 656 3500
★★★★ Hotel

Old Waverley Hotel
43 Princes Street, Edinburgh, EH2 2BY
Tel: 0131 556 4648
★★★ Hotel

One Royal Circus
1 Royal Circus, Edinburgh, EH3 6TL
Tel: 0131 225 5854
★★★★★ Exclusive Use Venue

Orwell Lodge Hotel
29 Polwarth Terrace, Edinburgh, EH11 1NH
Tel: 0131 229 1044
★★ Small Hotel

Osbourne Hotel
51-59 York Place, Edinburgh, EH1 3JD
Tel: 0131 556 5577
★ Hotel

46 Palmerston Place
Edinburgh, Midlothian, EH12 5BJ
Tel: 0131 226 3372
Awaiting Inspection

Parklands Guest House
20 Mayfield Gardens, Edinburgh, EH9 2BZ
Tel: 0131 667 7184
★★★ Guest House

Parliament House Hotel
15 Calton Hill, Edinburgh, EH1 3BJ
Tel: 0131 478 4000
★★★ Hotel

Piries Hotel
4-8 Coates Gardens, Edinburgh, EH12 5LB
Tel: 0131 337 1108
★★★ Hotel

The Point Hotel
34 Bread Street, Edinburgh, EH3 9AF
Tel: 0131 221 5555
★★★ Hotel

Directory of all VisitScotland Quality Assured Serviced Establishments

Portobello House
2 Pittville Street, Edinburgh, EH15 2BY
Tel: 0131 669 6067
★★★ Guest House

Premier Travel Inn
82 Lauriston Place, Edinburgh, Lothian, EH3 9HZ
Tel: 0131 221 7130
Awaiting Inspection

Prestonfield House Hotel
Priestfield Road, Edinburgh, Lothian, EH16 5UT
Tel: 0131 668 3346
★★★★★ Hotel

Priestville Guest House
10 Priestfield Road, Edinburgh, EH16 5HJ
Tel: 0131 667 2435
★★★ Guest House

The Quality Hotel Edinburgh Airport
Ingliston,by Edinburgh, Midlothian, EH28 8AU
Tel: 0131 333 4331
★★★ Hotel

Radisson SAS Hotel, Edinburgh
80 High Street, The Royal Mile, Edinburgh, EH1 1TH
Tel: 0131 473 6590
★★★★ Hotel

Ramada Mount Royal Hotel
53 Princes Street, Edinburgh, EH2 2DG
Tel: 0131 225 7161
★★★ Hotel

Ravensdown Guest House
248 Ferry Road, Edinburgh, Midlothian, EH5 3AN
Tel: 0131 552 5438
★★★ Guest House

Richmond House Hotel
20 Leopold Place, Edinburgh, EH7 5LB
Tel: 0131 556 3556
★★ Small Hotel

Ritz Hotel
14-18 Grosvenor Street, Edinburgh, EH12 5EG
Tel: 0131 337 4315
★★ Hotel

Robb's Guest House
5 Granville Terrace, Edinburgh, EH10 4PQ
Tel: 0131 229 2086
★★ Guest House

Robertson Guest House
5 Hartington Gardens, Edinburgh, EH10 4LD
Tel: 0131 229 2652
★★★ Guest House

The Rosebery Hotel
13 Rosebery Crescent, Edinburgh, EH12 5JY
Tel: 0131 337 1085
★ Guest House

Rosehall Hotel
101 Dalkeith Road, Newington, Edinburgh, EH16 5AJ
Tel: 0131 667 9372
★★★ Small Hotel

Roselea Guest House
4 Kew Terrace, Edinburgh, EH12 5JE
Tel: 0131 467 4166
★★ Guest House

Rosevale House
15 Kilmaurs Road, Edinburgh, EH16 5DA
Tel: 0131 667 4781
★★ Guest House

Rothesay Hotel
8 Rothesay Place, Edinburgh, EH3 7SL
Tel: 0131 225 4125
★ Hotel

Rowan Guest House
13 Glenorchy Terrace, Edinburgh, EH9 2DQ
Tel: 0131 667 2463
★★★ Guest House

Roxburghe Hotel
38 Charlotte Square, Edinburgh, EH2 4HG
Tel: 0131 240 5500
★★★★ Hotel

Royal British Hotel
20 Princes Street, Edinburgh, EH2 2AN
Tel: 0131 556 4901
★★★ Hotel

The Royal Over-Seas League
100 Princes Street, Edinburgh, EH2 3AB
Tel: 0131 225 1501
★★ Small Hotel

The Royal Scots Club
30 Abercromby Place, Edinburgh, Lothian, EH3 6QE
Tel: 0131 556 4270
★★★ Hotel

The Royal Scotsman
Edinburgh Waverley Station, Edinburgh
★★★★★ Train

Royal Terrace Hotel
18 Royal Terrace, Edinburgh, EH7 5AQ
Tel: 0131 557 3222
Hotel

The St Valery
36 Coates Gardens, Edinburgh, EH12 5LE
Tel: 0131 337 1893
★★★ Guest House

Sakura House
18 West Preston Street, Edinburgh, EH8 9PU
Tel: 0131 668 1204
★ Guest House

Sandaig Guest House
5 East Hermitage Place, Leith Links, Edinburgh, EH6 8AA
Tel: 0131 554 7357
★★★★ Guest House

Sandilands House
25 Queensferry Road, Edinburgh, EH4 3HB
Tel: 0131 332 2057
★★★ Guest House

San Marco
24 Mayfield Gardens, Edinburgh, EH9 2BZ
Tel: 0131 667 8982
★★★ Guest House

The Scotsman Hotel
20 North Bridge, Edinburgh, EH1 1YT
Tel: 0131 556 5565
★★★★★ Hotel

Shalimar Guest House
20 Newington Road, Edinburgh, EH9 1QS
Tel: 0131 6672827
★★ Guest House

Sheraton Grand Hotel & Spa
1 Festival Square, Edinburgh, EH3 9SR
Tel: 0131 229 9131
★★★★★ Hotel

Sheridan Guest House
1 Bonnington Terrace, Edinburgh, EH6 4BP
Tel: 0131 554 4107
★★★ Guest House

Sherwood Guest House
42 Minto Street, Edinburgh, EH9 2BR
Tel: 0131 667 1200
★★★ Guest House

Six Marys Place Guest House
Raeburn Place, Stockbridge, Edinburgh, EH4 1JH
Tel: 0131 332 8965
★★★ Guest House

Smiths' Guest House
77 Mayfield Road, Edinburgh, EH9 3AA
Tel: 0131 667 2524
★★★ Guest House

Sonas Guest House
3 East Mayfield, Edinburgh, EH9 1SD
Tel: 0131 667 2781
★★★ Guest House

Southside
8 Newington Road, Edinburgh, EH9 1QS
★★★★ Guest House

St Albans Lodge
St Albans Road, Edinburgh, Midlothian, EH9 2PA
Tel: 0131 667 6302
Awaiting Inspection

Ben Cruachan
17 McDonald Road, Edinburgh, Midlothian, EH7 4LX
Tel: 0131 556 3709
★★★ Guest House

Star Villa
36 Gilmore Place, Edinburgh, EH3 9NQ
Tel: 0131 229 4991
★★★ Guest House

St Bernards Guest House
22 St Bernards Crescent, Edinburgh, EH4 1NS
Tel: 0131 332 2339
★★ Guest House

St Conan's Guest House
30 Minto Street, Edinburgh, EH9 1SB
Tel: 0131 667 8393
★★★ Guest House

Strathallan Guest House
44 Minto Street, Edinburgh, Lothian, EH9 2BR
Tel: 0131 667 6678
★★★ Guest House

Stra'ven Guest House
3 Brunstane Road North, Edinburgh, EH15 2DL
Tel: 0131 669 5580
★★★ Guest House

Stuart House
12 East Claremont Street, Edinburgh, EH7 4JP
Tel: 0131 557 9030
★★★★ Guest House

Sunnyside Guest House
13 Pilrig Street, Edinburgh, EH6 5AN
Tel: 0131 553 2084
★★ Guest House

Tania Guest House
19 Minto Street, Edinburgh, EH9 1RQ
Tel: 0131 667 4144
★ Guest House

Tankard Guest House
40 East Claremont Street, Edinburgh, EH7 4JR
Tel: 0131 556 4218
★ Guest House

Terrace Hotel
37 Royal Terrace, Edinburgh, EH7 5AH
Tel: 0131 556 3423
★★ Guest House

Teviotdale House
53 Grange Loan, Edinburgh, EH9 2ER
Tel: 0131 667 4376
★★★ Guest House

Thistle Edinburgh
107 Leith Street, Edinburgh, EH1 3SW
Tel: 0870 3339153
★★★★ Hotel

Thistle Hotel
59 Manor Place, Edinburgh, EH3 7EG
Tel: 0131 225 6144
★★ Small Hotel

Thistle House
1 Kilmaurs Terrace, Edinburgh, EH16 5BZ
Tel: 0131 667 2002
Awaiting Inspection

Thrums Hotel
14-15 Minto Street, Edinburgh, EH9 1RQ
Tel: 0131 667 5545
★★ Guest House

Toby Carvery & Innkeepers Lodge Edin
114-116 St Johns Road, Edinburgh, EH12 8AX
Tel: 0131 334 8235
★★★ Inn

The Town House
65 Gilmore Place, Edinburgh, EH3 9NU
Tel: 0131 229 1985
★★★★ Guest House

Turret Guest House
8 Kilmaurs Terrace, Edinburgh, EH16 5DR
Tel: 0131 667 6704
★★★★ Guest House

Valentine Guest House
19 Gilmore Place, Tollcross, Edinburgh, EH3 9NE
Tel: 0131 229 5622
★★ Guest House

Clan Walker Guest House
96 Dalkeith Road, Edinburgh, Lothian, EH16 5AF
Tel: 0131 667 1244
★★★ Guest House

The Walton Hotel
79 Dundas Street, Edinburgh, Lothian, EH3 6SD
Tel: 0131 556 1137
★★★★ Guest House

West End Hotel
35 Palmerston Place, Edinburgh, EH12 5AU
Tel: 0131 225 3656
★★★ Small Hotel

Western Manor House Hotel
92 Corstorphine Road, Murrayfield, Edinburgh, EH12 6JG
Tel: 0131 538 7490
★★★ Guest House

BY EDINBURGH

Dalhousie Castle & Spa
Cockpen Road, Bonnyrigg, Edinburgh, Midlothian, EH19 3JB
Tel: 01875 820153
★★★★ Hotel

GIFFORD

Tweeddale Arms Hotel
High Street, Gifford, East Lothian, EH41 4QU
Tel: 01620 810240
★★★ Small Hotel

GOREBRIDGE

Ivory House
14 Vogrie Road, Gorebridge, Midlothian, EH23 4HH
Tel: 01875 820755
★★★★ Guest House

GULLANE

Greywalls
Muirfield, Gullane, East Lothian, EH31 2EG
Tel: 01620 842144
★★★★ Hotel

Mallard Hotel
East Links Road, Gullane, East Lothian, EH31 2AF
Tel: 01620 843288
★★ Small Hotel

HADDINGTON

Browns Hotel
1 West Road, Haddington, EH41 3RD
Tel: 01620 822254
★★★★ Small Hotel

Maitlandfield House Hotel
24 Sidegate, Haddington, East Lothian, EH41 4BZ
Tel: 01620 826513
★★★ Hotel

KIRKNEWTON

The Marriott Dalmahoy Hotel and Country Club
Kirknewton, Midlothian, EH27 8EP
Tel: 0131 333 1845
★★★★ Hotel

LINLITHGOW

The Bonsyde House Hotel
Bonsyde, By Linlithgow, West Lothian, EH49 7NU
Tel: 01506 842229
★★ Small Hotel

Lumsdaine
Lanark Road, Linlithgow, West Lothian, EH49 6QE
Tel: 01506 845001
Awaiting Inspection

West Port Hotel
West Port, Linlithgow,
West Lothian, EH49 7AZ
Tel: 01506 847456
★★ Small Hotel

LIVINGSTON

Ramada Jarvis Livingston
Almondview, Livingston,
West Lothian, EH54 6QB
Tel: 01506 431222
★★★ Hotel

LOANHEAD

Aaron Glen Guest House
7 Nivensknowe Road, Loanhead,
Midlothian, EH20 9AU
Tel: 0131 440 1293
★★★ Guest House

MUSSELBURGH

Arden House
26 Linkfield Road, Musselburgh,
East Lothian, EH21 7LL
Tel: 0131 665 0663
★★★ Guest House

Carberry Conference Centre
Carberry Tower, Musselburgh,
East Lothian, EH21 8PY
Tel: 0131 665 3135/3488
★★ Guest House

NORTH BERWICK

The County Hotel
High Street, North Berwick,
East Lothian, EH39 4HH
Tel: 01620 892989
Awaiting Inspection

The Golf Hotel
34 Dirleton Avenue,
North Berwick, East Lothian,
EH39 4BH
Tel: 01620 892202
★★ Small Hotel

The Marine Hotel
Cromwell Road, North Berwick,
East Lothian, EH39 4LZ
Tel: 0870 400 8129
Hotel

Nether Abbey Hotel
20 Dirleton Avenue, North
Berwick, EH39 4BQ
Tel: 01620 892802
★★ Small Hotel

NORTH MIDDLETON

Borthwick Castle
North Middleton, Gorebridge,
Midlothian, EH23 4QY
Tel: 01875 820514
★★★ Small Hotel

PATHHEAD

The Stair Arms Hotel
Ford, Patthead, Midlothian,
EH37 5TX
Tel: 01875 320277
Awaiting Inspection

PENICUIK

Ptarmigan
Nine Mile Burn, by Penicuik,
Midlothian, EH26 9LZ
Tel: 01968 675933
Awaiting Inspection

ROSLIN

Original Rosslyn Inn
Main Street, Roslin, Midlothian,
EH25 9LE
Tel: 0131 440 2384
★★ Small Hotel

SOUTH QUEENSFERRY

Priory Lodge
8 The Loan, South Queensferry,
West Lothian, EH30 9NS
Tel: 0131 331 4345
★★★★ Guest House

TRANENT

Rosebank Guest House
161 High Street, Tranent,
East Lothian, EH33 1LP
Tel: 01875 610967
★★★ Guest House

UPHALL

Houstoun House Hotel
Uphall, West Lothian, EH52 6JS
Tel: 01506 853831
★★★★ Hotel

WHITBURN

Hilcroft Hotel
East Main Street, Whitburn,
West Lothian, EH47 0JU
Tel: 01501 740818
★★★ Hotel

GREATER GLASGOW AND CLYDE VALLEY

ABINGTON

Abington Hotel
Carlisle Road, Abington,
Lanarkshire, ML12 6SD
Tel: 01864 502467
★★ Hotel

AIRDRIE

Knight's Rest
150 Clark Street, Airdrie,
Lanarkshire, ML6 6DZ
Tel: 01236 606193
★★ Guest House

BARRHEAD, GLASGOW

Dalmeny Park Hotel
Lochlibo Road, Barrhead,
Renfrewshire, G78 1LG
Tel: 0141 881 9211
★★★ Small Hotel

BIGGAR

Cornhill House Hotel
Cornhill Road, Coulter, Biggar,
Clyde Valley, ML12 6QE
Tel: 01899 220001
★★★ Small Hotel

Shieldhill Hotel
Quothquan, Biggar, Lanarkshire,
ML12 6NA
Tel: 01899 220035
★★★★ Hotel

BISHOPTON

Mar Hall
Mar Estate, Bishopton,
Renfrewshire, PA7 5PU
Tel: 0141 812 9999
★★★★★ Hotel

CALDERBANK, BY AIRDRIE

Calder Guest House
13 Main Street, Calderbank,
by Airdrie, Lanarkshire,
ML6 9SG
Tel: 01236 769077
★★★ Guest House

CARLUKE

Burnhead Farm
Carluke, Lanarkshire, ML8 4QN
Tel: 01555 771360
Awaiting Inspection

CARNWATH

Wester Walston Lodge
Walston, Nr Carnwarth,
South Lanarkshire, ML11 8NF
Awaiting Inspection

COATBRIDGE

Georgian Hotel
26 Lefroy Street, Coatbridge,
Lanarkshire, ML5 1LZ
Tel: 01236 421888
★★ Small Hotel

BY COATBRIDGE

Auchenlea
153 Langmuir Road, Bargeddie,
Lanarkshire, G69 7RT
Tel: 0141 771 6870
★★★ Guest House

CRAWFORD

William's Rest House Hotel
115 Carlisle Road, Crawford,
Biggar, ML12 6TP
Tel: 01864 502590
★★ Small Hotel

EAGLESHAM, BY GLASGOW

Eglinton Arms Hotel
Gilmour Street, Eaglesham,
Glasgow, G76 0LG
Tel: 01355 302631
★★★ Hotel

EAST KILBRIDE

The Bruce Hotel
35 Cornwall Street, East Kilbride, G74 1AF
Tel: 01355 229771
Hotel

Crutherland House Hotel
Strathaven Road, East Kilbride, Lanarkshire, G75 0QJ
Tel: 01355 577000
★★★★ Hotel

Torrance Hotel
Torrance Road, East Kilbride, Lanarkshire, G74 4LN
Tel: 013552 25241
★★ Small Hotel

ERSKINE

Erskine Bridge Hotel
Erskine, Renfrewshire, PA8 6AN
Tel: 0141 812 0123
★★★ Hotel

GLASGOW

The Alamo Guest House
46 Gray Street, Glasgow, G3 7SE
Tel: 0141 339 2395
★ Guest House

Albion Hotel
405 North Woodside Road, Glasgow, G20 6NN
Tel: 0141 339 8620
★★★ Small Hotel

Alison Guest House
26 Circus Drive, Glasgow, G31 2JH
Tel: 0141 556 1431
★★ Guest House

Ambassador Hotel
7 Kelvin Drive, Glasgow, G20 8QG
Tel: 0141 946 1018
★★★ Hotel

Argyll Hotel
973 Sauchiehall Street, Glasgow, G3 7TQ
Tel: 0141 337 3313
★★★ Hotel

Arthouse Hotel
129 Bath Street, Glasgow, G2 2SZ
Tel: 0141 221 6789
★★★★ Hotel

Artto Hotel
37-39 Hope Street, Glasgow, G2 6AE
Tel: 0141 2482480
★★★ Hotel

Belgrave Guest House
2 Belgrave Terrace, Hillhead, Glasgow, G12 8JD
Tel: 0141 337 1850
★★ Guest House

The Belhaven Hotel
15 Belhaven Terrace, Glasgow, G12 OTG
Tel: 0141 339 3222
★★★ Small Hotel

Bewleys Hotel
110 Bath Street, Glasgow, G2 2EN, Fax:0141 353 0900
Tel: 0845 234 5959
★★★ Hotel

Bothwell Bridge Hotel
89 Main Street, Bothwell, Glasgow, G71 8EU
Tel: 01698 852246
★★★ Hotel

Buchanan Hotel
185 Buchanan Street, Glasgow, G1 2JY
Tel: 0141 332 7284
★ Hotel

Burnside Hotel
East Kilbride Road, Rutherglen, Glasgow, G73 5EA
Tel: 0141 634 1276
★★ Small Hotel

Busby Hotel
Field Road, Clarkston, Glasgow, G76 8RX
Tel: 0141 644 2661
★★ Hotel

Campanile Hotel Glasgow
Tunnel Street, Glasgow, G3 8HL
Tel: 0141 287 7700
★★★ Hotel

Carlton George Hotel
44 West George Street, Glasgow, G2 1DH
Tel: 0141 353 6373
★★★★ Hotel

Cathedral House
28-32 Cathedral Square, Glasgow, G4 0XA
Tel: 0141 552 3519
★★ Small Hotel

City Inn Glasgow
Finnieston Quay, Glasgow, G3 8HN
★★★ Hotel

Corus Hotel Glasgow
377 Argyle Street, Glasgow, Dunbartonshire, G2 8LL
Tel: 0141 2482355
★★★ Hotel

Craigpark Guest House
33 Circus Drive, Glasgow, G31 2JG
Tel: 0141 554 4160
★★ Guest House

Devoncove Hotel
931 Sauchiehall Street, Glasgow, G3 7TQ
Tel: 0141 334 4000
★★★ Hotel

1 Devonshire Gardens
Glasgow, G12 0UX
Tel: 0141 339 2001
★★★★★ Hotel

The Enterprise Hotel
144 Renfrew Street, Glasgow, G3 6RF
Tel: 0141 332 8095
Awaiting Inspection

Ewington Hotel
132 Queen's Drive, Queen's Park, Glasgow, G42 8QW
Tel: 0141 423 1152
★★ Hotel

Express by Holiday Inn
Theatreland, 165 West Nile Street, Glasgow, Lanarkshire, G1 2RL
Tel: 0141 331 6800
★★★ Hotel

Express by Holiday Inn Glasgow
122 Stockwell Street, Glasgow, G1 4LT
Tel: 0141 548 5000
★★★ Hotel

Garfield House Hotel
Cumbernauld Road, Stepps, Glasgow, Lanarkshire, G33 6HW
Tel: 0141 779 2111
★★★ Hotel

The Georgian House
29 Buckingham Terrace, Great Western Road, Hillhead, Glasgow, G12 8ED
Tel: 0141 339 0008
★★ Guest House

Glasgow Marriott
500 Argyle Street, Glasgow, G3 8RR
Tel: 0141 226 5577
★★★★ Hotel

Glasgow Moat House
Congress Road, Glasgow, G3 8QT
Tel: 0141 306 9988
★★★★ Hotel

Hampton Court Hotel
230 Renfrew Street, Glasgow, G3 6TX
Tel: 0141 332 6623
★★ Guest House

The Heritage Hotel
4-5 Alfred Terrace, Glasgow, G12 8RF
Tel: 0141 339 6955
★★★ Guest House

Hillhead Hotel
32 Cecil Street, Glasgow, G12 8RJ
Tel: 0141 339 7733
★ Guest House

Hilton Glasgow Grosvenor
Grosvenor Terrace, Glasgow, G12 OTA
Tel: 0141 339 8811
★★★★ Hotel

Directory of all VisitScotland Quality Assured Serviced Establishments

Hilton Hotel Glasgow
1 William Street, Glasgow,
G3 8HT
Tel: 0141 204 5555
★★★★★ Hotel

Hilton Strathclyde
Pheonix Crescent, Bellshill,
North Lanarkshire, ML4 3JQ
Tel: 01698 395500
★★★★ Hotel

Holiday Inn Glasgow City West
Bothwell Street, Glasgow,
G2 7EN
Tel: 0870 4009032
★★★ Hotel

Holiday Inn Glasgow City Centre
Theatreland, 161 West Nile
Street, Glasgow, G1 2RL
Tel: 0141 352 8300
★★★★ Hotel

Ibis Hotel Glasgow
220 West Regent Street,
Glasgow, G2 4DQ
Tel: 0141 225 6000
★★ Hotel

The Inn on the Green
25 Greenhead Street, Glasgow,
Lanarkshire, G40 1ES
Tel: 0141 554 0165
★★★ Small Hotel

Jurys Glasgow Hotel
Great Western Road, Glasgow,
G12 0XP
Tel: 0141 334 8161
★★ Hotel

Jurys Inn Glasgow
Jamaica Street, Glasgow, G1 4QE
Tel: 0141 314 4800
★★★ Hotel

Kelvingrove Hotel
944 Sauchiehall Street,
Glasgow, G3 7TH
Tel: 0141 339 5011
★★★ Guest House

Kelvin Hotel
15 Buckingham Terrace,
Glasgow, G12 8EB
Tel: 0141 339 7143
★★ Guest House

Kirkland House
42 St Vincent Crescent,
Glasgow, G3 8NG
Tel: 0141 248 3458
★★ Guest House

Kirklee Hotel
11 Kensington Gate, Glasgow,
G12 9LG
Tel: 0141 334 5555
★★★ Guest House

Langs Hotel
2 Port Dundas Place, Glasgow,
G2 3LD
Tel: 0141 330 1500
★★★★ Hotel

Lees Guest House
3 Bank Street, Glasgow, G12 8JQ
Tel: 0141 337 7000
Awaiting Inspection

McLays Guest House
268 Renfrew Street, Glasgow,
G3 6TT
Tel: 0141 332 4796
★ Guest House

The Malmaison
278 West George Street,
Glasgow, G2 4LL
Tel: 0141 572 1000
★★★★ Hotel

Manor Park Hotel
28 Balshagray Drive, Glasgow,
G11 7DD
Tel: 0141 339 2143
★★★ Small Hotel

The Millennium Glasgow Hotel
George Square, Glasgow, G2
1DS
Tel: 0141 332 6711
★★★★ Hotel

Milton Hotel & Spa, Glasgow
27 Washington Street, Glasgow,
G3 8AZ
Tel: 0141 222 2929
★★★★ Hotel

Newton House Hotel
248-252 Bath Street, Glasgow,
G2 4JW
Tel: 0141 332 1666
Awaiting Inspection

Novotel Glasgow Centre
181 Pitt Street, Glasgow, G2 4DT
Tel: 0141 222 277
★★★ Hotel

Radisson SAS Hotel Glasgow
301 Argyle Street, Glasgow,
G2 8DL
Tel: 0141 204 3333
★★★★★ Hotel

The Ramada Glasgow City
201 Ingram Street, Glasgow,
G1 1DQ
Tel: 0141 248 4401
★★★ Hotel

Saint Judes
190 Bath Street, Glasgow,
Strathclyde, G2 4HG
Tel: 0141 3528800
★★★ Small Hotel

The Sandyford Hotel
904 Sauchiehall Street,
Glasgow, G3 7TF
Tel: 0141 334 0000
★★★ Lodge

Seton Guest House
6 Seton Terrace, Dennistoun,
Glasgow, G31 2HY
Tel: 0141 556 7654
★★ Guest House

Sherbrooke Castle Hotel
11 Sherbrooke Avenue, Glasgow,
G41 4PG
Tel: 0141 427 4227
★★★ Hotel

Smiths Hotel
3 David Donnelly Place,
Kirkintilloch, Glasgow, G66 1DD
Tel: 0141 775 0398
★★★ Small Hotel

Smiths Hotel
963 Sauchiehall Street,
Glasgow, G3 7TQ
Tel: 0141 339 6363
★ Guest House

University of Strathclyde
Residence and Catering
Services,, 50 Richmond Street,
Glasgow, G1 1XP
Tel: 0141 553 4148
★ Campus

Swallow Hotel
517 Paisley Road West,
Glasgow, G51 1RW
Tel: 0141 427 3146
★★ Hotel

Thistle Glasgow
36 Cambridge Street, Glasgow,
G2 3HN
Tel: 0141 332 3311
★★★★ Hotel

The Town House
4 Hughenden Terrace, Glasgow,
G12 9XR
Tel: 0141 3570862
★★★ Guest House

Tulip Inn Glasgow
80 Ballater Street, Glasgow,
G5 0TW
Tel: 0141 429 4233
★★★ Hotel

Willow Hotel
228 Renfrew Street, Glasgow,
G3 6TX
Tel: 0141 332 2332
★★ Guest House

BY GLASGOW

The Westerwood
St Andrews Drive, Cumbernauld,
by Glasgow, G68 0EW
Tel: 01236 457171
★★★ Hotel

NR GLASGOW

Uplawmoor Hotel
Neilston Road, Uplawmoor,
Glasgow, G78 4AF
Tel: 01505 850565
★★★ Small Hotel

Wallace Hotel
1 Yieldshields Road, Carluke,
Lanarkshire, ML8 4QG
Tel: 01555 773000
★★ Restaurant with Rooms

GLASGOW AIRPORT

Holiday Inn Glasgow Airport
Abbotsinch, Paisley, Glasgow, Renfrewshire, PA3 2TR
Tel: 0870 4009031
★★★ Hotel

Ramada Glasgow Airport
Marchburn Drive, Glasgow Airport Business Park, Paisley, PA3 2SJ
Tel: 0141 840 2200
★★★ Hotel

GOUROCK

Ramada Jarvis Gourock
Cloch Road, Gourock, Renfrewshire, PA15 1AR
Tel: 01475 634671
★★★ Hotel

Spinnaker Hotel
121 Albert Road, Gourock, Renfrewshire, PA19 1BU
Tel: 01475 633107
★★ Small Hotel

GREENOCK

Express by Holiday Inn
Cartsburn, Greenock, PA15 4RT
Tel: 01475 786666
★★★ Hotel

Lindores Manor
61 Newark Street, Greenock, Renfrewshire, PA16 7TE
Tel: 01475 783075
★★★ Small Hotel

Tontine Hotel
6 Ardgowan Square, Greenock, Renfrewshire, PA16 8NG
Tel: 01475 723316
★★★ Hotel

HAMILTON

Avonbridge Hotel
Carlisle Road, Hamilton, Lanarkshire, ML3 7DG
Tel: 01698 420525
★★★ Hotel

Clydesdale Hotel
12 Clydesdale Street, Hamilton, Lanarkshire, ML3 0DP
Tel: 01698 891897
★★★ Small Hotel

Thorndale Guest House
Manse Road, Stonehouse, Lanarkshire, ML9 3NX
Tel: 01698 791133
★★★ Guest House

The Villa Hotel
49/51 Burnbank Road, Hamilton, Lanarkshire, ML3 9AQ
Tel: 01698 891777
★★★ Small Hotel

HARTHILL, BY SHOTTS

Blairmains Guest House
Harthill, Shotts, Lanarkshire, ML7 5TJ
Tel: 01501 751278
★★ Guest House

HOWWOOD

Bowfield Hotel & Country Club
Howwood, Renfrewshire, PA9 1DB
Tel: 01505 705225
★★★ Hotel

INVERKIP

Inverkip Hotel
Main Street, Inverkip, Renfrewshire, PA16 0AS
Tel: 01475 521478
★★★ Small Hotel

JOHNSTONE

Lynnhurst Hotel
Park Road, Johnstone, Renfrewshire, PA5 8LS
Tel: 01505 324331
★★★★ Hotel

LANARK

Cartland Bridge Country House Hotel
Glasgow Road, Lanark, ML11 9UE
Tel: 01555 664426
★★★ Small Hotel

LANGBANK

Gleddoch House Hotel
Langbank, Renfrewshire, PA14 6YE
Tel: 01475 540711
★★★ Hotel

BY LARKHALL

Shawlands Hotel
Ayr Road, Canderside Toll, by Larkhall, Lanarkshire, ML9 2TZ
Tel: 01698 791111
★★★ Lodge

MILNGAVIE, GLASGOW

A[DBest Foot Forward West, Milngavie
1 Dougalston Gardens South, Milngavie, Glasgow, G62 6HS
Tel: 0141 956 3046
★★ Guest House

MILTON OF CAMPSIE, BY KIRKINTILLOCH

Kincaid House Hotel
Milton of Campsie, Glasgow, G65 8BZ
Tel: 0141 776 2226
★★★ Small Hotel

MOTHERWELL

The Alona Hotel
Strathclyde Country Park, Motherwell, North Lanarkshire, ML1 3RT
Tel: 01698 303031
★★★★ Hotel

The Bentley Hotel
19 High Road, Motherwell, ML1 3HU
Tel: 01698 265588
★★★ Small Hotel

Dalziel Park Hotel and Conference Centre
100 Hagen Drive, Motherwell, Lanarkshire, ML1 5RZ
Tel: 01698 862862
★★★ Small Hotel

Moorings Hotel
114 Hamilton Road, Motherwell, ML1 3DG
Tel: 01698 258131
★★★ Hotel

Motherwell College - Stewart Halls of Residence
Dalzell Drive, Motherwell, Lanarkshire, ML1 2DD
Tel: 01698 261890
★ Campus

NEW LANARK, BY LANARK

New Lanark Mill Hotel
New Lanark, Lanarkshire, ML11 9DB
Tel: 01555 667200
★★★★ Hotel

PAISLEY

Ardgowan House
92 Renfrew Road, Paisley, Renfrewshire, PA3 4BJ
Tel: 0141 889 4763
★★ Guest House

Ardgowan Town House Hotel
94 Renfrew Road, Paisley, Renfrewshire, PA3 4BJ
Tel: 0141 889 4763
★★★ Small Hotel

Ashtree House
9 Orr Square, Paisley, Renfrewshire, PA1 2DL
Tel: 0141 848 6411
★★★★ Guest House

Dryesdale Guest House
37 Inchinnan Road, Paisley, Renfrewshire, PA3 2PR
Tel: 0141 889 7178
★★ Guest House

Express by Holiday Inn Glasgow Airport
St Andrews Drive, Paisley, PA3 2TJ
Tel: 0141 842 1100
★★★ Hotel

Makerston House + Spa
19 Park Road, Paisley, Renfrewshire, PA2 6JP
Tel: 0141 884 2520
★★★ Guest House

Directory of all VisitScotland Quality Assured Serviced Establishments

Watermill Hotel
1 Lonend, Paisley, Renfrewshire, PA1 1SR
Tel: 0141 889 3201
★★ Hotel

RENFREW

Dean Park Hotel
91 Glasgow Road, Renfrew, PA4 8YB
Tel: 0141 886 3771
★★ Hotel

Glynhill Hotel
169 Paisley Road, Renfrew, Near Glasgow Airport, Renfrewshire, PA4 8XB
Tel: 0141 886 5555
★★★ Hotel

The Normandy
Inchinnan Road, Renfrew, Renfrewshire, PA4 5EJ
Tel: 0141 886 4100
★★ Hotel

ROSEBANK

Popinjay Hotel
Lanark Road, Rosebank, Lanarkshire, ML8 5QB
Tel: 01555 860441
★★★★ Hotel

STRATHAVEN

Springvale Hotel
18 Lethame Road, Strathaven, Lanarkshire, ML10 6AD
Tel: 01357 521131
★★★ Small Hotel

Strathaven Hotel
Hamilton Road, Strathaven, Lanarkshire, ML10 6JA
Tel: 01357 521778
★★★★ Hotel

SYMINGTON, BY BIGGAR

Tinto Hotel
Biggar Road, Symington, Lanarkshire, ML12 6FT
Tel: 01899 308454
★★ Hotel

Wyndales House Hotel
Wyndales, Symington, Lanarkshire, ML12 6JU
Tel: 01899 308207
★★ Hotel

UDDINGSTON

Redstones Hotel
8-10 Glasgow Road, Uddingston, Glasgow, G71 7AS
Tel: 01698 813744
★★★ Small Hotel

WISHAW

Herdshill Guest House
224 Main Street, Bogside, Wishaw, Lanarkshire, ML2 8HA
Tel: 01698 381579
★★★ Guest House

WEST HIGHLANDS & ISLANDS, LOCH LOMOND, STIRLING AND TROSSACHS

ABERFOYLE

Altskeith
Loch Ard Road, Kinlochard,by Aberfoyle, Stirlingshire, FK8 3TL
Tel: 01877 387266
★★★ Guest House

Crannaig House
Trossachs Road, Aberfoyle, Stirlingshire, FK8 3SR
Tel: 01877 382276
★★★ Guest House

Creag-Ard House
Aberfoyle, Stirling, FK8 3TQ
Tel: 01877 382297
★★★★ Guest House

Fielbarachan Guest House
Lochard Road, Aberfoyle, Stirlingshire, FK8 3SZ
Tel: 01877 382536
★★ Guest House

Forest Hills Hotel
Kinlochard, By Aberfoyle, Stirlingshire, FK8 3TL
Tel: 01877 387277
★★★★ Hotel

Rob Roy Hotel
Aberfoyle, Stirlingshire, FK8 3UX
Tel: 01877 382245
★★ Hotel

AIRTH, BY FALKIRK

Airth Castle Hotel & Spa Resort
Airth, By Falkirk, Stirlingshire, FK2 8JF
Tel: 01324 831411
★★★ Hotel

ALEXANDRIA

De Vere Cameron House
Loch Lomond, Alexandria, Dunbartonshire, G83 8QZ
Tel: 01389 755565
★★★★★ Hotel

ALLOA

The Royal Oak Hotel
7 Bedford Place, Alloa, Clackmannanshire, FK10 1LJ
Tel: 01259 722423
★★★ Small Hotel

ARDEN

Duck Bay Hotel & Marina
Loch Lomond, Arden,by Alexandria, Dunbartonshire, G83 8QZ
Tel: 01389 751234
★★★ Hotel

ARDEONAIG, BY KILLIN

The Ardeonaig Hotel
South Loch Tay, Killin, Perthshire, FK21 8SU
★★★ Small Hotel

ARDLUI

Ardlui Hotel
Ardlui, Loch Lomond, Argyll, G83 7EB
Tel: 01301 704269
★★★ Small Hotel

Beinglas Farm Campsite
Inverarnan, Ardlui, G83 7DX
Tel: 01301 704281
★★★ Guest House

ARDRISHAIG, BY LOCHGILPHEAD

Allt-Na-Craig House
Tarbert Road, Ardrishaig, Argyll, PA30 8EP
Tel: 01546 603245
★★★★ Small Hotel

Bridge House Hotel
St Clair Road, Ardrishaig, Argyll, PA30 8HB
Tel: 01546 606379
★★ Small Hotel

ARDUAINE

Loch Melfort Hotel
Arduaine, Argyll, PA34 4XG
Tel: 01852 200233
★★★★ Hotel

ARROCHAR

Arrochar Hotel
Arrochar, Dunbartonshire, G83 7AU
Tel: 01301 702484
Awaiting Inspection

Claymore Hotel
Arrochar, Argyll & Bute, G83 7BB
Tel: 01301 702238
Awaiting Inspection

Fascadail Country Guest House
Shore Road, Arrochar, Dunbartonshire, G83 7AB
Tel: 01301 702344
★★★ Guest House

Loch Long Hotel
Arrochar, Dunbartonshire, G83 7AA
Tel: 01301 702434
★★★ Hotel

Lochside Guest House
Main Street, Arrochar,
Dunbartonshire, G83 7AA
Tel: 01301 702467
★★★ Guest House

AVONBRIDGE, BY FALKIRK

The Smithy
Hillhead, Avonbridge,
West Lothian, FK1 2NL
Tel: 01324 861555
Awaiting Inspection

BALLOCH

Anchorage Guest House
31 Balloch Road, Balloch,
Loch Lomond, G83 8SS
Tel: 01389 753336
★★ Guest House

Gowanlea
Drymen Road, Balloch,
Dunbartonshire, G83 8HS
Tel: 01389 752456
★★★★ Guest House

Norwood Guest House
60 Balloch Road, Balloch,
Dunbartonshire, G83 8LE
Tel: 01389 750309
★★★ Guest House

Palombo's of Balloch
40 Balloch Road, Balloch,
Alexandria, West
Dunbartonshire, G83 8LE
Tel: 01389 752243
Awaiting Inspection

The Reivers
Drymen Road, Balloch, G83 8HS
Tel: 01204 362606
Awaiting Inspection

Time Out
24 Balloch Road, Balloch,
Dunbartonshire, G83 8SR
Tel: 07748 174889
★★★ Guest House

The Water House Inn
34 Balloch Road, Balloch,
Dunbartonshire, G83 8LE
Tel: 01389 752120
Awaiting Inspection

BALMAHA

Northwood Cottage
Sallochy, Rowardennan,
Balmaha, Stirlingshire,
G63 0AW
Tel: 01360 870351
Awaiting Inspection

BALQUHIDDER

King's House Hotel
Balquhidder, Perthshire,
FK19 8NY
Tel: 0877 384646
★★ Small Hotel

Monachyle Mhor
Balquhidder, Lochearnhead,
Perthshire, FK19 8PQ
Tel: 0877 384622
★★★★ Small Hotel

BELLOCHANTUY, BY CAMPBELTOWN

Argyll Hotel
Bellochantuy,by Campbeltown,
Argyll, PA28 6QE
Tel: 01583 421212
★★ Small Hotel

Hunting Lodge Hotel
Bellochantuy, Kintyre, Argyll,
PA28 6QE
Tel: 01583 421323
★★ Small Hotel

BENDERLOCH, BY OBAN

Dun Na Mara
Benderloch, Oban, Argyll,
PA37 1RT
Tel: 01631 720233
★★★★ Guest House

Innis Chonain
Benderloch, by Oban, Argyll,
PA37 1RT
Tel: 01631 720550
Awaiting Inspection

BO'NESS

Carriden House
Carriden Brae, Bo'ness,
West Lothian, EH51 9SN
Tel: 01506 829811
★★★ Guest House

BRIDGE OF ALLAN

Knockhill Guest House
Bridge of Allan, Stirling,
FK9 4ND
Tel: 01786 833123
Awaiting Inspection

The Queen's Hotel
24 Henderson Street, Bridge of
Allan, Stirlingshire, FK9 4HP
Tel: 01786 833268
★★★★ Small Hotel

Royal Hotel
55 Henderson Street, Bridge of
Allan, Stirlingshire, FK9 4HG
Tel: 01786 832284
★★★ Hotel

ARDBEG, ISLE OF BUTE

Ardmory House Hotel & Restaurant
Ardmory Road, Ardbeg,
Isle of Bute, PA20 0PG
Tel: 01700 502346
★★★ Small Hotel

KILCHATTAN BAY

St Blane's Hotel
Kilchattan Bay, Isle of Bute,
PA20 9NW
Tel: 01700 831224
★★ Small Hotel

NORTH BUTE

Chandlers
Ascog Bay, Isle of Bute, Argyll,
PA20 9ET
Tel: 01700 505577
Small Hotel

ROTHESAY, ISLE OF BUTE

Ardbeg Lodge
23 Marine Place, Ardbeg,
Rothesay, Isle of Bute, PA20 0LF
Tel: 01700 505448
★★★ Small Hotel

The Ardyne Hotel
38 Mountstuart Road, Rothesay,
Isle of Bute,, PA20 9EB
Tel: 01700 502052
★★★ Hotel

Argyle House
3 Argyle Place, Rothesay,
Isle of Bute, PA20 0AZ
Tel: 01700 502424
★★ Guest House

Bayview Hotel
21-22 Mountstuart Road,
Rothesay, Isle of Bute, PA20 9EB
Tel: 01700 505411
★★★ Small Hotel

The Boat House
15 Battery Place, Rothesay,
Argyll & Bute, PA20 9DP
Tel: 01700 702696
★★★ Guest House

Bute House Hotel
4 West Princess Street,
Rothesay, Isle of Bute, PA20 9AF
Tel: 01700 502481
★★ Guest House

Cannon House Hotel
Battery Place, Rothesay,
Isle of Bute, PA20 9DP
Tel: 01700 502819
★★★★ Small Hotel

The Commodore
12 Battery Place, Rothesay,
Isle of Bute, PA20 9DP
Tel: 01700 502178
★★★ Guest House

Glenburn Hotel
Mount Stuart Road, Rothesay,
Isle of Bute, PA20 9JB
Tel: 01942 824824
★★★ Hotel

Glendale Guest House
20 Battery Place, Rothesay,
Isle of Bute, PA20 9DU
Tel: 01700 502329
★★★★ Guest House

Lyndhurst Guest House
29 Battery Place, Rothesay,
Isle of Bute, PA20 9DU
Tel: 01700 504799
★★ Guest House

Palmyra Hotel
12 Ardbeg Road, Rothesay, Isle of Bute, PA20 0NJ
Tel: 01700 502929
★★★ Guest House

The Regent Hotel
23 Battery Place, Rothesay, Isle of Bute, PA20 9DU
Tel: 01700 502006
★★★ Small Hotel

CAIRNDOW

Cairndow Stagecoach Inn
Cairndow, Argyll, PA26 8BN
Tel: 01499 600286
★★ Inn

CALLANDER

Annfield Guest House
North Church Street, Callander, Perthshire, FK17 8EG
Tel: 01877 330204
★★★ Guest House

Arden House
Bracklinn Road, Callander, Perthshire, FK17 8EQ
Tel: 01877 330235
★★★★ Guest House

Coppice Hotel
Leny Road, Callander, Perthshire, FK17 8AL
Tel: 01877 330188
★★ Small Hotel

The Crags Hotel
101 Main Street, Callander, Perthshire, FK17 8BQ
Tel: 01877 330257
★★★ Guest House

Craigburn House
North Church Street, Callander, Perthshire, FK17
Tel: 01877 330332
★★★ Guest House

East Mains House
Manse Lane, Bridgend, Callander, Perthshire, FK17 8AG
Tel: 01877 330535
★★★ Guest House

Elmbank Guest House
157 Main Street, Callander, Perthshire, FK17 8BH
Tel: 01877 330205
★★★ Guest House

The Knowe
Ancaster Road, Callander, Perthshire, FK17 8EL
Tel: 01877 330076
★★★★ Guest House

Lubnaig House
Leny Feus, Callander, Perthshire, FK17 8AS
Tel: 01877 330376
★★★★ Guest House

The Old Rectory Guest House
Leny Road, Callander, Perthshire, FK17 8AL
Tel: 01877 339215
★★★ Guest House

Poppies Hotel and Restaurant
Leny Road, Callander, Perthshire, FK17 8AL
Tel: 01877 330329
★★★ Small Hotel

Riverview Guest House
Leny Road, Callander, Perthshire, FK17 8AL
Tel: 01877 330635
★★★ Guest House

Roman Camp Hotel
Main Street, Callander, Perthshire, FK17 8BG
Tel: 01877 330003
★★★★ Small Hotel

Southfork Villa
25 Cross Street, Callander, Perthshire, FK17 8EA
Tel: 01877 330831
★★★★ Guest House

CAMPBELTOWN

Ardshiel Hotel
Kilkerran Road, Campbeltown, Argyll, PA28 6JL
Tel: 01586 552133
★★ Small Hotel

Craigard House
Low Askomil, Campbeltown, Argyll, PA28 6EP
Tel: 01586 554242
★★★ Small Hotel

Dellwood Hotel
Drumore, Campbeltown, Argyll, PA28 6HD
Tel: 01586 552465
★★ Small Hotel

Rosemount
Low Askomil, Campbeltown, Argyll, PA28 6EN
Tel: 01586 553552
Awaiting Inspection

Seafield Hotel
Kilkerran Road, Campbeltown, Argyll, PA28 6JL
Tel: 01586 554385
Awaiting Inspection

Westbank Guest House
Dell Road, Campbeltown, Argyll, PA28 6JG
Tel: 01586 553660
★★★ Guest House

CARDROSS

Old Mill Cottage
2 Mill Cottages, Cardross, Dunbartonshire, G83 5JY
Tel: 01389 842157
Awaiting Inspection

CARRADALE

Ashbank Hotel
Carradale, by Campbeltown, Argyll, PA28 6RY
Tel: 01583 431650
★★★ Small Hotel

Carradale Hotel
Carradale, Argyll, PA28 6RY
Tel: 01583 431223
★★★ Small Hotel

Dunvalanree
Portrigh Bay, Carradale, Argyll, PA28 6SE
Tel: 01583 431226
★★★★ Small Hotel

CASTLECARY VILLAGE, BY CUMBERNAULD

Castlecary House Hotel
Castlecary Road, Castlecary, Cumbernauld, G68 0HD
Tel: 01324 840233
★★★ Hotel

CLYDEBANK

Beardmore Hotel
Beardmore Street, Clydebank, Greater Glasgow, G81 4SA
Tel: 0141 951 6000
★★★★ Hotel

Boulevard Hotel
1710 Great Western Road, Clydebank, West Dunbartonshire, G81 2XT
Tel: 01389 879803
★★ Small Hotel

Radnor Park Hotel
Kilbowie Road, Clydebank, Dunbartonshire, G81 2AP
Tel: 0141 952 3427
★★ Hotel

COLINTRAIVE

Colintraive Hotel
Colintraive, Argyll, PA22 3AS
Tel: 01700 841207
★★★ Small Hotel

COLL, ISLE OF

Coll Hotel
Arinagour, Isle of Coll, Argyll, PA78 6SZ
Tel: 01879 230334
★★★ Small Hotel

CONNEL

Greenacre
Connel, by Oban, Argyll, PA31 1PJ
Tel: 01631 710756
★★ Guest House

Ronebhal Guest House
Connel, Argyll, PA37 1PJ
Tel: 01631 710310
★★★★ Guest House

CRIANLARICH

Ben More Lodge Hotel
Crianlarich, Perthshire,
FK20 8QP
Tel: 01838 300210
★★ Inn

Ewich House
Strathfillan, Crianlarich,
Perthshire, FK20 8RU
Tel: 01838 300300
★★★ Guest House

Glenardran Guest House
Crianlarich, Perthshire,
FK20 8QS
Tel: 01838 300236
★★★ Guest House

Highland Hotel
Crianlarich, Perthshire,
FK20 8RW
Tel: 01838 300272
★★★ Hotel

Inverardran House
A85, Crianlarich, Perthshire,
FK20 8QS
Tel: 01838 300240
★★★ Guest House

The Lodge House
Crianlarich, Perthshire,
FK20 8RU
Tel: 01838 300276
★★★★ Guest House

The Luib Hotel
Glendochart, Crianlarich,
Perthshire, FK20 8QT
Tel: 01567 820664
Awaiting Inspection

Riverside Guest House
Tigh Na Struith, Crianlarich,
Perthshire, FK20 8RU
Tel: 01838 300235
★★ Guest House

Suie Lodge Hotel
Luib, Glen Dochart, Crianlarich,
Perthshire, FK20 8QT
Tel: 01567 820417
★★ Small Hotel

CRINAN, BY LOCHGILPHEAD

Crinan Hotel
Crinan, Argyll, PA31 8SR
Tel: 01546 830261
★★★★ Small Hotel

DALMALLY

Craig Villa Guest House
Dalmally, Argyll, PA33 1AX
Tel: 01838 200255
★★★ Guest House

Dalmally Hotel
Dalmally, Argyll, PA33 1AY
Tel: 01838 200444
★★★ Hotel

Glenorchy Lodge Hotel
Dalmally, Argyll, PA33 1AA
Tel: 018382 00312
★★★ Small Hotel

DOLLAR

Castle Campbell Hotel
Bridge Street, Dollar,
Clackmannanshire, FK14 7DE
Tel: 01259 742519
★★★ Small Hotel

DRYMEN

Buchanan Arms Hotel & Leisure Club
Main Street, Drymen,
Stirlingshire, G63 0BQ
Tel: 01360 660588
★★★ Hotel

Burnbank Cottage
Croftamie Post Office,
Croftamie, Drymen, G63 0EZ
Tel: 01360 660378
Awaiting Inspection

The Clachan Inn
2 The Square, Drymen, G63 0BG
Tel: 01360 660824
Awaiting Inspection

Winnock Hotel
The Square, Drymen,
Stirlingshire, G63 0BL
★★★ Hotel

DUMBARTON

The Abbotsford Hotel
Stirling Road, Dumbarton,
G82 2PJ
Tel: 01389 733304
★★★ Hotel

Dumbuck House Hotel
Glasgow Road, Dumbarton,
Dunbartonshire, G82 1EG
Tel: 01389 734336
★★★ Hotel

DUNBLANE

Dunblane Hydro
Perth Road, Dunblane,
Perthshire, FK15 0HG
Tel: 01786 822551
★★★★ Hotel

BY DUNBLANE

Cromlix House
Kinbuck, Dunblane, Perthshire,
FK15 9JT
Tel: 01786 822125
★★★★★ Small Hotel

DUNOON

Abbot's Brae Hotel
West Bay, Dunoon, Argyll,
PA23 7QJ
Tel: 01369 705021
★★★★ Small Hotel

The Ardtully Hotel
297 Marine Parade, Hunters
Quay, Dunoon, Argyll, PA23 8HN
Tel: 01369 702478
★★★ Guest House

Argyll Hotel
Argyll Street, Dunoon, Argyll,
PA23 7NE
Tel: 01369 702059
★ Hotel

Bay House Hotel
West Bay Promenade, Dunoon,
Argyll, PA23 7HU
Tel: 01369 704832/702348
★★★ Small Hotel

The Cedars
51 Alexandra Parade, East Bay,
Dunoon, Argyll, PA23 8AF
Tel: 01369 702425
★★★★ Guest House

Craigen Hotel
85 Argyll Street, Dunoon,
PA23 7DH
Tel: 01369 702307
★★ Guest House

Craigieburn Hotel
Alexandra Parade, East Bay,
Dunoon, Argyll, PA23 8AN
Tel: 01369 702048
★★ Guest House

Dhailling Lodge
155 Alexandra Parade, Dunoon,
Argyll, PA23 8AW
Tel: 01369 701253
★★★★ Guest House

Enmore Hotel
Marine Parade, Kirn, Dunoon,
Argyll, PA23 8HH
Tel: 01369 702230
★★★★ Small Hotel

Esplanade Hotel
West Bay, Dunoon, Argyll,
PA23 7HU
Tel: 01369 704070
★★★ Hotel

Hunters Quay Hotel
Marine Parade, Dunoon, Argyll,
PA23 8HJ
Tel: 01369 707070
★★★★ Small Hotel

McColl's Hotel
West Bay, Dunoon, Argyll,
PA23 7HN
Tel: 01369 702764/08702
403080
★ Hotel

Milton Tower Hotel
West Bay, Dunoon, Argyll,
PA23 7LD
Tel: 01369 705785
★★★ Small Hotel

Park Hotel
3 Glenmorag Avenue, Dunoon, Argyll, PA23 7LG
Tel: 01369 702383
★★★ Hotel

Rosscairn Private Hotel
51 Hunter Street, Kirn, Dunoon, Argyll, PA23 8JR
Tel: 01369 704344
★★★ Guest House

Royal Marine Hotel
Hunter's Quay, Dunoon, Argyll, PA23 8HJ
Tel: 01369 705810
★★★ Hotel

Sebright
41A Alexandra Parade, Dunoon, Argyll, PA23 8AF
Tel: 01369 702099
★★ Guest House

St Ives Hotel
West Bay, Dunoon, Argyll, PA23 7HU
Tel: 01369 702400/704825
★★★ Small Hotel

West End Hotel
54 Victoria Parade, Dunoon, Argyll, PA23 7HU
Tel: 01369 702907
★★ Small Hotel

The Western Hotel
60 Victoria Parade, Dunoon, Argyll, PA23 7LD
Tel: 01369 704468
★ Guest House

DUNTOCHER, GLASGOW

West Park Hotel
Great Western Road, Duntocher, Clydebank, G81 6DB
Tel: 01389 872333
★★ Hotel

FALKIRK

Ashbank
105 Main Street, Redding, Falkirk, Stirlingshire, FK2 9UQ
Tel: 01324 716649
★★★★ Guest House

Best Western Park Hotel
Camelon Road, Falkirk, FK1 5RY
Tel: 01324 628331
★★★ Hotel

Cladhan Hotel
Kemper Avenue, Falkirk, Stirlingshire, FK1 1UF
Tel: 01324 627421
★★★ Hotel

Graeme Hotel
40 Grahams Road, Falkirk, FK1 1HR
Tel: 01324 628576
★★ Small Hotel

Rosie's B&B
115 Oswald Street, Falkirk, Stirlingshire, FK1 1QL
Tel: 01324 634108
Awaiting Inspection

FINTRY

Culcreuch Castle Hotel
Fintry, Glasgow, G63 0LW
Tel: 01360 860555
★★★ Small Hotel

FORD, BY LOCHGILPHEAD

Ford House
Ford, By Lochgilphead, Argyll, PA31 8RH
Tel: 01546 810273
★★★ Guest House

GARELOCHHEAD

Rock House
Garelochhead, Argyll & Bute, G84 0AN
Tel: 01436 810082
Awaiting Inspection

GARTMORE

Gartmore House
Gartmore, Stirling, FK8 3SZ
Tel: 01877 382991
Awaiting Inspection

GARTOCHARN

Badshalloch Farm House
Badshalloch Farm, Gartocharn, Alexandria, G83 8SB
Tel: 01360 661167
Awaiting Inspection

Ross Priory Guest House
Ross Loan, Gartocharn, by Alexandria, Dunbartonshire, G83 8NL
Tel: 01389 830398
★★★ Guest House

GIGHA, ISLE OF

Gigha Hotel & Cottages
Isle of Gigha, Argyll, PA41 7AA
Tel: 01583 505254
★★★ Small Hotel

GRANGEMOUTH

Grangeburn House
55 Bo'ness Road, Grangemouth, Stirlingshire, FK3 9BJ
Tel: 01324 471301
★★★★ Guest House

Grange Manor Hotel
Glensburgh Road, Grangemouth, Stirlingshire, FK3 8XJ
Tel: 01324 474836
★★★★ Hotel

Leapark Hotel
130 Bo'ness Road, Grangemouth, FK3 9BX
Tel: 01324 486733
★★★ Hotel

HELENSBURGH

Commodore Hotel
112-117 West Clyde Street, Helensburgh, Dunbartonshire, G67 3EA
Tel: 01436 676924
Awaiting Inspection

Sinclair House
91/93 Sinclair Street, Helensburgh, Argyll & Bute, G84 8TR
Tel: 0800 1646301
★★★★ Guest House

INNELLAN, BY DUNOON

The Osborne Hotel
44 Shore Road, Innellan, By Dunoon, Argyll, PA23 7TJ
Tel: 01369 830445
★★ Small Hotel

INVERARAY

Argyll Hotel
Front Street, Inveraray, Argyll, PA32 8XB
Tel: 01499 302466
★★★★ Hotel

Fernpoint Hotel
By the Pier, Inveraray, Argyll, PA32 8UX
Tel: 01499 302170
Small Hotel

Killean Farm House
Inveraray, Argyll, PA32 8XT
Tel: 01499 302474
★★★ Guest House

Loch Fyne Hotel
Newtown, Inveraray, Argyll, PA32 8XJ
Tel: 01499 302148
★★★ Hotel

INVERSNAID

Inversnaid Hotel
Inversnaid, by Aberfoyle, Stirlingshire, FK8 3TU
Tel: 01877 386223
★★★ Hotel

IONA, ISLE OF

Argyll Hotel
Iona, Isle of Iona, Argyll, PA76 6SJ
Tel: 01681 700334
★★★ Small Hotel

St Columba Hotel
Isle of Iona, Argyll, PA76 6SL
Tel: 01681 700304
★★ Hotel

BALLYGRANT, ISLE OF ISLAY

Kilmeny
Ballygrant, Isle of Islay, PA45 7QW
Tel: 01496 840668
★★★★★ Guest House

BOWMORE, ISLE OF ISLAY

Lambeth Guest House
Jamieson Street, Bowmore, Isle of Islay, Argyll, PA43 7HL
Tel: 01496 810597
★★★ Guest House

Lochside Hotel
Shore Street, Bowmore,
Isle of Islay, PA43 7LB
Tel: 01496 810244
★★★ Small Hotel

BRIDGEND, ISLE OF ISLAY

Bridgend Hotel
Bridgend, Isle of Islay, PA44 7PJ
Tel: 01496 810212
★★★ Small Hotel

PORT ASKAIG, ISLE OF ISLAY

Port Askaig Hotel
Port Askaig, Isle of Islay,
PA46 7RB
Tel: 01496 840 245
★ Small Hotel

Torrabus Cottage
Port Askaig, Isle of Islay, Argyll,
PA46 7RN
Tel: 01496 840249
Awaiting Inspection

PORT CHARLOTTE, ISLE OF ISLAY

The Port Charlotte Hotel
Main Street, Port Charlotte,
Isle of Islay, PA48 7TU
Tel: 01496 850360
★★★★ Small Hotel

PORT ELLEN, ISLE OF ISLAY

Machrie Hotel
Port Ellen, Islay, Argyll,
PA42 7AN
Tel: 01496 302310
★★ Small Hotel

The Trout Fly Guest House
8 Charlotte Street, Port Ellen,
Isle of Islay, PA42 7DF
Tel: 01496 302204
★★ Guest House

White Hart Hotel
1 Charlotte Street, Port Ellen,
Isle of Islay, PA42 7DF
Tel: 01496 300120
Hotel

JURA, ISLE OF

Jura Hotel
Isle of Jura, Argyll, PA60 7XU
Tel: 01496 820243
★★ Small Hotel

KILCHRENAN

Ardanaiseig Hotel
Kilchrenan, by Taynuilt, Argyll,
PA35 1HE
Tel: 01866 833333
★★★★ Small Hotel

Taychreggan Hotel
Kilchrenan,by Taynuilt, Argyll,
PA35 1HQ
Tel: 01866 833211
★★★★ Hotel

KILFINAN

Kilfinan Hotel
Kilfinan, Tighnabruaich, Argyll,
PA21 2EP
Tel: 01700 821201
★★★ Small Hotel

KILLIN

Breadalbane House
Main Street, Killin, Perthshire,
FK21 8UT
Tel: 01567 820134
★★★ Guest House

Craigbuie Guest House
Main Street, Killin, Perthshire,
FK21 8UH
Tel: 01567 820439
★★★ Guest House

Dall Lodge Country House
Main Street, Killin, Perthshire,
FK21 8TN
Tel: 01567 820217
★★★★ Guest House

Invertay House
Main Road, Killin, Perthshire,
FK21 8TN
Tel: 01567 820492
★★★ Guest House

Killin Hotel
Main Street, Killin, Perthshire,
FK21 8TP
Tel: 01567 820296
★★ Hotel

Morenish Lodge Hotel
Morenish, Killin, Perthshire,
FK21 8TX
Tel: 01567 820258
★★★ Small Hotel

KILNINVER, BY OBAN

Knipoch Hotel
Kilninver, by Oban, Argyll,
PA34 4QT
Tel: 01852 316251
★★★★ Hotel

LEDAIG, BY OBAN

Isle of Eriska Hotel
Ledaig, Argyll, PA37 1SD
Tel: 01631 720371
★★★★★ Hotel

LOCHAWE

Loch Awe Hotel
Loch Awe, Dalmally, Argyll,
PA33 1AQ
Tel: 01838 200261
★★★ Hotel

BY LOCHAWESIDE

Eredine House
Eredine, Lochaweside,
By Dalmally, Argyll, PA33 1BP
Tel: 01866 844207
★★★ Guest House

LOCHEARNHEAD

Lochearnhead Hotel
Lochside, Lochearnhead,
FK19 8PN
Tel: 01567 830229
★★ Small Hotel

Lochearn House
Lochearnhead, Perthshire,
FK19 8NR
Tel: 01567 830380
Awaiting Inspection

LOCHGILPHEAD

Stag Hotel
Argyll Street, Lochgilphead,
Argyll, PA31 8NE
Tel: 01546 602496
★★ Small Hotel

BY LOCHGILPHEAD

Cairnbaan Hotel
Cairnbaan, by Lochgilphead,
Argyll, PA31 8SJ
Tel: 01546 603668
★★★★ Small Hotel

LOCHGOILHEAD

Drimsynie House Hotel
Lochgoilhead, Argyll, PA24 8AD
Tel: 01301 703247
★★★ Small Hotel

Lochwood House
Lochgoilhead, Argyll, PA24 8AE
Tel: 01301 703288
Awaiting Inspection

The Shore House Inn
Lochgoilhead, Argyll, PA24 8AD
Tel: 01301 703340
Awaiting Inspection

LUSS

Colquhoun Arms Hotel
Luss,by Alexandria,
Dunbartonshire, G83 8NY
Tel: 01436 860282
★★ Small Hotel

Culag Lochside Guest House
Luss, Loch Lomond, G83 8PD
Tel: 01436 860248
★★★★ Bed & Breakfast

The Lodge on Loch Lomond
Luss, Alexandria, G83 8PA
Tel: 01436 860201
★★★ Hotel

BUNESSAN, ISLE OF MULL

Ardachy House Hotel
Uisken, by Bunessan,
Isle of Mull, Argyll, PA67 6DS
Tel: 01681 700505
★★★ Small Hotel

CRAIGNURE, ISLE OF MULL

Isle of Mull Hotel
Craignure, Isle of Mull, Argyll,
PA65 6BB
Tel: 01680 812351
★★★ Hotel

Pennygate Lodge
Craignure, Isle of Mull, Argyll,
PA65 6AY
Tel: 01680 812333
★★★ Guest House

DERVAIG, ISLE OF MULL

Druimard Country House
Dervaig, Tobermory, Isle of Mull,
PA75 6QW
Tel: 01688 400345
★★★★ Small Hotel

Druimnacroish Hotel
Dervaig, Isle of Mull, PA75 6QW
Tel: 01688 400274
★★★ Small Hotel

BY DERVAIG, ISLE OF MULL

The Calgary Hotel
by Dervaig, Isle of Mull, Argyll,
PA75 6QW
Tel: 01688 400256
★★★ Small Hotel

FIONNPHORT, ISLE OF MULL

Achaban House
Fionnphort, Isle of Mull, Argyll,
PA66 6BL
Tel: 01681 700205
★★★ Guest House

Staffa House
Fionnphort, Isle of Mull, Argyll,
PA66 6BL
Tel: 01681 700677
★★★ Guest House

LOCHDON, ISLE OF MULL

Wild Cottage
Lochdon, Isle of Mull,
Argyll & Bute, PA64 6AP
Tel: 01680 812105
Awaiting Inspection

PENNYGHAEL, ISLE OF MULL

Pennyghael Hotel
Pennyghael, Isle of Mull,
PA70 6HB
Tel: 01681 704288
★★★★ Small Hotel

SALEN, AROS, ISLE OF MULL

Ard Mhor House
Pier Road, Salen, Isle of Mull,
PA72 6JL
Tel: 01680 300255
★★★ Guest House

Salen Hotel
Salen, Isle of Mull, Argyll,
PA72 6JE
Tel: 01680 300324
★★ Small Hotel

TIRORAN, ISLE OF MULL

Tiroran House
Tiroran, Isle of Mull, Argyll,
PA69 6ES
Tel: 01681 705232
Small Hotel

TOBERMORY, ISLE OF MULL

Baliscate Guest House
Salen Road, Tobermory,
Isle of Mull, Argyll, PA75 6QA
Tel: 01688 302048
★★★ Guest House

Carnaburg Hotel
55 Main Street, Tobermory,
Isle of Mull, PA75 6NT
Tel: 01688 302479
★★ Guest House

Drovers Lodge
Dervaig, Tobermory, Isle of Mull,
PA75 6QR
Tel: 01688 400362
★★★★ Guest House

Failte Guest House
Main Street, Tobermory,
Isle of Mull, Argyll, PA75 6NU
Tel: 01688 302495
★★★ Guest House

Fairways Lodge
Erray Road, Tobermory,
Isle of Mull, Argyll, PA75 6PS
Tel: 01688 302792
★★★★ Guest House

Gramercy
Tobermory, Isle of Mull,
PA75 6QA
Tel: 01688 302150
Awaiting Inspection

Highland Cottage
Breadalbane Street, Tobermory,
Isle of Mull, PA75 6PD
Tel: 01688 302030
★★★★ Small Hotel

Sunart View Guest House
Eas Brae, Tobermory,
Isle of Mull, Argyll, PA75 6QA
Tel: 01688 302439
★★★ Guest House

Tobermory Hotel
Main Street, Tobermory,
Isle of Mull, PA75 6NT
Tel: 01688 302091
★★★ Small Hotel

The Western Isles Hotel
Tobermory, Isle of Mull, Argyll,
PA75 6PR
Tel: 01688 302012
★★★ Hotel

NORTH CONNEL

Lochnell Arms Hotel
North Connel, Argyll, PA37 1RP
Tel: 01631 710239
★★★ Small Hotel

OBAN

Alexandra Hotel
The Esplanade, Oban, Argyll,
PA34 5AA
1838200444
★★★ Hotel

Alltavona
Corran Esplanade, Oban, Argyll,
PA34 5AQ
Tel: 01631 565067
★★★★ Guest House

Alt Na Craig
Colenmore Road, Oban, Argyll,
PA34 4PG
Tel: 01631 563637
★★★★ Guest House

Ayres Guest House
3 Victoria Street, Esplanade,
Oban, Argyll, PA34 5JL
Tel: 01631 562 260
★★ Guest House

Balmoral Inn
4 Craigard Road, Oban, Argyll,
PA34 5NP
Tel: 01631 562731
★★ Inn

The Barriemore Hotel
Corran Esplanade, Oban, Argyll,
PA34 5AQ
Tel: 01631 566356
★★★★ Guest House

Beech Grove Guest House
Croft Road, Oban, Argyll,
PA34 5JL
Tel: 01631 66111
★★★★ Guest House

Corriemar House
6 Corran Esplanade, Oban,
Argyll, PA34 5AQ
Tel: 01631 562476
★★★★ Guest House

Don-Muir
Pulpit Hill, Oban, Argyll,
PA34 4LX
Tel: 01631 564536
★★★★ Guest House

Dungallan House Hotel
Gallanach Road, Oban, Argyll,
PA34 4PD
Tel: 01631 563799
★★★★ Small Hotel

Foxholes Country Hotel
Cologin, Lerags, Oban, Argyll,
PA34 4SE
Tel: 01631 564982
★★★★ Small Hotel

Ganavan Sands Holiday Village
Ganavan Road, Oban, Argyll,
PA34 5TU
Tel: 01631 566479
★★★ Guest House

Glenbervie Guest House
Dalriach Road, Oban, Argyll,
PA34 5JD
Tel: 01631 564770
★★★★ Guest House

Glenburnie House
Esplanade, Oban, Argyll,
PA34 5AQ
Tel: 01631 562089
★★★★ Guest House

Glengorm
Dunollie Road, Oban, Argyll,
PA34 5PH
Tel: 01631 564386
★★★ Guest House

Glenrigh Guest House
Corran Esplanade, Oban, Argyll,
PA34 5AQ
Tel: 01631 562991
★★★ Guest House

Glenroy Guest House
Rockfield Road, Oban, Argyll,
PA34 5DQ
Tel: 01631 562 585
★★★ Guest House

Gramarvin Guest House
Breadalbane Street, Oban,
Argyll, PA34 5PE
Tel: 01631 564622
★★★ Guest House

Great Western Hotel
Corran Esplanade, Oban, Argyll,
PA34 5PP
Tel: 01942 824824
★★★ Hotel

Greencourt Guest House
Benvoullin Road, Oban, Argyll,
PA34 5EF
Tel: 01631 563987
★★★★ Guest House

Hawthornbank Guest House
Dalriach Road, Oban, Argyll,
PA34 5JE
Tel: 01631 562041
★★★★ Guest House

Herbridean Princess
South Pier, Oban
★★★★★ Cruise Ship

Kathmore Guest House
Soroba Road, Oban, Argyll,
PA34 4JF
Tel: 01631 562104
★★★ Guest House

Kelvin Hotel
Shore Street, Oban, Argyll,
PA34 4LQ
Tel: 01631 562150
★ Guest House

The Kimberley Hotel, Bachler's Conservatory
3 Dalriach Road, Oban, Argyll,
PA34 5EQ
Tel: 01631 571115
★★★★ Small Hotel

Kings Knoll Hotel
Dunollie Road, Oban, PA34 5JH
Tel: 01631 562536
★★★ Small Hotel

Manor House
Gallanoch Road, Oban, Argyll,
PA34 4LS
Tel: 01631 562087
★★★★ Small Hotel

Maridon House
Dunuaran Road, Oban, Argyll,
PA34 4NE
Tel: 01631 562670
★★★ Guest House

Oban Bay Hotel
Esplanade, Oban, Argyll,
PA34 5AE
Tel: 01631 562051
★★ Hotel

The Oban Caledonian Hotel
Waterfront, Oban, Argyll,
PA34 5RT
Tel: 0871 222 3415
★★★★ Hotel

The Old Manse Guest House
Dalriach Road, Oban, Argyll,
PA34 5JE
Tel: 01631 564886
★★★★ Guest House

Queens Hotel
Esplanade, Oban, Argyll,
PA34 5AG
Tel: 01631 562505
Awaiting Inspection

Regent Hotel
Esplanade, Oban, Argyll,
PA34 5PZ
Tel: 01631 562341
Awaiting Inspection

Roseneath Guest House
Dalriach Road, Oban, Argyll,
PA34 5EQ
Tel: 01631 562929
★★★★ Guest House

Royal Hotel
Argyll Square, Oban, Argyll,
PA34 4BE
Tel: 01631 563021
★★ Hotel

Sgeir Mhaol Guest House
Soroba Road, Oban, Argyll,
PA34 4JF
Tel: 01631 562650
★★★ Guest House

St Anne's Guest House
Dunollie Road, Oban, Argyll,
PA34 5PH
Tel: 01631 562743
★★★ Guest House

Strathnaver Guest House
Dunollie Road, Oban, Argyll,
PA34 5JQ
Tel: 01631 63305
★★★ Guest House

Sutherland Hotel
Corran Esplanade, Oban, Argyll,
PA34 5PN
Tel: 01631 562539
★★★ Guest House

Thornloe Guest House
Albert Road, Oban, Argyll,
PA34 5JD
Tel: 01631 562879
★★★★ Guest House

Ulva Villa
Soroba Road, Oban, Argyll,
PA34 4JF
Tel: 01631 563042
★★★ Guest House

Viewbank
Breadalbane Lane, Oban, Argyll,
PA34 5PF
Tel: 01631 562328
★★★★ Guest House

Wellpark House
Esplanade, Oban, Argyll,
PA34 5AQ
Tel: 01631 562948
★★★ Guest House

BY OBAN

Ards House
Connel, Oban, Argyll, PA37 1PT
Tel: 01631 710255
★★★★ Guest House

Loch Etive House
Main Street, Connel, Oban,
Argyll, PA37 1PH
Tel: 01631 710400
★★ Guest House

Willowburn Hotel
Clachan Seil, by Oban, Argyll,
PA34 4TJ
Tel: 01852 300276
★★★★ Small Hotel

POLMONT, BY FALKIRK

Inchyra Grange Hotel
Grange Road, Polmont,
Stirlingshire, FK2 0YB
Tel: 01324 711911
★★★★ Hotel

PORT APPIN

The Airds Hotel
Port Appin, Appin, Argyll,
PA38 4DF
Tel: 01631 730236
★★★★ Small Hotel

PORT OF MENTEITH

Currach
Currach Cottage, Port of
Menteith, Stirling, FK8 3RA
Tel: 01877 385699
Awaiting Inspection

ROSNEATH

Easter Garth
The Clachan, Rosneath,
Argyll & Bute, G84 0RF
Tel: 01436 831007
★★★ Guest House

ROWARDENNAN

Rowardennan Hotel
Rowardennan, By Drymen,
Stirlingshire, G63 0AR
Tel: 01360 870273
★★★ Small Hotel

ST CATHERINES

Thistle House
St Catherines, Argyll, PA25 8AZ
Tel: 01499 302209
Awaiting Inspection

STIRLING

Allan Park Hotel
20 Allan Park, Stirling,
Stirlingshire, FK8 2QG
Tel: 01786 473598
★★ Small Hotel

156 Bannockburn Road
Stirling, FK7 0EW
Tel: 01786 812098
Awaiting Inspection

Burns View
1 Albert Place, Stirling,
Stirlingshire, FK8 2QL
Tel: 01786 451002
★★★ Guest House

Cambria Guest House
141 Bannockburn Road, Stirling,
FK7 0EP
Tel: 01786 814603
★★★★ Guest House

Castlecroft B&B
Ballengiech Road, Stirling,
Stirlingshire, FK8 1TN
Tel: 01786 474933
★★★ Guest House

Express by Holiday Inn - Stirling
Springkerse Business Park,
Stirling, Stirlingshire, FK7 7XH
Tel: 01786 449922
★★★ Hotel

Garfield Guesthouse
12 Victoria Square, Stirling,
Stirlingshire, FK8 2QZ
Tel: 01786 473730
★★★ Guest House

King Robert Hotel
Glasgow Road, Bannockburn,
Stirlingshire, FK7 0LJ
Tel: 01786 811666
★★★ Hotel

Linden Guest House
22 Linden Avenue, Stirling,
Stirlingshire, FK7 7PQ
Tel: 01786 448850
★★★★ Guest House

Munro Guest House
14 Princes Street, Stirling,
FK8 1HQ
Tel: 01786 472685
★★★ Guest House

The Park Lodge Country House Hotel
32 Park Terrace, Stirling,
FK8 2JS
Tel: 01786 474862
★★★ Small Hotel

The Portcullis
Castle Wynd, Stirling, FK8 1AG
Tel: 01786 472290
★★★ Small Hotel

Ravenswood Guest House
94 Causewayhead Road,
Stirling, Stirlingshire, FK9 5HJ
Tel: 01786 475291
★★★ Guest House

The Royal Hotel and Royal Lodge Conference Centre
55+103 Henderson Street,
Bridge of Allan, Stirlingshire,
FK9 4HG
Tel: 01786 832284
★★★ Small Hotel

The Stirling Highland Hotel
Spittal Street, Stirling, FK8 1DU
Tel: 01786 272727
★★★★ Hotel

Stirling Management Centre
Stirling University, Stirling,
FK9 4LA
Tel: 01786 451666
★★★ Hotel

St Thomas's Well House
St Thomas's Well, Stirling,
FK7 9PR
Tel: 01786 475788
Awaiting Inspection

Terraces Hotel
4 Melville Terrace, Stirling,
Stirlingshire, FK8 2ND
Tel: 01786 472268
★★★ Small Hotel

Wallaceview
4 Causewayhead Road, Stirling,
Stirlingshire, FK9 5EN
Tel: 01786 475447
★★★ Guest House

Whitegables
112 Causewayhead Road,
Stirling, Stirlingshire, FK9 5HJ
Tel: 01786 479838
★★★ Guest House

The Whitehouse
13 Glasgow Road, Stirling,
Stirlingshire, FK7 0PA
Tel: 01786 462636
★★★ Guest House

STRACHUR

The Creggans Inn
Strachur, Argyll, PA27 8BX
Tel: 01369 860279
★★★ Small Hotel

STRATHYRE

Creagan House Restaurant with Accommodation
Strathyre, Callander, Perthshire,
FK18 8ND
Tel: 01877 384638
★★★★ Restaurant with Rooms

Rosebank House
Main Street, Strathyre,
Perthshire, FK18 8NA
Tel: 01877 384208
★★★ Guest House

TARBERT, LOCH FYNE

Balinakill Country House Hotel
Clachan, by Tarbet, Kintyre,
PA29 6XL
Tel: 01880 740206
★★★ Small Hotel

The Columba Hotel
East Pier Road, Tarbert, Argyll,
PA29 6UF
Tel: 01880 820808
★★★ Small Hotel

Stonefield Castle Hotel
Tarbert, Loch Fyne, Argyll,
PA29 6YJ
Tel: 01880 820836
Hotel

TARBET, BY ARROCHAR

Tarbet Hotel
Tarbert, Arrochar, Loch Lomond,
Argyll & Bute, G83 7DE
Tel: 01942 824824
★★ Hotel

TAYNUILT

Taynuilt Hotel
Main Road, Taynuilt, Argyll,
PA35 1JN
Tel: 01866 822437
★★★ Small Hotel

TIGHNABRUAICH

The Royal at Tighnabruaich
Shore Road, Tighnabruaich,
Argyll, PA21 2BE
Tel: 01700 811239
★★★★ Small Hotel

TILLICOULTRY

Harviestoun Country Hotel
Dollar Road, Tillicoultry,
Clackmannanshire, FK13 6PQ
Tel: 01259 752522
★★★ Small Hotel

GOTT BAY

Kirkapol Guest House
Gott Bay, Isle of Tiree, Argyll,
PA77 6TW
Tel: 01879 220729
★★★ Guest House

ISLE OF TIREE

Glebe House Tiree
Gott Bay, Isle of Tiree, Argyllshire, PA77 6TN
Tel: 01879 220758
★★★★ Guest House

SCARINISH

Tiree Scarinish Hotel
Scarinish, Isle of Tiree, Argyll, PA77 6UH
Tel: 01879 220308
★★ Small Hotel

TROSSACHS, BY CALLANDER

Loch Achray Hotel
by Callander, Stirlingshire, FK17 8HZ
Tel: 01877 376229
★★★ Hotel

TYNDRUM, BY CRIANLARICH

Ben Doran Hotel
Tyndrum, Perthshire, FK20
Tel: 01838 400373
★★★ Hotel

Dalkell Cottages
Lower Station Road, Tyndrum, Perthshire, FK20 8RY
Tel: 01838 400285
★★★ Guest House

Invervey Hotel
Tyndrum, by Crianlarich, Perthshire, FK20 8RY
Tel: 01838 400219
★★ Small Hotel

Royal Hotel
Tyndrum,by Crianlarich, Perthshire, FK20 8RZ
Tel: 01838 400272
★★★ Hotel

PERTHSHIRE, ANGUS AND DUNDEE AND THE KINGDOM OF FIFE

ABERDOUR

Aberdour Hotel
38 High Street, Aberdour, Fife, KY3 0SW
Tel: 01383 860325
★★★ Small Hotel

The Cedar Inn
20 Shore Road, Aberdour, Fife, KY3 0TR
Tel: 01383 860310
★★ Inn

The Woodside Hotel
High Street, Aberdour, Fife, KY3 0SW
Tel: 01383 860328
★★★ Small Hotel

ABERFELDY

Balnearn House
Crieff Road, Aberfeldy, Perthshire, PH15 2BJ
Tel: 01887 820431
★★★ Guest House

The Moness House Hotel & Country Club
Crieff Road, Aberfeldy, Perthshire, PH15 2DY
Tel: 0870 4431460
★★★ Small Hotel

Old Police Station
30 Chapel Street, Aberfeldy, Perthshire, PH15 2AS
Tel: 01887 822980
Awaiting Inspection

The Palce Hotel
Breadalbane Terrace, Aberfeldy, Perthshire, PH15 2AG
Tel: 01887 820359
Awaiting Inspection

Tigh'n Eilean Guest House
Taybridge Drive, Aberfeldy, Perthshire, PH15 2BP
Tel: 01887 820109
★★★★ Bed & Breakfast

BY ABERFELDY

The Weem Hotel
Weem, By Aberfeldy, Perthshire, PH15 2LD
Tel: 01887 820381
★★★ Small Hotel

ALYTH

Airlie Mount Mansion House
2 Albert Street, Alyth, Blairgowrie, Perthshire, PH11 8AX
Tel: 01828 632986
Awaiting Inspection

Alyth Hotel
6 Commercial Street, Alyth, Perthshire, PH11 8AT
Tel: 01828 632447
Awaiting Inspection

Lands of Loyal Hotel
Loyal Road, Alyth, Blairgowrie, PH11 8JQ
Tel: 01828 633151
★★★★ Small Hotel

Tigh Na Leigh
22-24 Airlie Street, Alyth, Perthshire, PH11 8AD
Tel: 01828 632372
★★★★ Guest House

ANSTRUTHER

Craw's Nest Hotel
Bankwell Road, Anstruther, Fife, KY10 3DS
Tel: 01333 310691
★★★ Hotel

ARBROATH

Cliffburn Hotel
Cliffburn Road, Arbroath, Angus, DD11 5BT
Tel: 01241 873432
Awaiting Inspection

Harbour Nights Guest House
4 Shore, Arbroath, Angus, DD11 1PB
Tel: 01241 434343
★★★★ Guest House

Rosely Country House Hotel
Forfar Road, Arbroath, Angus, DD11 3RB
Tel: 01241 876828
★★ Small Hotel

Towerbank Guest House
9 James Street, Arbroath, Angus, DD11 1JP
Tel: 01241 431343
Awaiting Inspection

Viewfield Hotel
1 Viewfield Road, Arbroath, DD11 2BS
Tel: 01241 872446
★★★ Small Hotel

AUCHTERARDER

Cairn Lodge Hotel
Orchil Road, Auchterarder, Perthshire, PH3 1LX
Tel: 01764 662634
★★★★ Small Hotel

Collearn House Hotel
High Street, Auchterarder, Perthshire, PH3 1DF
Tel: 01764 663553
★★★★ Small Hotel

Duchally Country Estate
Duchally Country Estate, Duchally, Auchterarder, Perthshire, PH3 1PN
Tel: 01764 663071
★★★ Small Hotel

The Gleneagles Hotel
Auchterarder, Perthshire, PH3 1NF
Tel: 01764 662231
★★★★★ International Resort

AUCHTERMUCHTY

Myres Castle
Auchtermuchty, Fife, KY14 7EW
Tel: 01337 828350
★★★★★ Exclusive Use Venue

Directory of all VisitScotland Quality Assured Serviced Establishments

BALLINLUIG, BY PITLOCHRY

Cuil -an- Daraich
2 Cuil -an- Daraich, Logierait, Pitlochry, Perthshire, PH9 0LH
Tel: 01796 482750
★★★ Guest House

BLACKFORD

Blackford Hotel
Moray Street, Blackford, Perthshire, PH4 1QF
Tel: 01764 682497
★★★ Small Hotel

BLAIR ATHOLL

Atholl Arms Hotel
Old North Road, Blair Atholl, Perthshire, PH18 5SG
Tel: 01796 481205
★★★ Hotel

Bridge of Tilt Hotel
Bridge of Tilt, Blair Atholl, Perthshire, PH18 5SU
Tel: 01796 481333
★★ Hotel

Dalgreine Guest House
St Andrews Crescent, Blair Atholl, Perthshire, PH18 5SX
Tel: 01796 481276
★★★★ Guest House

The Firs
St Andrews Crescent, Blair Atholl, by Pitlochry, PH18 5TA
Tel: 01796 481256
★★★ Guest House

BLAIRGOWRIE

Altamount House Hotel
Coupar Angus Road, Blairgowrie, Perthshire, PH10 6JN
Tel: 01250 873512
★★★ Small Hotel

Angus Hotel
Wellmeadow, Blairgowrie, Perthshire, PH10 6NQ
Tel: 01250 872455
★★★ Hotel

Broadmyre Motel
Carsie, Blairgowrie, Perthshire, PH10 6QW
Tel: 01250 873262
★★ Guest House

Dalmore Hotel
Rosemount, Blairgowrie, Perthshire, PH10 6QB
Tel: 01250 872150
★★ Small Hotel

Duncraggan
Perth Road, Blairgowrie, Perthshire, PH10 6EJ
Tel: 01250 872082
★★★★ Guest House

Glenshieling House Hotel
Hatton Road, Blairgowrie, Perthshire, PH10 7HZ
Tel: 01250 874605
★★★★ Guest House

Kintrae House Hotel
52 Balmoral Road, Blairgowrie, Perthshire, PH10 7AH
Tel: 01250 872106
★★ Small Hotel

Rosebank House
Balmoral Road, Blairgowrie, Perthshire, PH10 7AF
Tel: 01250 872912
★★★ Guest House

The Rosemount Golf Hotel
Golf Course Road, Rosemount, Blairgowrie, Perthshire, PH10 6LJ
Tel: 01250 872604
★★★ Small Hotel

Royal Hotel
53 Allan Street, Blairgowrie, Perthshire, PH10 6AB
Tel: 01250 872226
AWAIT INSPECTION

BY BLAIRGOWRIE

Kinloch House Hotel
Blairgowrie, Perthshire, PH10 6SG
Tel: 01250 884237
★★★★★ Hotel

Moorfield House Hotel
Myreriggs Road, Coupar Angus, Perthshire, PH13 9HS
Tel: 01828 627303
★★★ Small Hotel

BRECHIN

Northern Hotel
2 Clerk Street, Brechin, Angus, DD9 6AE
Tel: 01356 625400
★★★ Small Hotel

BRIDGE OF EARN

The Last Cast Hotel
Main Street, Bridge of Earn, Perthshire, PH2 9PL
Tel: 01738 812578
★★ Guest House

BROUGHTY FERRY

Redwood Guest House
89 Monifieth Road, Broughty Ferry, Dundee, DD5 2SB
Tel: 01382 736550
★★★★ Guest House

Sands
6 The Esplanade, Broughty Ferry, Dundee, DD6 2EL
Tel: 01382 860956
Awaiting Inspection

BURNTISLAND

Kingswood Hotel
Kinghorn Road, Burntisland, Fife, KY3 9LL
Tel: 01592 872329
★★★ Small Hotel

CARNOUSTIE

Carnoustie Golf Course Hotel & Resort
The Links, Carnoustie, Angus, DD7 7JE
Tel: 01241 411999
★★★★ Hotel

Carnoustie Links Hotel
8 Links Parade, Carnoustie, Angus, DD7 7JF
Tel: 01241 853273
★★★ Small Hotel

Kinloch Arms Hotel
27 High Street, Carnoustie, Angus, DD7 6AN
Tel: 01241 853127
★★ Small Hotel

Lochlorian House Hotel
13 Philip Street, Carnoustie, DD7 6ED
Tel: 01241 852182
★★★ Small Hotel

Lochtybank House
20 High Street, Carnoustie, Angus, DD7 6AQ
Tel: 01241 854849
★★★ Guest House

Seaview Private Hotel
29 Ireland Street, Carnoustie, Angus, DD7 6AS
Tel: 01241 851092
★★★★ Small Hotel

Station Hotel
Station Road, Carnoustie, Angus, DD7 6AR
Tel: 01241 852447
★★ Small Hotel

CHARLESTOWN, BY DUNFERMLINE

The Elgin Hotel and Restaurants
Charlestown, by Dunfermline, Fife, KY11 3EE
Tel: 01383 872257
★★★ Small Hotel

COMRIE

Mossgiel House
Burrell Street, Comrie, Perthshire, PH6 2JP
Tel: 01764 670438
Awaiting Inspection

The Royal Hotel
Melville Square, Comrie, Perthshire, PH6 2DN
Tel: 01764 679200
★★★★ Small Hotel

COUPAR ANGUS

Red House Hotel
Station Road, Coupar Angus, Blairgowrie, PH13 9AL
Tel: 01828 628500
★★★ Hotel

COWDENBEATH

Struan Bank Hotel
74 Perth Road, Cowdenbeath, Fife, KY4 9BG
Tel: 01383 511057
★★ Guest House

CRAIL

Balcomie Links Hotel
Balcomie Road, Crail, Fife, KY10 3TN
Tel: 01333 450237
★★ Small Hotel

Caiplie House
53 High Street, Crail, Fife, KY10 3RA
Tel: 01333 450564
★★★ Guest House

The Golf Hotel
4 High Street, Crail, Fife, KY10 3TD
Tel: 01333 450206
★★★ Small Hotel

Marine Hotel
54 Nethergate, Crail, Fife, KY10 3TZ
Tel: 01333 450207
★★★ Guest House

Selcraig Guest House
47 Nethergate, Crail, Fife, KY10 3TX
Tel: 01333 450697
★★★ Guest House

CRIEFF

Ardo Howe
31 Burrell Street, Crieff, Perthshire, PH7 4DT
Tel: 01764 652825
★★★ Guest House

Arduthie House Hotel
Perth Road, Crieff, Perthshire, PH7 3EQ
Tel: 01764 653113
★★★ Small Hotel

Comely Bank Guest House
32 Burrell Street, Crieff, Perthshire, PH7 4DT
Tel: 01764 653409
★★★ Guest House

The Crieff Hotel
45-47 East High Street, Crieff, Perthshire, PH7 3HY
Tel: 01764 652632
★★ Small Hotel

Crieff Hydro Hotel
Crieff, Perthshire, PH7 3LQ
Tel: 01764 655555
★★★★ Hotel

Fendoch Guest House
Sma' Glen, Crieff, Perthshire, PH7 3LW
Tel: 01764 653446
★★★ Guest House

Galvelbeg House
Perth Road, Crieff, Perthshire, PH7 3EQ
Tel: 01764 655061
★★★ Guest House

Glenearn House
Perth Road, Crieff, Perthshire, PH7 3EQ
Tel: 01764 650000
★★★★ Guest House

Kingarth
Perth Road, Crieff, Perthshire, PH7 3EQ
Tel: 01764 652060
★★★ Guest House

Leven House Hotel
Comrie Road, Crieff, PH7 4BA
Tel: 01764 652529
★★ Small Hotel

Murraypark Hotel
Connaught Terrace, Crieff, Perthshire, PH7 3DJ
Tel: 01764 653731
★★★ Hotel

Roundelwood Health Spa
Drummond Terrace, Crieff, Perthshire, PH7 4AN
Tel: 01764 653806
★★★ Small Hotel

CROSSFORD, BY DUNFERMLINE

Pinewood Lodge Guest House
2 Main Street, Crossford, Dunfermline, KY12 8NJ
Tel: 01383 737541
★★★ Guest House

DUNDEE

Aberlaw Guest House
230 Broughty Ferry Road, Dundee, Angus, DD4 7JP
Tel: 01382 456929
★★★ Guest House

Anderson's Guest House
285 Perth Road, Dundee, Tayside, DD2 1JS
Tel: 01382 668585
★★★ Guest House

Apex City Quay Hotel & Spa
1 West Victoria Dock Road, Dundee, DD1 3JP
Tel: 0845 365 0000
★★★★ Hotel

Auld Steeple Guest House
94 Nethergate, Dundee, Angus, DD1 4EL
Tel: 01382 200302
★ Guest House

Craigtay Hotel
101 Broughty Ferry Road, Dundee, Angus, DD3 9EJ
Tel: 01382 451142
★★ Small Hotel

Cullaig Guest House
1 Rosemount Terrace, Dundee, Tayside, DD3 6JQ
Tel: 01382 322154
★★★ Guest House

Dunlaw House Hotel
10 Union Terrace, Dundee, Angus, DD3 6JD
Tel: 01382 221703
★★ Small Hotel

The Fishermans Tavern Hotel
10-16 Fort Street, Broughty Ferry, Dundee, Angus, DD5 2AD
Tel: 01382 775941
★★ Small Hotel

The Fort Hotel
58-60 Fort Street, Broughty Ferry, Dundee, Angus, DD5 2AB
Tel: 01382 737999
★★ Small Hotel

Grampian Hotel
295 Perth Road, Dundee, DD2 1JS
Tel: 01382 667785
★★★ Guest House

Grosvenor Hotel
1 Grosvenor Road, Dundee, Angus, DD2 1LF
Tel: 01382 642991
★★ Guest House

Hilton Dundee
Earl Grey Place, Dundee, DD1 4DE
Tel: 01382 229271
★★★★ Hotel

Hotel Broughty Ferry
16 West Queen Street, Broughty Ferry, Dundee, DD5 1AR
Tel: 01382 480027
★★★★ Small Hotel

Invercarse Hotel
371 Perth Road, Dundee, DD2 1PG
Tel: 01382 669231
★★★ Hotel

Park House Hotel
40 Coupar Angus Road, Dundee, Angus, DD2 3HY
Tel: 01382 611151
★★★ Small Hotel

Queens Hotel
160 Nethergate, Dundee, Angus, DD1 4DU
Tel: 01382 322515
★★★ Hotel

Shaftesbury Hotel
1 Hyndford Street, Dundee, Angus, DD2 1HQ
Tel: 01382 669216
★★★ Small Hotel

St Leonard B&B
22 Albany Terrace, Dundee, Angus, DD3 6HR
Tel: 01382 227146/227461
★ Guest House

Strathdon Guest House
277 Perth Road, Dundee, Angus, DD2 1JS
Tel: 01382 665648
★★★ Guest House

Swallow Hotel
Kingsway West, Invergowrie, Dundee, Angus, DD2 5JT
Tel: 01382 641122
★★★ Hotel

Taychreggan Hotel
4 Ellieslea Road, Broughty Ferry, Dundee, Angus, DD5 1JG
Tel: 01382 778626
★★★ Small Hotel

Woodlands Hotel
13 Panmure Terrace, Barnhill, Dundee, DD5 2QL
Tel: 01382 480033
★★★ Hotel

DUNFERMLINE

Best Western Keavil House
Crossford, Fife, KY12 8QW
Tel: 01383 736258
★★★ Hotel

Clarke Cottage Guest House
139 Halbeath Road, Dunfermline, Fife, KY11 4LA
Tel: 01383 735935
★★★ Guest House

Davaar House Hotel
126 Grieve Street, Dunfermline, Fife, KY12 8DW
Tel: 01383 721886
★★★ Small Hotel

Garvock House Hotel
St Johns Drive, Dunfermline, KY12 7TU
Tel: 01383 621067
★★★★ Small Hotel

King Malcolm Hotel
Queensferry Road, Dunfermline, Fife, KY11 8DS
Tel: 01383 722611
★★★ Hotel

Pitbauchlie House Hotel
Aberdour Road, Dunfermline, KY11 4PB
Tel: 01383 722282
★★★ Hotel

Pitreavie Guest House
3 Aberdour Road, Dunfermline, Fife, KY11 4PB
Tel: 01383 724244
★★★★ Guest House

Rooms at 29 Bruce Street
29-35 Bruce Street, Dunfermline, Fife, KY12 7AG
Tel: 01383 840041
★★★ Small Hotel

DUNKELD

Atholl Arms Hotel
Tay Street, Bridgehead, Dunkeld, Perthshire, PH8 OAQ
Tel: 01350 727219
★★★ Small Hotel

The Birnam Guest House
4 Murthly Terrace, Birnam, By Dunkeld, Perthshire, PH8 0BG
Tel: 01350 727201
★★★ Guest House

Hilton Dunkeld
Dunkeld, Perthshire, PH8 0HX
Tel: 01350 727771
★★★★ Hotel

Royal Dunkeld Hotel
Atholl Street, Dunkeld, PH8 0AR
Tel: 01350 727322
★★★ Hotel

Waterbury Guest House
Murthly Terrace, Birnam, by Dunkeld, Perthshire, PH8 OBG
Tel: 01350 727324
★★★★ Guest House

BY DUNKELD

Kinnaird
Kinnaird Estate, Dalguise, by Dunkeld, Perthshire, PH8 0LB
Tel: 01796 482440
★★★★★ Small Hotel

EDZELL

Glenesk Hotel
High Street, Edzell, Tayside, DD9 7TF
Tel: 01356 648319
★★★ Hotel

Panmure Arms Hotel
52 High Street, Edzell, Angus, DD9 7TA
Tel: 01356 648950
★★★ Small Hotel

ELIE

The Elms
14 Park Place, Elie, Fife, KY9 1DH
Tel: 01333 330404
★★★ Guest House

FORTINGALL

Fortingall Hotel
Fortingall, By Aberfeldy, Perthshire, PH15 2NQ
07855 782356
Awaiting Inspection

FREUCHIE

Lomond Hills Hotel and Leisure Centre
Parliament Square, Freuchie, Fife, KY15 7EY
Tel: 01337 857329
★★ Hotel

GLAMIS

Castleton House Hotel
Eassie, Glamis, Angus, DD8 1SJ
Tel: 01307 840340
★★★★ Small Hotel

GLEN CLOVA, BY KIRRIEMUIR

Glen Clova Hotel
Glen Clova, by Kirriemuir, Angus, DD8 4QS
Tel: 01575 550350
★★★ Small Hotel

GLENDEVON

Tormaukin Hotel
Glendevon, by Dollar, Clackmannanshire, FK14 7JY
Tel: 0125 9781 252
★★★ Small Hotel

GLENISLA

Glenmarkie Guest House
Health Spa & Riding Centre, Glenisla, Perthshire, PH11 8QB
Tel: 01575 582295
★★★★ Guest House

GLENROTHES

Balgeddie House Hotel
Balgeddie Way, Glenrothes, Fife, KY6 3ET
Tel: 01592 742511
Hotel

Express by Holiday Inn
Leslie Road, Glenrothes, KY7 6XX
Tel: 01592 745509
★★★ Hotel

GLENSHEE

Dalmunzie
Spittal of Glenshee, Blairgowrie, Perthshire, PH10 7QG
Tel: 01250 885224
★★★ Small Hotel

KENMORE

Kenmore Hotel
The Square, Kenmore, Perthshire, PH15 2NU
Tel: 01887 830205
★★★ Hotel

KILLIECRANKIE

Killiecrankie House Hotel
Killiecrankie, Perthshire, PH16 5LG
Tel: 01796 473220
★★★★ Small Hotel

KINLOCH RANNOCH

Bunrannoch House
Kinloch Rannoch, Perthshire, PH16 5QB
Tel: 01882 632407
★★★ Guest House

Dunalastair Hotel
The Square, Kinloch Rannoch, Perthshire, PH16 5PW
Tel: 01882 632218
★★★ Hotel

Loch Rannoch Hotel
Kinloch Rannoch, Perthshire, PH16 5PS
Tel: 01882 632201
★★★ Hotel

KINROSS

The Green Hotel
2 The Muirs, Kinross, KY13 8AS
Tel: 01577 863467
★★★★ Hotel

Grouse and Claret Restaurant
Heatheryford, Kinross, KY13 0NQ
Tel: 01577 864212
★★★ Restaurant with Rooms

Kirklands Hotel
20 High Street, Kinross, Perthshire, KY13 8AN
Tel: 01577 863313
★★★ Small Hotel

Roxburghe Guest House
126 High Street, Kinross, KY13 8DA
Tel: 01577 862498
★★ Guest House

The Well Country Inn
Main Street, Scotlandwell, Kinross, KY13 9JA
Tel: 01592 840444
★★★ Small Hotel

Windlestrae Hotel
The Muirs, Kinross, Perthshire, KY13 8AS
Tel: 01577 863217
★ Hotel

BY KINROSS

Gartwhinzean Hotel
Powmill, By Dollar, Clackmannanshire, FK14 7NW
Tel: 01577 840595
★★ Hotel

KIRKCALDY

Arboretum
20 Southerton Road, Kirkcaldy, Fife, KY2 5NB
Tel: 01592 643673
★★★ Bed & Breakfast

Auld Post Hotel
1 Hunter Street, Kirkcaldy, Fife, KY1 1ED
Tel: 01592 204040
★★ Small Hotel

The Belvedere Hotel
Coxstool, West Wemyss, Fife, KY1 4SL
Tel: 01592 654167
★★★ Small Hotel

Dean Park Hotel
Chapel Level, Kirkcaldy, Fife, KY2 6QW
Tel: 01592 261635
★★★ Hotel

Dunnikier House Hotel
Dunnikier Park, Kirkcaldy, Fife, KY1 3LP
Tel: 01592 268393
★★★ Hotel

Mintella
38 Bennochy Road, Kirkcaldy, Fife, KY2 5RB
Tel: 01592 593446
★★ Guest House

Parkway Hotel
6 Abbotshall Road, Kirkcaldy, Fife, KY2 5PQ
Tel: 01592 262 143
★★ Hotel

KIRKMICHAEL

The Log Cabin Hotel
Glen Derby, Kirkmichael, Blairgowrie, Perthshire, PH10 7NA
Tel: 01250 881288
★★ Small Hotel

KIRRIEMUIR

Airlie Arms Hotel
No 4 St. Malcolms Wynd, Kirriemuir, Angus, DD8 4HB
Tel: 01575 572847
★★★ Small Hotel

Thrums Hotel
25 Bank Street, Kirriemuir, Angus, DD8 4BE
Tel: 01575 572758
★★★ Small Hotel

LADYBANK

Redlands Country Lodge
Pitlessie Road, By Ladybank, Fife, KY7 7SH
Tel: 01337 831091
★★★ Guest House

LESLIE

Rescobie House Hotel
6 Valley Drive, Leslie, Fife, KY6 3BQ
Tel: 01592 749555
★★★ Small Hotel

BY LEUCHARS

Drumoig Hotel & Golf Resort
Drumoig, Leuchars, by St Andrews, Fife, KY16 0BE
Tel: 01382 541800
★★★ Hotel

LEVEN

Dunclutha Guest House
16 Victoria Road, Leven, Fife, KY8 4EX
Tel: 01333 425515
★★★★ Guest House

Fluthers Wood
Cupar Road, Leven, Fife, KY8 5NN
Tel: 01333 351167
Awaiting Inspection

LOCH EARN

Achray House Hotel
St Fillans, Perthshire, PH6 2NF
Tel: 01764 685231
★★★ Small Hotel

The Four Seasons Hotel
St Fillans, Perthshire, PH6 2NF, info@thefourseasonshotel.co.uk www.thefourseasonshotel.co.uk
Tel: 01764 685333
★★★ Small Hotel

LOCH RANNOCH

Talladh-a-Bheithe Lodge
Loch Rannoch,by Pitlochry, Perthshire, PH17 2QW
Tel: 01882 633203
★★★ Guest House

LOWER LARGO

Crusoe Hotel
2 Main Street, Lower Largo, Fife, KY8 6BT
Tel: 01333 320759
★★★ Small Hotel

LUNDIN LINKS

Lundin Links Hotel
Leven Road, Lundin Links, Fife, KY8 6AP
Tel: 01333 320207
★★★ Hotel

Swallow Old Manor Hotel
55 Leven Road, Lundin Links, Fife, KY8 6AJ
Tel: 01333 320368
★★★★ Hotel

MARKINCH

Balbirnie House
Balbirnie Park, Markinch, Fife, KY7 6NE
Tel: 01592 610066
★★★★ Hotel

MEIKLEOUR, BY PERTH

Meikleour Hotel
Meikleour, Perthshire, PH2 6EB
Tel: 01250 883206
★★★★ Inn

MONIFIETH, BY DUNDEE

Panmure Hotel
Tay Street, Monifieth, Angus, DD5 4AX
Tel: 01382 532911
★★ Small Hotel

Directory of all VisitScotland Quality Assured Serviced Establishments

MONTROSE

Best Western Links Hotel
Midlinks, Montrose, Angus, DD10 8RL
Tel: 01674 671000
★★★★ Hotel

George Hotel
22 George Street, Montrose, DD10 8EW
Tel: 01674 675050
★★ Hotel

The Limes Guest House
15 King Street, Montrose, Angus, DD10 8NL
Tel: 01674 677236
★★★ Guest House

Park Hotel
61 John Street, Montrose, Angus, DD10
Tel: 01674 663400
★★ Hotel

BY NORTH QUEENSFERRY

Corus Hotel
Edinburgh North, St Margarets Head, North Queensferry, Fife, KY11 1HP
Tel: 01383 410000
Hotel

PERTH

Aberdeen Guest House
13 Pitcullen Terrace, Perth, Perthshire, PH2 7HT
Tel: 01738 633183
★★★★ Guest House

Achnacarry Guest House
3 Pitcullen Crescent, Perth, PH2 7HT
Tel: 01738 621421
★★★★ Guest House

Ackinnoull Guest House
5 Pitcullen Crescent, Perth, PH2 7HT
Tel: 01738 634165
★★★★ Guest House

Adam Guest House
6 Pitcullen Crescent, Perth, PH2 7HT
Tel: 01738 627179
★★★ Guest House

Almond Villa Guest House
51 Dunkeld Road, Perth, PH1 5RP
Tel: 01738 629356
★★★★ Guest House

Ardfern House
15 Pitcullen Crescent, Perth, Perthshire, PH2 7HT
Tel: 01738 637031
★★★★ Guest House

Arisaig Guest House
4 Pitcullen Crescent, Perth, PH2 7HT
Tel: 01738 628240
★★★★ Guest House

Ballathie House Sportsman's Lodge
Kinclaven, Stanley, Perthshire, PH1 4QN
Tel: 01250 883268
★★★ Lodge

Beechgrove Guest House
Dundee Road, Perth, PH2 7AQ
Tel: 01738 636147
★★★★ Guest House

The Bield at Blackruthven
Blackruthven House, Tibbermore, Perthshire, PH1 1PY
Tel: 01738 583238
★★★ Guest House

Cherrybank Inn
210 Glasgow Road, Perth, PH2 ONA
Tel: 01738 624349
★★★ Inn

Clifton House
36 Glasgow Road, Perth, Perthshire, PH2 0PB
Tel: 01738 621997
Awaiting Inspection

Clunie Guest House
12 Pitcullen Crescent, Perth, PH2 7HT
Tel: 01738 623625
★★★ Guest House

Dunallan
10 Pitcullen Crescent, Perth, Perthshire, PH2 7TH
Tel: 01738 622551
★★★★ Guest House

The Gables
24-26 Dunkeld Road, Perth, PH1 5RW
Tel: 01738 624717
★★★ Guest House

Hazeldene Guest House
Strathmore Street, Perth, Perthshire, PH2 7HP
Tel: 01738 623550
★★★ Guest House

Heidl Guest House
43 York Place, Perth, Perthshire, PH2 8EH
Tel: 01738 635031
★★ Guest House

Huntingtower Hotel
Crieff Road, Perth, Perthshire, PH1 3JT
Tel: 01738 583771
★★★★ Hotel

Iona Guest House
2 Pitcullen Crescent, Perth, Perthshire, PH2 7HT
Tel: 01738 627261
★★★ Guest House

Kinnaird Guest House
5 Marshall Place, Perth, Perthshire, PH2 8AH
Tel: 01738 628021
★★★★ Guest House

Lorne Villa Guest House
65 Dunkeld Road, Perth, Perthshire, PH1 5RP
Tel: 01738 628043
★★★ Guest House

Lovat Hotel
Glasgow Road, Perth, Perthshire, PH2 0LT
Tel: 01738 636555
★★★ Hotel

New County Hotel
26 County Place, Perth, PH2 8EE
0738 623355
★★★ Hotel

Parklands Hotel
2 St Leonards Bank, Perth, PH2 8EB
Tel: 01738 622451
★★★★ Small Hotel

Pitcullen Guest House
17 Pitcullen Crescent, Perth, PH2 7HT
Tel: 01738 626506
★★★ Guest House

Queens Hotel
Leonard Street, Perth, PH2 8HB
Tel: 01738 442222
★★★ Hotel

Ramada Hotel
West Mill Street, Perth, Perthshire, PH1 5QP
Tel: 01738 628281
★★★ Hotel

Rowanlea
87 Glasgow Road, Perth, Perthshire, PH2 0PQ
Tel: 01738 621922
★★★★ Guest House

The Royal George
Tay Street, Perth, PH1 5LD
Tel: 01738 624455
★★★ Hotel

Salutation Hotel
34 South Street, Perth, PH2 8PH
Tel: 01738 630066
★★ Hotel

Sunbank House Hotel
50 Dundee Road, Perth, Perthshire, PH2 7BA
Tel: 01738 624882
★★★★ Small Hotel

Tigh Mhorag Guest House
69 Dunkeld Road, Perth, PH1 5RP
Tel: 01738 622902
★★ Guest House

Westview Bed & Breakfast
49 Dunkeld Road, Perth, PH1 5RP
Tel: 01738 627787
★★★★ Bed & Breakfast

WoodLea Hotel
23 York Place, Perth, Perthshire, PH2 8EP
Tel: 01738 621744
★★★ Small Hotel

PERTH BY

Ballathie House Hotel
Kinclaven, Stanley, Perthshire, PH1 4QN
Tel: 01250 883268
★★★★ Hotel

Murrayshall Hotel
Scone, Perth, Perthshire, PH2 7PH
Tel: 01738 551171
★★★★ Hotel

Newton House Hotel
Glencarse, Perthshire, PH2 7LX
Tel: 01738 860250
★★★ Small Hotel

PITLOCHRY

Acarsaid Hotel
8 Atholl Road, Pitlochry, Perthshire, PH16 5BX
01796 47 2389
★★★ Hotel

Almond Lee
East Moulin Road, Pitlochry, Perthshire, PH16 5HU
Tel: 01796 474048
★★★ Guest House

Annslea Guest House
164 Atholl Road, Pitlochry, Perthshire, PH16 5AR
Tel: 01796 472430
★★★ Guest House

Atholl Palace
Pitlochry, Perthshire, PH16 5LY
Tel: 01796 472400
★★★★ Hotel

Atholl Villa Guest House
29/31 Atholl Road, Pitlochry, Perthshire, PH16 5BX
Tel: 01796 473820
★★★ Guest House

Balrobin Hotel
Higher Oakfield, Pitlochry, PH16 5HT
Tel: 01796 472901
★★★ Small Hotel

Bendarroch House
Strathtay, Perthshire, PH9 0PG
Tel: 01887 840420
★★★ Guest House

Birchwood Hotel
2 East Moulin Road, Pitlochry, Perthshire, PH16 5DW
Tel: 01796 472477
★★★ Small Hotel

Claymore Hotel
162 Atholl Road, Pitlochry, Perthshire, PH16 5AR
Tel: 01796 472888
★★★ Small Hotel

Craigatin House & Courtyard
165 Atholl Road, Pitlochry, Perthshire, PH16 5QL
Tel: 01796 472478
★★★★ Guest House

Craigmhor Lodge
27 West Moulin Road, Pitlochry, Perthshire, PH16 5EF
Tel: 01796 472123
★★★★ Guest House

Craigvrack Hotel
38 West Moulin Road, Pitlochry, Perthshire, PH16 5EQ
Tel: 01796 472399
★★★ Small Hotel

Donavourd House Hotel
Pitlochry, Perthshire, PH16 5JS
Tel: 01796 472100
★★★★ Small Hotel

Dundarach Hotel
Perth Road, Pitlochry, Perthshire, PH16 5DJ
Tel: 01796 472862
★★★ Hotel

Dunmurray Lodge Guest House
72 Bonnethill Road, Pitlochry, Perthshire, PH16 5ED
Tel: 01796 473624
★★★★ Guest House

Easter Croftinloan Farmhouse
Croftloan Farm, Pitlochry, Perthshire, PH16 5JN
Tel: 01796 473 454
Awaiting Inspection

East Haugh House Country Hotel & Res
East Haugh, by Pitlochry, Perthshire, PH16 5JS
Tel: 01796 473121
★★★★ Small Hotel

Fasganeoin Country House
Perth Road, Pitlochry, PH16 5DJ
Tel: 01796 472387
★★★ Guest House

Fishers Hotel
75-79 Atholl Road, Pitlochry, Perthshire, PH16 5BN
Tel: 01796 472000
★★★ Hotel

The Green Park Hotel
Clunie Bridge Road, Pitlochry, Perthshire, PH16 5JY
Tel: 01796 473248
★★★★ Hotel

Knockendarroch House Hotel
Higher Oakfield, Pitlochry, Perthshire, PH16 5HT
Tel: 01796 473473
★★★★ Small Hotel

Macdonald's Restaurant & Guest House
140 Atholl Road, Pitlochry, Perthshire, PH16 5AG
Tel: 01796 472170
★★★ Guest House

Moulin Hotel
11-13 Kirkmichael Road, by Pitlochry, Perthshire, PH16 5EH
Tel: 01796 472196
★★★ Inn

Pine Trees Hotel
Strathview Terrace, Pitlochry, Perthshire, PH16 5QR
Tel: 01796 472121
★★★★ Small Hotel

Pitlochry Hydro Hotel
Knockard Road, Pitlochry, Perthshire, PH16 5JH
Tel: 01942 824824
★★★ Hotel

The Poplars
27 Lower Oakfield, Pitlochry, Perthshire, PH16 5DS
Tel: 01796 472911
★★★ Guest House

Rosehill
47 Atholl Road, Pitlochry, Perthshire, PH16 5BX
Tel: 01796 472958
★★★ Guest House

Rosemount Hotel
12 Higher Oakfield, Pitlochry, Perthshire, PH16 5HT
Tel: 01796 472302
★★★ Hotel

Scotlands Hotel
40 Bonnethill Road, Pitlochry, Perthshire, PH16 5BT
Tel: 01796 472292
★★★ Hotel

Strathgarry Hotel
113 Atholl Road, Pitlochry, Perthshire, PH16 5AG
Tel: 01796 472469
★★★ Small Hotel

Tigh Na Cloich Hotel
Larchwood Road, Pitlochry, Perthshire, PH16 5AS
Tel: 01796 472216
★★★ Small Hotel

Tir Aluinn
10 Higher Oakfield, Pitlochry, Perthshire, PH16 5HT
Tel: 01796 473811
★★★ Guest House

Torrdarach House
Golf Course Road, Pitlochry, Perthshire, PH16 5AU
Tel: 01796 472136
★★★★ Guest House

The Well House
11 Toberargan Road, Pitlochry, Perthshire, PH16 5HG
Tel: 01796 472239
★★★ Guest House

Westlands Hotel
160 Atholl Road, Pitlochry, Perthshire, PH16 5AR
Tel: 01796 472266
★★★ Hotel

ROSYTH

Cochranes Hotel
Hilton Road, Rosyth, Fife, KY11 2BA
Tel: 01383 420101
Hotel

ST ANDREWS

The Albany Hotel
56 North Street, St Andrews, Fife, KY16 9AH
Tel: 01334 477737
★★★ Small Hotel

Amberside
4 Murray Park, St Andrews, Fife, KY16 9AW
Tel: 01334 474644
★★★ Guest House

Anderson House
122 Lamond Drive, St Andrews, Fife, KY16 8DA
Tel: 01334 477286
Awaiting Inspection

Annandale Guest House
23 Murray Park, St Andrews, Fife, KY16 9AW
Tel: 01334 475310
★★★ Guest House

Ardgowan Hotel
2 Playfair Terrace, St Andrews, Fife, KY16 9HX
Tel: 01334 472970
★★★ Small Hotel

Arran House
5 Murray Park, St Andrews, Fife, KY16 9AW
Tel: 01334 474 724
★★★ Guest House

Aslar House
120 North Street, St Andrews, Fife, KY16 9AF
Tel: 01334 473460
★★★★ Guest House

Bell Craig
8 Murray Park, St Andrews, Fife, KY16 9AW
Tel: 01334 472962
★★ Guest House

Bramley House
10 Bonfield Road, Strathkinness, by St Andrews, KY16 9RP
Tel: 01334 850362
★★★★ Bed & Breakfast

Brownlees Guest House
7 Murray Place, St Andrews, Fife, KY16 9AP
Tel: 01334 473868
★★★ Guest House

Burness House
1 Murray Park, St Andrews, Fife, KY16 9AW
Tel: 01334 474314
★★★★ Guest House

Cameron House
11 Murray Park, St Andrews, Fife, KY16 9AW
Tel: 01334 72306
★★★★ Guest House

Charlesworth House
9 Murray Place, St Andrews, KY16 9AP
Tel: 01334 476528
★★★ Guest House

Cleveden House
3 Murray Place, St Andrews, Fife, KY16 9AP
Tel: 01334 474212
★★★ Guest House

Craigmore Guest House
3 Murray Park, St Andrews, Fife, KY16 9AW
Tel: 01334 472142
★★★★ Guest House

Doune House
5 Murray Place, St Andrews, Fife, KY16 9AP
Tel: 01334 475195
★★★ Guest House

Dunvegan Hotel
7 Pilmour Place, North Street, St Andrews, Fife, KY16 9HZ
Tel: 01334 473105
★★★ Small Hotel

Feddinch Mansion Country Guest House
St Andrews, Fife, KY16 8NR
Tel: 01334 470888
★★★★ Guest House

Five Pilmour Place
North Street, St Andrews, Fife, KY16 9HZ
Tel: 01334 478665
★★★★ Guest House

Glenderran Guest House
9 Murray Park, St Andrews, Fife, KY16 9AW
Tel: 01334 477951
★★★★ Guest House

Hazelbank Hotel
28 The Scores, St Andrews, Fife, KY16 9AS
Tel: 01334 472466
★★★ Small Hotel

Lorimer House
19 Murray Park, St Andrews, Fife, KY16 9AW
Tel: 01334 476599
★★★★ Guest House

Macdonald Rusacks Hotel
Pilmour Links, St Andrews, Fife, KY16 9JQ
Tel: 0870 4008128
★★★★ Hotel

Montague Guest House
21 Murray Park, St Andrews, Fife, KY16 9AW
Tel: 01334 479 287
★★★ Guest House

Nethan House
17 Murray Park, St Andrews, Fife, KY16 9AW
Tel: 01334 472104
★★★★ Guest House

New Hall, University of St Andrews
North Haugh, St Andrews, Fife,, KY16 9XW
Tel: 01334 467000
★★★ Hotel

Old Course Hotel, Golf Resort & Spa
St Andrews, Fife, KY16 9SP
Tel: 01334 474371
★★★★★ International Resort

The Old Station Country Guest House
Stratvithie Bridge, St Andrews, KY16 8LR
Tel: 01334 880505
★★★★ Guest House

Riverview Guest House
Edenside, St Andrews, Fife, KY16 9SQ
Tel: 01334 838009
★★★ Guest House

Rufflets Country House Hotel
Strathkinness Low Road, St Andrews, Fife, KY16 9TX
Tel: 01334 472594
★★★★★ Hotel

The Russell Hotel
26 The Scores, St Andrews, Fife, KY16 9AS
Tel: 01334 473447
★★★ Small Hotel

Scores Hotel
76 The Scores, St Andrews, Fife, KY16 9BB
Tel: 01334 472451
★★★ Hotel

Shandon House
10 Murray Place, St Andrews, Fife, KY16 9AP
Tel: 01334 472412
★★★ Guest House

St Andrews Bay Golf Resort & Spa
St Andrews, Fife, KY16 8PN
Tel: 01334 837000
★★★★★ International Resort

St Andrews Golf Hotel
40 The Scores, St Andrews, Fife, KY16 9AS
Tel: 01334 472611
★★★★ Hotel

West Acre Guest House
2 West Acre, St Andrews, Fife, KY16 9UD
Tel: 01334 476720
Awaiting Inspection

West Park House
5 St Marys Place, St Andrews, Fife, KY16 9UY
Tel: 01334 475933
★★★ Guest House

Whitecroft Guest House
33 Strathkinness High Road, St Andrews, Fife, KY16 9UA
Tel: 01334 474448
★★★★ Guest House

Yorkston Guest House
68-70 Argyle Street, St Andrews, Fife, KY16 9BU
Tel: 01334 472019
★★★ Guest House

BY ST ANDREWS

Edenside House
Edenside, By St Andrews, Fife, KY16 9QS
Tel: 01334 83 8108
★★★ Guest House

The Inn At Lathones
By Largoward, St Andrews, Fife, KY9 1JE
Tel: 01334 840494
★★★★ Inn

Pinewood Country House
Tayport Road, St Michaels, Fife, KY16 0DU
Tel: 01334 839860
★★★★ Guest House

ST FILLANS

Drummond Hotel Ltd
St Fillans, Perthshire, PH6 2NF
Tel: 01764 685212
★★ Hotel

STANLEY

The Tayside Hotel
51 Mill Street, Stanley, Perth, PH1 4NL
Tel: 01738 828249
★★★ Small Hotel

TUMMEL BRIDGE

Kynachan Loch Tummel Hotel
Tummel Bridge, Perthshire, PH16 5SB
Tel: 01796 484848
★★★ Hotel

WORMIT

Sandford Country House Hotel
Newton Hill, Wormit, Newport-on-Tay, Fife, DD6 8RG
Tel: 01382 541802
★★★ Hotel

ABERDEEN AND GRAMPIAN HIGHLANDS – SCOTLAND'S CASTLE AND WHISKY COUNTRY

ABERDEEN

Abbotswell Guest House
28 Abbotswell Crescent, Aberdeen, AB12 5AR
Tel: 01224 871788
★★★ Guest House

Aberdeen City Hotel
43-45 Market Street, Aberdeen, AB11 5EL
Tel: 01224 582255
★★ Hotel

Aberdeen Guest House
218 Great Western Road, Aberdeen, AB10 6PD
Tel: 01224 211733
★★★ Guest House

Aberdeen Marriott Hotel
Riverview Drive, Farburn, Dyce, Aberdeenshire, AB21 7AZ
Tel: 0870 400 7291
★★★★ Hotel

Aberdeen Northern Hotel
1 Great Northern Road, Aberdeen, AB24 3PS
Tel: 01224 483342
★★★ Hotel

Aberdeen Patio Hotel
Beach Boulevard, Aberdeen, AB24 5EF
Tel: 01224 633339
★★★★ Hotel

Aberdeen Springdale Guest House
404 Great Western Road, Aberdeen, AB10 6NR
Tel: 01224 316561
★★★ Guest House

Adelphi Guest House
8 Whinhill Road, Aberdeen, AB11 7XH
Tel: 01224 583078
★★★ Guest House

Albany Guest House
18 Whinhil Road, Aberdeen, Aberdeen-shire, AB11 7XH
Tel: 01224 571703
★★★ Guest House

Allan Guest House
56 Polmuir Road, Aberdeen, AB11 7RT
Tel: 01224 584484
★★★★ Guest House

The Angel Islington Guest House
191 Bon Accord Street, Aberdeen, AB116UA
Tel: 01224 587043
★★★ Guest House

Antrim Guest House
157 Crown Street, Aberdeen, AB11 6HT
Tel: 01224 590987
★★ Guest House

Arden Guest House
61 Dee Street, Aberdeen, Aberdeenshire, AB10 2EE
Tel: 01224 580700
★★★ Guest House

Ardoe House Hotel
South Deeside Road, Blairs, Aberdeen, Aberdeenshire, AB12 5YP
Tel: 01224 867355
★★★★ Hotel

Arkaig Guest House
43 Powis Terrace, Aberdeen, AB25 3PP
Tel: 01224 638872
★★★ Guest House

Armadale Guest House
605 Holburn Street, Aberdeen, AB10 7JN
Tel: 01224 580636
★★★ Guest House

Ashgrove Guest House
34 Ashgrove Road, Aberdeen, AB25 3AD
Tel: 01224 484861
★★★ Guest House

Atholl Hotel
54 Kings Gate, Aberdeen, AB15 4YN
Tel: 01224 323505
★★★★ Hotel

Balvenie Guest House
9 St Swithin Street, Aberdeen, Aberdeenshire, AB10 6XB
Tel: 01224 322559
★★ Guest House

Directory of all VisitScotland Quality Assured Serviced Establishments

Beeches Private Hotel
193 Great Western Road,
Aberdeen, AB10 6PS
Tel: 01224 586413
★★★ Guest House

Belhaven
152 Bon-Accord Street,
Aberdeen, AB11 6TX
Tel: 01224 588384
★★★ Guest House

Bimini Guest House
69 Constitution Street,
Aberdeen, AB24 5ET
Tel: 01224 646912
★★★ Guest House

Brentwood Hotel
101 Crown Street, Aberdeen,
AB11 6HH
Tel: 01224 595440
★★★ Hotel

Brentwood Villa
560 King Street, Aberdeen,
Grampian, AB24 5SR
Tel: 01224 480633
★★★ Guest House

Britannia Hotel
Malcolm Road, Aberdeen,
Grampian, AB21 9LN
Tel: 01224 409988
★★★ Hotel

The Burnett Arms Hotel
25 High Street, Banchory,
Aberdeenshire, AB31 5TD
Tel: 01330 824944
★★★ Small Hotel

Butler's Islander Guest House
122 Crown Street, Aberdeen,
Aberdeenshire, AB11 6HJ
Tel: 01224 212411
★★★ Guest House

Cedars Private Hotel
339 Great Western Road,
Aberdeen, AB10 6NW
Tel: 01224 583225
★★★ Guest House

Cloverleaf Hotel
Kepplehills Road, Bucksburn,
Aberdeen, AB21 9DG
Tel: 01224 714294
★ Hotel

Copthorne Hotel Aberdeen
122 Huntly Street, Aberdeen,
AB10 1SU
Tel: 01224 630404
★★★★ Hotel

Craighaar Hotel
Waterton Road, Bucksburn,
Aberdeen, AB21 9HS
Tel: 01224 712275
★★★ Hotel

Crown Private Hotel
10 Springbank Terrace,
Aberdeen, AB11
Tel: 01224 586842
★★★ Guest House

Crynoch Guest House
164 Bon-Accord Street,
Aberdeen, AB10 2TX
Tel: 01224 582743
★★★ Guest House

Cults Hotel
328 North Deeside Road,
Aberdeen, AB15 9SE
Tel: 01224 867632
★★★ Small Hotel

Dunavon House Hotel
60/62 Victoria Street, Dyce,
Aberdeenshire, AB21 7EE
Tel: 01224 722483
★★★ Hotel

Dunnydeer Guest House
402 Great Western Road,
Aberdeen, AB10 6NR
Tel: 01224 312821
★★★ Guest House

Dunrovin Guest House
168 Bon-Accord Street,
Aberdeen, AB10 2TX
Tel: 01224 586081
★★★ Guest House

Dyce Skean Dhu Hotel
Farburn Terrace, Dyce,
Aberdeenshire, AB21 7DW
Tel: 01224 723101
★★★ Hotel

Ellenville Guest House
50 Springbank Terrace,
Aberdeen, AB11 6LR
Tel: 01224 213334
★★★ Guest House

Express by Holiday Inn
Chapel Street, Aberdeen,
AB10 1SQ
Tel: 01224 623500
★★★ Hotel

Furain Guest House
92 North Deeside Road,
Peterculter, Aberdeen,
AB14 0QN
Tel: 01224 732189
★★★ Guest House

Granville Guest House
401 Great Western Road,
Aberdeen, AB10 6NY
Tel: 01224 313043
★★★ Guest House

376 Great Western Road
Aberdeen, Aberdeenshire,
AB10 6PH
Tel: 01224 313678
★★★ Guest House

Greyholme Guest House
35 Springbank Terrace,
Aberdeen, AB11 6LR
Tel: 01224 587081
★★★ Guest House

Hilton Aberdeen Treetops
161 Springfield Road, Aberdeen,
AB15 7AQ
Tel: 01224 313377
★★★★ Hotel

Holiday Inn
Claymore Drive, Aberdeen,
AB23 8GP
Tel: 08704 003046
★★★ Hotel

The Jays Guest House
422 King Street, Aberdeen,
AB24 3BR
Tel: 01224 638295
★★★★ Guest House

Kildonan Guest House
410 Great Western Road,
Aberdeen, AB10 6NR
Tel: 01224 316 115
★★★ Guest House

University of Aberdeen, King's Hall
College Bounds, Aberdeen,
AB24 3TT
Tel: 01224 273444
★★ Campus

Lillian Cottage
442 King Street, Aberdeen,
Aberdeenshire, AB24 3BS
Tel: 01224 636947
★★★ Guest House

Lonicera Guest House
261 Great Western Road,
Aberdeen, AB10 6PP
Tel: 01224 583200
★★★ Guest House

Marcliffe at Pitfodels
North Deeside Road, Pitfodels,
Aberdeen, AB15 9YA
Tel: 01224 861000
★★★★★ Hotel

Mariner Hotel
349 Great Western Road,
Aberdeen, AB10 6NW
Tel: 01224 588901
★★★ Hotel

Maryculter House Hotel
South Deeside Road,
Maryculter, Aberdeenshire,
AB12 5GB
Tel: 01224 732124
★★★ Hotel

Merkland Guest House
12 Merkland Road East,
Aberdeen, AB24 5PR
Tel: 01224 634451
★★ Guest House

Norwood Hall Hotel
Garthdee Road, Aberdeen, AB15 9NX
Tel: 01224 868951
★★★★ Hotel

Palm Court Hotel
81 Seafield Road, Aberdeen, AB15 7YX
Tel: 01224 310351
★★★ Hotel

Penny Meadow Private Hotel
189 Great Western Road, Aberdeen, AB10 6PS
Tel: 01224 588037
★★★★ Guest House

The Queen's Hotel
49-53 Queen's Road, Aberdeen, AB15 4YP
Tel: 01224 209999
★★★★ Hotel

Roselea Hotel
12 Springbank Terrace, Aberdeen, AB10 2LS
Tel: 01224 583060
★★★ Guest House

Royal Crown Guest House
111 Crown Street, Aberdeen, AB11 2HN
Tel: 01224 586461
★★★ Guest House

Royal Hotel
1-3 Bath Street, Aberdeen, AB11 6BJ
Tel: 01224 585152
★★ Hotel

Simpson's Hotel
59 Queens Road, Aberdeen, Aberdeen-shire, AB15 4YP
Tel: 01224 327777
★★★★ Hotel

Speedbird Inn
Argyll Road, Aberdeen Airport, Dyce, AB21 0AF
Tel: 01224 772883
★★★ Hotel

St Ola Guest House
421 Great Western Road, Aberdeen, AB10 6NJ
Tel: 01224 317186
★★★ Guest House

Strathisla Guest House
408 Great Western Road, Aberdeen, AB10 6NR
Tel: 01224 321026
★★★ Guest House

Thistle Aberdeen Airport Hotel
Argyll Road, Aberdeen, Aberdeenshire, AB21 0AF
Tel: 01224 725252
★★★★ Hotel

Thistle Aberdeen Altens
Soutarhead Road, Altens, Aberdeen, Aberdeenshire, AB12 3LF
Tel: 01224 877000
★★★ Hotel

Thistle Aberdeen Caledonian
10-14 Union Terrace, Aberdeen, Aberdeenshire, AB10 1WE
Tel: 01224 640233
★★★★ Hotel

Crombie Johnston Hall
University of Aberdeen, Aberdeen, AB24 3TT
Tel: 01224 273444
★ Campus

West Lodge Guest House
Norwood Hall, Garthdee Road, Cults, Aberdeen, AB15 9FX
Tel: 01224 861936
★★★ Guest House

NR ABERDEEN

The Belvedere Hotel
41 Evan Street, Stonehaven, Aberdeenshire, AB39 2ET
Tel: 01569 762672
★★ Small Hotel

Old Mill Inn
South Deeside Road, Maryculter, Aberdeen, AB12 5FX
Tel: 01224 733212
★★★ Small Hotel

Strathburn Hotel
Burghmuir Drive, Inverurie, Aberdeenshire, AB51 4GY
Tel: 01467 624422
★★★★ Hotel

ABERLOUR

Dowans Hotel
Aberlour, Banffshire, AB38 9LS
Tel: 01340 871488
★★★ Small Hotel

BY ALFORD

Forbes Arms Hotel
Alford, Aberdeenshire, AB33 8QJ
Tel: 01975 562108
★★★ Small Hotel

ARCHIESTOWN

Archiestown Hotel
Archiestown, by Aberlour, Moray, AB38 7QL
Tel: 01340 810218
★★★ Small Hotel

BALLATER

Alexandra Hotel
12 Bridge Square, Ballater, Aberdeenshire, AB35 5QJ
Tel: 01339 755376
★★★ Small Hotel

Allargue Arms Hotel
Corgarff, Strathdon, Aberdeenshire, AB36 8YP
Tel: 019756 51410
★ Inn

Auld Kirk Hotel & Johnson's Restaurant
Braemar Road, Ballater, Aberdeenshire, AB35 5RQ
Tel: 013397 55762
★★★ Restaurant with Rooms

Balgonie Country House
Braemar Place, Ballater, Aberdeenshire, AB35 5NQ
Tel: 013397 55482
★★★★ Small Hotel

Cambus O'May Hotel
nr Ballater, Aberdeenshire, AB35 5SE
Tel: 013397 55428
★★★ Small Hotel

Darroch Learg Hotel
Braemar Road, Ballater, Aberdeenshire, AB35 5UX
Tel: 013397 55443
★★★★ Small Hotel

Deeside Hotel
Braemar Road, Ballater, Aberdeenshire, AB35 5RQ
Tel: 013397 55420
★★★ Small Hotel

Glen Lui Hotel
Invercauld Road, Ballater, Aberdeenshire, AB35 5PP
Tel: 01339 755402
★★★ Small Hotel

The Gordon Guest House
Station Square, Ballater, Aberdeenshire, AB35 5QB
Tel: 013397 55996
★★★★ Guest House

Hilton Craigendarroch Hotel
Braemar Road, Ballater, Aberdeenshire, AB35 5RQ
Tel: 013397 55858
★★★ Hotel

Moorside Guest House
26 Braemar Road, Ballater, Aberdeenshire, AB35 5RL
Tel: 013397 55492
★★★★ Guest House

Morvada House
28 Braemar Road, Ballater, Deeside, AB35 5RL
Tel: 013397 56334
★★★★ Guest House

Netherley Guest House
2 Netherley Place, Ballater, Aberdeenshire, AB35 5QE
Tel: 013397 55792
★★★ Guest House

BY BALLATER

Loch Kinord Hotel
Ballater Road, Dinnet, Royal Deeside,, Aberdeenshire, AB34 5JY
Tel: 013398 85229
★★★ Hotel

BANCHORY

Crossroads Hotel
Lumphanan, by Banchory, Kincardineshire, AB31 4RH
Tel: 013398 83275
★★ Small Hotel

Douglas Arms Hotel
22 High Street, Banchory,
Aberdeenshire, AB31 5SR
Tel: 01330 822547
★★ Small Hotel

Raemoir House Hotel
Banchory, Aberdeenshire,
AB31 4ED
Tel: 01330 824884
★★★★ Hotel

BY BANCHORY

Learney Arms Hotel
The Square, Torphins,
Kincardineshire, AB31 4JP
Tel: 01339 882202
★★ Small Hotel

BANFF

Banff Links Hotel
Swordanes, Banff,
Aberdeenshire, AB45 2JJ
Tel: 01261 812414
★★ Small Hotel

Banff Springs Hotel
Golden Knowes Road, Banff,
Banffshire, AB45 2JE
Tel: 01261 812881
★★★ Hotel

Carmelite House Hotel
Low Street, Banff, AB45 1AY
Tel: 01261 812152
★★ Small Hotel

Fife Lodge Hotel
Sandyhill Road, Banff, AB45 1BE
Tel: 01261 812436
★★★ Small Hotel

BRAEMAR

Braemar Lodge Hotel
Glenshee Road, Braemar,
Aberdeenshire, AB35 5YQ
Tel: 013397 41627
★★★ Guest House

Callater Lodge Guest House
9 Glenshee Road, Braemar,
Aberdeenshire, AB35 5YQ
Tel: 013397 41275
★★★★ Guest House

Clunie Lodge Guest House
Cluniebank Road, Braemar,
Aberdeenshire, AB35 5ZP
Tel: 013397 41330
★★★ Guest House

Cranford Guest House
15 Glenshee Road, Braemar,
Aberdeenshire, AB35 5YQ
Tel: 01339 741675
★★★ Guest House

Invercauld Arms
Main Street, Braemar,
Aberdeenshire, AB35 5YR
Tel: 01942 824824
★★★ Hotel

Schiehallion House
10 Glenshee Road, Braemar,
Aberdeenshire, AB35 5YQ
Tel: 013397 41679
★★★ Guest House

BUCKIE

The Old Coach House Hotel
26 High Street, Buckie,
Banffshire, AB56 1AR
Tel: 01542 836266
★★ Hotel

CRAIGELLACHIE

Craigellachie Hotel
Victoria Street, Craigellachie,
Aberlour, Banffshire, AB38 9SR
Tel: 01340-881 204
★★★★ Hotel

Highlander Inn
Victoria Street, Craigellachie,
Speyside, AB38 9SR
Tel: 01340 881446
Awaiting Inspection

CRATHIE

The Inver Hotel
Crathie, by Ballater,
Aberdeenshire, AB35 5XN
Tel: 01339 742345
Awaiting Inspection

CRUDEN BAY

Kilmarnock Arms Hotel
Bridge Street, Cruden Bay,
by Peterhead, AB42 0HD
Tel: 01779 812213
★★★ Small Hotel

CULLEN

Norwood House
11 Seafield Place, Cullen,
Banffshire, AB56 4TE
Tel: 01542 840314
★★★ Guest House

The Seafield Hotel
Seafield Street, Cullen,
Banffshire, AB56 4SG
Tel: 01542 840791
★★★ Hotel

DUFFTOWN

Fife Arms Hotel
2 The Square, Dufftown,
Nr Keith, Banffshire, AB55 4AD
Tel: 01340 820220
★ Small Hotel

Tannochbrae Guest House & Scotts Restaurant
22 Fife Street, Dufftown,
Banffshire, AB55 4AL
Tel: 01340 820541
★★★ Guest House

ELGIN

West End Guest House
282 High Street, Elgin, IV30 1AQ
Tel: 01343 549629
★★★ Guest House

Auchmillan Guest House
12 Reidhaven Street, Elgin,
IV30 1QG
Tel: 01343 549077
★★★ Guest House

Eight Acres Hotel & Leisure Club
Morriston Road, Elgin, Moray,
IV30 6UL
Tel: 01343 543077
★★★ Hotel

Laichmoray Hotel
Maisondieu Road, Elgin, Moray,
IV30 1QR
Tel: 01343 540045
★★★ Hotel

The Lodge
Duff Avenue, Elgin, Moray,
IV30 1QS
Tel: 01343 549981
★★★★ Guest House

The Mansefield Hotel
Mayne Road, Elgin, Moray,
IV30 1NY
Tel: 01343 540883
★★★★ Hotel

The Mansion House Hotel
The Haugh, Elgin, Moray,
IV30 1AW
Tel: 01343 548811
★★★ Hotel

Moraydale
276 High Street, Elgin,
Morayshire, IV30 1AG
Tel: 01343 546381
★★★ Guest House

Royal Hotel
Station Road, Elgin, Moray,
IV30 1QW
Tel: 01343 542320
★★★ Hotel

Southbank Guest House
36 Academy Street, Elgin,
Moray, IV30 1LP
Tel: 01343 547132
★★★ Guest House

Sunninghill Hotel
Hay Street, Elgin, Moray,
IV30 1NH
Tel: 01343 547799
★★★ Hotel

ELLON

Station Hotel
Station Brae, Ellon,
Aberdeenshire, AB41 9BD
Tel: 01358 720209
★★ Small Hotel

FORRES

April Rise
16 Forbes Road, Forres, Moray, IV36 1HP
Tel: 01309 674066
★★★ Bed & Breakfast

Cluny Bank Hotel
St Leonards Road, Forres, Morayshire, IV36 1DW
Tel: 01309 674304
★★★★ Small Hotel

Knockomie Hotel
Grantown Road, Forres, Moray, IV36 2SG
Tel: 01309 673146
★★★★ Small Hotel

Morven
Caroline Street, Forres, Moray, IV36 1AN
Tel: 01309 673788
★★★ Bed & Breakfast

Ramnee Hotel
Victoria Road, Forres, Moray, IV36 3BN
Tel: 01309 672410
★★★★ Hotel

FRASERBURGH

Findlays Hotel & Restaurant
Smiddyhill Road, Fraserburgh, Aberdeenshire, AB43 9WL
Tel: 01346 519547
★★★ Small Hotel

GLENLIVET

Minmore House Hotel
Glenlivet, Ballindalloch, Banffshire, AB37 9DB
Tel: 01807 590378
★★★ Small Hotel

HUNTLY

Castle Hotel
Huntly, Aberdeenshire, AB54 4SH
Tel: 01466 792696
★★★★ Small Hotel

Gordon Arms Hotel
The Square, Huntly, Aberdeenshire, AB54 8AF
Tel: 01466 792288
★★ Small Hotel

INVERURIE

Ardennan House Hotel
Kemnay Road, Port Elphinstone, Inverurie, Aberdeenshire, AB51 3XD
Tel: 01467 621502
★★★ Small Hotel

Breaslann Guest House
Old Chapel Road, Inverurie, Aberdeenshire, AB51 4QN
Tel: 01467 621608
★★★ Guest House

Grant Arms Hotel
Monymusk, Inverurie, Aberdeenshire, AB51 7HJ
Tel: 01467 651226
Awaiting Inspection

Swallow Thainstone House Hotel
Thainstone Estate, Inverurie Road, Inverurie, Aberdeenshire, AB51 5NT
Tel: 01467 621643
★★★★ Hotel

BY INVERURIE

Pittodrie House Hotel
Pitcaple, Aberdeenshire, AB51 5HS
Tel: 01467 681444
★★★ Hotel

KEMNAY

Bennachie Lodge Hotel
Victoria Terrace, Kemnay, Aberdeenshire, AB51 5RL
Tel: 01467 642789
★★★ Small Hotel

Burnett Arms Hotel
Bridge Street, Kemnay, Aberdeenshire, AB51 5QT
Tel: 01467 642208
Awaiting Inspection

KILDRUMMY

Kildrummy Castle Hotel
Kildrummy, Alford, Aberdeenshire, AB33 8RA
Tel: 019755 71288
★★★★ Hotel

KINGSTON-ON-SPEY, BY ELGIN

Bayview
Beach Road, Kingston-on-Spey, Moray, IV32 7NP
1343
Awaiting Inspection

KINTORE

Torryburn Hotel
School Road, Kintore, Aberdeenshire, AB51 0XP
Tel: 01467 632269
★★★ Small Hotel

LAURENCEKIRK

Marykirk Hotel
Main Street, Marykirk, Laurencekirk, Aberdeenshire, AB30 1UT
Tel: 01674 840239
★★★ Inn

LOSSIEMOUTH

Ardivot House B&B
Ardivot Farm, Lossiemouth, Moray, IV31 6RY
Tel: 01343 811076
Awaiting Inspection

Skerry Brae
Stotfield Road, Lossiemouth, Moray, IV31 6QS
Tel: 01343 812040
Awaiting Inspection

MACDUFF

The Highland Haven
Shore Street, Macduff, Aberdeenshire, AB44 1UB
Tel: 01261 832408
★★★ Hotel

Knowes Hotel
78 Market Street, Macduff, Banffshire, AB44 1LL
Tel: 01261 832229
★★ Small Hotel

The Park Hotel
Fife Street, Macduff, Banffshire, AB44 1YA
Tel: 01261 832265
★★★ Guest House

Waterfront Hotel
25 Union Road, MacDuff, Aberdeen-shire, AB44 1UD
Tel: 01261 831661
Awaiting Inspection

NEWBURGH

Udny Arms Hotel
Main Street, Newburgh, Aberdeenshire, AB41 0BL
Tel: 01358 789444
★★★ Hotel

Ythan Hotel
Main Street, Newburgh, Aberdeenshire, AB41 6BP
Tel: 01358 789257
★★★ Small Hotel

OLDMELDRUM

Meldrum Arms Hotel
The Square, Oldmeldrum, Aberdeenshire, AB51 0AE
Tel: 01651 832238
★ Small Hotel

The Redgarth
Kirk Brae, Oldmeldrum, Aberdeenshire, AB51 0DJ
Tel: 01651 872353
★★★★ Inn

OLD RAYNE

The Lodge Hotel
Old Rayne, Insch, Aberdeenshire, AB52 6RY
Tel: 01464 851 205
★★ Small Hotel

PETERHEAD

Carrick Guest House
16 Merchant Street, Peterhead, Aberdeenshire, AB42 1DU
Tel: 01779 470610
★★ Guest House

Invernettie Guest House
South Road, Peterhead,
Aberdeenshire, AB42 0YX
Tel: 01779 473530
★★★ Guest House

Palace Hotel
Prince Street, Peterhead,
Aberdeenshire, AB42 6PL
Tel: 01779 474821
★★★ Hotel

Waterside Inn
Fraserburgh Road, Peterhead,
Aberdeenshire, AB42 3BN
0779 471121
★★★ Hotel

PORT ELPHINSTONE

Ashdon Guest House
Old Kemney Road, Port
Elphinstone, Inverurie,
Aberdeenshire, AB51 5XJ
Tel: 01467 620980
★★★ Guest House

PORTSOY

The Boyne Hotel Portsoy
2 North High Street, Portsoy,
Aberdeenshire, AB45 2PA
Tel: 01261 842242
★★ Small Hotel

The Station Hotel Portsoy
Seafield Street, Portsoy,
Aberdeenshire, AB45 2QT
Tel: 01261 842327
★★ Small Hotel

ROTHES

The Ben Aigen Hotel
51 New Street, Rothes, Moray,
AB38 7BJ
Tel: 01340 831240
★★ Small Hotel

ROTHIENORMAN

Rothie Inn
Main Street, Rothienorman,
Aberdeenshire, AB51 8UD
Tel: 01651 821206
★★★ Inn

ST COMBS, BY FRASERBURGH

The Tufted Duck Hotel
Corsekelly Place, St Combs,
Aberdeenshire, AB43 8ZS
Tel: 01346 582481
★★ Small Hotel

SPEY BAY

Spey Bay Hotel
Spey Bay, Fochabers,
Morayshire, IV32 7PJ
Tel: 01343 820424
★★★ Small Hotel

STONEHAVEN

Arduthie Guest House
Ann Street, Stonehaven,
Kincardineshire, AB39
Tel: 01569 762381
★★★★ Guest House

County Hotel and Squash Club
Arduthie Road, Stonehaven,
Kincardineshire, AB39 2EH
Tel: 01569 764386
★★ Small Hotel

Heugh Hotel
Westfield Road, Stonehaven,
Aberdeenshire, AB39 2EE
Tel: 01569 762379
★★★ Small Hotel

Woodside of Glasslaw
Stonehaven, Aberdeenshire,
AB39 3XQ
Tel: 01569 763799
★★★ Guest House

STRATHDON

Colquhonnie Hotel
Strathdon, Aberdeenshire,
AB36 8UN
Tel: 01975 651210
★★★ Small Hotel

TOMINTOUL

The Gordon Hotel
The Square, Tomintoul,
Aberdeenshire, AB37 9ET
Tel: 01807 580206
★★★ Hotel

Richmond Hotel
The Square, Tomintoul,
Aberdeenshire, AB37 9ET
Tel: 01807 580777
★ Hotel

TURRIFF

Deveron Lodge B&B Guesthouse
Bridgend Terrace, Turriff,
Aberdeenshire, AB53 4ES
Tel: 1888 563613
★★★★ Guest House

THE HIGHLANDS AND SKYE

ACHARACLE

Clanranald Hotel
Mingarry, Acharacle, Argyll,
PH36 4JX
Tel: 01967 431662
Awaiting Inspection

ACHNASHEEN

Ledgowan Lodge Hotel
Ledgowan, Achnasheen,
Ross-shire, IV22 2EJ
Tel: 01445 720252
★★★ Small Hotel

ALNESS

Teaninich Castle
Teaninich, Alness, Ross-Shire,
IV17 0XB
Tel: 01349 883231
★★★ Small Hotel

ARDELVE, BY DORNIE

Caberfeidh House
Caberfeidh House, Upper
Ardelve, by Kyle of Lochalsh,
Ross-shire, IV40 8DY
Tel: 01599 555293
★★★ Guest House

Conchra House
Sallachy Road, Ardelve, by Kyle,
Ross-shire, IV40 8DZ
Tel: 01599 555 233
★★★ Guest House

ARDNAMURCHAN

Feorag House
Glenborrodale, Acharacle,
Argyll, PH36 4JP
Tel: 01972 500248
★★★★★ Guest House

ARISAIG

The Arisaig Hotel
Arisaig, Inverness-shire,
PH39 4NH
Tel: 01687 450210
Awaiting Inspection

Cnoc-na-Faire Hotel
Back of Keppoch, Arisaig,
Inverness-shire, PH39 4NS
Tel: 01687 450249
★★★★ Small Hotel

AULTBEA

Aultbea Hotel
Aultbea, Ross-shire, IV22 2HX
Tel: 01445 731201
★★ Small Hotel

Cartmel Guest House
Birchburn Road, Aultbea,
Ross-shire, IV22 2HZ
Tel: 01445 731375
★★★★ Guest House

Drumchork Lodge
Aultbea, Wester Ross, IV22 2HU
Tel: 01445 731242
★★ Small Hotel

AVIEMORE

Ardlogie Guest House
Dalfaber Road, Aviemore,
Inverness-shire, PH22 1PU
Tel: 01479 810747
★★★ Guest House

Aviemore Four Seasons
Aviemore, Inverness-shire,
PH22 1PJ
Tel: 01479 815100
Hotel

Cairngorm Hotel
Grampian Road, Aviemore,
PH22 1PE
Tel: 01479 810233
★★★ Hotel

Cairngorm Guest House
Grampian Road, Aviemore,
Inverness-shire, PH22 1RP
Tel: 01479 810630
★★★ Guest House

Corrour House Hotel
Inverdruie, Aviemore,
Inverness-shire, PH22 1QH
Tel: 01479 810220
★★★★ Small Hotel

Hilton Coylumbridge Hotel
Coylumbridge, by Aviemore,
Inverness-shire, PH22 1QN
Tel: 01479 810661
★★★ Hotel

Kinapol Guest House
Dalfaber Road, Aviemore,
Inverness-shire, PH22 1PY
Tel: 01479 810513
★★ Guest House

MacDonald Highlands Hotel
Aviemore Centre, Aviemore,
Inverness-shire, PH22 1PJ
Tel: 01479 810771
★★★★ Hotel

Ravenscraig Guest House
Grampian Road, Aviemore,
Inverness-shire, PH22 1RP
Tel: 01479 810278
★★★ Guest House

The Rowan Tree Country Hotel
Loch Alvie, Aviemore,
Inverness-shire, PH22 1QB
Tel: 01479 810207
★★★ Small Hotel

BADACHRO

Dry Island B&B
Dry Island, Badachro, Gairloch,
Ross-shire, IV21 2AB
Tel: 01445 741263
Awaiting Inspection

BALLACHULISH

Ballachulish Hotel & Bulas Bar & Bistro
Ballachulish, nr Fort William,
Argyll, PH49 4JY
Tel: 0871 222 3415
★★★ Hotel

Ballachulish House
Ballachulish, Argyll, PH49 4JX
Tel: 01855 811266
★★★★★ Small Hotel

Craiglinnhe House
Lettermore, Ballachulish, Argyll,
PH49 4JD
Tel: 01855 811270
★★★★ Guest House

Fern Villa Guest House
Loanfern, Ballachulish,
PH49 4JE
Tel: 01855 811393
★★★ Guest House

Isles of Glencoe Hotel & Leisure Centre
Ballachulish, nr Fort William,
Argyll, PH49 4HL
0871 222 3415
★★★★ Hotel

Lyn Leven Guest House
Ballachulish, Argyll, PH49 4JP
Tel: 01855 811392
★★★★ Guest House

BANAVIE, BY FORT WILLIAM

Banavie House
Locheil Crescent, Banavie,
by Fort William, Inverness-shire,
PH33 7LY
Tel: 01397 772 531
★★ Guest House

BOAT OF GARTEN

The Boat Hotel
Boat of Garten, Inverness-shire,
PH24 3BH
Tel: 01479 831258
★★★★ Hotel

Heathbank House
Drumuillie Road,
Boat of Garten, Inverness-shire,
PH24 3BD
Tel: 01479 831234
★★★ Guest House

Moorfield House
Deshar Road, Boat of Garten,
Inverness-shire, PH24 3BN
Tel: 01479 831646
★★★★ Guest House

BRACKLA, LOCH NESS-SIDE

Loch Ness Clansman Hotel
Brackla, Loch Ness Side,
Inverness-shire, IV3 8LA
Tel: 01456 450326
★★★ Hotel

BRORA

Royal Marine Hotel
Golf Road, Brora, Sutherland,
KW9 6GS
Tel: 01408 621252
★★★★ Hotel

CARRBRIDGE

Cairdeas Guest House
Main Street, Carrbridge,
Inverness-shire, PH23 3AA
Tel: 01479 841271
★★★★ Guest House

The Cairn Hotel
Main Road, Carrbridge,
Inverness-shire, PH23 3AS
Tel: 01479 841212
★★★ Inn

Carrmoor Guest House
Carr Road, Carrbridge,
Inverness-shire, PH23 3AD
Tel: 01479 841244
★★★ Guest House

Craigellachie House
Main Street, Carrbridge,
Inverness-shire, PH23 3AS
Tel: 01479 841641
★★★ Guest House

Dalrachney Lodge Hotel
Carrbridge, Inverness-shire,
PH23 3AT
Tel: 01479 841252
★★★★ Small Hotel

Fairwinds Hotel
Carrbridge, Inverness-shire,
PH23 3AA
Tel: 01479 841240
★★★★ Small Hotel

CASTLETOWN, BY THURSO

St Clair Arms Hotel
Main Street, Castletown,
Caithness, KW14 8TP
Tel: 01847 821656
★★ Hotel

CORPACH, BY FORT WILLIAM

Braeburn
Badabrie, Fort William,
Inverness-shire, PH33 7LX
Tel: 01397 77 772047
★★★ Guest House

CROMARTY

Royal Hotel
Marine Terrace, Cromarty,
Ross-shire, IV11 8YN
Tel: 01381 600217
★★★ Small Hotel

CULBOKIE

Ben Wyvis Views
Bydand, Culbokie, Ross-shire,
IV7 8JH
Awaiting Inspection

DALWHINNIE

The Inn at Loch Ericht
Dalwhinnie, Inverness-shire,
PH19 1AG
Tel: 01528 522257
★ Inn

DINGWALL

Tulloch Castle Hotel
Tulloch Castle Drive, Dingwall,
Ross-shire, IV15 9ND
Tel: 01349 861325
★★★★ Hotel

Directory of all VisitScotland Quality Assured Serviced Establishments

BY DINGWALL

Kinkell Country House
Easter Kinkell, by Conon Bridge, Ross-shire, IV7 8HY
Tel: 01349 861270
★★★ Small Hotel

DORNIE, BY KYLE OF LOCHALSH

Dornie Hotel
Francis Street, Dornie, Ross-shire, IV40 8DT
Tel: 01599 555205
★★★ Small Hotel

Eilean A-Cheo
Dornie, by Kyle of Lochalsh, Ross-shire, IV40 8DY
Tel: 01599 555485
★★★ Bed & Breakfast

Loch Duich Hotel
Ardelve, By Kyle of Lochalsh, Ross-shire, IV40 8DY
Tel: 01599 555213
★★ Small Hotel

DORNOCH

Burghfield House Hotel
Dornoch, Sutherland, IV25 3HN
Tel: 01862 810212
★★ Hotel

Dornoch Hotel
Grange Road, Dornoch, IV25 3LD
Tel: 01942 824824
★★ Hotel

Dornoch Castle Hotel
Castle Street, Dornoch, Sutherland, IV25 3SD
Tel: 01862 810216
★★★ Hotel

Eagle Hotel
Dornoch, Sutherland, IV25 3SR
Tel: 01862 810008
★★★ Small Hotel

Royal Golf Hotel
Grange Road, Dornoch, Sutherland, IV25 3LD
Tel: 01667 452301
★★★ Hotel

DRUMBEG

Drumbeg Hotel & Restaurant
Drumbeg, by Lochinver, Sutherland, IV27 4NW
Tel: 01571 833236
★★★ Small Hotel

DRUMNADROCHIT

Drumbuie Farm
Loch Ness, Drumnadrochit, Inverness-shire, IV63 6XP
Tel: 01456 450634
Awaiting Inspection

Drumnadrochit Hotel
Drumnadrochit, Inverness-shire, IV63 6TU
Tel: 01456 450218
Awaiting Inspection

Clunebeg Lodge Guest House
Clunebeg Estate, Drumnadrochit, Inverness-shire, IV63 6US
Tel: 01456 450387
★★★ Guest House

Loch Ness Lodge Hotel
Drumnadrochit, Inverness-shire, IV63 6TU
Tel: 01456 450342
★★★ Hotel

DULNAIN BRIDGE, BY GRANTOWN-ON-SPEY

Muckrach Lodge Hotel + Restaurant
Dulnain Bridge, Grantown on Spey, Inverness-shire, PH26 3LY
Tel: 01479 851257
★★★★ Small Hotel

Tigh Na Sgiath Country House Hotel
Skye of Curr, Dulnain Bridge, Inverness-shire, PH26 3PA
Tel: 01479 851345
★★★ Small Hotel

DURNESS

MacKays
Durness, Sutherland, IV27 4PN
Tel: 01971 511209
★★★★ Small Hotel

BY EVANTON

Kiltearn House
Kiltearn House, Kiltearn, by Evanton, Ross-shire, IV16 9UY
Tel: 01349 830 617
★★★★ Guest House

FARR, BY INVERNESS

The Steadings Hotel
Flichity, Farr, Inverness-shire, IV2 6XD
Tel: 01808 521314
Awaiting Inspection

FESHIE BRIDGE, BY KINCRAIG

March House Guest House
Feshiebridge, Kincraig, Inverness-shire, PH21 1NA
Tel: 01540 651388
★★★ Guest House

FORT AUGUSTUS

Auchterawe Country House
Auchterawe, Fort Augustus, Inverness-shire, PH32 4BT
Tel: 01320 366228
★★ Guest House

Caledonian Hotel
Fort Augustus, Inverness-shire, PH32 4BQ
Tel: 01320 366256
★★ Small Hotel

Inchnacardoch Lodge Hotel
Loch Ness, by Fort Augustus, Inverness-shire, PH32 4BL
Tel: 01320 366258
★★★ Small Hotel

The Lovat Arms Hotel
Fort William Road, Fort Augustus, Inverness-shire, PH32 4DU
Tel: 01320 366366
Awaiting Inspection

FORT WILLIAM

Alexandra Hotel
The Parade, Fort William, PH33 6AZ
Tel: 01397 702241
★★ Hotel

Bank Street Lodge
Bank Street, Fort William, Inverness-shire, PH33 0AY
Tel: 01397 700070
Awaiting Inspection

Ben Nevis Hotel & Leisure Club
North Road, Fort William, Inverness-shire, PH33 6TG
Tel: 01397 702331
★★ Hotel

Ben View Guest House
Belford Road, Fort William, Inverness-shire, PH33 6ER
Tel: 01397 702966
★★★ Guest House

Berkeley House
Belford Road, Fort William, Inverness-shire, PH33 6BT
Tel: 01397 701185
★★★ Guest House

Caledonian Hotel
Achintore Road, Fort William, Inverness-shire, PH33 6RW
Tel: 01942 824824
★★★ Hotel

Clan MacDuff Hotel
Achintore Road, Fort William, Inverness-shire, PH33 6RW
Tel: 01397 702341
★★★ Hotel

Constantia House
Costantia, Fassifern Road, Fort William, Inverness-shire, PH33 6BD
Tel: 01397 702893
★★ Guest House

Craig Nevis West
Belford Road, Fort William, Inverness-shire, PH33 6BU
Tel: 01397 702023
★★ Guest House

Cruachan Hotel
Achintore Road, Fort William, Inverness-shire, PH33 6RQ
Tel: 01397 702022
★★ Hotel

Distillery Guest House
Nevis Bridge, Fort William, Inverness-shire, PH33 6LR
Tel: 01397 700103
★★★★ Guest House

Glenlochy Guest House
Nevis Bridge, Fort William, Inverness-shire, PH33 6LP
Tel: 01397 702909
★★★ Guest House

Glentower Lower Observatory
Achintore Road, Fort William, Inverness Shire, PH33 6PQ
Tel: 01397 704007
★★★★ Guest House

Grand Hotel
Gordon Square, Fort William, Inverness-shire, PH33 6DX
Tel: 01397 702928
★★★ Hotel

Guisachan Guest House
Alma Road, Fort William, Inverness-shire, PH33 6HA
Tel: 01397 703797
Guest House

Highland Hotel
Union Road, Fort William, Inverness-shire, PH33 6QT
Tel: 01397 702291
Awaiting Inspection

The Inn at Ardgour
Ardgour, by Fort William, Inverness-shire, PH33 7AA
Tel: 01855 841225
★★★ Small Hotel

Inverlochy Castle Hotel
Torlundy, Fort William, Inverness-shire, PH33 6SN
Tel: 01397 702177
★★★★★ Hotel

Lime Tree Studio
Achintore Road, Fort William, Inverness-shire, PH33 6RQ
Tel: 01397 701806
Awaiting Inspection

Lochiel Villa Guest House
Achintore Road, Fort William, Inverness-shire, PH33 6RQ
Tel: 01397 703616
★★★ Guest House

Lochview House
Heathercroft, off Argyll Terrace, Fort William, Inverness-shire, PH33 6RE
Tel: 01397 703149
★★★ Guest House

Mansefield Guest House
Corpach, Fort William, Inverness-shire, PH33 7LT
Tel: 01397 772262
★★★ Guest House

Moorings Hotel
Banavie, Fort William, PH33 7LY
Tel: 01397 772797
★★★★ Hotel

The Neuk
Corpach, Fort William, Inverness-shire, PH33 7LR
Tel: 01397 772244
★★★ Guest House

Nevis Bank Hotel
Belford Road, Fort William, Inverness-shire, PH33 6BY
Tel: 01397 705721
★★ Hotel

Orchy Villa Guest House
Alma Road, Fort William, Inverness-shire, PH33 6HA
Tel: 01397 702445
★ Guest House

Stronchreggan View Guest House
Achintore Road, Fort William, Inverness-shire, PH33 6RW
Tel: 01397 704644
★★★ Guest House

West End Hotel
Achintore Road, Fort William, PH33 6ED
Tel: 01397 702614
★★★ Hotel

BY FORT WILLIAM

Carinbrook
Banavie, Fort William, Inverness-shire, PH33 7LX
Tel: 01397 772318
★★★ Guest House

Glen Loy Lodge
Banavie, Fort William, Inverness-shire, PH33 7PD
Tel: 01397 712 700
★ Guest House

Old Pines Hotel & Restaurant
Spean Bridge, by Fort William, PH34 4EG
Tel: 01397 712324
★★★★ Small Hotel

NR FORT WILLIAM

The Tailrace Inn
Riverside Road, Kinlochleven, Argyll, PA40 4QH
Tel: 01855 831777
★★ Inn

GAIRLOCH

Gairloch Hotel
Gairloch, Highland Region, IV21 2BL
Tel: 01942 824824
★★★ Hotel

Millcroft Hotel
Strath, Gairloch, Ross-shire, IV21 2BT
Tel: 01445 712376
★★ Small Hotel

Myrtle Bank Hotel
Low Road, Gairloch, Ross-shire, IV21 2BS
Tel: 01445 712004
★★ Small Hotel

The Old Inn
Gairloch, Ross-shire, IV21 2BD
Tel: 01445 712006
★★★ Inn

Shieldaig Lodge Hotel
Gairloch, Wester Ross, IV21 2AW
Tel: 01445 741250
Awaiting Inspection

BY GARVE

Inchbae Lodge
By Garve, Ross-shire, IV23 2PH
Tel: 01997 455269
Awaiting Inspection

GLENCOE

Clachaig Inn
Glencoe, Argyll, PH49 4HX
Tel: 01855 811252
★★ Inn

Dorrington Lodge
6 Tigh Phuirst, Glencoe, Argyll, PH49 4HN
Tel: 01855 811653
★★★ Guest House

Glencoe Hotel
Glencoe, West Highlands, PH49 4HW
Tel: 01855 811245
★★ Small Hotel

MacDonald Hotel
Fort William Road, Kinlochleven, Argyll, PH50 4QL
Tel: 01855 831539
★★★ Small Hotel

Scorrybreac Guest House
Glencoe, Argyll, PH49 4HT
Tel: 01855 811354
★★★ Guest House

Strathassynt Guest House
Loan Fern, Ballachulish, Argyll, PH49 4JB
Tel: 01855 811261
★★★ Guest House

GLENFINNAN

The Princes' House Hotel
Glenfinnan, Inverness-shire, PH37 4LT
Tel: 01397 722246
★★★ Small Hotel

GLENMORISTON

Cluanie Inn
Glenmoriston, Inverness-shire, IV63 7YW
Tel: 01320 340238
★★★ Small Hotel

GLEN NEVIS, BY FORT WILLIAM

Corrie Duff Guest House
Glen Nevis, Fort William, Inverness-shire, PH33 6AB
Tel: 01397 701412
Guest House

GLENSHIEL, BY KYLE OF LOCHALSH

Kintail Lodge Hotel
Glenshiel, Ross-shire, IV40 8HL
Tel: 01599 511275
★★★ Small Hotel

GLEN URQUHART

Glenurquhart House
Glenurquhart, Drumnadrochit, Inverness-shire, IV63 6TJ
Tel: 01456 476234
★★★ Small Hotel

GOLSPIE

The Golf Links Hotel
Church Street, Golspie, Sutherland, KW10 6TT
Tel: 01408 633 408
★★ Small Hotel

Granite Villa Guest House
Fountain Road, Golspie, Sutherland, KW10 6TH
Tel: 01408 633146
★★★ Guest House

GRANTOWN-ON-SPEY

An Cala Guest House
Woodlands Terrace, Grantown on Spey, Moray, PH26 3JU
Tel: 01479 873293
★★★★ Guest House

Ben Mhor Hotel
53-57 High Street, Grantown on Spey, Moray, PH26 3EG
Tel: 01479 872056
★★ Hotel

Craiglynne Hotel
Woodlands Terrace, Grantown-on-Spey, Morayshire, PH26 3JX
Tel: 01479 872597
Awaiting Inspection

Culdearn House
Woodland Terrace, Grantown-on-Spey, Morayshire, PH26 3JU
Tel: 01479 872106
★★★★ Small Hotel

Dunallan House
Woodside Avenue, Grantown-on-Spey, Moray, PH26 3JN
Tel: 01479 872140
★★★★ Guest House

Firhall Guest House
Grant Road, Grantown-on-Spey, Moray, PH26 3LD
Tel: 01479 873097
★★★ Guest House

Garden Park Guest House
Woodside Avenue, Grantown-on-Spey, Moray, PH26 3JN
Tel: 01479 873235
★★★★ Guest House

Garth Hotel
The Square, Grantown-on-Spey, Moray, PH26 3HN
Tel: 01479 872836
★★★ Small Hotel

Grant Arms Hotel
The Square, Grantown-on-Spey, Morayshire, PH21 3HF
Tel: 01479 872526
★★ Hotel

Holmhill House
Woodside Avenue, Grantown on Spey, Morayshire, PH26 3JR
Tel: 01479 873977
★★★ Guest House

Kinross House
Woodside Avenue, Grantown-on-Spey, Moray, PH26 3JR
Tel: 01479 872042
★★★★ Guest House

Parkburn Guest House
High Street, Grantown-on-Spey, Moray, PH26 3EN
Tel: 01479 873116
★★★ Guest House

The Pines
Woodside Avenue, Grantown-on-Spey, Moray, PH26 3JR
Tel: 01479 872092
★★★★ Small Hotel

Ravenscourt House Hotel
Seafield Avenue, Grantown-on-Spey, Morayshire, PH26 3JG
Tel: 01479 872286
★★★★ Small Hotel

Rosegrove Guesthouse
Skye of Curr, Dulnain Bridge, Grantown on Spey, Inverness-shire, PH26 3PA
Tel: 01479 851335
★★★ Guest House

Rosehall Guest House
13 The Square, Grantown On Spey, Morayshire, PH26 3HG
Tel: 01479 872721
Awaiting Inspection

Rossmor Guest House
Woodlands Terrace, Grantown on Spey, Moray, PH26 3JU
Tel: 01479 872201
★★★★ Guest House

Seafield Lodge Hotel
Woodside Avenue, Grantown-on-Spey, Morayshire, PH26 3JN
Tel: 01479 872152
★★★ Small Hotel

Strathallan House
Grant Road, Grantown-on-Spey, Moray, PH26 3LD
Tel: 01479 872165
★★★ Guest House

Willowbank
High Street, Grantown on Spey, Morayshire, PH26 3EN
Tel: 01479 872089
★★★ Guest House

HALKIRK

Ulbster Arms Hotel
Bridge Street, Halkirk, Caithness, KW12 6XY
Tel: 01847 831641
★ Hotel

HELMSDALE

Kindale House
5 Lilleshall Street, Helmsdale, Sutherland, KW8 6JF
Tel: 01431 821415
★★★★ Guest House

Kintrye Family B&B
Trentham Street, Helmsdale, Sutherland, KW8 6JD
Tel: 01431 821590
Awaiting Inspection

INVERGARRY

Ardgarry Farm
Faichem, Invergarry, Inverness-shire, PH35 4HG
Tel: 01809 501226
Awaiting Inspection

Glengarry Castle Hotel
Invergarry, Invernes-shire, PH35 4HW
Tel: 01809 501254
★★★★ Hotel

INVERGORDON

Kincraig House Hotel
Invergordon, Ross-shire, IV18 0LF
Tel: 01349 852587
★★★ Hotel

INVERNESS

Abermar Guest House
25 Fairfield Road, Inverness, IV3 5QD
Tel: 01463 239019
★★★ Guest House

Ach Aluinn Guest House
27 Fairfield Road, Inverness, IV3 5QD
Tel: 01463 230127
★★★★ Guest House

Acorn House
Bruce Gardens, Inverness, Inverness-shire, IV3 5ED
Tel: 01463 717021
★★★ Guest House

Alban House
Bruce Gardens, Inverness, IV3 5EN
Tel: 01463 714301
★★★ Guest House

The Alexander
16 Ness Bank, Inverness, Inverness-shire, IV2 4SF
Tel: 01463 231151
★★★ Guest House

Ardconnel House
21 Arconnel Street, Inverness, Inverness-shire, IV2 3EU
Tel: 01463 240455
★★★★ Guest House

Ardross House
18 Ardross Street, Inverness, Inverness-shire, IV3 5NS
Tel: 01463 241740
★★★ Guest House

Avalon Guest House
79 Glenurquhart Road, Inverness, IV3 5PB
Tel: 01463 239075
★★★★ Guest House

Ballifeary House Hotel
10 Ballifeary Road, Inverness, IV3 5PJ
Tel: 01463 235572
★★★★ Guest House

Beaufort Hotel
11 Culduthel Road, Inverness, IV2 4AG
Tel: 01463 222897
Awaiting Inspection

Best Western Inverness Palace Hotel & Spa
Ness Walk, Inverness, IV3 5NG
Tel: 01463 223243
★★★ Hotel

Brae Ness Hotel
Ness Bank, Inverness, IV2 4SP
Tel: 01463 712266
Awaiting Inspection

Bunchrew House Hotel
Bunchrew, Inverness, IV3 8TA
Tel: 01463 234917
★★★★ Small Hotel

Castleview Guest House
2A Ness Walk, Inverness, Inverness-shire, IV3 5NE
Tel: 01463 241443
★★ Guest House

Cedar Villa Guest House
33 Kenneth Street, Inverness, IV3 5DH
Tel: 01463 230477
★★★ Guest House

Columba Hotel
Ness Walk, Inverness, IV3 5NF
Tel: 01463 231391
★★★ Hotel

Copperfield
Culloden Road, Westhill, Inverness, IV2 5BP
Tel: 01463 792251
★★★ Guest House

Craigmonie Hotel
9 Annfield Road, Inverness, Inverness-shire, IV2 3HX
Tel: 01463 231649
★★★ Hotel

Craignay House
16 Ardross Street, Inverness, IV3 5NS
Tel: 01463 226563
★★★ Guest House

Craigside Lodge
4 Gordon Terrace, Inverness, IV2 3HD
Tel: 01463 231576
★★★ Guest House

Crown Court Hotel
25 Southside Road, Inverness, IV2 3BG
Tel: 01463 234816
★★★ Small Hotel

Crown Guest House
19 Ardconnel Street, Inverness, Inverness-shire, IV2 3EU
Tel: 01463 231135
★★★ Guest House

Cuchullin Lodge Hotel
43 Culduthel Road, Inverness, Inverness-shire, IV2 4HQ
Tel: 01463 231945
★★★★ Small Hotel

Culloden House Hotel
Milton of Culloden, Inverness, IV1 2NZ
Tel: 01463 790461
★★★★ Hotel

Drumossie Hotel
Old Perth Road, Inverness, IV2 5BE
Tel: 01463 236451
★★★★ Hotel

Dunain Park
Inverness, IV3 8JN
Tel: 01463 230512
★★★★ Small Hotel

East Dene
6 Ballifeary Road, Inverness, IV3 5PJ
Tel: 01463 232976
★★★ Guest House

Eden House
8 Ballifeary Road, Inverness, Inverness-shire, IV3 5PJ
Tel: 01463 230278
★★★★ Guest House

Eildon Guest House
29 Old Edinburgh Road, Inverness, Inverness-shire, IV2 3HJ
Tel: 01463 231969
Awaiting Inspection

Eskdale House
41 Greig Street, Inverness, IV3 5PX
Tel: 01463 240933
★★★ Guest House

Felstead House
18 Ness Bank, Inverness, Inverness-shire, IV2 4SF
Tel: 01463 231634
★★★★ Guest House

Fraser House
49 Huntly Street, Inverness, IV3 5HS
Tel: 01463 716488
★★★ Guest House

Glencairn
19 Ardross Street, Inverness, IV3 5NS
Tel: 01463 232965
★★★ Guest House

Glendruidh House Hotel
Old Edinburgh Road South, Inverness, IV2 6AR
Tel: 01463 226499
★★★★ Small Hotel

Glen Mhor Hotel & Restaurant
8-13 Ness Bank, Inverness, IV2 4SG
Tel: 01463 234308
★★★ Hotel

Glenmoriston Town House
20 Ness Bank, Inverness, Inverness-shire, IV2 4SF
Tel: 01463 223777
★★★★ Hotel

Inverglen
7 Abertarff Road, Inverness, IV2 3NW
Tel: 01463 236281
★★★ Guest House

Inverness Marriott Hotel
Culcabock Road, Inverness, IV2 3LP
Tel: 01463 237166
★★★★ Hotel

Ivybank Guest House
28 Old Edinburgh Road, Inverness, IV2 3HJ
Tel: 01463 232796
★★★★ Guest House

Kessock Hotel
North Kessock, Ross-shire, IV1 1XN
Tel: 01463 731208
★★★ Small Hotel

Larchfield House
15 Ness Bank, Inverness, IV2 4SF
Tel: 01463 233874
★★★ Guest House

Lochardil House Hotel
Stratherrick Road, Inverness, Inverness-shire, IV2 4LF
Tel: 01463 235995
★★★★ Small Hotel

Loch Ness House Hotel
Glenurquhart Road, Inverness, IV3 8JL
Tel: 01463 231248
★★★ Hotel

MacDougall Clansman Hotel
103 Church Street, Inverness, IV1 1ES
Tel: 01463 713702
★ Small Hotel

Maple Court Hotel
Ness Walk, Inverness, IV3 5SQ
Tel: 01463 230330
★★★ Small Hotel

Melrose Villa
35 Kenneth Street, Inverness, IV3 5DH
Tel: 01463 233745
★★★ Guest House

Moray Park House
Island Bank Road, Inverness, IV2 4SX
Tel: 01463 233528
★★★ Guest House

Moyness House
6 Bruce Gardens, Inverness, IV3 5EN
Tel: 01463 233836
★★★★ Guest House

Ness Bank Guest House
7 Ness Bank, Inverness, Inverness-shire, IV2 4SF
Tel: 01463 232939
★★★ Guest House

The Old Rectory
9 Southside Road, Inverness, IV2 3BG
Tel: 01463 220969
★★★★ Guest House

The Old Royal Guest House
10 Union Street, Inverness, IV1 1PL
Tel: 01463 230 551
★ Guest House

Pitfaranne
57 Crown Street, Inverness, IV2 3AY
Tel: 01463 239338
★★★ Guest House

The Priory Hotel
The Square, Beauly, Inverness-shire, IV4 7BX
Tel: 01463 782309
★★★ Hotel

Ramada Jarvis Inverness
Church Street, Inverness, Inverness-shire, IV1 1DX
Tel: 01463 235181
★★★ Hotel

Riverview Guest House
2 Moray Park, Island Bank Road, Inverness, Inverness-shire, IV2 4SX
Tel: 01463 235557
★★★ Guest House

Roseneath Guest House
39 Greig Street, Inverness, IV3 5PX
Tel: 01463 220201
★★★ Guest House

The Royal Highland Hotel, Ash Restaurant
Station Square, 18 Academy Street, Inverness, IV1 1LG
Tel: 01463 231926
★★★ Hotel

Royston Guest House
16 Millburn Road, Inverness, IV2 3PS
Tel: 01463 231243
★★★ Guest House

St Ann's House
37 Harrowden Road, Inverness, IV3 5QN
Tel: 01463 236157
★★★ Guest House

Silverwells Guest House
28 Ness Bank, Inverness, IV2 4SF
Tel: 01463 232113
★★★★ Guest House

Talisker House
25 Ness Bank, Inverness, Inverness-shire, IV2 4SF
Tel: 01463 236221
★★★ Guest House

Thistle Inverness
Millburn Road, Inverness, Inverness-shire, IV2 3TR
Tel: 01463 239666
★★★ Hotel

Tower Hotel
4 Ardross Terrace, Inverness, IV3 5NQ
Tel: 01463 232765
★★★ Small Hotel

Trafford Bank Guest House
96 Fairfield Road, Inverness, Inverness-shire, IV3 5LL
Tel: 01463 241414
★★★★ Guest House

Waterside Hotel
Ness Bank, Inverness, Inverness-shire, IV2 4SF
Tel: 01463 233065
★★★ Hotel

Whinpark Guest House
17 Ardross Street, Inverness, Inverness-shire, IV3 5NS
Tel: 01463 232549
★★★ Guest House

White Lodge
15 Bishops Road, Inverness, IV3 5SB
Tel: 01463 230693
★★★★ Guest House

Winston Guest House
10 Ardross Terrace, Inverness, Inverness-shire, IV3 5NQ
Tel: 01463 234477
★★★ Guest House

JOHN O'GROATS

Caber Feidh Guest House
John O'Groats, Wick, Caithness, KW1 4YR
Tel: 01955 611219
★★ Guest House

John O'Groats Guest House
The Broo, John O'Groats, Caithness, KW1 4YR
Tel: 01955 611251
★★ Guest House

Seaview Hotel
John O'Groats, Caithness, KW1 4YR
Tel: 01955 611220
★★ Small Hotel

KENTALLEN, BY APPIN

Holly Tree Hotel
Kentallen, Appin, Argyll, PA38 4BY
Tel: 01631 740292
★★★ Small Hotel

KINCRAIG, BY KINGUSSIE

Braeriach Guest House
Braeriach Road, Kincraig, by Kingussie, Inverness-shire, PH21 1NA
Tel: 01540 651369
★★★★ Guest House

Suie Hotel
Kincraig, Inverness-shire, PH21 1NA
Tel: 01540 651 344
★★★ Guest House

KINGUSSIE

Arden House
Newtonmore Road, Kingussie, Inverness-shire, PH21 1HE
Tel: 01540 661369
★★★★ Guest House

Columba House Hotel & Garden Restaurant
Manse Road, Kingussie, Inverness-shire, PH21 1JF
Tel: 01540 661402
★★★ Small Hotel

Duke of Gordon Hotel
Kingussie, Inverness-shire, PH21 1HE
Tel: 01540 661302
★★★ Hotel

The Hermitage Guest House
Spey Street, Kingussie, Inverness-shire, PH21 1HN
Tel: 01540 662137
★★★★ Guest House

Homewood Lodge
Newtonmore Road, Kingussie, Inverness-shire, PH21 1HD
Tel: 01540 661507
★★★★ Guest House

The Osprey Hotel
Ruthven Road, Kingussie, Inverness-shire, PH21 1EN
Tel: 01540 661510
★★★ Small Hotel

The Scot House Hotel
Newtonmore Road, Kingussie, Inverness-shire, PH21 1HE
Tel: 01540 661351
★★★ Small Hotel

KINLOCHBERVIE

The Kinlochbervie Hotel
Kinlochbervie, Sutherland, IV27 4RP
Tel: 01971 521275
★★ Small Hotel

Old School Hotel
Inshegra, Kinlochbervie, Sutherland, IV27 4RH
Tel: 01971 521383
★★★ Guest House

KINLOCHEWE

Kinlochewe Hotel
Kinlochewe, By Achnasheen, Wester Ross, IV22 2PA
Tel: 01445 760253
★ Small Hotel

KINLOCHLEVEN

Mamore Lodge Hotel
Kinlochleven, Argyll, PH50 4QN
Tel: 01855 831 213
★ Small Hotel

Tigh-Na-Cheo Guest House
Garbhein Road, Kinlochleven, PH50 4SE
Tel: 01855 831434
★★★ Guest House

KYLE OF LOCHALSH

Kyle Hotel
Main Street, Kyle of Lochalsh, Ross-shire, IV40 8AB
Tel: 01599 534204
★★★ Hotel

KYLESKU

Newton Lodge
Kylesku, Sutherland, IV27 4HW
Tel: 01971 502070
★★★★ Small Hotel

LAGGAN BRIDGE, BY NEWTONMORE

Monadhliath Hotel
Laggan Bridge, nr Newtonmore, Inverness-shire, PH20 1BT
Tel: 01528 544276
★★★ Small Hotel

LAIRG

Altnaharra Hotel
Altnaharra, By Lairg, Sutherland, IV27 4UE
Tel: 01549 411222
★★★ Small Hotel

Carnbren
Station Road, Lairg, Sutherland, IV27 4AY
Tel: 01549 402259
★★★ Bed & Breakfast

The Nip Inn
Main Street, Lairg, Sutherland, IV27 4DB
Tel: 01549 402243
★★★ Small Hotel

BY LAIRG

The Overscaig House Hotel
Loch Shin, Sutherland, IV27 4NY
Tel: 01549 431203
★★★ Small Hotel

LOCHINVER

The Albannach
Baddidarroch, Lochinver, Sutherland, IV27 4LP
Tel: 01571 844407
★★★★ Small Hotel

Inver Lodge Hotel
Lochinver, Sutherland, IV27 4LU
Tel: 01571 844496
★★★★ Hotel

Kylesku Hotel
Kylesku, by Lochinver, Sutherland, IV27 4HW
Tel: 01971 502231
★★★ Small Hotel

Polcraig Guest House
Lochinver, Sutherland, IV27 4LD
Tel: 01571 844429
★★★★ Guest House

Ruddyglow Park
Loch Assynt, By Lairg, Sutherland, IV27 4HB
Tel: 01571 822216
Awaiting Inspection

LOCH MAREE

The Old Mill Highland Lodge
Talladale, Loch Maree, Achnasheen, Ross-shire, IV22 2HL
Tel: 01445 760271
★★★★ Small Hotel

LOCH NESS

Craigdarroch House Hotel
Foyers, South Loch Ness, Inverness-shire, IV2 6XU
Tel: 01456 486400
★★★★ Small Hotel

Foyers Bay House
Lower Foyers, Inverness, IV2 6YB
Tel: 01456 486624
★★★ Guest House

Whitebridge Hotel
Whitebridge, Inverness-shire, IV2 6UN
Tel: 01456 486226
★★ Small Hotel

LYBSTER

Swallow Portland Arms Hotel
Lybster, Caithness, KW3 6BS
Tel: 01593 721721
★★★ Small Hotel

MALLAIG

Garramore House
South Morar, Mallaig, Inverness-shire, PH40 4PD
Tel: 01687 450268
★★ Guest House

The Moorings
East Bay, Mallaig, Inverness-shire, PH41 4PQ
Tel: 01687 462225
★★★ Guest House

Morar Hotel
Morar, nr Mallaig, PH40 4PA
Tel: 01687 462346
★★ Hotel

Seaview
Main Street, Mallaig, Inverness-shire, PH41 4QS
Tel: 01687 462059
★★★ Guest House

Western Isles
East Bay, Mallaig, Inverness-shire, PH41 4QG
Tel: 01687 462320
★★★ Guest House

West Highland Hotel
Mallaig, Inverness-shire, PH41 4QZ
Tel: 01687 462210
★★★ Hotel

MARYBANK

Fairburn Activity Centre
Urray, Muir of Ord, Ross-shire, IV6 7UT
Tel: 01997 433397
★★★ Small Hotel

MELVICH

Bighouse Lodge
Melvich, by Thurso, Sutherland, KW14 7YJ
Tel: 01641 531207
★★★★ Small Hotel

Melvich Hotel
Melvich, Sutherland, KW14 7YJ
Tel: 01641 531206
★★ Small Hotel

MEY

Castle Arms Hotel
Mey,by Thurso, Caithness, KW14 8XH
Tel: 01847 851244
★★ Small Hotel

MUIR OF ORD

The Dower House
Highfield, Muir of Ord, Ross-shire, IV6 7T
Tel: 01463 870090
★★★★ Small Hotel

Ord House Hotel
Muir of Ord, Ross-shire, IV6 7UH
Tel: 01463 870492
★★ Small Hotel

MUNLOCHY

Anwoth
Littleburn Road, Munlochy, Ross-shire, IV8 8NN
Tel: 01463 811674
Awaiting Inspection

NAIRN

Alton Burn Hotel
Alton Burn Road, Nairn, Inverness-shire, IV12 5ND
Tel: 01667 452 051
★ Hotel

Ascot House
7 Cawdor Street, Nairn, Inverness-shire, IV12 4QD
Tel: 01667 455855
★★★ Guest House

Directory of all VisitScotland Quality Assured Serviced Establishments

Aurora Hotel
2 Academy Street, Nairn,
Nairn-shire, IV12 4RJ
Tel: 01667 453551
★★ Small Hotel

Bracadale House
Albert Street, Nairn, IV12 4HF
Tel: 01667 452547
★★★★ Guest House

Braeval Hotel
Crescent Road, Nairn, IV12 4NB
Tel: 01667 452341
★★ Small Hotel

Claymore House Hotel
Seabank Road, Nairn, IV12 4EY
Tel: 01667 453731
★★★★ Small Hotel

Glen Lyon Lodge
19 Waverley Road, Nairn,
Nairnshire, IV12 4RH
Tel: 01667 452780
★★★ Guest House

Golf View Hotel
Seabank Road, Nairn,
Inverness-shire, IV12 4HD
Tel: 01667 452301
★★★★ Hotel

Greenlawns
13 Seafield Street, Nairn,
Inverness-shire, IV12 4HG
Tel: 01667 452738
★★★★ Guest House

Invernairne Guest House
Thurlow Road, Nairn,
Inverness-shire, IV12 4EZ
Tel: 01667 452039
★★★ Guest House

Newton Hotel
Nairn, Inverness-shire, IV12 4RX
Tel: 01667 453144
★★★★ Hotel

Sunny Brae Hotel
Marine Road, Nairn, IV12 4EA
Tel: 01667 452309
★★★★ Small Hotel

Windsor Hotel
Albert Street, Nairn, IV12 4HP
Tel: 01667 453108
★★★ Hotel

NETHY BRIDGE

Mount View Hotel
Nethy Bridge, Inverness-shire,
PH25 3EB
Tel: 01479 821 248
★★★ Small Hotel

Nethybridge Hotel
Nethybridge, Inverness-shire,
PH25 3DP
Tel: 01479 821203
★★★ Hotel

NEWTONMORE

Alvey House Hotel
Golf Course Road, Newtonmore,
Inverness-shire, PH20 1AT
Tel: 01540 673260
★★★ Small Hotel

Balavil Sport Hotel
Main Street, Newtonmore,
Inverness-shire, PH20 1DL
Tel: 01540 673220
★★ Hotel

Coig Na Shee
Fort William Road, Newtonmore,
Inverness-shire, PH20 1DG
Tel: 01540 670109
★★★★ Guest House

Crubenbeg House
Falls of Truim, By Newtonmore,
PH20 1BE
Tel: 01540 673300
★★★★ Guest House

ONICH, BY FORT WILLIAM

Allt-Nan-Ros Hotel
Main Road, Onich,
Inverness-shire, PH33 6RY
Tel: 01855 821462
Awaiting Inspection

Camus House
Lochside Lodge, Onich,
Inverness-shire, PH33 6RY
Tel: 01855 821200
★★★ Guest House

Creag Mhor Lodge
Onich, Fort William,
Inverness-shire, PH33 6RY
Tel: 01855 821379
★★★ Guest House

Cuilcheanna House
Onich, Inverness-shire,
PH33 6SD
Tel: 01855 821226
★★★★ Small Hotel

Lodge on the Loch Hotel
Onich, nr Fort William,
Inverness-shire, PH33 6RY
Tel: 01855 821237
★★★★ Small Hotel

Onich Hotel
Onich, by Fort William,
PH33 6RY
Tel: 01855 821214
★★★★ Hotel

PLOCKTON

The Haven Hotel
Innes Street, Plockton,
Ross-shire, IV52 8TW
Tel: 01599 544 223
★★★ Small Hotel

Plockton Hotel
Harbour Street, Plockton,
Ross-shire, IV52 8TN
Tel: 01599 544274
★★★ Small Hotel

POOLEWE

Poolewe Hotel
Main Street, Poolewe, IV22 2JX
Tel: 01445 781241
★★★ Small Hotel

Pool House
Poolewe, Rosshire, IV22 2LD
Tel: 01445 781272
★★★★ Small Hotel

PORTMAHOMACK

Caledonian Hotel
Main Street, Portmahomack,
Tain, Ross-shire, IV20 1YS
Tel: 01862 871345
★★ Small Hotel

RAASAY, ISLE OF

Isle of Raasay Hotel
Raasay, Kyle of Lochalsh,
Ross-shire, IV40 8PB
Tel: 01478 660222
★★ Small Hotel

RHICONICH

Rhiconich Hotel
Rhiconich, Sutherland,
IV27 4RN
Tel: 01971 521224
★★★ Small Hotel

ROTHIEMURCHUS

The Old Ministers House
Rothiemurchus, Aviemore,
Inverness-shire, PH22 1QH
Tel: 01479 812181
★★★★ Guest House

ROY BRIDGE

Glenspean Lodge Hotel
Roy Bridge, Inverness-shire,
PH31 4AW
Tel: 01397 712223
★★★★ Small Hotel

SCOURIE

Eddrachilles Hotel
Badcall Bay, Scourie,
Sutherland, IV27 4TH
Tel: 01971 502080
★★★ Small Hotel

Scourie Hotel
Scourie, Sutherland, IV27 4SX
Tel: 01971 502396
★★★ Small Hotel

ARDVASAR, SLEAT, ISLE OF SKYE

Ardvasar Hotel
Ardvasar, Isle of Skye, IV45 8RS
Tel: 01471 844223
★★★ Small Hotel

BERNISDALE, BY PORTREE, ISLE OF SKYE

Rubislaw
34 Bernisdale, Portree, Isle of
Skye, Inverness-shire, IV51 9NS
Tel: 01470 532 212
Awaiting Inspection

BROADFORD, ISLE OF SKYE

Dunollie Hotel
Broadford, Isle of Skye,
Inverness-shire, IV49 9AE
Tel: 01471 822253
Awaiting Inspection

Seaview
Main Street, Broadford,
Isle of Skye, IV49 9AB
Tel: 01471 820308
★★★ Guest House

BY BROADFORD, ISLE OF SKYE

The Skye Picture House
Ard Dorch, Broadford, Isle of Skye, Inverness-shire, IV49 9AJ
Tel: 01471 822531
★★★ Guest House

DUNVEGAN, ISLE OF SKYE

Atholl House Hotel
Dunvegan, Isle of Skye,
IV55 8WA
Tel: 01470 521219
★★★ Small Hotel

Dunorin House Hotel
2 Herebost, Dunvegan, Isle of Skye, Inverness-shire, IV55 8GZ
Tel: 01470 521488
★★★★ Small Hotel

Dunvegan Hotel
Main Street, Dunvegan,
Isle of Skye, IV55 8WA
Tel: 01470 521497
★★★ Small Hotel

Roskhill House
Roskhill, Dunvegan,
Isle of Skye, IV55 8ZD
Tel: 01470 521317
★★★★ Guest House

The Tables Hotel
Main Street, Dunvegan, Isle of Skye, Inverness-shire, IV55 8WA
Tel: 01470 521404
★★ Small Hotel

EDINBANE, ISLE OF SKYE

Ashaig B&B
3 Kildonan, Edinbane,
Isle of Skye, IV51 9PU
Tel: 01470 582336
Awaiting Inspection

ISLEORNSAY, ISLE OF SKYE

5 Drumfearn
Isleornsay, Isle of Skye,
IV43 8QZ
Tel: 01471 820171
Awaiting Inspection

KYLEAKIN, ISLE OF SKYE

King's Arms Hotel
Kyleakin, Isle of Skye,
Inverness-shire, IV41 8PH
Tel: 01599 534109
Awaiting Inspection

Mackinnon Country House Hotel
Old Farm Road, Kyleakin, Isle of Skye, Inverness-shire, IV41 8PQ
Tel: 01599 534180
★★★ Small Hotel

PORTREE, ISLE OF SKYE

An Airidh
6 Fisherfield, Portree,
Isle of Skye, IV51 9EU
Tel: 01478 612250
★★★ Guest House

Balloch
Viewfield Road, Portree, Isle of Skye, Inverness-shire, IV51 9ES
Tel: 01478 612093
★★★★ Guest House

The Bosville Hotel
10 Bosville Terrace, Portree,
Isle of Skye, Inverness-shire,
IV51 9DG
Tel: 01478 612846
★★★★ Hotel

Cuillin Hills Hotel
Portree, Isle of Skye, IV51 9QU
Tel: 01478 612003
★★★★ Hotel

Givendale Guest House
Heron Place, Portree,
Isle of Skye, IV51 9GU
Tel: 01478 612183
★★★ Guest House

Green Acres Guest House
Viewfield Road, Portree,
Isle of Skye, IV51 9EU
Tel: 01478 613175
★★★★ Guest House

Peinmore House
By Portree, Isle of Skye,
IV51 9LG
Awaiting Inspection

The Pink Guest House
1 Quay Street, Portree, Isle of Skye, Inverness-shire, IV51 9BT
Tel: 01478 612263
★★★ Guest House

Portree House Hotel
Home Farm Road, Portree,
Isle of Skye, IV51 9LX
Tel: 01478 611711
Awaiting Inspection

Quiraing Guest House
Viewfield Road, Portree, Isle of Skye, Inverness-shire, IV51 9ES
Tel: 01478 612870
★★★★ Guest House

Rosebank House
Springfield Road, Portree,
Isle of Skye, Inverness-shire,
IV51 9QX
Tel: 01478 612282
★★★ Guest House

Rosedale Hotel
Beaumont Crescent, Portree,
Isle of Skye, IV51 9DB
Tel: 01478 613131
★★★ Hotel

Royal Hotel
Bank Street, Portree, Isle of Skye, Inverness-shire, IV51 9BU
Tel: 01478 612525
★★★ Hotel

Viewfield House Hotel
Portree, Isle of Skye, IV51 9EU
Tel: 01478 612217
★★★ Small Hotel

BY PORTREE, ISLE OF SKYE

Greshornish House Hotel
Edinbane, By Portree,
Isle of Skye, IV51 9PN
Tel: 01470 582266
★★★ Small Hotel

SCONSER, ISLE OF SKYE

Sconser Lodge Hotel
Sconser, Isle of Skye,
Inverness-shire, IV48 3TD
Tel: 01478 650 333
★★★ Small Hotel

SKEABOST, ISLE OF SKYE

Skeabost Country House Hotel
Skeabost Bridge, Isle of Skye,
IV51 9NP
Tel: 01470 532202
★★★ Hotel

SLEAT, ISLE OF SKYE

Hotel Eilean Iarmain
Sleat, Isle of Skye, IV43 8QR
Tel: 01471 833332
★★★ Small Hotel

Kinloch Lodge
Sleat, Isle of Skye, IV43 8QY
Tel: 01471 833214
★★★★ Small Hotel

Toravaig House Hotel & Iona Restaurant
Knock Bay, Sleat, Isle of Skye,
IV44 8RE
Tel: 01471 833231
★★★★ Small Hotel

STAFFIN, ISLE OF SKYE

Flodigarry Country House Hotel
Staffin, Isle of Skye, IV51 9HZ
Tel: 01470 552203
★★★★ Small Hotel

Glenview Hotel
Culnacnoc, Staffin, Isle of Skye,
IV51 9JH
Tel: 01470 562248
★★ Small Hotel

UIG, ISLE OF SKYE

Uig Hotel
Uig, Isle of Skye,
Inverness-shire, IV51 9YE
Tel: 01470 542205
★★★ Small Hotel

Woodbine House
Uig, Portree, Isle of Skye,
IV51 9XP
Tel: 01470 542243
★★★ Guest House

WATERNISH, ISLE OF SKYE

Stein Inn
Macleod's Terrace, Waternish,
Isle of Skye, Inverness-shire,
IV55 8GA
Tel: 01470 592362
★★★ Inn

SPEAN BRIDGE

Aonach Mor Hotel
North Road, Spean Bridge, Inverness-shire, PH34 4ES
Tel: 01397 712351
★★ Small Hotel

The Braes Guest House
Spean Bridge, Inverness-shire, PH34 4EU
Tel: 01397 71243
★★★ Guest House

Coire Glas Guest House
Roybridge Road, Spean Bridge, Inverness-shire, PH34 4EU
Tel: 01397 712272
★★ Guest House

Corriegour Lodge Hotel
Loch Lochy, by Spean Bridge, Inverness-shire, PH34 4EA
Tel: 01397 712685
★★★★ Small Hotel

The Heathers
Invergloy Halt, Spean Bridge, Inverness-shire, PH34 4DY
Tel: 01397 712077
★★★★ Guest House

Inverour Guest House
Roy Bridge Road, Spean Bridge, Inverness-shire, PH34 4EU
Tel: 01397 712218
★★★ Guest House

Letterfinlay Lodge Hotel
Loch Lochy, Spean Bridge, Inverness-shire, PH34 4DZ
Tel: 01397 712622
★★ Small Hotel

Smiddy House
Roy Bridge Road, Spean Bridge, Inverness-shire, PH34 4EU
Tel: 01397 712335
★★★★ Guest House

Spean Bridge Hotel
Main Road, Spean Bridge, Inverness-shire, PH34 4ES
Tel: 01397 712250
★★ Hotel

BY STRATHCARRON

Tigh an Eilean Hotel
Shieldaig, by Strathcarron, Ross-shire, IV54 8XN
Tel: 01520 755251
★★★★ Small Hotel

STRATHPEFFER

Ben Wyvis Hotel
Strathpeffer, Ross-shire, IV14 9DN
Tel: 01997 421323
★★ Hotel

Brunstane Lodge Hotel
Golf Road, Strathpeffer, Ross-shire, IV14 9AT
Tel: 01997 421261
★★★ Small Hotel

Coul House Hotel
Contin, by Strathpeffer, Ross-shire, IV14 9ES
Tel: 01997 421487
★★★ Hotel

Highland Hotel
Strathpeffer, Highland Region, IV14 9AN
Tel: 01942 824824
★★★ Hotel

STRONTIAN

Ben View Hotel
Strontian, Acharacle, Argyll, PH36 4HY
Tel: 01967 402333
★★★ Small Hotel

Kilcamb Lodge Hotel
Strontian, Argyll, PH36 4HY
Tel: 01967 402257
★★★★ Small Hotel

The Strontian Hotel
Strontian, Acharacle, Argyll, PH36 4HZ
Tel: 01967 402029
★★ Small Hotel

STRUY, BY BEAULY

Cnoc Hotel
Struy, By Beauly, Inverness-shire, IV4 7JU
Tel: 01463 761 264
★★★ Small Hotel

TAIN

Dunbius Guest House
Morangie Road, Tain, Ross-shire, IV19 1HP
Tel: 01862 894902
★★★★ Guest House

Glenmorangie Highland Home at Cadboll
Fearn, by Tain, Ross-shire, IV20 1XP
Tel: 01862 871671
★★★★★ Small Hotel

Golf View Guest House
13 Knockbreck Road, Tain, Ross-shire, IV19 1BN
Tel: 01862 892856
★★★★ Guest House

Mansfield Castle
Scotsburn Road, Tain, Ross-shire, IV19 1PR
Tel: 01862 892052
★★★★ Hotel

Swallow Morangie House Hotel
Morangie Road, Tain, Ross-shire, IV19 1PY
Tel: 01862 892281
★★★★ Hotel

THURSO

Forss House Hotel
Forss, by Thurso, Caithness, KW14 7XY
Tel: 01847 861201
★★★★ Small Hotel

Holborn Hotel
Princess Street, Thurso, Caithness, KW14 7JA
Tel: 01847 892771
Awaiting Inspection

Park Hotel
Thurso, KW14 8RE
Tel: 01847 893251
★★★ Small Hotel

Pentland Hotel
Princes Street, Thurso, Caithness, KW14 7AA
Tel: 01847 893202
★★★ Hotel

Sheigra
6 Macdonald Green, Thurso, Caithness, KW14 7EL
Tel: 01847 892559
Awaiting Inspection

Station Hotel
54 Princes Street, Thurso, Caithness, KW14 7DH
Tel: 01847 892003
★★★ Hotel

Weigh Inn Hotel
Burnside, Thurso, KW14 7UG
Tel: 01847 893722
★★★ Hotel

TOMICH

Tomich Hotel
Tomich, by Cannich, near Beauly, Inverness-shire, IV4 7LY
Tel: 01456 415399
★★★ Small Hotel

TONGUE

Ben Loyal Hotel
Main Street, Tongue, Sutherland, IV27 4XE
Tel: 01847 611216
★★★ Small Hotel

Borgie Lodge Hotel
Skerray, By Tongue, Sutherland, KW14 7TH
Tel: 01641 521332
★★★★ Small Hotel

Tongue Hotel
Tongue, by Lairg, Sutherland, IV27 4XD
Tel: 01847 611206
★★★★ Small Hotel

TORRIDON

Loch Torridon Hotel
Torridon, Achnasheen, Ross-shire, IV22 2EY
Tel: 01445 791242
★★★★ Small Hotel

ULLAPOOL

Caledonian Hotel
Ullapool, Ross-shire, IV26 2UG
Tel: 01854 612306
Awaiting Inspection

Dromnan Guest House
Garve Road, Ullapool, Ross-shire, IV26 2SX
Tel: 01854 612333
★★★★ Guest House

Eilean Donan Guest House
14 Market Street, Ullapool,
Ross-shire, IV26 2XE
Tel: 01854 612524
★★★ Guest House

Glenfield Hotel
North Road, Ullapool,
Ross-shire, IV26 2XL
Tel: 01854 612314
Awaiting Inspection

Harbour Lights Hotel
Garve Road, Ullapool,
Ross-shire, IV26 2SX
Tel: 01854 612222
Awaiting Inspection

Point Cottage Guest House
22 West Shore Street, Ullapool,
Ross-shire, IV26 2UR
Tel: 01854 612494
★★★★ Guest House

Riverside
Quay Street, Ullapool,
Ross-shire, IV26 2UE
Tel: 01854 612239
★★★ Guest House

Strathmore House
Morefield, Ullapool, Ross-shire,
IV26 2TH
Tel: 01854 612423
★★★ Guest House

Ullapool Hotel
Garve Road, Ullapool,
Wester Ross, IV26 2SX
Tel: 01854 612905
★★ Small Hotel

Westlea Guest House
2 Market Street, Ullapool,
Ross-shire, IV26 2XE
Tel: 01854 612594
★★★★ Guest House

WICK

Bramhill Guest House
9 Francis Street, Wick,
Caithness, KW1 5PZ
Tel: 01955 602136
Awaiting Inspection

Impala Craigie Highland Home
Broadhaven Road, Wick,
Caithness, KW1 4RF
Tel: 01955 602194
★★ Guest House

Mackays Hotel
46 Union Street, Wick,
Caithness, KW1 5ED
Tel: 01955 602323
★★★ Hotel

Nethercliffe Hotel
Louisburgh Street, Wick,
Caithness, KW1 4NS
Tel: 01955 602044
★★ Small Hotel

Norseman Hotel
Riverside, Wick, Caithness,
KW1 4NL
Tel: 01955 603344
Awaiting Inspection

Queens Hotel
16 Francis Street, Wick,
Caithness, KW1 5PZ
Tel: 01955 602992
★★ Small Hotel

OUTER ISLANDS

Outer Hebrides, Orkney, Shetland

CASTLEBAY, ISLE OF BARRA

Castlebay Hotel
Castlebay, Isle of Barra,
HS9 5XD
Tel: 01871 810223
★★★ Small Hotel

Craigard Hotel
Castlebay, Barra, Outer
Hebrides, HS9 5XD
Tel: 01871 810200
★★★ Small Hotel

Terranova
Nask, Castlebay, Isle of Barra,
Outer Hebrides, HS9 5XN
Tel: 01871 810458
Awaiting Inspection

TANGASDALE, ISLE OF BARRA

Isle of Barra Hotel
Tangasdale Beach, Isle of Barra,
Western Isles, HS9 5XW
Tel: 01871 810383
★★★ Hotel

BENBECULA, ISLE OF

Lionacleit Guest House
27 Liniclate, Benbecula,
Western Isles, HS7 5PY
Tel: 01870 602179
★★★ Guest House

CREAGORRY, ISLE OF BENBECULA

Creagorry Hotel
Creagorry, Isle of Benbecula,
Western Isles, HS7 5PG
Tel: 01870 602024
★★★ Hotel

LINICLATE, ISLE OF BENBECULA

Dark Island Hotel
Liniclate, Isle of Benbecula,
Western Isles, HS7 5PJ
Tel: 01870 603030
★★★ Hotel

ARDHASAIG, ISLE OF HARRIS

Ardhasaig House
Ardhasaig, Isle of Harris,
HS3 3AJ
Tel: 01859 502066
★★★★ Small Hotel

KYLES HARRIS, ISLE OF HARRIS

Rodel Hotel
Rodel, Isle of Harris, HS5 3TW
Tel: 01859 520 210
★★★ Small Hotel

LEVERBURGH, ISLE OF HARRIS

Grimisdale
Leverburgh, Isle of Harris,
Western Isles, HS5 3TS
Tel: 01859 520460
★★★★ Guest House

SCALPA, ISLE OF HARRIS

Highcroft
6 Ardnakillie, Scalpay,
Isle of Harris, HS4 3YB
Tel: 01859 540305
Awaiting Inspection

SCARISTA, ISLE OF HARRIS

Scarista House
Scarista, Isle of Harris, HS3 3HX
Tel: 01859 550238
★★★★ Guest House

TARBERT, ISLE OF HARRIS

Harris Hotel
Tarbert, Isle of Harris, Western
Isles, HS3 3DL
Tel: 01859 502154
★★ Hotel

Leachin House
Tarbert, Harris, Western Isles,
HS3 3AH
Tel: 01859 502157
★★★★ Guest House

MacLeod Motel
Pier Road, Tarbert, Isle of Harris,
HS3 3DG
Tel: 01859 502364
★★ Inn

ACHMORE, ISLE OF LEWIS

Cleascro House
Achmore, Isle of Lewis,
HS2 9DU
Tel: 01851 860302
★★★★ Guest House

BACK, ISLE OF LEWIS

Banagher House
43 Vatisker, Back, Isle of Lewis,
HS2 0LF
Awaiting Inspection

Ravenstar
24 Vatisker, Back, Isle of Lewis,
HS2 0JS
Tel: 01851 820517
Awaiting Inspection

BREASCLEIT

Loch Roag Guest House
22A Breasclete, Isle of Lewis,
Western Isles, HS2 9EF
Tel: 01851 621357
★★★ Guest House

CALLANISH, ISLE OF LEWIS

Eshcol Guest House
Breasclete, Callanish,
Isle of Lewis, HS2 9ED
Tel: 01851 621357
★★★★ Guest House

CARLOWAY, ISLE OF LEWIS

Doune Braes Hotel
Doune, Carloway, Isle of Lewis,
HS2 9AA
Tel: 01851 643252
★★★ Small Hotel

LOCHS, ISLE OF LEWIS

Claitair Hotel
Shieldinish, Isle of Lewis, HS2 9RA
Tel: 01851 830473
Awaiting Inspection

SOUTH GALSON, ISLE OF LEWIS

Galson Farm Guest House
South Galson, Lewis, Western Isles, HS2 0SH
Tel: 01851 850492
★★★★ Guest House

STORNOWAY, ISLE OF LEWIS

Braighe House
20 Braighe Road, Stornoway, Isle Of Lewis, HS2 0BQ
Tel: 01851 705287
★★★★ Guest House

Cabarfeidh Hotel
Manor Park, Stornoway, Lewis, Western Isles, HS1 2EU
Tel: 01851 702604
★★★ Hotel

Caladh Inn
James Street, Stornoway, Isle of Lewis, HS1 2QN
Tel: 01851 702604
★★ Hotel

Cuanna House
29 Francis Street, Stornoway, Isle of Lewis, HS1 2NF
Tel: 01851 703482
★★★★ Guest House

Greenacres
8 Smith Avenue, Stornoway, Isle of Lewis, Western Isles, HS1 2PY
Tel: 01851 706383
★★★ Guest House

Hal-O The Wynd
2 Newton Street, Stornoway, Isle of Lewis, HS1 2RE
Tel: 01851 706073
★★★ Guest House

The Haven
12 Guershader, Stornoway, Isle of Lewis, HS2 0DP
Tel: 01851 700211
Awaiting Inspection

Hebridean Guest House
61 Bayhead, Stornoway, Isle of Lewis, HS1 2DZ
Tel: 01851 702268
★★★ Guest House

Park Guest House
30 James Street, Stornoway, Isle of Lewis, HS1 2QN
Tel: 01851 702485
★★★ Guest House

CARINISH, NORTH UIST

Temple View Hotel
Carinish, Isle of North Uist, Western Isles,, HS6 5EJ
Tel: 01876 580676
★★★★ Small Hotel

LOCHEPORT, NORTH UIST

Langass Lodge
Locheport, North Uist, Western Isles, HS6 5HA
Tel: 01876 580285
★★★ Small Hotel

LOCHMADDY, NORTH UIST

Lochmaddy Hotel
Lochamddy, North Uist, Western Isles, HS6 5AA
Tel: 01876 500331
★★ Hotel

Tigh Dearg Hotel
Lochmaddy, Isle of North Uist, Western Isles, HS6 5AE
Tel: 01876 500700
Awaiting Inspection

BURRAY, ORKNEY

Sands Hotel
Burray, Orkney, KW17 2SS
Tel: 01856 731298
★★★★ Small Hotel

DOUNBY, ORKNEY

Smithfield Hotel
Dounby, Orkney, KW17 2HT
Tel: 01856 771215
Awaiting Inspection

EVIE, ORKNEY

Woodwick House
Evie, Orkney, KW17 2PQ
Tel: 01856 751330
★★★ Small Hotel

HARRAY, ORKNEY

Merkister Hotel
Loch Harray, Orkney, KW17 2LF
Tel: 01856 771366
★★★ Hotel

HOY, ORKNEY

Stromabank
Hoy, Orkney, KW16 3PA
Tel: 01856 701494
★★★ Small Hotel

KIRKWALL, ORKNEY

Albert Hotel
Mounthoolie Lane, Kirkwall, Orkney, KW15 1JZ
Tel: 01856 876000
★★ Hotel

Ayre Hotel
Ayre Road, Kirkwall, Orkney, KW15 1QX
Tel: 01856 873001
★★★ Hotel

Brekkness Guest House
Muddisdale Road, Kirkwall, Orkney, KW15 1RS
Tel: 01856 874317
★★★ Guest House

Dunedin
Springfield Drive, Berstane Road, Kirkwall, Orkney , KW15 1XU
Tel: 01856 872967
Awaiting Inspection

Eastbank House
East Road, Kirkwall, Orkney, KW15 1LX
Tel: 01856 870179
★★ Guest House

Foveran Hotel
St Ola, Kirkwall, Orkney, KW15 1SF
Tel: 01856 872389
★★★ Small Hotel

Kirkwall Hotel
Harbour Street, Kirkwall, Orkney, KW15 1LF
Tel: 01856 872232
★★★ Hotel

Lav'rockha Guest House
Inganess Road, Kirkwall, Orkney, KW15 1SP
Tel: 01856 876103
★★★★ Guest House

Lynnfield Hotel
Holm Road, Kirkwall, Orkney, KW15 1SU
Tel: 01856 872505
★★★ Small Hotel

No 5 Ingale
Kirkwall, Orkney, KW15 1UY
Tel: 01856 875721
Awaiting Inspection

Orkney Hotel
Victoria Street, Kirkwall, Orkney, KW15
Tel: 01856 873477
★★★ Hotel

Polrudden Guest House
Peerie Sea Loan, Kirkwall, Orkney, KW15 1UH
Tel: 01856 874761
★★★ Guest House

Royal Oak Guest House
Holm Road, Kirkwall, Orkney, KW15 1PY
Tel: 01856 873487
★★★ Guest House

Sanderlay Guest House
2 Viewfield Drive, Kirkwall, Orkney, KW15 1RB
Tel: 01856 875587
★★ Guest House

St Ola Hotel
Harbour Street, Kirkwall, Orkney, KW15 1LE
Tel: 01856 875090
★★★ Guest House

West End Hotel
14 Main Street, Kirkwall, Orkney, KW15 1BU
Tel: 01856 872368
★★ Small Hotel

NORTH RONALDSAY, ORKNEY

Observatory Guest House
North Ronaldsay, Orkney, KW17 2BE
Tel: 01857 633200
★★★ Guest House

PAPA WESTRAY, ORKNEY

Beltane House
Papay Community Cooperative Ltd, Papa Westray, Orkney, KW17 2BU
Tel: 01857 644321
★★ Guest House

SHAPINSAY

Balfour Castle
Balfour Village, Shapinsay, Orkney, KW17 2DY
Tel: 01856 711282
★★★ Small Hotel

STENNESS, ORKNEY

Standing Stones Hotel
Stenness, Stromness, Orkney, KW16 3JX
Tel: 01856 850449
Awaiting Inspection

STROMNESS

Millers House & Harbourside B&B
7 & 13 John Street, Stromness, Orkney, KW16 3AD
Tel: 01856 851969
★★★ Guest House

Orca Hotel
76 Victoria Street, Stromness, Orkney, KW16 3BS
Tel: 01856 850447
★★ Guest House

Royal Hotel
55-57 Victoria Street, Stromness, Orkney, KW16 3BS
Tel: 01856 850342
★★ Small Hotel

Stromness Hotel
The Pier Head, Stromness, Orkney, KW16 3AA
Tel: 01856 850298
★★★ Hotel

WESTRA, ORKNEYY

Cleaton House
Cleaton, Westray, Orkney, KW17 2DB
Tel: 01857 677508
★★★★ Small Hotel

BRAE, NORTH MAINLAND, SHETLAND

Busta House Hotel
Busta, North Mainland, Shetland, ZE2 9QN
Tel: 01806 522506
★★★ Hotel

FAIR ISLE, SHETLAND

Fair Isle Bird Observatory Lodge
Fair Isle, Shetland, ZE2 9JU
Tel: 01595 760258
★★ Guest House

LERWICK, SHETLAND

Alderlodge Guest House
6 Clairmont Place, Lerwick, Shetland, ZE1 0BR
Tel: 01595 695705
★★★ Guest House

Bonavista Guest House
26 Church Road, Lerwick, Shetland, ZE1 0AE
Tel: 01595 692269
★★★ Guest House

Breiview
43 Kanterstead Road, Lerwick, Shetland, ZE1 0RJ
Tel: 01595 695956
★★★ Guest House

Eddlewood Guest House
8 Clairmont Place, Lerwick, Shetland, ZE1 0BR
Tel: 01595 692772
★★★ Guest House

Fort Charlotte Guest House
1 Charlotte Street, Lerwick, Shetland, ZE1 0JL
Tel: 01595 692140
★★★ Guest House

Glen Orchy Guest House
20 Knab Road, Lerwick, Shetland, ZE1 0AX
Tel: 01595 692031
★★★ Guest House

Grand Hotel
Commercial Street, Lerwick, Shetland, ZE1 0HX
Tel: 01595 692826
★★★ Hotel

Kveldsro House Hotel
Greenfield Place, Lerwick, Shetland, ZE1 0AN
Tel: 01595 692195
★★★★ Small Hotel

Lerwick Hotel
15 South Road, Lerwick, Shetland, ZE1 0RB
Tel: 01595 692166
★★★ Hotel

No 4 Punds
Lerwick, Shetland, ZE1 0LP
Tel: 01595 692155
Awaiting Inspection

Queen's Hotel
Commercial Street, Lerwick, Shetland, ZE1 0AB
Tel: 01595 692826
★★★ Hotel

Shetland Hotel
Holmsgarth Road, Lerwick, Shetland, ZE1 0PW
Tel: 01595 695515
★★★ Hotel

Solheim Guest House
34 King Harald Street, Lerwick, Shetland, ZE1 0EQ
Tel: 01595 695275
★★★ Guest House

Westhall
Ness of Sound, Lerwick, Shetland, ZE1 0RN
Tel: 01595 694247
Awaiting Inspection

SCALLOWAY, SHETLAND

Scalloway Hotel
Main Street, Scalloway, Shetland, ZE1 0RT
Tel: 01595 880444
★★ Small Hotel

SCOUSBURGH, SHETLAND

Spiggie Hotel
Scouseburgh, Shetland Isles, ZE2 9JE
Tel: 01950 460409
★★★ Small Hotel

SUMBURGH, SHETLAND

Sumburgh Hotel
Sumburgh, Virkie, Shetland, ZE3 9JN
Tel: 01950 60201
★★★ Hotel

TINGWALL, SHETLAND

Herrislea House
Veensgarth, Tingwall, Shetland, ZE2 9SB
Tel: 01595 840208
★★★★ Small Hotel

UNST, SHETLAND

The Baltasound Hotel
Baltasound, Unst, Shetland, ZE2 9DS
Tel: 01957 711334
★★ Hotel

Ordale Guest House
Baltasound, Unst, Shetland, ZE2 9DT
Tel: 01957 711867
★★ Guest House

WALLS, SHETLAND

Burrastow House
Walls, Shetland, ZE2 9PD
Tel: 01595 809307
★★★★ Guest House

DALIBURGH, SOUTH UIST

Borrodale Hotel
Daliburgh, South Uist, Western Isles, HS8 5SS
Tel: 0878 700444
★★★ Small Hotel

EOCHDAR, SOUTH UIST

Anglers Retreat
1 Ardmore, Iochdar, South Uist, HS8 5QY
Tel: 01870 610325
★★ Guest House

LOCHBOISDALE, SOUTH UIST

Brae Lea House
Lasgair, Lochboisdale, Isle of South Uist, HS8 5TH
Tel: 01878 700497
★★★ Guest House

LOCHCARNAN, SOUTH UIST

Orasay Inn
Lochcarnan, South Uist, Outer Hebrides, HS8 5PD
Tel: 01870 610298
★★★ Small Hotel

MILTON, SOUTH UIST

Caloraidh
Milton, South Uist, HS8 5RY
Tel: 01878 710365
Awaiting Inspection

Index

By location

Area Codes

A	South of Scotland: Ayrshire and Arran, Dumfries and Galloway, Scottish Borders	2
B	Edinburgh and Lothians	21
C	Greater Glasgow and Clyde Valley	52
D	West Highlands & Islands, Loch Lomond, Stirling and Trossachs	66
E	Perthshire, Angus and Dundee and the Kingdom of Fife	90
F	Aberdeen and Grampian Highlands – Scotland's Castle and Whisky Country	120
G	The Highlands and Skye	138
H	Outer Islands: Outer Hebrides, Orkney, Shetland	182

Location	Area code	Page no.
Aberdeen	F	126
by Aberdeen	F	130
Aberdour	E	96
Aberfeldy	E	96
Aberfoyle	D	72
Alexandria	D	83
Alyth	E	97
Ardchattan	A	83
Ardhasaig, Isle of Harris	H	188
Ardlui	D	72
Ardrishaig, by Lochgilphead	D	72
Auchencairn, by Castle Douglas	A	9
Auchterarder	E	97
Aultbea	G	144
Aviemore	G	144
Ayr	A	9
Ballachulish	G	145
Ballater	F	131
by Ballater	F	131
Balloch	D	72
Banchory	F	132
Banff	F	132
Biggar	C	58
Blackwaterfoot, Isle of Arran	A	8
Blair Atholl	E	98
Blairgowrie	E	98
by Blairgowrie	E	98
Boat of Garten	G	146
Boness	D	72
Bowmore, Isle of Islay	D	92
Brackla, Loch Ness-side	G	147
Braemar	F	132
Brodick, Isle of Arran	A	8
Broxburn	B	27
Bunessan, Isle of Mull	D	81
Burntisland	E	99
Cairndow	D	73
Callander	D	74
Callanish, Isle of Lewis	H	189
Carinish	H	189
Carnoustie	E	99
Carradale	D	75
Carrbridge	G	148
Castlebay, Isle of Barra	H	188

Location	Area code	Page no.	Location	Area code	Page no.
Castle Douglas	A	10	Fintry	D	78
Colintraive	D	75	Forres	F	135
Coll, Isle of	D	75	Fort Augustus	G	150
Colvend	A	11	Fort William	G	150
Comrie	E	99	by Fort William	G	154
Coupar Angus	E	99	Freuchie	E	104
Cowdenbeath	E	100	Gairloch	G	154
Craignure, Isle of Mull	D	81	Galashiels	A	12
Crail	E	100	Gatehouse of Fleet	A	12
Creagorry	H	188	Gigha, Isle of	D	78
Creetown	A	11	Girvan	A	13
Crianlarich	D	76	Glasgow	C	58
Crieff	E	100	Glasgow Airport	C	63
Crocketford	A	11	nr Glasgow	B	63
Cromarty	G	148	by Glasgow	C	63
Cullen	F	134	Glencoe	G	156
Cruden Bay	F	133	Glenfinnan	G	157
Dalkeith	B	27	Glenshee	E	104
Dalrymple	A	11	Glenshiel, by Kyle of Lochalsh	G	157
Dalwhinnie	G	149	Glen Urquhart	G	157
Dervaig, Isle of Mull	D	81	Grantown-on-Spey	G	158
by Dervaig, Isle of Mull	D	82	Gretna Green	A	13
Dornie, by Kyle of Lochalsh	G	149	Gullane	B	50
Dornoch	G	149	Haddington	B	50
Drumnadrochit	G	149	Harthill, by Shotts	C	64
Dulnain Bridge	G	150	by Hawick	A	13
Dumfries	A	12	Invergarry	G	159
Dunbar	B	27	Invergordon	G	160
Dunblane	D	76	Inverkip	C	64
Dundee	E	101	Inverness	G	160
Dunfermline	E	103	Iona, Isle of	D	79
Dunkeld	E	103	nr Irvine	A	14
Dunoon	D	76	Isle of Whithorn	A	14
Dunvegan, Isle of Skye	G	173	Jedburgh	A	14
East Calder	B	27	John O'Groats	G	164
Edinburgh	B	28	Jura, Isle of	D	80
Edzell	E	104	Kelso	A	14
Elgin	F	134	Kildonan, Isle of Arran	A	8
Ettrick Bridge, by Selkirk	A	12	Kildrummy	F	136
Falkirk	D	77	Killin	D	80

Index

By location

Location	Area code	Page no.
Kingussie	G	164
Kinlochleven	G	165
Kinloch Rannoch	E	104
by Kinloch Rannoch	E	104
Kinross	E	105
Kirkcaldy	E	106
Kirkwall	H	190
Kirriemuir	E	106
Kyle of Lochalsh	G	165
Laggan Bridge, by Newtonmore	G	166
Lairg	G	166
by Lairg	G	166
Largs	A	15
by Larkhall	B	64
Laurencekirk	F	136
Leven	E	106
Liniclate	H	188
Loch Earn	E	106
Lochearnhead	D	80
Locheport, Isle of North Uist	H	190
Lochinver	G	167
Loch Ness	G	168
Lochranza, Isle of Arran	A	8
Lockerbie	A	15
Luss	D	81
Lybster	G	168
Macduff	F	136
Mallaig	G	169
Markinch	E	107
Meikleour	E	107
Melrose	A	15
by Melrose	A	16
Moffat	A	16
Montrose	E	108
Motherwell	C	64
Muir of Ord	G	170
Nairn	G	170
Newtonmore	G	171
Newton Stewart	A	18
North Berwick	B	51
Oban	D	83
by Oban	D	87
Oldmeldrum	F	136
Onich, by Fort William	G	172
Paisley	C	65
Peebles	A	18
by Peebles	A	19
Pennyghael, Isle of Mull	D	82
Perth	E	108
by Perth	E	111
Peterhead	F	136
Pitlochry	E	111
Poolewe	G	172
Port Ellen, Isle of Islay	D	80
Portree, Isle of Skye	G	174
by Portree, Isle of Skye	G	175
Portsoy	F	137
Prestwick	A	19
Rhiconich	G	172
Rothesay, Isle of Bute	D	73
Rothienorman	F	157
St Andrews	E	114
by St Andrews	E	118
Scourie	G	173
Skeabost	G	175
Sleat, Isle of Skye	G	175
South Queensferry	B	51
Spean Bridge	G	177
Staffin, Isle of Skye	G	176
Stanley	E	119
Stirling	D	87
by Stirling	D	88
Stornoway, Isle of Lewis	H	189
Strachur	D	89
Stranraer	A	19
by Stranraer	A	19
by Strathcarron	G	178
Strathpeffer	G	178
Strathyre	D	89

Location	Area code	Page no.
Stromness, Orkney	H	190
Strontian	G	179
Swinton	A	19
Tain	G	179
Tangasdale, Isle of Barra	H	188
Tarbert, Isle of Harris	H	189
Tarbet, by Arrochar	D	89
Thurso	G	179
Tobermory, Isle of Mull	D	82
Tongue	G	180
Troon	A	19
Turnberry	A	20
Uddingston	C	65
Ullapool	G	181
Uphall	B	51
Waternish, Isle of Skye	G	177

Notes

Notes